"In our age of alternative truths in politics as well as finance, HOLT has proven to be one of very few truthful voices in analyzing corporate performance."

Henrik Andersson, Fund Manager, Didner & Gerge

BEYOND EARNINGS

BEYOND EARNINGS

Applying the HOLT CFROI®
and Economic Profit Framework

David A. Holland

Bryant A. Matthews

WILEY

Published by John Wiley & Sons, Inc., Hoboken, New Jersey.
Published simultaneously in Canada.

CFROI is a trademark of CSFB HOLT LLC.

For general information on our other products and services or for technical support, please contact our Customer Care Department within the United States at (800) 762-2974, outside the United States at (317) 572-3993, or fax (317) 572-4002.

Wiley publishes in a variety of print and electronic formats and by print-on-demand. Some material included with standard print versions of this book may not be included in e-books or in print-on-demand. If this book refers to media such as a CD or DVD that is not included in the version you purchased, you may download this material at http://booksupport.wiley.com. For more information about Wiley products, visit www.wiley.com.

Library of Congress Cataloging-in-Publication Data is Available:

ISBN 9781119440482 (Hardcover)
ISBN 9781119440505 (ePDF)
ISBN 9781119440529 (ePub)

Cover Design: Wiley
Cover Image: © De Space Studio/Shutterstock

Printed in the United States of America

10 9 8 7 6 5 4 3 2 1

This book is dedicated to the memory of Bob Hendricks who passed away on May 28, 2017. The global success of the HOLT CFROI framework never would have been realized without Bob's vision, persistence, and uncanny marketing skills. Bob brought the CFROI framework to life for countless fund managers, corporate clients and HOLT employees. He distilled the art of stock selection to its essence in his famous 2-minute drills. He reminded us that investing was fun but required many hours of attention.

Bob was an amazing presenter – one of the best we've seen. To be on the same presentation bill with him was daunting. We recall having to precede him at a seminar in Germany after he had retired. Bob was the keynote speaker. After a full day of lectures on the mechanics of financial performance analysis and equity valuation, when listeners were surely mentally exhausted, he held the audience of fund managers spellbound. Bob de-mystified stock analysis, breezed through 2-minute drills, and told tales from his forty years in the financial industry. At the end of his speech, the audience jumped out of their seats and enthusiastically applauded. The Director of Research at a distinguished fund manager told us that he leapt up wondering why Bob Hendricks hadn't been awarded a Nobel prize only to realize after calm reflection that the presentation simply described the skilled application of a discounted cash flow model. Bob brought the subject of investing to life!

CONTENTS

Contents

Contents

Contents

III   Value Driver Forecasting

8   The Competitive Life-Cycle of Corporate Evolution

9   The Persistence of Corporate Profitability

Contents

Contents

INTRODUCTION

THE PRICING PUZZLE: FOUNDATIONAL HOLT CONCEPT AND A KEY TO BETTER VALUATION

On May 13, 2017, the *Financial Times* reported that "investors wiped $4.6bn from the market value of the U.S. department store sector in the space of two days, as concern mounted about sliding sales and the effects of online competition." U.S. department stores suffered an astonishing fall in market value of over 16% in two days.[1] Who is responsible for this vaporization of shareholder value? All fingers were pointed at Amazon, the biggest online retailer, which accounts for 5% of retail spending in the United States, and is presently the world's fifth most valuable company.[2]

In 1994, Amazon was just a fledgling start-up. The Internet was beginning to take off as a vehicle for commerce, and growth rates were forecast to be into the *hundreds* of percent. Seeing an opportunity, Jeff Bezos launched Amazon as an online retail bookstore from his garage. Over the last decade, Amazon has grown its revenue to almost 13 times from where it started for a compound annual growth of 29%.[3] To say it is disrupting traditional retailers and ways of doing business is an understatement.

---

[1] Adam Samson, Mamta Badkar, and Nicole Bullock, "US Retail Sector's Misery—In Charts," *Financial Times*, May 13, 2017.
[2] Reported in "Primed," *The Economist*, March 25, 2017, pp. 24–26.
[3] Even as late as 2014 when we began writing this book, we would have been skeptical of Amazon increasing its sales from $74bn in 2013 to $136bn in 2016. According to our study of sales growth in Chapter 10, Amazon only had a 13% probability of growing sales at this rate or higher over three years.

Amazon's share price has increased 63,990% since its IPO on May 15, 1997, versus 300% in total return for the S&P 500 over the same period.[4] Amazon surpassed the mighty Wal-Mart in 2015 as the most valuable retailer in America. Despite this stellar performance, Amazon regularly posts poor earnings numbers and a subpar return on equity (ROE) yet consistently trades at a price-to-book (P/B) ratio in the neighborhood of 20. Is there something missing in the accounting figures?

Jeff Bezos, CEO and founder of Amazon, gives us a clue in his 1997 Letter to Shareholders: "When forced to choose between optimizing the appearance of our GAAP accounting and maximizing the present value of future cash flows, we'll take the cash flows." Treating Amazon's research and development (R&D) cost as a long-term investment instead of an accounting expense provides a completely different perspective on the company's economic profitability and value. The capitalization of R&D is explored in the Asset Life section of Chapter 3. Accounting data does not convey a clear picture of a firm's economic performance, and is becoming less relevant as intangible assets become more important than physical assets in generating economic value.[5] A framework that focuses on economic returns and ties them to intrinsic value is crucial for equity investors and corporate managers when pricing assets and strategies. We show how cash flow return on investment (CFROI) improves upon accounting measures of profitability in Chapter 3, using Amazon's 2013 annual report. We explore discounted cash flow (DCF) and discounted economic profit (EP) valuation methods in Chapters 4 and 6. The tools and techniques are the same for fund and corporate managers, and we welcome both groups to apply this book's lessons in valuing companies and assessing their profitability.

A thread that runs throughout the book from its opening is the importance of capital allocation and investing in positive net present value (NPV) strategies. We demonstrate the connection between project economics and corporate valuation. Company managers who focus on making positive

---

[4]Nicole Bullock, and Mamta Badkar, "Amazon's 20 Years as 'Pre-Eminent Disrupter of Retail,'" *Financial Times*, May 16, 2017.
[5]For more on the increasing irrelevance of accounting numbers, see Baruch Lev and Feng Gu, *The End of Accounting and the Path Forward for Investors and Managers*, John Wiley & Sons, 2016.

NPV investments will increase the economic profit and intrinsic value of their firms. Beware when acquisitions and investments are made for "strategic" reasons. This excuse often means that financial reasons are lacking. Capital allocation, NPV, EP, and intrinsic value are intimately linked.

Successful equity investing requires an ability to gauge the expectations of others (what's priced into the stock) and to skillfully weigh this expectation against the likelihood of success. Accurately predicting a company's future profitability doesn't necessarily lead to outperformance. Instead, large gains accrue to investors who identify stocks that will beat expectations. It doesn't matter if the expectations are for failure or enormous success: If a company can better those expectations, shareholders will reward the company by pushing its share price higher.

The professional employer services firm Automatic Data Processing (ADP) makes this point clear. Since 1991, ADP has earned impressive operating margins that rank it in the top twentieth percentile of profitability in the world. ADP ranks as one of the 50 most profitable firms over the past 25 years.

Despite ADP's impressive track record of performance, price expectations as of April 2004 showed investors were anticipating even greater success. And investors got it right! Over the next 10 years, ADP outpunched rivals and steadily earned increasing profits. What an impressive achievement: Investors anticipated this success and embedded it into the stock price as early as 2004. But here's the key point: ADP's shareholder returns over this ten-year period were lackluster, and investors earned no more than benchmark performance despite ADP's stunning record of profitability. How could this happen? It's simple, really: If you bought ADP in April of 2004, you paid for stellar future operating performance. ADP met this expectation; it did *not* exceed it. Instead of reaping huge gains as profits rose, shareholders earned exactly what they paid for in the form of benchmark returns. Upon reflection, this should be viewed as an entirely reasonable outcome: If stocks are priced efficiently, then companies that meet expectations should return only their cost of equity.

Starbucks, the purveyor of fine coffee, had similarly high expectations in January 2009. Its cash flow return on investment (CFROI) was expected to rise from 8.5% to 9.3% over the ensuing five years. This seemingly small upward improvement was empirically a 20% probability event, meaning that 80% of firms with similar profitability throughout history were unable to lift CFROI above 9.3%. This placed the odds of success at 1-in-4 (0.2/0.8). But, instead of just meeting expectations, Starbucks brewed profits well above this level, pushing CFROI over the brim toward 12%. This success was unanticipated, and Starbucks share price leapt ahead of its benchmark, nearly quadrupling it by 2013. Finding stocks that can beat expectations is the key to earning large returns. We explore how to evaluate market expectations in Chapter 11.

The ultimate aim of equity analysts and portfolio managers is to select future winners and avoid tomorrow's losers. This requires a considerable measure of predictive skill (or luck). Like a garden, forecasting skill can be cultivated to yield greater output. We provide empirical results for the behavior of corporate growth and profitability in Chapters 8, 9, and 10, and show how you can improve your forecasts of growth and profitability. Growth and profitability both exhibit reversion to the mean, which we describe and model as "fade."

A key to superior stock picking is utilizing a framework that facilitates consistent and rigorous evaluation of an investment's positive and negative merits. The HOLT framework is designed to help investors do a better job at grading stock ideas. At the heart of this objective is an effort to de-bias the investor by exposing a stock's embedded price expectations. HOLT's framework is a proven and reliable system that has been rigorously field tested by investment professionals for over 40 years.

This book relies on the Pricing Puzzle as a useful aid for thinking critically about the intrinsic value of a firm (Exhibit I.1). The Pricing Puzzle contains all of the key elements that influence a stock's price, including fundamental and behavioral drivers. Familiarity with this tool can help you quickly and effectively think through how changes in fundamental drivers are likely to influence the value of a company.

EXHIBIT I.1 The Pricing Puzzle and chapter that corresponds to each driver.

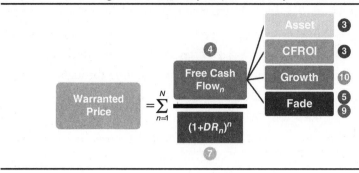

HOLT's valuation model is predicated on a life-cycle perspective of corporate evolution. From start-up to mature veteran or restructuring candidate, empirical evidence shows that companies share similar traits at each state of development and that these traits can be helpful in predicting future profitability and growth. Few firms can sustain high profitability for decades. Most companies become cost-of-capital operations within five to ten years.

HOLT's valuation model embeds competitive fade (reversion to the mean) into forecasts of future profitability and growth. Beginning with a firm's asset base, stated in current dollars, the principle drivers of corporate value are the firm's economic rate of return (CFROI), asset growth rate, and its likely fade rate in profitability. These three drivers are used to estimate a firm's free cash flows. Over time, profitability converges toward the cost of capital and growth converges toward a long-term sustainable level.

The Pricing Puzzle can be elegantly stated as a simple but powerful formula that estimates a mature firm's value. We call this the Fundamental Pricing Model:

$$P = B\frac{(ROC_1 - g + f)}{(r - g + f)}$$

where B is book value, ROC is the forward return on capital, g is the asset growth rate, and f is the rate at which profitability fades to the cost of

EXHIBIT I.2 **Perspectives for application of the Fundamental Pricing Model.**

Perspective:	Equity Holders	Capital Providers (Conventional)	Capital Providers (HOLT)
P:	Equity value	Enterprise value	Enterprise value
B:	Book equity value	Invested capital	Inflation-adjusted gross investment (IAGI)
ROC:	ROE	ROIC	CFROI
g:	Growth in book equity	Growth in invested capital	Real growth in IAGI
r:	Cost of equity, r_e	Weighted-average cost of capital (WACC)	Real cost of capital, HOLT DR
f:	ROE fades to r_e	ROIC fades to WACC	CFROI fades to HOLT DR

capital r.[6] Exhibit I.2 shows the corresponding variables for different perspectives.[7] Consistency is paramount!

This equation introduces a vital component missing from traditional valuation models, such as the Gordon Growth Model: *fade (f)* is the rate at which profitability reverts toward the mean. The slower the fade, the longer the competitive advantage period (CAP) of a firm with attractive profitability and the greater its intrinsic value. Shifting B to the left-hand side of the equation restates the formula as price-to-book, P/B, which can be calculated on the back of an envelope for stable, mature firms.

Note that when the return on capital equals the cost of capital, growth and fade create no value since no excess rents are earned and P/B equals 1. When CFROI is greater than the cost of capital, P/B is greater than 1. When fade is high, profitability changes quickly. Fade *drives down* or reduces the intrinsic value of a profitable firm, but *drives up* or enhances the value of an unprofitable one. The strong statistical relationship between

---

[6] The HOLT framework uses the inflation-adjusted gross assets as the asset base to minimize accounting and inflationary distortions. To obtain the intrinsic enterprise value, the inflation-adjusted accumulated depreciation must be subtracted from the calculated price, which represents a gross value in the HOLT formulation. These nuances and their benefits are explored in the book.

[7] The earnings form of the model is: $P = E_1 \dfrac{\left(1 - \left[\frac{g-f}{ROC_1}\right]\right)}{(r-g+f)}$, where the forward earnings E_1 is net income, NOPAT, or gross cash flow for the equity, invested capital and HOLT perspectives respectively. For the full derivation, see our report "Don't Suffer from a Terminal Flaw, Add Fade to your DCF" issued by Credit Suisse HOLT in June 2016.

EXHIBIT I.3 The Pricing Puzzle using Economic Profit and the chapter that corresponds to each driver.

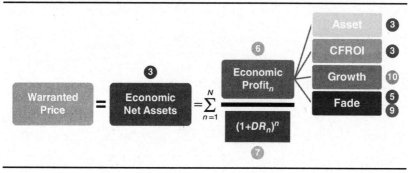

HOLT P/B and CFROI supports the utility of this pricing equation.[8] The Fundamental Pricing Model is worth remembering; every student and practitioner of finance should commit it to memory. We explore the use of this equation in Chapter 5 to quickly and effectively estimate a firm's value, understand its competitive advantage period, and gauge expectations embedded in a stock's price.

We praise the virtue of cash flow over earnings throughout the book, which begs the question: Is negative free cash flow a bad thing in the short to medium term if a company has a host of positive NPV strategies to invest in? The answer is a resounding "No!" Capital providers will excitedly queue to invest in positive NPV projects, each of which increases the company's intrinsic value by the expected value of its NPV. For this reason, it is generally easier for company managers to think in terms of economic profit, where a capital charge is subtracted from operating profit. Firms investing in positive NPV projects will create positive economic profit regardless of whether the short to medium term free cash flow is negative. We cover this topic in detail in Chapter 6. The Prizing Puzzle can also be written in terms of economic profit (Exhibit I.3).

---

[8] R^2 values are typically above 0.7, making CFROI a significant variable in explaining a stock's market enterprise value. We use HOLT P/B and economic P/E, which is HOLT P/B divided by CFROI, as screening variables and stock-picking factors. Economic PE provides an excellent signal of relative attractiveness.

OVERVIEW OF BOOK CHAPTERS

This book is divided into three sections and 11 chapters, with each focusing on a particular aspect of the Pricing Puzzle.

Section I: Financial Performance Assessment

In Chapter 1, we emphasize a core principle for corporate managers and investors: Always pursue positive NPV strategies. The NPV Rule states that any project that delivers returns in excess of its opportunity cost has merit. Managers should continually strive to create value by maximizing NPV. They can accomplish this by focusing their talents and efforts on building a sustainable competitive advantage for their firm. To be clear, short-term pursuit of profits should not dominate long-term value creation. Any tension that might arise between short-term and long-term objectives is resolvable when managers align their core responsibilities with the purpose of the firm. This logical and useful connection between the two is summarized by Bart Madden: "Maximizing shareholder value is best positioned not as the purpose of the firm, but as the result of achieving the firm's purpose."[9] Peter Drucker said, "The purpose of business is to create and keep a customer." He concluded that a firm retains customers, creates its competitive advantage and generates excess profits through innovation and marketing.

Chapter 2 reviews popular profitability metrics and discusses how these measures can be gamed by managers and how investors can sidestep some of these weaknesses. We show the relationship between P/E and a DCF valuation. We introduce the principles of value creation.

In Chapter 3, we describe how CFROI, HOLT's measure of a firm's economic return on investment, is determined from accounting information. We use Amazon as a case study and show how CFROI can be calculated from standard financial reporting statements and the notes from annual filings. We explain the adjustments and their economic reasons.

---

[9] Bartley J. Madden, *Value Creation Thinking*, LearningWhatWorks, Naperville, IL, 2016.

Section II: Discounted Cash Flow and Economic Profit Valuation

Chapter 4 shows how to value a firm. The present value of free cash flows, not earnings, is the ultimate measure of a firm's intrinsic worth. Companies that earn returns on investment in excess of their opportunity cost will trade at a premium to book because they are generating economic value from their assets that exceeds the cost of their use. Companies that earn returns on investment below their opportunity cost waste investor capital and destroy shareholder value.

Chapter 5 explains the connection between a firm's competitive advantage period (CAP) and its fade in profitability. We show how the fade rate can be easily incorporated into a DCF model. The impact of changes in CAP on intrinsic value can be assessed. The fade rate is a critical value driver when valuing successful companies whose return on capital exceeds their cost of capital.

Chapter 6 describes HOLT's measure of economic profit. Economic profit is the earnings that a firm generates in excess of its opportunity cost. Firms that earn positive economic profits generate significant economic value for investors. Valuations from the free cash flow and economic profit methods are equal for a given forecast. We demonstrate the equivalence. The goal for a company is not to increase earnings but rather to increase economic profit. Management bonuses should be tied to increases in economic profit.

In Chapter 7, we focus on investors' required rate of return. This chapter examines popular measures of the cost of capital. We demonstrate how HOLT's market-implied approach is related to these measures. This is a must-read chapter for HOLT veterans and newcomers who desire a better understanding of risk.

Section III: Value Driver Forecasting

In Chapter 8, we examine the importance of the competitive life-cycle as a framework for thinking about a firm's likely future evolution. Instead of classifying firms as *value* or *growth*, we split them into four groups based on profitability and expected economic growth: Question Marks, Stars, Cash Cows, and Dogs. We share our research on the probabilities of transitioning from one group to another.

Chapter 9 introduces the concept of fade, or what academics call persistence. This is a ground-breaking chapter that explores the notion of reversion to the mean in corporate profitability. We offer detailed evidence of mean-reversion in corporate profitability and show how investors can distinguish between random profitability, sustained profitability, and reversion to the mean. This is an essential chapter for directors of research, portfolio managers, and analysts who wish to improve the plausibility of their forecasts.

In Chapter 10 we investigate the persistence of revenue, earnings, and asset growth. We find overwhelming evidence that growth rates are volatile and quickly revert to the mean. Earnings growth is like white noise and reveals little of predictive value. Forecasts of sustained earnings growth are typically worthless. Few firms maintain high growth rates for long periods.

Finally, in Chapter 11 we wrap it up by focusing on how investors can effectively gauge the expectations embedded in a firm's stock price. HOLT provides several valuable tools to aid in this effort. This is an essential chapter for investors who seek to hone their skills at picking winning stocks using HOLT Lens.

WHO ARE WE AND WHAT DO WE HOPE TO ACHIEVE

We are valuation practitioners. We have worked with corporate and fund managers to value decisions, divisions, stocks, and strategies. Both sides can use the same metrics and valuation approaches to perform fundamental company analysis. Because we work closely with fund managers and equity analysts, we have focused much of our Credit Suisse HOLT research on refining fundamental valuations by improving forecasts of value drivers. Better probabilistic forecasts result in more accurate valuations.

Our purpose in writing this book is to improve:

- Financial performance analysis for corporate and fund managers when assessing a company's historical and forecast profitability
- The pricing model and its assumptions when performing discounted cash flow and economic profit valuations
- Value driver forecasting to improve fundamental valuation and stock picking

Return on equity (ROE) is a poor measure of a firm's profitability since it focuses only on equity investors and not the quality of the firm's operations. Earnings can be gamed by accounting shenanigans and are also dependent on a firm's leverage. In short, ROE is not to be trusted. Return on invested capital (ROIC) is a better measure of profitability but liable to accounting distortions. Although it takes more effort to calculate cash flow return on investment (CFROI), it is a comprehensive measure of a company's profitability. Because CFROI reverses accounting distortions and adjusts for inflation, it is comparable across borders and industries and over time. This is highly advantageous to corporate and fund managers when assessing profitability and the plausibility of forecast profitability. What's the upside? A better measure of profitability results in improved capital allocation decisions and fundamental valuation.

Earnings and P/E ratios are too unreliable for valuation, so we take you beyond earnings in this book. Although we prefer CFROI as a measure of profitability, the valuation methods we derive are general and can also utilize ROE, ROIC, or other metrics. Asset light businesses might not require the rigor of the CFROI inflation adjustments but will probably necessitate the capitalization of intangible assets such as R&D. It is essential that consistency reigns when measuring financial performance and valuing companies. Amazon provides an excellent case study, and is used throughout the book. We prefer the economic profit approach when discussing valuations since the present value of future economic profits equals the total NPV of all present and future investments. The relationship is one-to-one and connects project economics to corporate valuation. A relentless focus on this connection will lead to improvements in capital allocation for corporate executives and their boards. We explore the nuances of using net assets (invested capital) versus inflation-adjusted gross investment in the assessment of economic profit.

The final section of the book is targeted at fundamental stock pickers but should be of interest to corporate managers and strategists trying to assess the plausibility of a forecast or determine a company's market-implied expectations. Knowing what's in the price of suppliers, competitors, customers, and entire industries is valuable information. Better forecasts of the value drivers, CFROI, asset growth, and fade, should result in more accurate valuations and improved performance for stock pickers. We share our latest thinking and empirical findings from many years of observations.

When deciding which metrics and valuation approach to use for a specific company or investment decision process, it is best to recall the words of Albert Einstein: "Everything should be as simple as it can be but not simpler."

Section I

Financial Performance Assessment

1

NEVER FORGET THE GOLDEN RULE: PURSUE STRATEGIES WITH POSITIVE NPV

"Cash flow is a fact, earnings an opinion."

—written on a subway wall

KEY LEARNING POINTS

- Rational investors prefer more value to less.
- The responsibilities of corporate financial managers are varied but revolve around making decisions that increase economic value.
- Accounting value is what's been put into a business while economic value is what can be taken out in future cash flows. Don't confuse earnings and cash flow.
- The golden rule of finance is to pursue strategies and projects with a positive net present value.

- The growing annuity equation is useful for back-of-the-envelope valuations.
- Decision trees help visualize and value the outcomes from decisions and chance events.
- The price of short-termism can be high. Investors pay for the long term.
- The Law of Conservation of Value specifies that if expected cash flows don't change, then the intrinsic value shouldn't change.

INTRODUCTION

If we offered you the chance to buy a crisp $100 bill for $80, you would undoubtedly accept the deal since its immediate profit, or net present value (NPV), is $20 in your favor. You would surely decline an opportunity to purchase a $100 bill for $120. The NPV would be a loss of $20, resulting in an immediate decline in your wealth. Simply stated, rational investors prefer more value to less.

This statement might strike you as blindingly obvious, but there is no shortage of corporate examples where it has been violated. A National Bureau of Economic Research study estimated that shareholders lose $5.90 for every $100 spent on acquiring public companies.[1] Sprint, a U.S. telecommunications company, paid $36 billion in 2005 to acquire Nextel in a deal many thought was richly valued. It proved disastrous. They failed to integrate their networks and cultures. Sprint wrote off $30bn on the purchase in 2008, and the name Sprint Nextel became extinct in 2013 after years of very poor performance relative to the S&P 500.

Hewlett-Packard (HP), the famed Silicon Valley pioneer, paid $10.3 billion for the UK software company Autonomy in 2011, and wrote off $8.8 billion of the value one year after the acquisition. The premium it paid was 79% and considered excessive at the time. How did HP get it so wrong? According to Bloomberg, "One former HP executive who worked

---

[1]S.B. Moeller, F.P. Schlingemann, and R.M. Stulz. "Do Shareholders of Acquiring Firms Gain from Acquisitions?" NBER Working Paper No. 9523, March 2003.

there at the time says it appeared that Apotheker (HP's CEO) and the board didn't know what to do and were trying anything they could think of. 'It wasn't a strategy,' he says. 'It was total chaos.'"[2] HP paid $100 for a $10 bill.

Fund investors are also guilty of forgetting that rational investors prefer more value to less. Andrew Ang provides ample evidence in his excellent book on asset management that mutual funds, hedge funds, and private equity investments don't pay off for most investors after all the fees and risks are taken into account.[3] The fees are lower and your odds of better relative performance are higher when buying an S&P 500 ETF rather than an actively managed fund with the S&P 500 as its benchmark. Active funds are suffering massive outflows from their portfolios into those of passive funds.

Despite different opinions and time frames, all shareholders will agree that they are better off if a company's managers make decisions that increase the value of their shares. Rational investors prefer corporate managers to invest in wealth creating projects and to increase the value of their company.

One reason managers and investors forget this simple rule is because they confuse earnings and cash flow. An obsessive fixation with earnings influences markets from closing in Tokyo to opening on Wall Street. Earnings and accounting-based performance metrics are easily gamed and can destroy shareholder value when executives get rewarded for hitting them as targets. CEOs who are rewarded for growing earnings per share (EPS) can do it quite easily by repurchasing shares instead of paying dividends.

There is an antidote. Modern finance provides ample evidence that stock prices are based on long-term cash flow expectations, not short-term caprice. HOLT's cash flow return on investment (CFROI) framework pierces the veil of accounting gimmickry and attempts by corporate executives at window dressing, and offers a reliable system for investment analysis.

---

[2] Aaron Ricadela, "Why Hewlett-Packard's Impulse Buy Didn't Pay Off," *Bloomberg*, November 30, 2012. According to the article, Larry Ellison, the CEO of Oracle, described Autonomy's asking pricing as "absurdly high."

[3] Andrew Ang, *Asset Management: A Systematic Approach to Factor Investing*, Oxford University Press, 2014.

Cash is king and discounted cash flow (DCF) analysis is the appropriate way to value projects and corporations. There is a clear connection between decisions that managers make and the value of their company. Both corporate and fund managers can use the same tools to estimate the intrinsic value of their decisions.

WHAT DO CORPORATE FINANCIAL MANAGERS DO DURING THE DAY?

To appreciate how equity investors value companies, it helps to understand how companies value their decisions. The main responsibilities of corporate financial managers are:

- Deciding what investments to make
- Deciding how the corporation is financed
- Managing the corporation's cash needs
- Reporting the health of the business to its stockholders

Financial managers help decide in which strategies and projects the firm invests. Projects include expansion, outsourcing, licensing, R&D, business or product development, mergers, acquisitions, and disposals.

Financial managers report the firm's operating results to stakeholders and offer guidance on its prospects. This requires an estimate of the likely value of present and future projects. Risks, opportunities, and alternate scenarios need to be assessed so that corporate executives can make high-quality, rational decisions.[4] The purpose of the firm is to prosper by building a sustainable competitive advantage and selecting the most valuable portfolio of projects, strategies, and businesses from its palette of choices. Shareholder value will be maximized if the firm and its directors remain vigilant in this pursuit.

---

[4] For an excellent introduction to the art and science of decision analysis, and how to improve decision quality, see Peter McNamee and John Celona (2007), *Decision Analysis for the Professional*, 4th edition, SmartOrg, Inc.

Financial managers decide on and manage the firm's capital structure—its mix of equity, debt, and hybrid instruments such as convertible debt to fund the firm's investments. In a perfect capital market of no taxes or market frictions, Modigliani and Miller demonstrated that a firm's market value is independent of capital structure.[5] The value of a firm cannot be altered by changing capital structure or dividend policy in a perfect capital market. Any effects on value from changes in capital structure or dividend policy are due to frictions such as taxes, government policy, and transaction costs. Because interest payments on debt are tax deductible in many countries, it is valuable for firms to use debt. Unfortunately, there's no such thing as a free lunch. As the proportion of debt increases, the firm's ability to service its debt is threatened due to the rising possibility of default. A corporate finance team manages the issuance of debt and equity to fund investment, as well as the firm's overall debt level. It is vital to consider the trade-off between the tax benefits of debt and the costs of financial distress.

Financial managers must cope with the need for cash to run the business. The terms and conditions extended to customers and negotiated with creditors must be directed and administered. Short-term financing to buy inventory and respond to seasonal spikes in sales is an important task. The intelligent management of working capital is a key contributor to a firm's profitability, return on capital, and value.

Executives and line managers require management reports to monitor operations and remind themselves of targets. The results of individual projects are consolidated into the firm's aggregate financial reports. These management accounts are confidential and remain inside the firm to provide timely and critical information about the company's performance. Publicly listed firms provide investors four main financial statements on an annual basis:

---

[5] For more on Modigliani and Miller's Propositions I and II, see Jonathan Berk and Peter DeMarzo (2014), *Corporate Finance*, 3rd edition, Pearson, 478–501. For the ground-breaking original paper, see F. Modigliani and M. Miller (1958), "The Cost of Capital, Corporation Finance and the Theory of Investment," *American Economic Review* 48(3), 261–297.

- The balance sheet, or what's officially termed the *statement of financial position*
- The income statement, now known as the *statement of comprehensive income*, and commonly called the profit and loss account, or simply the P&L
- The *statement of cash flows*, or more commonly, the cash flow statement
- The *statement of changes in shareholders' equity*

Performance metrics should align employees and managers with the goal of building a sustainable competitive advantage and maximizing the value of the firm.[6] Metrics matter because they influence behavior. As the old medical saying goes, "What gets measured, gets managed." Financial managers play a central role in communicating operating results to both internal and external stakeholders. Investors and analysts will be confused and less interested in owning stock if the chief financial officer (CFO) can't clearly connect the firm's decisions and operating performance to its intrinsic value when communicating the firm's results, plans, and expectations. Meaningful financial metrics indicate the economic performance of the firm and help judge the plausibility of its expectations. The best place to look for what drives executive behavior is the annual financial statement's section on remuneration. Are reward metrics aligned with value creation or accounting shenanigans?

WHAT IS VALUE?

Suppose you have a chance to buy a new car from Cash Is King Motors or Royal Earnings Carport. You have agreed on a price of $50,000 for the

---

[6]It is our view that maximizing shareholder value is best positioned not as the purpose of the firm, but as the result of achieving the firm's purpose (see Madden). However, to gauge performance and assess the potential of alternate strategies, the NPV rule dominates all other methods by linking *opportunity cost* to *net value creation*. It is incumbent upon business managers to carefully weigh the value potential of short-term investments versus long-term bets whose value effects may be meaningfully larger but more difficult to quantify. Real options and decision models can be helpful in quantifying and visualizing them.

same model, but the salesman from Royal Earnings is under pressure to hit his sales target and throws in a sweetener. He says you can have the car for $50k if you sign now and pay within 365 days. That's a no brainer, right? If you have cash, you place $50k in a savings account, pay for the car in 364 days, and pocket the interest. The time value of money makes this deal attractive to you, and you would wait until the last minute to complete the transaction.

How does this deal work its way through Royal Earnings financial reports? Their income statement reports a profit after the sale despite no cash in the till. Thus, earnings are up, but so are accounts receivable on the balance sheet, which have to be collected at a future date. Let's assume the salesman is paid a commission of 2% and the cost of the car is $47,000. The recorded gross profit is plus $2,000, and managers congratulate themselves when they see it reported on the P&L statement:

$$Gross\ Profit = \$50,000 - \$47,000 - 0.02 \times \$50,000 = \$2,000$$

But not everyone is happy. The financial manager gets a headache because she has profit but no cash. To top it off, she is losing the time value of money and is exposed to credit risks and the possibility of losing any profit if you are unable to pay. Assuming a 10% cost of capital, we can calculate today's cash equivalent of receiving $50k in 364 days by discounting this amount. The net present value (NPV) in today's cash would be:

$$NPV = \frac{\$50,000}{1.10} - \$47,000 - 0.02 \times \$50,000 = -\$2,545.45$$

Accounting earnings are up (+$2,000), but the economic value of Royal Earnings is down (−$2,545). Economic value represents the residual value after imposing a charge on capital that could have earned a return by being invested elsewhere. In this case, Royal Earnings suffers a current dollar loss of value. To make matters worse, Royal Earnings might have to pay tax on the reported earnings before being paid in cash by the customer.

This example highlights a fundamental difference between financial economics and accounting. The former concerns itself with cash and the timing of those cash flows while the latter attempts to match revenue and expenses in an income statement, and tallies the net value in a balance sheet. Warren Buffett explains that "book value is an accounting concept, recording the accumulated financial input from both contributed capital and retained earnings. Intrinsic business value is an economic concept, estimating future cash output discounted to present value. Book value tells you what has been put in; intrinsic business value estimates what can be taken out."[7] Cash receipts and accounting income are rarely the same. Following the money is the best way to understand value since you want to be paid in cash, not promises.

The difference between a firm's assets and liabilities is shareholders' equity, which can be found on the balance sheet. This is also known as book value of equity. It is an accounting measure of the net worth of the firm. It is not an economic or market value of the firm's equity. While shareholders' equity is measured strictly in dollars, many of the firm's most valuable assets are not captured on the balance sheet:

- The expertise of employees
- The firm's reputation
- Relationships with customers and suppliers
- The value of future projects
- Quality of management and corporate culture
- The value of its brands

The market value of a company does not depend on the cost of its assets, which is a sunk cost. It depends on the present value of cash flows that investors expect those assets to produce in the future. Exhibits 1.1 and 1.2 show how a balance sheet differs from the perspective of a financial accountant and that of a financial economist.

Let's consider the case of Amazon from both an accounting and economic point of view. Amazon may trade in books but it certainly does not trade at book. Its price-to-book ratio (P/B) is 21 compared to 2 for an

---

[7] Warren E. Buffett, "1983 Letter to Shareholders," Berkshire Hathaway 1983 Annual Report.

EXHIBIT 1.1 The accountant's balance sheet equation is Total Assets equals Total Liabilities plus Shareholders' Equity. The latter is what remains in book terms.

Current assets
• Cash
• Accounts receivables
• Inventory
• Other current assets

=

Shareholders' equity
• Common stock
• Retained earnings
• Treasury stock
• Other equity

Current liabilities
• Short-term debt
• Accounts payable
• Other current liabilities

Long-term assets
• Net PP&E
• Goodwill
• Investments
• Other long-term assets

Long-term liabilities
• Long-term debt
• Deferred taxes
• Other long-term liabilities

EXHIBIT 1.2 The financial economist's balance sheet equation is Market Value of Assets equals Market Value of Total Liabilities plus Market Value of Shareholders' Equity. The latter is better known as market capitalization, or market cap.

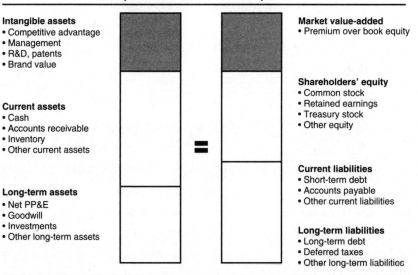

Intangible assets
• Competitive advantage
• Management
• R&D, patents
• Brand value

Market value-added
• Premium over book equity

Current assets
• Cash
• Accounts receivable
• Inventory
• Other current assets

=

Shareholders' equity
• Common stock
• Retained earnings
• Treasury stock
• Other equity

Current liabilities
• Short-term debt
• Accounts payable
• Other current liabilities

Long-term assets
• Net PP&E
• Goodwill
• Investments
• Other long-term assets

Long-term liabilities
• Long-term debt
• Deferred taxes
• Other long-term liabilitioc

11

average U.S. company because investors expect the company to generate attractive cash flows well into the future.[8] You might be shocked to learn that Amazon reported negative shareholders' equity from 2000 to 2004 and paltry operating earnings, yet investors never considered the company insolvent. Shareholders weren't bothered by the seemingly dreadful state of Amazon's accounting statements. Jeff Bezos has maintained since his 1997 Letter to Shareholders that, "When forced to choose between optimizing the appearance of our GAAP accounting and maximizing the present value of future cash flows, we'll take the cash flows."

Let's shift from ratios to absolute amounts to bring home this essential point. Amazon's equity book value was $11.8bn on June 30, 2015, and its market cap was $252bn on September 17, 2015. It was priced to generate $240bn of economic value in current dollars on its existing and future businesses (market premium equals market cap minus equity book value (252 − 12 = 240)).

The market value of equity can also be less than its book value. This occurs in depressed industries where profitability is low and there is excess capacity, or for firms with grim prospects.

THE GOLDEN RULE OF FINANCIAL DECISION MAKING

Hindustan Unilever's guiding maxim is "what is good for the people of India is good for Hindustan." Similarly, what is good for the sustainable competitive advantage of a firm is good for the investors of a firm. And, what is good for investors is to increase their economic wealth since they have a choice of investment opportunities. A business decision whose benefits exceed its costs is valuable. Comparing benefits and costs is often complicated because they occur at different points in time, could be in different currencies, or may have different risks associated with them. At its essence, value is the money you make minus the total cost of making

---

[8]P/B ratio for Amazon on September 17, 2015, based on the most recent quarter.

that money, or simply what's left in the cash box after the transaction is complete. Paying additional charges for interest, collection fees, refunds, and product recalls reduces the cash in the till that can be paid as dividends to shareholders. Shortsightedness is not in the best interest of long-term investors.

Corporate finance is concerned with the present value of an investment, which represents today's cash value of future cash flows. To compare cash flows at different points in time, we need to state them in a single period's cash-equivalent value. It is standard to state cash flows in today's value. As an example, consider exchanging a bond that matures in six months for cash today, or an oil futures contract that matures in one year. In either case, discussing the value of the bond or futures contract in today's dollar value allows for comparison between investments and instant appreciation of their relative merit.

The fundamental measure of value creation is net present value (NPV), which is the present value of all future and present cash inflows and out-flows related to a strategy or project. Cash outflows are negative and inflows are positive.

$$NPV = PV\ of\ Benefits - PV\ of\ Costs$$

If the expected NPV of an investment is negative, it should be rejected. You wouldn't trade £10,000 for $10,000 if the exchange rate were $1.60 per £, nor would you invest £10,000 in a risky venture if you were only guaranteed £10,000 in one year's time. A decision increases the value of a firm when its expected NPV is positive. **The Golden Rule of Finance is to pursue projects that are NPV positive**. This objective necessarily includes a comprehensive examination of all the costs and profits associated with the project, those that occur today as well as those that may occur many years into the future, such as cleanup costs and the probability of stranded assets.

This is important because investment decisions and their associated NPVs are related to the market value of a company's equity. The market cap of a company equals its book value plus the NPV of *all* its present and future projects, even those yet to be imagined:[9]

$$Market\ Value\ of\ Equity = Book\ Value\ of\ Equity + Market\ Premium$$

$$Market\ Premium = NPV\ of\ All\ Projects$$

If a company is growing but all its growth is into projects that create zero NPV, then growth is irrelevant and the company should trade at its book value. Growth can decrease the value of a firm if investments are poured into negative NPV projects. You will be reminded of this point throughout the book. Growth is not always value additive.

The *Law of One Price*—or the absence of arbitrage—is central to modern finance. Investments that offer the same payoff must trade at the same price in well-functioning markets. In a perfect market, the NPV of financial transactions will be zero. Exchanging currencies, commodities, or financial instruments at a discount suggests arbitrage (risk-free profit), which is rapidly eliminated whenever it appears. It is rare to find a $100 note lying on the ground because anyone seeing it is instantly wealthier after picking it up.

By extension, the NPV decision rule states that when considering investments, take the alternative with the highest NPV.[10] Choosing this alternative is equivalent to receiving its NPV in cash today. Because present value is additive, the NPV of a firm is the sum of its strategies' NPVs. This is precisely what connects project economics to the value of the corporation and is properly known as the *value additivity principle*. The NPV decision rule helps maximize the value of the firm by aligning management's goals with strategies best suited for commercial and long-term financial success. Decisions and their expected values matter.

---

[9]We are assuming that the book value of equity is a fair estimate of its liquidation value in this formulation.

[10]We stress, again, that the NPV decision rule must be guided by an honest and ethical assessment of all associated costs, those that occur now and many years into the future. For instance, the decision to extract coal from a profitable mine cannot ignore the potentially damaging long-term effects on the local geography and the significant costs that might be associated with cleanup and restoration.

Investment projects are either mutually exclusive or independent. A mutually exclusive decision involves choosing one project from among a group of projects. Examples include choosing one plant or product design; in-house manufacturing instead of outsourcing; or acquiring one company rather than another. The NPV rule for mutually exclusive decisions is to choose the one with the highest NPV because that is the investment that will maximize the corporation's total value. Though this statement seems blatantly obvious, it often eludes corporate executives when they make investment decisions. For example, there is significant evidence that acquisitions tend to destroy economic value for the acquiring shareholders. Hubris and nebulous "strategic reasons" often result in an overly optimistic assessment of synergies and the expected value creation from mergers and acquisitions. Directors of the firm choose unwisely when they seek to diversify the firm's risk on behalf of its investors, who are capable of doing it at a far lower cost and with far more relevance to their individual portfolios.

Independent projects are trickier, but the rules remain the same. To maximize the value of the entire firm, managers should make decisions that maximize NPV. All positive NPV projects should be accepted until reasonable constraints such as lack of skilled employees interfere. When budget constraints get in the way of accepting all of them, then projects should be ranked and those with the lowest net present value should be rejected or delayed. Metrics such as profitability index (PI) help with the ranking but the rule is clear. If management is convinced that an investment will generate positive net present value, then the CFO should pick up the phone and raise capital.[11]

BACK-OF-THE-ENVELOPE BASICS

By converting all cash flows to a common point in time, we can compare the costs and benefits of an investment, and calculate its NPV, which is the

---

[11] Just because NPV is positive doesn't necessarily mean that a project should be commenced immediately. A project might be worth more if waiting is valuable. Decision analysis and real options are useful for understanding the value implications of waiting, gathering more information, and flexibility.

net benefit of the project in terms of cash today.

$$NPV = \sum_{n=0}^{N} \frac{CF_n}{(1+r)^n} \tag{1.1}$$

The variable CF_n is the cash flow in year n, N is the life of the project, and r is the discount rate, or opportunity cost of the funds provided.

Three basic rules apply when translating cash flows:

1. Only cash flows occurring at the same point in time can be compared or combined.
2. To move cash flow forward in time, you must compound it.

$$FV_n = PV \times (1+r)^n$$

3. To move cash flow backward in time, you must discount it.

$$PV = \frac{FV_n}{(1+r)^n}$$

To compound the value of cash (move it forward in time), apply an interest rate. If you wish to know a company's expected total shareholder return in one year's time, then compound today's share price by the company's cost of equity. To discount the value of cash (move it backward in time), apply a discount rate. If you wish to know the present value of a special dividend in one year's time, then discount it by the company's cost of equity.

At this stage, it is useful to derive a few simple relationships. A constant annual payment that lasts forever is called a *perpetuity*. It has a surprisingly simple solution called the *perpetuity equation*.[12]

$$PV = \sum_{n=1}^{\infty} \frac{CF}{(1+r)^n} = \frac{CF}{r} \tag{1.2}$$

If DivCo pays a constant dividend of $2bn into perpetuity and its risk-adjusted cost of equity is 10%, then its market cap should trade at

---

[12]This can be proved by multiplying PV times $(1 + r)$ and then subtracting PV from it. $PV \times (1 + r) - PV = r \times PV$. The summation times $(1 + r)$ equals $CF + PV$, thus $r \times PV = CF + PV - PV$, which simplifies to $PV = CF/r$.

$20bn in a competitive market. Similarly, if DivCo could take out $2bn in after-tax costs on a sustainable basis, its market cap would rise by $20bn minus the investment needed to take out the costs. Let's assume an investment of $5bn is necessary. The NPV of the investment would be $15bn:

$$NPV = -\$5bn + \frac{\$2bn}{0.10} = \$15bn$$

The value of the firm would increase to $35bn based on the value additivity principle. Because it is a positive NPV project, the firm should invest. It can issue $5bn worth of equity to pay for it. Assuming the firm starts with 1 billion shares, its market cap would immediately jump to $35bn after the announcement ($20bn + $15bn = $35bn). Existing shareholders would pocket the full gain as the share price jumps from $20 to $35 ($20bn/1bn shares = $20/share to $35bn/1bn shares = $35/share). The firm would only have to issue 143 million shares to pay for the investment ($5bn/($35/share) = 143m shares). The dividend per share would increase to $4bn divided by the total number of shares outstanding, 1.143bn, which equals $3.50 per share, or according to the perpetuity equation, a share price of $35 (P = $3.50/0.10 = $35 per share) (Exhibit 1.3).

The value of clear communication to investors should not be underestimated. In this example, announcing the savings initiative is critical. If the potential upside of an investment is properly communicated, existing shareholders will get all the additional expected value. If DivCo were to issue shares without announcing the savings, the share price would remain at $20 instead of immediately jumping to $35. Existing shareholders would share the gain with those who bought the issued shares, i.e., 250m shares would be issued at $20 per share and the share price would eventually settle at $32, costing existing shareholders $3 per share in potential gain due to poor communication. New shareholders would delight in their luck and the blunder of management in failing to publicize the savings.

An important equation to remember is the formula for valuing a growing annuity in which cash flow grows at a constant rate g for N years, and then stops. An annuity is a fixed sum. The growing annuity formula meets

EXHIBIT 1.3 DivCo has an opportunity to save $2bn per year and increase its dividend. It issues shares to fund a $5bn investment to generate the savings.

Timeline	Start	Announce	Reaction	Issue	Result
Dividend ($bn)	2		2		4
Shares (bn)	1		1		1.143
DPS ($/share)	2.00		2.00		3.50
Cost of equity	10%		10%		10%
Market cap ($bn)	20		35		40
Share price ($/share)	20.00		35.00		35.00
Savings announcement					
After-tax savings ($bn)		2			
PV of savings ($bn)		20			
Investment ($bn)		−5			
NPV ($bn)		15			
Share issuance					
Issue shares ($bn)				5	
Issue price ($/share)				35.00	
Shares (bn)				0.143	

the requirements of Herbert Stein's law, "If something cannot go on forever, it will stop."

$$PV = \sum_{n=1}^{N} \frac{CF_1 \times (1+g)^n}{(1+r)^n} = \frac{CF_1}{(r-g)} \left[1 - \frac{(1+g)^N}{(1+r)^N} \right] \quad (1.3)$$

This equation should be permanently stamped into your memory or placed on standby in your tablet! The first term is simply a growing perpetuity. The compound term accounts for the truncation of cash flow after N years. If N is infinity, it simplifies to the growing perpetuity equation, $PV = CF_1/(r-g)$. If g is zero and N is infinity, it simplifies to the perpetuity equation, $PV = CF_1/r$. From the growing annuity equation, we can quickly determine the perpetuity, growing perpetuity, and annuity equations. This opens a whole new world to performing back-of-the-envelope calculations!

Suppose Bad Karma Pharma has just learned that it will have to pull a valuable cash cow product from the market. The CEO calls you in, the eager financial analyst sporting a pen, envelope, and calculator. He is clearly upset and asks you to calculate the hit on the share price, explaining that after-tax cash flow will be reduced by $800m a year forever and the cost of equity is 10%. In a jiffy, you realize this is a perpetuity and tell him the market cap will take a hit of $8bn once the news is public. There goes the yacht he planned to buy with stock options.

$$PV = \frac{CF_1}{(r-g)}\left[1 - \frac{(1+g)^N}{(1+r)^N}\right] = \frac{CF}{r} = \frac{-\$800m}{0.10} = -\$8bn$$

The CFO interjects that it might be worse since the product's cash flow has been growing with inflation at 2%, which is expected to persist. No problem, plenty of space on your envelope. This is a growing perpetuity.

$$PV = \frac{CF_1}{(r-g)}\left[1 - \frac{(1+g)^N}{(1+r)^N}\right] = \frac{CF_1}{(r-g)} = \frac{-\$800m}{(0.10-0.02)} = -\$10bn$$

The CEO turns pale when you quickly respond that this increases the total hit to the market cap to $10bn. The Sales Director says it won't be that bad since she expects only 10 more years of cash flow before the product becomes uncompetitive. You mutter to yourself, "No sweat," but this will require a calculator and the envelope.

$$PV = \frac{CF_1}{(r-g)}\left[1 - \frac{(1+g)^N}{(1+r)^N}\right]$$
$$= \frac{-\$800m}{(0.10-0.02)}\left[1 - \frac{(1+0.02)^{10}}{(1+0.10)^{10}}\right] = -\$5.3bn$$

The CEO sighs with relief when you say the total hit reduces to $5.3bn. The Director of Research adds with an air of authority that there is a 30% chance the findings were incorrect and that the product won't have to be pulled, but that it will cost $190m to contest the findings. The CEO winces at the expense and asks if it is a wise decision to contest the findings. You sketch a probability tree and calculate an expected loss of $3.9bn (Exhibit 1.4).[13] You add that he can pay up to $1.59bn to contest the findings, which is the value of perfect information, making the $190m

---

[13] A decision tree is useful for mapping and valuing decisions, uncertainties, and real options. Squares represent decision points such as invest, delay, or kill. Circles represent uncertainties such as the likelihood of success or potential values.

EXHIBIT 1.4 **Bad Karma Pharma NPV Tree. Squares represent decision points, and circles represent uncertainties and their probabilities. The path with the greatest expected value should be chosen.**

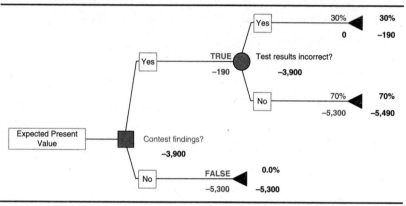

expenditure seem like a bargain.[14] The CEO realizes the news is bad but now knows what he can expect when the market opens. He authorizes the expenditure to contest the findings and thanks you profusely for making such complicated financial calculations under fire and in a pinch.

IS THE NPV RULE FOOLPROOF?

Don't let the rule fool with your head. Let's take the case of Woody Rock, a music impresario, who combs the clubs of London looking for up-and-coming bands. He wears an easy smile and possesses that rare quality of understanding the music business. You meet him at a club and wonder if the NPV rule applies to the music business. He tells you that one out of ten bands he signs has a successful first release. He typically invests £10,000 to record a band. Nine turn out to be duds that claw back

---

[14] The value of perfect information is the maximum amount that should be paid for the decision maker to be indifferent to contesting the findings. An expense greater than $1.59 would lead to a negative expected value: Value of perfect information = 5.3bn – (0.3 × 0 + 0.7 × 5.3bn) = 1.59bn. It is worthwhile to contest the findings unless it costs more than $1.59bn, thus a cost of $190m is a wise expenditure.

half of the investment and one band proves to be commercially successful, grossing £55,000 for his production company. You run the numbers in your head and conclude that it is breakeven. He explains that it takes a year until he sees any cash flow. You scribble the NPV on a napkin, assuming a 10% discount rate.

$$NPV = -10 \times 10,000 + \frac{9 \times 5,000}{1.10} + \frac{1 \times 55,000}{1.10} = -£9,091$$

You're scratching your head. The more he invests in bands, the more value he destroys, yet Rock's wearing the best money can buy on Bond Street. This is not making sense and perhaps a fitting occasion to give up on modern finance.

You decide to explain the NPV rule and show him the napkin. Rock has no idea what you're babbling about but is intrigued because he likes making money while messing with the establishment. "Mate, when I sign a band, I have an option to produce the next two albums." You press ahead with a few questions about probabilities and expected earnings. "I only continue with bands that succeed with their first album. Most get the same result with the second album, but 25% of the time the next album grosses 10 times as much while another 25% turn out to be flash-in-the-pans that gross one-tenth as much." You draw the probability tree in your tablet and re-commit yourself to the NPV rule. Despite the poor odds (90% of his signings generate a negative NPV), Rock's expected NPV per signing is £49,466 for the first three releases (Exhibit 1.5). With a committed team and a lot of luck, he'll win at the start, scale up, and watch his options pay off!

Options have value and should be part and parcel of investment analyses. Just because a project has a negative NPV doesn't mean that subsequent contingent options don't have attractive value. Just like record companies, pharmaceutical firms bet on many potential products but have few actual winners. When the investments succeed, the payoff can be huge.

EXHIBIT 1.5 **Woody Rock's NPV. Real options have value. All values shown are net present values.**

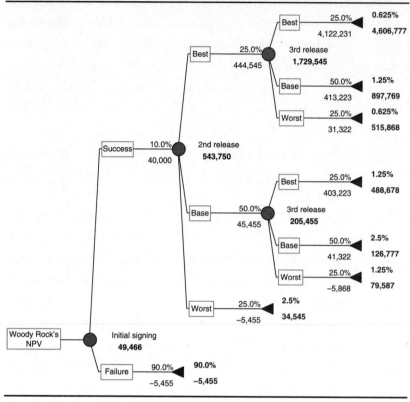

THE PRICE OF SHORT-TERMISM

According to David Larcker of Stanford University, "Companies want long-term shareholders in particular because it allows them to implement their corporate strategy and make long-term investments without the distraction and short-term performance pressures that come from active traders."[15] Most companies believe their share price would trade 15% higher on average with a volatility that is 20% lower if they were able to attract their ideal shareholder base. This is an extraordinary finding.

[15]Anne Beyer, David F. Larcker, and Brian Tayan, "2014 Study on How Investment Horizon Expectations of Shareholder Base Impact Corporate Decision-Making," Rock Center for Corporate Governance at Stanford University and NIRI.

It implies that corporate investor relations professionals have recognized the connection between decisions, value, and communication but are unsuccessful in convincing investors of the merits of their companies' long-term plans. Is the market so shortsighted or inefficient that it prefers accounting gimmicks and short-term earnings over decisions that increase NPV over the long term? Numerous studies point to the opposite, namely that the market sees through actions intended to increase accounting earnings without increasing cash flow.[16]

We wonder who is responsible for this specious issue of having the wrong shareholders. In a famous survey, Graham, Harvey, and Rajgopal found that 80% of CFOs would cut spending on discretionary future-oriented activities such as marketing and R&D to meet short-term earnings targets.[17] We have personally experienced situations where group executives pressure managers to book revenue and earnings within the artificial constraint of a financial year even if it means offering better terms and discounts. Financial analysts will spot this trick by comparing net income to operating cash flow. This is uneconomic behavior and not doing the "right thing" for long-term shareholders.

Academic research has shown that R&D intensive firms have generated substantial future risk-adjusted shareholder returns.[18] Cutting the R&D budget to boost short-term earnings would hurt the share prices of most successful technology and pharmaceutical companies. Paradoxically, successful firms can often surprise the market by an unexpected increase in their R&D expenditure and increase their share price while earnings drop.[19]

---

[16]Tim Koller, Marc Goedhart, and David Wessels (2010), *Valuation: Measuring and Managing the Value of Companies*, Chapter 16, John Wiley & Sons. The authors point out numerous examples.

[17]John R. Graham, Cam Harvey, and Shiva Rajgopal, "The Economic Implications of Corporate Financial Reporting," *Journal of Accounting and Economics*, 40 (2005), 3–73.

[18]Mustafa Ciftci, Baruch Lev, and Suresh Radhakrishnan, "Is Research and Development Mispriced or Properly Risk Adjusted?" *Journal of Accounting, Auditing & Finance* 26(1) (January 2011), 81–116.

[19]For an interesting case study on how an improved decision analysis process shifted SmithKline Beecham from cutting R&D to increasing it, see Paul Sharpe and Tom Keelin, "How SmithKline Beecham Makes Better Resource-Allocation Decisions," *Harvard Business Review*, March-April 1998.

As Mauboussin and Callahan point out in their study "A Long Look at Short-Termism," "concerns about short-termism have been around for a long time."[20] Here is a recent example that they cite:

> "... the shadow of short-termism has continued to advance—and the situation may actually be getting worse. As a result, companies are less able to invest and build value for the long term, undermining broad economic growth and lowering returns on investment for savers.
>
> The main source of the problem, we believe, is the continuing pressure on public companies from financial markets to maximize short-term results."[21]

Contrast this sentiment with Amazon's pitiful accounting earnings and superlative market rating, and what Jeff Bezos said in 1997 and reiterates every year, "We believe that a fundamental measure of our success will be the shareholder value we create over the long term." Amazon's average return on equity over the past five years is a meager 1.4% yet it trades at a price-to-book (P/B) multiple of 21.[22] It doesn't have a trailing price-to-earnings (P/E) ratio since it reported negative earnings in 2014. Its forward P/E is an astronomical 112 compared to a longer-term average of around 14 for most firms.

In Apple's release of its third quarter 2015 results, the world's most valuable and followed company beat analysts' expectations, yet its share price dropped 8%.

The *Financial Times* reported, "Revenues for the three months ending in June were up 33 per cent to $49.6bn with earnings up 45 per cent to $1.85—the ninth consecutive quarter that Apple has beaten earnings forecasts."[23]

Although Apple beat quarterly sales and earnings expectations, concerns about the iPhone's longer-term growth, and prospects for revenue growth

---

[20] Michael J. Mauboussin and Dan Callahan (2014), "A Long Look at Short-Termism: Questioning the Premise," Credit Suisse Global Financial Strategies.

[21] Dominic Barton and Mark Wiseman, "Focusing on the Long Run," *Harvard Business Review*, January 2014.

[22] Amazon's ROE based on average book equity from 2010 to 2014 was respectively: 4.8%, 2.2%, −0.1%, 0.8%, and −0.6%. The P/B and forward P/E values are as of September 17, 2015.

[23] Tim Bradshaw. "Apple Shares Tumble after Third Quarter Results," *Financial Times*, July 21, 2015.

from China and the Apple Watch, brought down the share price. Apple lost $30bn in market cap despite posting stellar numbers. Apple is expected to generate $525bn in NPV on its present and future as-yet-unknown businesses![24] The market is already paying for enormous value creation and growth. It is no wonder that investors get twitchy when it appears future growth engines might disappoint.

Mauboussin defines short-termism as "the tendency to make decisions that appear beneficial in the short term at the expense of decisions that have a higher payoff in the longer term." Although short-termism is often cited by the press as a plague infecting the investment and corporate community, it is difficult to prove. We maintain that investors prefer more value to less, and that they prefer decisions that increase the long-term NPV of the firm over short-term antics and accounting manipulation meant to fool investors. In fact, companies that frequently restate their financial reports tend to underperform the stock market.[25]

Corporate valuation is based on the present value of a firm's future cash flows. Fledgling companies that are burning cash and not yet making profits may trade at rich P/E and P/B ratios because investors are willing to pay juicy premiums for future growth and profitability that they expect from projects that have yet to break ground. High valuations relative to book value indicate that the market is paying for the long term. When investors have a short-term horizon, they are unwilling to pay much for the future. Most investors take a longer-term view, and are willing to pay for many years of cash flow when they purchase the shares of highly successful firms that demonstrate durable competitive advantages.

A simple example illustrates the connection between time and value (Exhibit 1.6). Franck Dangereux is an extraordinary chef from France who moved to Cape Town in the 1990s. His Foodbarn has been a favorite restaurant of this section's author for over a decade (mainly as a tourist

---

[24]On September 17, 2015, Apple's market cap was $650bn, and its book equity value was $126bn as of June 30, 2015. Apple is presently feeling pressure from activist shareholders since it holds $201bn in short- and long-term investments, and cash.
[25]Conversations with and studies performed by Ron Graziano of Credit Suisse HOLT.

EXHIBIT 1.6 **A simple example connecting time and value with the culinary delights of Cape Town's Foodbarn.**

Year	1	2	3	4	5	6	7	8	9	10
Gross Profit	2,500	2,700	2,916	3,149	3,401	3,673	3,967	4,285	4,627	4,998
x PV factor	0.909	0.826	0.751	0.683	0.621	0.564	0.513	0.467	0.424	0.386
= PV of Gross Profit	2,273	2,231	2,191	2,151	2,112	2,073	2,036	1,999	1,962	1,927
PV of Cumulative GP	2,273	4,504	6,695	8,846	10,958	13,031	15,067	17,066	19,028	20,955

but now as a resident).[26] What is the financial value of my visits to the restaurant?

Let's say I visit the Foodbarn four times a year with three other people. In the next year, the total bill for each visit will average R2,500 before tip and VAT. Let's assume a gross margin of 25% for Foodbarn, which is the difference between the price of the meals to me and the cost of the food and its preparation to Chef Dangereux. If I further assume a discount rate of 10%, the present value for the next year's gross profit is R2,273, which is stated in the currency of South African rand, R.

$$PV \ Gross \ Profit = \frac{4 \ visits \times R2,500 \ per \ visit \times 25\%}{1.10} = R2,273$$

The present value for five years of loyal dining is R10,958 if Franck can increase prices 8% annually due to demand. If he continues to inspire and delight customers for ten years, the present value leaps to R20,955. Every time I walk into Foodbarn, I am greeted as warmly as R21,000 in today's cash. And the free round of port at the meal's conclusion is a sound investment on Franck's part.

Five hundred like-minded foodies are worth R10.5m in today's cash. If every visit leads to enthusiastic recommendations and new customers for Franck, then Foodbarn's value multiplies and marketing is free. Let's assume that out of 4 visits per a year, a new loyal customer is smitten by Franck's culinary skill. Starting with me, the family tree grows to 16 in

---

[26] David Holland lived in Cape Town from 1995 to 2002 and moved back to Cape Town in 2012.

5 years for a present value of R66,497 and 512 in 10 years for a present value of R2m. The network effect compounds handsomely.

Loyal Customer Tree	1	2	4	8	16	32	64	128	256	512
Loyal Gross Profit	2,500	5,400	11,664	25,194	54,420	117,546	253,900	548,424	1,184,595	2,558,726
PV of Loyal GP	2,273	4,463	8,763	17,208	33,790	66,352	130,291	255,844	502,384	986,500
PV of Cumulative Loyal GP	2,273	6,736	15,499	32,707	66,497	132,849	263,140	518,983	1,021,368	2,007,867

If Franck's attention wanders, and food quality and service deteriorate, then the value of my visits drops to R2,273, and he loses a loyal, long-term fan. He'll have to spend money on advertising and offer discounted specials to attract new customers. Profits will shrink. His wallet will wither. Short-term tricks such as overbilling, using poorer quality ingredients, or reduced service will hurt long-term value. Aggressive expansion, which means taking his eye off his franchise restaurant, can easily backfire.

In addition to creating long-term value, Franck must also be socially responsible. If Franck were to begin treating his staff in a repulsive manner or expressing odious views in the local paper, patronage of his restaurant would fall. It is in his long-term interest to behave in a socially responsible manner.

A company can suffer tremendous economic loss when its reputation is damaged. The British public relations firm Bell Pottinger declared bankruptcy in 2017 after it was linked to a racially derisive PR campaign in South Africa. In 2015, Chipotle suffered share price losses totaling more than $10bn due to contamination of its chicken through _E. coli_ bacteria. In 1993, when four people died from _E. coli_ bacteria after eating hamburgers at Jack-in-the-Box, the firm's market value fell more than 30%. In 1982, someone put potassium cyanide in Tylenol capsules and placed the bottles back on the shelf. Seven people who took those capsules died. Johnson & Johnson, the maker of Tylenol, suffered a loss of two billion dollars in market value. Its direct costs to recall the product and in litigating lawsuits were a tenth of that. These firms all suffered a direct hit to the value of their long-term cash flows.

From a fundamental point of view, the long term clearly matters to investors. Because valuations are highly sensitive to changes in expectations about long-term profitability and growth, it is little wonder that share prices can be quite volatile. Essentially, investors make short-term bets on long-term outcomes. If your analysis leads you to conclude a stock is selling at the wrong price during the short term, there is an opportunity to create value for yourself in the long term by purchasing it today.

THINKING CLEARLY ABOUT ACTIONS, REACTIONS, AND VALUE

How can you digest everything from company announcements to government policy changes in a clear, uncluttered way without getting lost in distractions and abstractions? We find the *Law of Conservation of Value* to be enormously beneficial and an appropriate way to end this chapter. This law states that anything that doesn't change an asset's *expected* cash flows, or the riskiness of those cash flows, doesn't change the intrinsic value of the asset.

$$Value = \sum_{n=1}^{N} \frac{E[CF_n]}{(1 + r)^n} \tag{1.4}$$

The term $E[CF_n]$ is the expected cash flow in year n.

When an announcement is made or an event occurs, you should ask two simple questions about how the new information affects the numerator and denominator of this equation:

- Will the expected cash flows change?
- Will the riskiness of those cash flows change?

If the answer is no to both questions, then the intrinsic value shouldn't change no matter what an army of investment bankers or television pundits armed with P/E ratios might suggest. **If an action does not increase expected cash flows, then it should not increase value.**

Equipped with this law, you can disentangle countless arguments and sleights of hand:

- If a company axes R&D to increase next quarter's earnings—and the expected NPV from the R&D is positive—then future expected cash flows will be lower.

- Idle (excess) cash destroys value, and should be distributed to shareholders. Activist shareholders know this and press for it to extinguish the temptation of value-destroying acquisitions and investments. Yet according to Larcker et al. 87% of companies agree or strongly agree that activist shareholders are undesirable. Why should they be feared if they are presenting ideas to increase the share price? Activists are unlikely to attack companies that act in shareholders' best long-term interests. Companies get the shareholders they deserve.

- Don't be fooled by whether earnings are accretive or dilutive in a company takeover. If the expected increase in cash flow does not exceed the premium paid for the acquisition, then intrinsic value will be lower and destroy value for shareholders. Don't fall for arguments that hail diversification as a key benefit when mergers and acquisitions are promoted. As Brealey, Myers, and Allen point out, "Value additivity also means that you can't increase value by putting two whole companies together unless you thereby increase the total cash flow. In other words, there are no benefits to mergers solely for diversification."[27]

- Don't get suckered by the *sunk cost fallacy*. If the NPV of future cash flows is negative, it doesn't matter how much was invested—the project should be stopped at once and written off. It is for this reason that the market shrugs when companies write off billions in bad investments if the market has already taken a negative view on those investments. Mining giants BHP Billiton, Rio Tinto, and Anglo American made big bets during the commodity super cycle of the mid-noughties that were later written off when commodity prices crashed. Despite totaling

---

[27] Richard A. Brealey, Stewart C. Myers, and Franklin Allen, *Principles of Corporate Finance*, McGraw-Hill Education, 2014.

tens of billions of dollars, the write-offs didn't alter expected cash flows and share prices on their dates of announcement. Expectations for future cash flow and shares prices had already dropped in line with sinking commodity prices.

- If you wish to understand the impact of government policy on a company's value or country's wealth, follow the change in expected cash flow. Will the policy increase expected cash flow, or reduce uncertainty in any of the firm's projects? Margaret Thatcher earned a degree in chemistry and probably recalled scientific and economic conservation principles when she observed, "The problem with socialism is that you eventually run out of other people's money."

We suggest that you commit the Law of Conservation of Value and its two simple questions to memory. They will save you time, breath, and money.

When in doubt on how to think about or value a decision or strategy, always remember that the NPV rule is the golden rule of finance. Countless managers and investors live to regret forgetting it. Here's what the new CEO of the once mighty South African mining giant Anglo American had to say while the company was struggling to survive calamitous acquisitions, onerous debt obligations, and devastating shareholder returns: "The flaw in the strategy was growth that was not pinned to returns or affordability. You have to protect your balance sheet."[28] That is an astonishing admission of value destruction.

---

[28] Mark Cutifani, CEO of Anglo American, quoted in the *Financial Times* on February 14, 2016. In an earlier interview with *The Globe and Mail* in 2014, the article stated, "Today, the new focus is on boring but worthy pursuits, like capital discipline and shareholder value, not the fun but destructive activities like growth for the sake of growth. 'We were forcing growth through the system and that's partly how we got into trouble,' Mr. Cutifani says." The ignominious acquisition of Brazilian iron ore assets was over $10bn of trouble, but it was made on the previous CEO's account. See Eric Reguly, "The Lunch: At Helm of Anglo American, Consummate Miner Digs Deep for Savings," *The Globe and Mail*, April 25, 2014.

2

THE FLYING TRAPEZE OF PERFORMANCE METRICS

"As managements and board members improve their knowledge of the link between firms' economic performance and share price, they will increasingly look beyond accounting earnings. They will gain conviction that large investments in core competencies and long-lived, viable projects in which the firm has demonstrated skill can raise the company's stock price, even if near-term accounting results suffer from it."

—Bartley J. Madden[1]

KEY LEARNING POINTS

- Return on equity (ROE), a commonly used measure of profitability, is subject to numerous distortions and, therefore, unreliable.
- Return on invested capital (ROIC) is a better measure of a firm's profitability. It is not influenced by capital structure.

---

[1] Bartley J. Madden (1999), *CFROI Valuation: A Total System Approach to Valuing the Firm*, Butterworth–Heinemann.

- The P/E ratio can be related to a DCF model but is highly restrictive and subject to numerous distortions. Relative valuation metrics such as P/E and P/B should only be used as sanity checks.
- All things being equal, an increase in profitability results in an increase in value. All asset growth is not equal. Companies should only expand if they can generate returns on capital that exceed the cost of capital.
- The hallmarks of a sound economic performance and valuation framework are outlined.

MEASURES OF CORPORATE PERFORMANCE

Profit is a measure of gain from investment. Profitability is a measure of relative gain, typically scaled by the investment. A popular metric for assessing profitability is to compare reported or expected net income to the book value of stockholders' equity. This ratio is known as return on equity (ROE). Let's see how return on equity can be gamed.

Amazon traded at a price-to-earnings ratio (P/E) of 169 and price-to-book ratio (P/B) of 13.8 in December 2014 indicating that the market had buoyant expectations for the firm's profitability and growth.[2] Amazon spends billions of dollars on marketing, improving its technology, and investing in new areas like web services (Exhibit 2.1).[3]

EXHIBIT 2.1 Amazon increased the amount it spent on marketing and technology during this period.

Amazon	2011	2012	2013
Net Sales ($m)	48,077	61,093	74,452
Marketing ($m)	1,630	2,408	3,133
Marketing / Sales	3.4%	3.9%	4.2%
Technology & Content ($m)	2,909	4,564	6,565
T&C / Sales	6.1%	7.5%	8.8%

---

[2] Amazon's closing share price was $307.32, and its market cap was $142 billion on December 12, 2014. The P/E ratio is based on the expected FY2014 earnings and the P/B ratio on the most recent quarter. Both ratios were taken from www.bloomberg.com on the same day.
[3] These figures were taken from Amazon's FY2013 annual report.

Marketing expense increased from 3.4% of sales to 4.2% from 2011 to 2013. Amazon invested heavily in technology and content over this period, increasing that investment from 6.1% to 8.8% of sales.

RETURN ON EQUITY

Return on equity (ROE) is a traditional accounting metric used to assess the performance of companies.

$$ROE = \frac{Net\ Income}{Book\ Equity}$$

Most practitioners use average book equity since net income represents earnings for the entire financial year. Valuations should be based on the beginning-of-year (BOY) equity since all cash flows are relative to opening assets. Companies that can maintain an ROE that exceeds the cost of equity should trade at a premium to book value (P/B > 1), and companies that are unable to meet the cost of equity should trade at a discount (P/B < 1). Amazon's ROE suffered because investments were expensed rather than capitalized (Exhibit 2.2). Expenses that are expected to generate future cash flows are more accurately recognized as an investment (or an intangible asset), and as such, they are placed on the balance sheet. Over time, as revenue is recognized, the asset is amortized in keeping with the matching principle in accounting. This is known as a capital expense.

EXHIBIT 2.2 **Amazon's return on equity (ROE) and price-to-book ratio (P/B). Market capitalization is based on the December year-end value.**

Amazon	2011	2012	2013
Net Income ($m)	631	(39)	274
÷ Beginning Equity ($m)	7,757	8,192	9,746
= ROE (boy)		−0.5%	3.3%
= ROE (avg)		−0.5%	3.1%
Market cap ($m)	78,761	113,895	183,045
÷ Beginning Equity ($m)	7,757	8,192	9,746
= P/B	10.2	13.9	18.8

If earnings were the be-all and end-all of valuation, Amazon should have traded at a discount to its book value. Its fiscal year 2013 ROE of 3.1% is hardly the level of return investors get excited about and is more symptomatic of a mature company in a dying industry than a highly profitable star. Amazon's P/B of 18.8 at the end of 2013 tells a different story and is indicative of a firm with sky high returns and growth. Amazon could have improved its earnings by cutting its marketing and technology expenses, which were respectively 11× and 24× the 2013 reported net income. We would venture that the share price would have taken a hard knock since a cut in these expenses affects future growth and long-term cash flow generation (don't forget the Law of Conservation of Value described in Chapter 1). Clearly, neither Amazon nor its investors view technology and content as an operating expense but rather as an investment in the company's future.

If Amazon had cut spending on technology and content to zero, its 2013 ROE would have jumped to over 50% and the company would have reported record earnings (Exhibit 2.3). Wouldn't shareholders welcome the leap in ROE and earnings? Most certainly not, as the share price would have plummeted. There is an expectation by shareholders that Amazon's managers invest in positive NPV projects and that they will reduce

EXHIBIT 2.3 Amazon's ROE if it cut its technology and content spending to zero.

Cut Amazon's R&D	2011	2012	2013
Net Income	631	(39)	274
+ Technology & Content	2,909	4,564	6,565
− Tax Adjustment @ 35%	1,018	1,597	2,298
= Adjusted Net Income	2,522	2,928	4,541
÷ Book Equity ($m)	7,757	8,192	9,746
= ROE (boy)		37.7%	55.4%
= ROE (avg)		36.7%	50.6%

capital expenses as attractive projects dry up. If this expectation did not exist, Amazon would trade at a significantly lower price-to-book value.

Cutting the entire technology expense would be quite drastic. An astute analyst should parse the technology expense into a maintenance expense, and a development investment, and adjust earnings and the balance sheet accordingly. We will soon see that R&D is more appropriately treated as an investment and therefore capitalized on the balance sheet when calculating CFROI.

Reclassifying a short-term operating expense as a long-term capital expense will affect earnings and ROE, but it will not affect cash flow. The increase in earnings will be offset by an increase in investment, so the net cash flow will stay the same.[4] Reclassification will influence the accounting results and can be used to boost earnings, but it has no effect on the firm's economics, which is the chief focus of long-term investors.[5] Despite this fact, 80% of CFOs said they would cut discretionary spending on value-enhancing activities to meet short-term earnings targets.[6] This behavior is at odds with the rules of corporate finance we outlined in Chapter 1.

Jeff Bezos's thoughts on this topic and how they apply to Amazon are instructive, "We will continue to make investment decisions in light of long-term market leadership considerations rather than short-term prof-itability considerations or short-term Wall Street reactions."[7] Amazon's aim is to create value for its customers and shareholders, not to hit quarterly earnings targets and placate equity analysts.

---

[4]There is an immediate tax benefit to expensing R&D. Once the tax benefits are accounted for, there is no difference in cash flow if R&D is expensed or capitalized. The latter is preferable for financial performance analysis if the R&D expense is expected to result in long-term cash flows.

[5]WorldCom covered up its poor performance and inflated its earnings by capitalizing connection line costs, which were removed as operating expenses on the income statement and shifted to the balance sheet as sham assets. The asset base was inflated by some $11bn over three years. WorldCom's fraud ended in bankruptcy and a significant loss in wealth for its shareholders.

[6]John R. Graham, Cam Harvey, and Shiva Rajgopal (2005), "The Economic Implications of Corporate Financial Reporting," *Journal of Accounting and Economics*, 40, p. 3–73.

[7]Jeff Bezos, 1997 Letter to Shareholders, Amazon.com 1997 Annual Report.

WHAT ABOUT DEBT AND LEVERAGE?

Let's continue our investigation into measuring corporate performance by assessing three fictitious airlines with identical expectations regarding return on investment, growth, and the timing of cash flows, but different opinions on employing debt. We will demonstrate how accounting ratios can be distorted, making comparison difficult.

Safe Way is very conservative and employs no debt; Daedalus Way follows a middle route, employing a modest amount of debt, and thereby avoids flying too high or too low; and Icarus is run by blue sky daredevils who are deeply in debt. The airlines industry is highly competitive and no firm has a significant competitive advantage. Historically, the airlines industry has generated operating returns at or below its cost of capital, meaning it has generated profits below investors' expectations. Volatile earnings and operating returns are correlated to macroeconomic strength. When the economy is riding high, businessmen and tourists take to the skies and travel.

Each airline in this example has the same operating assets but different levels of gearing (Exhibit 2.4).[8] We consider two possible scenarios with equal chance that the economy will be either depressed or buoyant. The two economic scenarios are expressed as "low" and "high" in next year's potential earnings before interest and tax (EBIT), which is identical for each airline. Because they employ different levels of debt, their net income scenarios are different. Safe Way will earn either $16m if the economy tumbles or $49m if it booms on $775m of equity; Daedalus Way will earn $6m or $38m on $525m of equity; and Icarus Way will lose $4m or earn $29m on only $300m of equity. The results are summarized in Exhibit 2.4.

If the economy soars, then Icarus leads the way with an ROE of 9.6% while Safe Way gets by with an ROE of 6.3%. If the economy crashes, the ranking inverts: Icarus reports a loss and ROE of −1.2% while Safe Way leads the pack with a low but positive ROE of 2.1%.

---

[8] The term *gearing* is synonymous with leverage, and used commonly outside the United States.

EXHIBIT 2.4 **Flying high or low the Safe, Daedalus, and Icarus Way.**

Income statement	Safe Way			Daedalus Way			Icarus Way		
	Low	Expected	High	Low	Expected	High	Low	Expected	High
EBIT	23	47	70	23	47	70	23	47	70
Interest @ 6%	–	–	–	(15)	(15)	(15)	(29)	(29)	(29)
Tax @ 30%	(7)	(14)	(21)	(2)	(9)	(16)	2	(5)	(12)
Net income	16	33	49	6	22	38	(4)	13	29
Opening Balance sheet									
Current assets	250	250	250	250	250	250	250	250	250
Long-term assets	750	750	750	750	750	750	750	750	750
Total assets	1,000	1,000	1,000	1,000	1,000	1,000	1,000	1,000	1,000
Current liabilities	225	225	225	225	225	225	225	225	225
Long-term debt	–	–	–	250	250	250	475	475	475
Stockholders' equity	775	775	775	525	525	525	300	300	300
Total liabilities & equity	1,000	1,000	1,000	1,000	1,000	1,000	1,000	1,000	1,000
Metrics									
Debt / Equity	0.00	0.00	0.00	0.48	0.48	0.48	1.58	1.58	1.58
ROE	2.1%	4.2%	6.3%	1.1%	4.2%	7.3%	−1.2%	4.2%	9.6%
ROA	1.6%	3.3%	4.9%	0.6%	2.2%	3.8%	−0.4%	1.3%	2.9%
ROIC	2.1%	4.2%	6.3%	2.1%	4.2%	6.3%	2.1%	4.2%	6.3%

The impact of debt to shareholders depends on its cost and the debt-to-equity ratio (D/E). If a firm is exposed to highly volatile revenue and has a high fixed-cost base, that is, overhead costs which do not typically vary with revenue such as salaries and rent, its operating cash flow will also be highly volatile, which increases uncertainty. Debt adds value only if the firm is generating enough operating cash to cover its debt obligations in desperate scenarios. Not only do we see that debt can be a bane (low scenario) or boon (high scenario), but that it leads to a greater variance in the ROE, which can be seen in Exhibit 2.5. The standard deviation for Safe Way is 2.1%; for Daedalus, 3.1%; and for Icarus, 5.4%. An increase in debt makes returns to shareholders less predictable and this demands a higher cost of equity. Leverage comes with a cost.

EXHIBIT 2.5 **The effect of gearing on ROE for the high and low scenarios for each airline.**

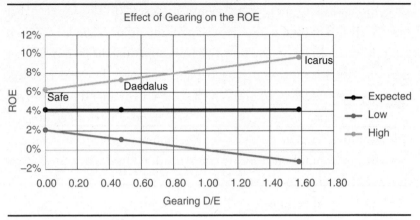

As a general rule, if the return on equity with no debt exceeds the after-tax cost of debt, then ROE will rise with increasing debt. On the other hand, if the return on equity with no debt is less than the after-tax cost of debt, then ROE will decrease as debt increases, eventually resulting in a loss in earnings. A firm with stable operating cash flow can carry more debt and take greater advantage of its tax benefit. Debt investors demand a higher interest rate for riskier loans. In our example, Safe Way can increase the market value of its equity by using debt to buy back shares or pay a special dividend. Icarus is too risky and needs to raise equity to lower its debt. Daedalus and its middle way is the most sensible and valuable approach.

If anything is clear, it is that ROE is not only distorted by accounting conventions but highly sensitive to and muddied by leverage. For these reasons, ROE is not a reliable measure of performance for industrial and service firms. Earnings and ROE are simply not comparable unless firms have identical risks and gearing, and if they trade in environments with similar inflation. There are ways to get around these issues and improve the performance metric.

RETURN ON ASSETS

One approach is to measure the return on assets (ROA), which is net income divided by total assets. The results for the airline example are shown in the Metrics section of Exhibit 2.4. When comparing the performance of two firms, ROA is superior to ROE because it removes the distortive effect of leverage embedded in equity. ROA has a short-coming: It measures the earnings of equity investors relative to assets funded by both equity and debt investors. Thus, its numerator and denominator are inconsistent and provide an incomplete perspective on the performance of the firm. ROA decreases as leverage increases in our example.

Metrics should be consistent with their intent. The numerator of ROA will be consistent with its denominator if interest paid is added back to net income.

$$ROA_{adj} = \frac{Net\ Income + Interest\ Paid}{Total\ Assets}$$

This measure is better than ROE when comparing the performance of firms but still prone to bias. If a firm were to increase current assets and current liabilities by the same amount, its ROA would drop without any change in cash flow.

The ROA and adjusted ROA calculations for Amazon are shown in Exhibit 2.6. Amazon's adjusted ROA in 2013 based on its assets at the beginning of year was an unimpressive 1.1%. This accounting metric doesn't explain why Amazon was trading at a multiple well above its book value.

RETURN ON INVESTED CAPITAL

Accounts payable and other non-interest-bearing current liabilities are essentially short-term sources of capital to fund a firm's operations, and should be subtracted from current assets to determine invested capital:

$$Net\ Working\ Capital = Current\ Assets - Current\ Liabilities$$

EXHIBIT 2.6 **Return on asset calculation for Amazon in 2012 and 2013.**

Amazon.com ($m)	2011	2012	2013
Net income	631	(39)	274
+ interest paid	65	92	141
= adjusted net income	696	53	415
Balance Sheet			
Total current assets	17,490	21,296	24,625
Property & equipment, net	4,417	7,060	10,949
Goodwill	1,955	2,552	2,655
Other assets	1,416	1,647	1,930
Total assets	25,278	32,555	40,159
Total current liabilities	14,896	19,002	22,980
Long-term debt	1,415	3,830	5,181
Other long-term liabilities	1,210	1,531	2,252
Total stockholders' equity	7,757	8,192	9,746
Liabilities & stockholders' equity	25,278	32,555	40,159
ROA (avg)		−0.1%	0.8%
Adjusted ROA (avg)		0.2%	1.1%

Excess cash and short-term debt (the current portion due on long-term liabilities) are usually removed from current assets and liabilities. They are shifted to the funding side of invested capital since they are not part of the firm's day-to-day operations.

$$Invested\ Capital = Equity + LT\ Debt + ST\ Debt$$
$$- Excess\ Cash + Other\ LT\ Liabilities$$

Invested capital can be tallied from either the operating (business) or funding (investor) points of view, which must balance.

$$Invested\ Capital = Net\ Working\ Capital + Net\ Fixed\ Assets$$
$$+ Other\ LT\ Assets$$

You can think of invested capital in two ways. It represents the amount of net assets a company needs to run its business (the left side of the balance sheet). But, it is also the amount of financing (money) a company's creditors and shareholders supply to fund those assets (the right side of the balance sheet). Since double-entry accounting requires that both sides of the balance sheet equal one another, there is no real difference in the two points of view. Our preference is to calculate invested capital from the asset side of the balance sheet to track how efficiently the company is using capital.[9] Also, it is easier to address issues such as goodwill and investments in associates from the asset side of the balance sheet.

Return on invested capital (ROIC) relates the net operating profit after tax (NOPAT) to the operating invested capital from all sources:

$$ROIC = \frac{NOPAT}{Invested\ Capital}$$

NOPAT can be derived from the top down (starting with revenue) or bottom up (starting with earnings) where T_c is the cash tax rate:

$$NOPAT = EBIT \times (1 - T_c)$$

$$NOPAT = Net\ Income + Net\ Interest\ Paid \times (1 - T_c)$$

Financing effects are eliminated by adding back the after-tax net interest paid to net income. NOPAT is a measure of unlevered profit and treats the firm as if it is independent of debt. This is essential for accurately comparing the operating performance of firms.

Return on invested capital is superior to ROE as a measure of corporate performance. It is the return to all providers of capital, which is a more sensible way of assessing the performance of a business since it is typically funded by both debt and equity investors. In the airline example, Exhibit 2.4 shows that leverage has no impact on ROIC, and that for the unlevered Safe Way, ROE and ROIC are identical. In conventional approaches to calculating the value of a business, the tax shield benefit of interest paid on debt is accounted for by using an after-tax cost of debt in the discount rate.

---

[9] Efficiency ratios such as asset utilization (Sales/Assets) and working capital turns (Sales/Working Capital) are helpful in understanding how many dollars of revenue are associated with each dollar of a particular asset classification.

Amazon's NOPAT, invested capital (IC), and ROIC are calculated in Exhibit 2.7.[10] Amazon was holding a significant amount of cash and cash equivalents, which we netted against debt. The other key adjustment was to remove short-term debt from current liabilities since short-term debt is really the current portion of long-term interest-bearing debt that has come due. Amazon receives a significant degree of funding from its operating creditors. Note that its net working capital in fiscal year 2013 was negative $5.3bn, which reduces the invested capital. Also note that the operating and funding sides of the balance sheet are equal. Despite the "free" creditor funding, Amazon's ROIC in 2013 was only 3.9%. Once again, this return on capital does not bear the *imprimatur* of a leading global wealth creator.

Consistency in measurement is essential. If assets are considered necessary to business operations, then all income related to those assets should be treated as operating income. Non-operating investments and assets are often excluded from the invested capital, which requires that any income associated with these assets be removed from operating income. We will demonstrate these adjustments for CFROI. Numerous textbooks demonstrate how to calculate invested capital and its associated metrics, such as ROIC.[11]

Firms need assets to operate. Decisions must be made about how a business will finance and acquire assets. This decision should not affect the operating economics of the business, though it may affect the financing economics through tax advantages or the risk of financial distress. When a

---

[10] Since investments and other assets are included in our invested capital tally, we have included investment income in NOPAT. Consistency is paramount. A better approach would be to separate financial investments from operating assets, which we will do later in the book. Besides a large cash balance, Amazon also had marketable securities of $3.364bn and $3.789bn sitting in its current assets for FY2012 and FY2013 respectively. We left this item in current assets and accordingly included any income associated with marketable securities in NOPAT.

[11] An excellent reference book is Aswath Damodaran (2012), *Investment Valuation: Tools and Techniques for Determining the Value of Any Asset*. 3rd edition, John Wiley & Sons. The most common adjustments are to exclude cash and short-term debt from invested capital and thus to exclude interest received and interest paid from NOPAT. Equity investments and joint ventures are usually excluded from invested capital and for the sake of consistency equity investment income and JV income must be excluded from NOPAT. Acquisition goodwill should be excluded from invested capital if the goal is to measure the financial performance of operating assets. If you wish to measure whether executives pay too much for acquisitions, then include goodwill and any impairments to goodwill in invested capital. McKinsey's *Valuation* is a handy source for adjustments to NOPAT and invested capital.

EXHIBIT 2.7 Return on invested capital calculation for Amazon in 2012 and 2013.

Amazon.com ($m)	2011	2012	2013
Income from operations	862	676	745
Other income	76	(80)	(136)
EBIT	938	596	609
− Cash taxes @ 35%	(328)	(209)	(213)
+ Investment income, net of tax	(12)	(155)	(71)
NOPAT	598	232	325
Employment of capital (operating)			
Total current assets	17,490	21,296	24,625
− Cash & cash equivalents	(5,269)	(8,084)	(8,658)
Current assets (operating)	12,221	13,212	15,967
− Total current liabilities	(14,896)	(19,002)	(22,980)
+ Short-term debt	524	1,134	1,736
− Current liabilities (operating)	(14,372)	(17,868)	(21,244)
Net working capital	(2,151)	(4,656)	(5,277)
Property & equipment, net	4,417	7,060	10,949
Goodwill	1,955	2,552	2,655
Other assets	1,416	1,647	1,930
Invested capital	**5,637**	**6,603**	**10,257**
Capital employed (funding)			
Short-term debt	524	1,134	1,736
+ Long-term debt	1,415	3,830	5,181
− Cash & cash equivalents	(5,269)	(8,084)	(8,658)
Net debt	(3,330)	(3,120)	(1,741)
Other long-term liabilities	1,210	1,531	2,252
Total stockholders' equity	7,757	8,192	9,746
Invested capital	**5,637**	**6,603**	**10,257**
ROIC (boy)		4.1%	4.9%
ROIC (avg)		3.8%	3.9%

business leases an asset, it will affect accounting figures but not operating efficiency.

Financial decisions serve the company and its investors by adjusting the timing and risk of cash flows. Financial transactions in normally functioning markets neither create nor destroy value—they are zero NPV transactions. Operating decisions influence the success and value of the firm. The separation of a firm's investment and financing choices is termed the *Separation Principle*.[12] We can evaluate projects and the firm without explicitly considering the different financing possibilities the firm might choose. Before we do, let's demonstrate the failings of P/E as a technique for estimating value.

P/E AS A VALUATION METRIC AND DISCOUNTED CASH FLOW VALUATION APPROACH

The most distressing area of confusion between accounting and economics is valuation. Often, once the accounting analysis is complete, a ratio based on that analysis is used to estimate value. For example, a forward P/E ratio relies on an earnings estimate but gives no thought to the *quality* of earnings or the balance sheet needed to support those earnings, that is, what it costs to generate those earnings. The use of a P/B ratio to perform a relative valuation requires no earnings estimate and less analysis.

What's Wrong with P/E?

It is possible to relate the P/E ratio to a DCF model for a mature, stable firm where the firm's growth cannot exceed the long-term growth of the economy. The derivation is worthwhile and leads to important lessons. Let's assume Cash Cow Dairy has a low growth g that remains constant into perpetuity. The growing perpetuity equation from Chapter 1 should spring to mind and might be naively written as:

$$P = \frac{E_1}{(r_e - g)}$$

The term r_e represents the cost of equity and E_1 is the forward earnings. Simple, right? If the firm can grow faster, its price should be higher.

---

[12]Berk and DeMarzo define the Separation Principle as "Security transactions in a normal market neither create nor destroy value on their own. Therefore, we can evaluate the NPV of an investment decision separately from the decision the firm makes regarding how to finance the investment or any other security transactions the firm is considering." Jonathan Berk, and Peter DeMarzo. *Corporate Finance*, 3rd edition, Pearson, 2014.

There is a critical error in the above P/E equation, namely that it does not account for the cost (investment required) to grow earnings. It implies that earnings growth is free and thus that the incremental ROE is infinite. Instead of discounting future earnings, we need to discount future cash flow to equity providers. In addition to the constant earnings growth g, let's also assume that the firm has a constant perpetual return on equity, ROE.

$$FCFE = Earnings - Change\ in\ Equity$$

$FCFE$ is the free cash flow to equity holders and the change in equity ΔB is the investment required to support growth:[13]

$$\Delta B_1 = g \times \frac{E_1}{ROE}$$

Instead of calculating the present value of a growing earnings stream, we calculate the present value of a growing $FCFE$ stream by courtesy of the growing perpetuity equation:[14]

$$P = \frac{E_1 \times (1 - g/ROE)}{(r_e - g)}$$

The forward P/E for our stable firm is:

$$P/E_1 = \frac{(1 - g/ROE)}{(r_e - g)} \tag{2.1}$$

The P/E ratio is a function of earnings growth and more importantly, the *quality* of earnings indicated by *ROE*. With a bit of algebra, the price-to-book ratio is easily derived (Exhibits 2.8 and 2.9).[15]

$$P/B_0 = \frac{(ROE - g)}{(r_e - g)} \tag{2.2}$$

---

[13] All things equal, i.e., ROE is constant forever, then earnings growth and equity growth are equivalent. The full algebraic derivation is: $\Delta B_1 = B_1 - B_0 = (1 + g) \times B_0 - B_0 = g \times B_0 = g \times \frac{E_1}{ROE}$

[14] The algebra follows: $P = \frac{FCFE_1}{(r_e-g)} = \frac{E_1 - g \times \frac{E_1}{ROE}}{(r_e-g)} = \frac{E_1 \times (1-g/ROE)}{(r_e-g)}$

[15] Gordon's dividend growth model can be readily derived from this equation. The sustainable dividend payout ratio D_1/E_1 equals $(1 - g/ROE)$, which leads to $P = D_1/(r_e - g)$. Earnings, equity, and dividends all grow at a constant rate g. If growth is zero, then the firm pays all earnings as a dividend, the dividend yield equals the cost of equity and the price never appreciates (unless the firm were to repurchase shares instead of paying dividends).

EXHIBIT 2.8 The P/E ratio for different combinations of constant growth and ROE assuming a 10% cost of equity. It decreases as growth increases for the value destroyer; equals the inverse of the cost of equity for value-neutral corks; and increases with growth for value creators.

P/E matrix		ROE		
		5%	10%	20%
	0%	10.0	10.0	10.0
Growth	2%	7.5	10.0	11.3
	4%	3.3	10.0	13.3

EXHIBIT 2.9 The P/B ratio for different combinations of perpetual growth and ROE assuming a 10% cost of equity. It decreases as growth increases for the value destroyer; equals unity when ROE equals the cost of equity; and increases with growth for value creators.

P/B matrix		ROE		
		5%	10%	20%
	0%	0.5	1.0	2.0
Growth	2%	0.4	1.0	2.3
	4%	0.2	1.0	2.7

Several fascinating insights can be discovered from these equations:

- If $g = 0$, then the P/E ratio is simply the inverse of the cost of equity, r_e. Conversely, the cost of equity equals the forward earnings yield, E/P. The P/B ratio equals ROE/r_e when there is no growth. If ROE equals the cost of equity, then P/B should equal 1. When ROE exceeds the cost of equity, then the price should exceed the book value. If the firm is not meeting its cost of equity, the P/B should be less than 1. This result should be obvious since the denominator will be larger than the numerator.

- If $g <$ ROE, then cash flow will be positive. The FCFE can be distributed to shareholders, used to fund more growth, or pay down debt. If growth exceeds the ROE, then funds must be raised, which is not sustainable in this growing annuity example since it implies a negative price.

- If ROE $= r_e$, then growth is irrelevant. This company is value neutral, it neither creates nor destroys value. P/E equals $1/r_e$ and P/B equals 1. The chief lesson is that mature firms meeting their cost of equity should focus on improving operating margins and increasing asset utilization (sales/assets) to improve ROE rather than growing their business. Earnings growth should come from efficiency improvements not expansion.

- As ROE decreases, the quality of earnings deteriorates along with the free cash flow to equity providers. This leads to an extraordinary bifurcation.

  – If ROE $> r_e$ then the P/E ratio **increases** with growth when $g <$ ROE.[16] The higher ROE is relative to the cost of equity, the higher the quality of earnings and subsequent P/E ratio. Firms that can generate returns greater than the cost of capital should reinvest and grow. In this case, investors want high return on equity AND earnings growth.

  – If ROE $< r_e$, then the P/E ratio **decreases** as growth increases. In other words, the more a firm with miserable profitability tries to grow, the more value it destroys. P/B also suffers, dropping farther below 1 as growth increases. Warren Buffett warns about investing in industries with poor economics. These are often the companies guiltiest of trying to grow out of a hole, which only makes the hole deeper. Unless there is a credible catalyst for change, low-quality firms are best avoided, especially those that are obsessed with growth.

---

[16] This does not mean that firms with this luxury should limit growth to ROE. It simply means they need to raise capital to fund all of their attractive growth opportunities. In these instances, capital is not a scarce resource. Once growth slows to a level below ROE, the firm will become cash flow positive and can pay dividends.

The quality of earnings clearly matters. Besides the highly restrictive assumptions in this derivation, earnings and the subsequent ROE can be altered by any number of accounting decisions:

- Asset aging and depreciation policy (changing earnings through the depreciation charge and net assets through accumulated depreciation)
- Leasing of assets (removing the asset from the balance sheet and increasing operating expenses on the income statement)
- Leverage and financial structure (altering the amount of equity on the balance sheet and the resulting net income)
- Historical acquisitions and goodwill amortization policy (altering both income statement and balance sheet)
- Timing of expenses and revenue (altering both income statement and balance sheet through the level of accruals)[17]

If that's not enough, there are additional problems created by firms having different strategies for tax and accounting purposes. To minimize taxes, earnings are reduced for the tax books, but inflated for reporting purposes to impress investors. This can lead to discrepancies in the effective and marginal tax rates. That, in turn, can increase the probability of predicting earnings that never materialize. If we had a choice, we would prefer the tax books and their lower earnings which can then be consistently adjusted.

Note how important ROE is to the P/E ratio. A higher return always improves P/E, all else being equal. The same cannot be said for growth. The quality of earnings should be an explicit consideration when using P/E ratios but is rarely mentioned. The lower the ROE, the more it costs the firm to grow its earnings. Empirical results agree with this conclusion.

---

[17] Booking sales in advance to enhance earnings is a common trick. If a sale is accompanied by a price discount to speed up the transaction, then the economic value of the transaction is reduced. Companies that booked earnings early to inflate reported net income include Tesco, Toshiba, WorldCom, Xerox, Global Crossing, and Sunbeam. Toshiba's executives manipulated the company's accounts over many years to the tune of hundreds of billions of Yen before unceremoniously taking a bow.

EXHIBIT 2.10 **Forward P/E versus forward earnings growth for U.S. firms with a market cap exceeding $5bn on September 24, 2015.**

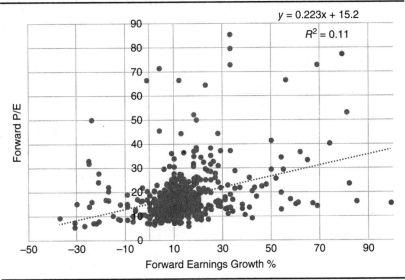

Exhibit 2.10 shows a plot of forward P/E versus forward earnings growth for U.S. firms with a market cap exceeding $5bn.

The relationship between earnings growth and P/E is weak at best with an R-squared of 0.11 for this winsorized sample. The point many forget when discussing earnings growth is that it has two components: investment growth and efficiency growth (Exhibit 2.11). The latter is almost always desirable all things being equal. Investment growth is only positive if the firm is investing in positive NPV strategies, e.g., growth in earnings isn't due to paying excessive premiums for acquisitions to boost earnings that destroy shareholder value. It is important to understand the source of earnings growth. Growth due to efficiency gains is not sustainable and requires explicit forecasting.

If two firms are identical, then their multiples should match exactly. Identical in our example means they have the same ROE, growth, and equivalent risk to have the same P/E and P/B ratios. Thus, a critical weakness of relative valuation measures is that they do not account for differences in growth, profitability, risk, and accounting methods. If that's

EXHIBIT 2.11 Earnings growth is comprised of two components: investment and efficiency growth. The former is only value additive when investments are made in positive NPV projects. Efficiency growth can be accomplished by increasing margins and/or turns.

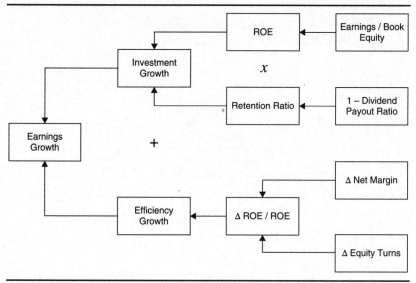

not enough to shake the intrepid investor, ROE is also highly dependent on inflation.[18] Multiples should be used only for sanity checks.

Professor Alfred Rappaport, a pioneer in developing the principles of shareholder value creation declared, "There is no greater enemy of stock market allocation efficiency than earnings obsession."[19] We have illustrated the relationship between measuring corporate performance and valuation, and how that link can be distorted by using traditional accounting figures such as earnings and ROE. Discounted cash flow methods offer the potential to be more accurate and to yield better insights. In addition, sensitivity analyses can be conducted on the firm's operating drivers to assess the impact

---

[18]Net income is in current dollars while book equity is in historical dollars. Inflation distorts the timing difference in this ratio, particularly if investments are lumpy in high-inflation environments. Imagine calculating the ROE on a fleet of power stations that were built thirty to forty years ago in a country that has experienced from 6% to 15% inflation over this period. We have, and CFROI resolved the dilemma. Unfortunately, our advice was not heeded by the controlling shareholder, which led to operating and financial distress.

[19]Alfred Rappaport, "The Economics of Short-Term Performance Obsession," *Financial Analysts Journal,* 61(3) (May/June 2005), 77.

on cash flow and corporate value. Models that measure economic performance and relate it to valuation aim to correct distortions caused by accounting. Don't forget that earnings are an opinion and cash flow is a fact.

HALLMARKS OF A SOUND ECONOMIC PERFORMANCE AND VALUATION MODEL

The hallmarks of a sound model of economic performance and valuation are:

- It should correct distortions caused by accounting so that the measure of operating performance mirrors the firm's underlying economics as closely as possible. We will show that CFROI reverses accounting distortions and places hidden assets (such as operating leases) back on the balance sheet.
- The measure of operating performance should mirror standard economic analyses used to evaluate projects and value their anticipated cash flow, such as NPV and internal rate of return (IRR). It should account for differences between non-depreciating assets (which do not wear out) and depreciating assets (which require replacement), and consider the life of the assets. We will show that CFROI is a cross-sectional weighted-average IRR measure, and that the present value of future economic profit (EP) equals the NPV of existing and future investments. We will show how the CFROI and HOLT EP valuation model reconciles to project economics.
- Inflationary effects should be removed from the measure of operating performance so that results are comparable over time, across borders and across industries. Although inflation is at modest levels in many developed economies, it has been high in the past and continues to distort important line items. Without adjusting for inflation, trend analysis across years and between companies from different countries becomes futile. Inflation artificially boosts earnings and accounting returns, which can

lead to uneconomic results and inferior decisions. CFROI is a real, inflation-adjusted measure.

- The valuation model should focus on determining the present value of future **cash flows**. Cash is king and the only true measure of a firm's value is based on its future cash flow potential. The HOLT CFROI valuation model is a discounted cash flow model which allows key value drivers such as investment growth, returns, and competitive advantage period to be flexed. Whether we discount future cash flows or economic profits, we obtain the same valuation for a given forecast.

- Competitive forces continuously bring about change, upheaval, and innovation. A competitive life-cycle process can be integrated into the valuation model to reflect that fortune and high returns decay over time. A key component of the HOLT CFROI valuation model is the notion of a competitive life-cycle.

The aim of a well-designed corporate performance measurement and valuation system is to provide a structured, economic way of thinking about the key drivers of value. The HOLT CFROI framework is a total system approach that enables users to compare historical corporate performance to market expectations in an efficient, comprehensive manner. Because CFROI is a real return (not nominal), it is possible to compare historical operating returns to forecast returns. This adds a new dimension of plausibility to forecasting and calibrating investor expectations. A firm's CFROI can be compared to its cost of capital to gauge whether the firm is creating or destroying economic value, which is imperative when assessing capital allocation choices.

Do empirical results provide evidence of a strong relationship between market-to-book value and profitability? You betcha. We plotted the HOLT price-to-book ratio versus CFROI for U.S. industrial and service companies in Exhibit 2.12. Note the highly significant R-squared of 0.74 between relative value (HOLT P/B) and the quality of earnings (CFROI).

Time to get started!

EXHIBIT 2.12 HOLT price-to-book ratio versus forward CFROI for U.S. industrial and service firms with a market cap exceeding $5bn on September 24, 2015. The HOLT price-to-book ratio is the market enterprise value divided by the inflation-adjusted net assets. A stock's premium is a function of the quality of its earnings (CFROI).

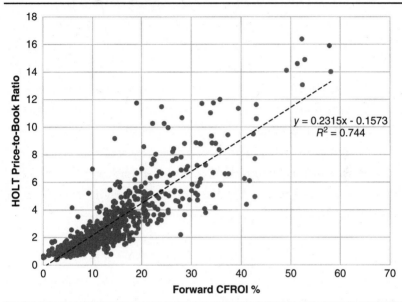

$y = 0.2315x - 0.1573$
$R^2 = 0.744$

CHAPTER APPENDIX

Be suspicious when terms such as "dilution" get thrown around by investment professionals. A common fallacy is that firms should take on debt instead of issuing shares since the latter dilutes the value of existing shares. If a firm issues new shares at a fair price, there will be no gain or loss to new or existing shareholders. The cash raised by the new shares exactly offsets the dilution of the shares.

Earnings dilution gets bandied about liberally by analysts and commentators when acquisitions are the subject of discussion. If an acquisition immediately dilutes EPS, then it is considered bad. The opposite occurs when an acquisition that grows EPS is considered a good one. The NPV rule remains the golden rule of finance when discussing the issuance,

EXHIBIT 2.13 Should Impress Industries buy Superstar or Superdud?

Impress Industries	Pre-raise	Post-raise	Superstar	Impress Star	Superdud	Impress Dud
Market cap	1,000	1,500	500	1,500	500	1,500
Earnings	80	80	25	105	50	130
Shares outstanding	20	30		30		30
Share price	50.00	50.00		50.00		50.00
EPS	4.00	2.67		3.50		4.33
P/E	12.5	18.8	20.0	14.3	10.0	11.5

repurchase or dilution of shares. Let's take the case of Impress Industries, a mature firm with no growth on the horizon but captained by an ambitious new CEO (Exhibit 2.13).

Impress is trading at $50 a share and has a market cap of $1bn (see column "Pre-raise"). Impress is expected to generate $4.00 a share and trades at a prosaic P/E of 12.5. The CEO convinces the market that he will not pay too much for an acquisition and raises $500m in preparation for the acquisition. The NPV of the cash raised is zero, and according to the Law of One Price, investors should be willing to purchase 10 million new shares for $50 a share (see column "Post-raise"). Although the share price remains the same and no value is created, the trailing EPS gets diluted from $4.00 a share to $2.67 a share. The share price does not take a beating due to the dilution since value has been neither created nor destroyed. Rather, the trailing P/E jumps from 12.5 to 18.8 to conserve value. Earnings dilution and P/E provide no insight into the economics of this event.

The CEO has two potential acquisition targets in mind but can only choose one:

1. Superstar Incorporated, which is growing and trades at a forward P/E of 20 (see column "Superstar" for its stand-alone numbers); or

2. Superdud Incorporated, which lives up to its reputation and trades at a P/E of 10 (see column "Superdud" for its stand-alone numbers).

Each target can be purchased at a fair market value of $500m and there is nothing Impress can do to enhance subsequent value.

Sure enough, the acquisition of Superstar results in earnings dilution for the new Impress Star Industries. EPS drops from a pre-raise value of $4.00 to post-merger value of $3.50, but the P/E increases from 12.5 to 14.3. Because the NPV of this acquisition is zero, the share price remains the same at $50.00. EPS dilution is a red herring.

The acquisition of Superdud provides an interesting ruse to excite accountants and analysts capitalizing earnings by P/E ratios. In this case, earnings are accretive and jump from a pre-raise EPS of $4.00 to a post-merger EPS of $4.33 (it is even more impressive if you consider the post-raise diluted EPS of $2.67 jumping to $4.33). The naive analyst might simply multiply the pre-raise P/E of 12.5 times the post-merger EPS of $4.33, and set his target price to $54.17 for an increase of 8.3% in the share price. This would be incorrect. The only way the share price should increase is if the NPV of the acquisition is greater than zero. Impress would have to increase the value of Superdud to $625m through merger synergies and cost savings to generate an NPV of $125m and share price of $54.17.

The next time somebody mentions dilution or accretion, please ask them for the expected NPV of the transaction. If accounting results change but future cash flows and their risk do not, then there should be no change in value. Anything that doesn't increase cash flows doesn't create value.

3

ACCOUNTING TO CASH FLOW RETURN ON INVESTMENT

"The CFROI measure was developed to minimize accounting distortions in measuring firms' economic performance, particularly distortions related to inflation. A time series of CFROIs helps in forecasting a firm's likely returns on future investments. The CFROI is best understood not as a stand-alone performance metric, but as part of a valuation model."

—Bartley J. Madden[1]

KEY LEARNING POINTS

- ROIC is influenced by asset age and can be increased by simply allowing assets to depreciate.
- CFROI is a comprehensive measure of operating performance. Accounting and inflationary distortions are reversed.

---

[1]Bartley J. Madden, *CFROI Valuation: A Total System Approach to Valuing the Firm,* Butterworth-Heinemann, 1999.

Depreciating assets and non-depreciating assets are separated. Asset life is an essential input.

- The calculation of CFROI requires four inputs: gross cash flow, inflation-adjusted gross investment, non-depreciating assets, and asset life. We show how each input is calculated using Amazon as an example.

- Investments in R&D and operating lease expenses should be capitalized to improve the understanding of a firm's economics and enhance comparability to peers.

- Inflationary effects can be significant, particularly for firms with long-life assets and countries with high inflation rates. CFROI is an inflation-adjusted measure of profitability, which makes it possible to compare companies over time and across borders.

- An improved measure of profitability is beneficial when assessing the plausibility of profitability forecasts.

IS CFROI A BETTER MEASURE OF PERFORMANCE?

To understand the logic and benefits of the cash flow return on investment (CFROI) operating performance measure, let us imagine a simple investment scenario. Suppose you invested £1m in your cousin Greg's "Braai Design & Build" business. *Braai* is the South African term for barbeque, where to *braai* with wood is a favorite national pastime.[2] Greg is passionate about braai equipment and outdoor cooking skills, and wishes to promote this custom in the UK. He requires an eight-year investment with £800,000 to support the shop and its fittings, and £200,000 for working capital. The shop equipment and fittings are depreciating assets that need to be replaced after eight years. The working capital will be used to purchase inventory and allow for day-to-day management of the business. You are the sole investor in this business and Greg's salary is an operating

---

[2]Braai is Afrikaans for barbeque or grill and is pronounced braī. It is used as a noun and verb to refer to barbeque activities throughout South Africa. A traditional braai uses wood. The use of gas is frowned upon and condescendingly referred to as a barbeque.

expense. He boldly promises that the business will generate a return of greater than 20%.

Since your cousin is a trustworthy fellow, you leave him to run the business and attend to your other investments. You receive a check for £200,000 every year, which is a 20% return on your original investment. After six-years, you decide to pay Greg a visit and check on your investment. When you arrive at his shop, business is booming and Greg exclaims that he expects the business to break through the 20% return barrier.

Greg apologizes for the slow start but confidently tells you that the business earned 20% last year and shows you his forward estimates of the return on invested capital (ROIC) with returns increasing to 33% (Exhibit 3.1). After pondering his apology and scratching your head over his rather astounding forecast, you attempt to deconstruct his financial analysis. You ask Greg, "How exactly did you arrive at that 20% return?" Greg answers, "The business earned £100,000 after tax on net assets of £500,000. Next year the return will increase to 25% and we'll really be coining it!"

EXHIBIT 3.1 **The evolution of CFROI and other financial performance metrics for Greg's Braai Design & Build business. Each return calculation is based on its beginning-of-year asset base.**

Year (£' 000)	0	1	2	3	4	5	6	7	8
Net income		100	100	100	100	100	100	100	100
+ Depreciation		100	100	100	100	100	100	100	100
Gross cash flow		200	200	200	200	200	200	200	200
Gross fixed assets	800	800	800	800	800	800	800	800	800
(Accum depreciation)		(100)	(200)	(300)	(400)	(500)	(600)	(700)	(800)
Net fixed assets	800	700	600	500	400	300	200	100	–
+ Working capital	200	200	200	200	200	200	200	200	–
Net assets	1,000	900	800	700	600	500	400	300	–
Gross assets	1,000	1,000	1,000	1,000	1,000	1,000	1,000	1,000	–
RONA ... (a÷h)		10.0%	11.1%	12.5%	14.3%	16.7%	20.0%	25.0%	33.3%
CROGA ... (c÷i)		20.0%	20.0%	20.0%	20.0%	20.0%	20.0%	20.0%	20.0%
CFROI ... (RATE(8,c,-i,g))		13.9%	13.9%	13.9%	13.9%	13.9%	13.9%	13.9%	13.9%
Net cash flow	(1,000)	200	200	200	200	200	200	200	400
IRR	**13.9%**								

This enigmatic discussion carries on to the pub where you call a friend who works for an investment bank. He tells you that ROIC is highly dependent on reinvestment and depreciation rates. He explains that investors are regularly fooled by trying to compare returns on new assets versus old assets. "The quickest way to increase returns is to cut capex for a few years. It might kill the business, but it'll look like the company is improving on paper and might command a higher price for a while. Don't be fooled by that trick, old chap." You explain this to Greg over a second pint and tell him that the investment banker suggested that they measure the cash return on gross assets (CROGA), which is the gross cash flow divided by the gross assets (Exhibit 3.1). Because you are the sole capital provider, the gross cash flow equals the net income plus the depreciation charge, which tallies to £200,000 in this example, and a constant 20% return.

Across the pub, you spot your private banker from Credit Suisse and decide to ask her for a second opinion. She laughs and tells you that she just attended a HOLT seminar where she learned that "you also have to account for asset life, and the split between non-depreciating and depreciating assets when performing a comprehensive return on capital analysis." Now you are at your wits end and order a final round to help translate the private banker's advice. After declining your kind offer, the Credit Suisse banker calculates an internal rate of return (IRR) of 13.9%, much lower than the return Greg promised. She explains that the fixed assets will have fully depreciated after eight years and will have little or no residual value. However, the business will be able to liquidate its non-depreciating assets, or working capital, after eight years. This argument makes sense and reminds you of the project analyses you did many years ago, studying corporate finance. The private banker then shows you how to calculate the single-period IRR, or cash flow return on investment (CFROI), for every financial year. The CFROI is a constant 13.9% which reconciles to the IRR and makes perfect sense since the business economics have been—and are expected to remain—constant. You thank the lady from Credit Suisse and stick Greg with the lunch bill.

This example illustrates the problem of measuring performance based on net assets, sometimes referred to as the "old plant trap."[3] As a business or project gets older, the return on net assets increases, all things being equal. Have the economics changed? No. Simple ROE, ROIC, and economic profit (EP) calculations increase only because fixed assets depreciate, which decreases the amount of net assets each year.[4] Metrics can be gamed, particularly accounting ratios, and mislead unwary investors. Since measurement influences behavior, investors and analysts need to carefully consider management's measures of performance, as well as their own. Inappropriate measurement promotes uneconomic behavior. Corporate managers who are rewarded on ROIC or EP might be inclined to cut capital expenditure (capex) and to resist investing in positive net present value (NPV) projects to maintain or increase the present ROIC. This is a classic agency conflict between shareholders (who hire managers to maximize the firm's value) and managers (who wish to maximize their own rewards). Managers are quite crafty when it comes to maximizing their pay.

Does this happen in the real world? Tesco introduced ROIC as a performance metric in 2002. It used property sales and lease-backs to artificially lower the invested capital on the balance sheet, and booked the profits on the disposals as an operating item. Performance didn't turn out well for shareholders. On the flipside, Wal-Mart and Walgreens act as responsible stewards of investor funds by capitalizing operating leases when calculating return on capital. Their income statements and balance sheets are consistent. Saint Gobain uses ROIC as a performance metric and relies on all the

[3] Fabozzi, F. J., and J. L. Grant, *Value-Based Metrics: Foundations and Practice*, New York, John Wiley & Sons, 2000. A sure-fire way to increase ROIC is to cut capex and allow the net plant, property, and equipment (PP&E) to reduce via depreciation. Although ROIC might increase, the sustainability of the business could be imperiled. Also, managers might be rejecting positive NPV projects to maintain a target ROIC.

[4] There are numerous acronyms for similar measures. Return on invested capital (ROIC), return on net assets (RONA), and return on capital employed (ROCE) typically measure the net operating profit after tax to all capital providers. Measures of gross cash flow to gross assets include CROGA, and cash return on capital invested (CROCI). The numerator and denominator should be consistent, for example, ROE is net income to shareholders divided by book equity.

tricks in the books to boost it: leases, aging assets, and asset impairments. EasyJet capitalizes the jets its leases.

Fund managers prefer performance metrics that are comparable across many firms and a valuation framework that objectively estimates intrinsic values. Corporate executives want the same properties but are much more interested in a simple measure that is easy to communicate and administer. Elimination of accounting and inflationary distortions enhances comparability across time, regions, and industries. Once the accounting distortions are cleaned up, we can evaluate if companies are creating or destroying value and perform more accurate valuations.

The HOLT CFROI and Economic Profit framework fits this description. The aim of CFROI is to mirror the IRR economic performance metric as closely as possible. The present value of HOLT EP is the firm's NPV, which clarifies decisions and action. There are four key inputs to IRR: gross investment, gross cash flow, asset life, and salvage value. Their analogs can be found in the CFROI calculation.

Return on Invested Capital (ROIC)

ROIC measures net operating profit after tax (NOPAT) divided by net assets. It is important to note that net operating profit is stated in current dollar value while net assets are stated at historical cost. This incongruity makes comparison between firms more difficult and ROIC less reliable unless the asset base is restated in current dollar value.

In year six, when you visit your cousin Greg, he calculates the return by dividing £100k of NOPAT by £500k of beginning-of-year net assets (NOPAT equals net income in this example since you are the sole supplier of capital). The result is the return of 20%. If you had solely relied on Greg's financial statements every year you would have had the misleading impression that he had increased the returns on his business from 10% to 20%, when in fact nothing changed in the economics of the business except net assets declined. Beware of the old plant trap! It shows up all the time in industries characterized by lumpy investments.

Cash Return on Gross Assets (CROGA)

CROGA improves on ROIC by measuring the gross cash flow in current dollars against the gross historical cost. Again, there is a mismatch in dollar values, but any misrepresentation caused by declining net plant is eliminated. In this example, the year 6 return is 20% (£200k/£1,000k). With CROGA, management is held accountable for the full investment albeit in historical dollars, and management cannot claim success by simply writing off some bad investments or changing the depreciation policy, thereby improving returns. Issues with CROGA are that it does not take into account the composition of assets and their useful life. It is also distorted by inflation.

Cash Flow Return on Investment (CFROI)

CFROI is based on the inflation-adjusted gross assets with two additional requirements: asset life and a separation of the gross investment into *depreciating* (PP&E) and *non-depreciating* (working capital) assets. CFROI is a comprehensive metric that takes account of the asset life and the asset release at the end of the project. Also, the gross investment is marked to current dollars instead of historical cost, which further refines and improves the reliability of this metric. CFROI is a single-period, inflation-adjusted hurdle rate which, if applied to a stream of cash flows and non-depreciating asset release, results in zero NPV.[5] Stated another way, CFROI is the clearing rate at which the present value of the cash flows and non-depreciating asset release exactly equals the investment. In the previous example, CFROI for Greg's business is constant and equals IRR. This result makes great sense since it is based on economic principles, not accounting conventions.

CFROI is conceptually equivalent to an IRR capital investment analysis, except the CFROI calculation is a real (inflation-adjusted) number. It is the

---

[5] In Excel spreadsheet terms the RATE function is used where RATE (nper, pmt, pv, fv) is the calculation for IRR, nper equals asset life, pmt equals gross cash flow, pv equals gross investment, and fv equals non-depreciating asset release.

weighted-average single-period IRR on all the firm's projects. Calculating CFROI requires four inputs:

- Present value (pv) of the total investment: Gross investment (IAGI) in the company adjusted for inflation. In Exhibit 3.2 it is the big down arrow and requires a negative sign in Excel's RATE function.
- Payment (pmt) or cash flow: Gross cash flow (GCF) adjusted for inflation and non-cash expenses. GCF can be thought of as the annual operating cash flow generated from the gross investment.
- Project life (nper): Asset life estimated by the depreciation expense and gross depreciating assets.
- Future value (fv): Non-depreciating assets which include working capital (current assets less current liabilities) and other non-depreciating assets such as land. The logic is that these non-depreciating assets are released at the end of the project and can be converted to cash.

Exhibit 3.2 shows the CFROI calculation for Greg's Braai Design & Build business. If £1,000k is invested in an eight-year project, that generates £200k per year and releases £200k in salvage value at the end of year eight; the resulting CFROI is 13.9%. You can perform the calculation in Excel:

$$CFROI = RATE(nper = 8, \ pmt = 200, \ pv = -1000, \ fv = 200)$$

$$= 13.9\%$$

Note that for CFROI, the use of debt or equity reflects a financing decision that does not affect the calculation of the operating return.[6]

---

[6]In reality since there is a tax advantage to debt, the financing of the firm will affect taxes, which in turn affects gross cash flow, which will have a minor impact on the CFROI calculation.

EXHIBIT 3.2 **CFROI / IRR equivalence for Greg's Braai Design & Build business.**

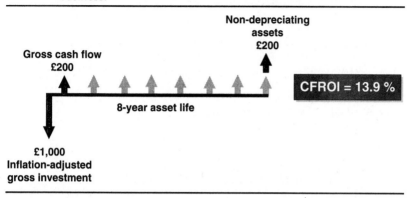

WARNING

If you are not interested in a detailed explanation of the adjustments necessary to calculate CFROI, then please skip to the Understanding the Relative Wealth Chart section.

CFROI ADJUSTMENTS USING AMAZON'S 2013 ANNUAL REPORT

Amazon describes itself in press releases as:

> "Amazon.com opened on the World Wide Web in July 1995. The company is guided by four principles: customer obsession rather than competitor focus, passion for invention, commitment to operational excellence, and long-term thinking. Customer reviews, 1-Click shopping, personalized recommendations, Prime, Fulfillment by Amazon, AWS, Kindle Direct Publishing, Kindle, Fire phone, Fire tablets, and Fire TV are some of the products and services pioneered by Amazon."

Investment in technology is crucial to Amazon's success and growth. It has expanded into web services via AWS. Here's a snippet from page 40 of Amazon's 2013 annual report:

> "We serve developers and enterprises of all sizes through AWS, which provides access to technology infrastructure that enables virtually any type of business."

Amazon has long held the view that its focus should be on long-term value creation and future cash flow. You can't get any clearer about this intention than this bullet point from the 1997 letter to shareholders, which has been reproduced in every annual report:

> "When forced to choose between optimizing the appearance of our GAAP accounting and maximizing the present value of future cash flows, we'll take the cash flows."

We will focus on Amazon's profitability and return on invested capital by assessing its CFROI. In this section, we discuss the logic behind the accounting adjustments necessary to calculate CFROI. In the HOLT framework, these adjustments and additional industry-specific modifications are systematically applied to all firms. We will use Amazon to demonstrate how each calculation is performed and indicate where the numbers come from. Our task will be to fill out the CFROI calculation template (Exhibit 3.3).

We will tackle each of the four key inputs separately. Let's begin with the inflation-adjusted gross investment (IAGI).

Inflation-Adjusted Gross Investment

The inflation-adjusted gross investment (IAGI) represents the total capital invested in the firm as of December 2013.

EXHIBIT 3.3 Inputs for calculating Amazon's 2013 CFROI.

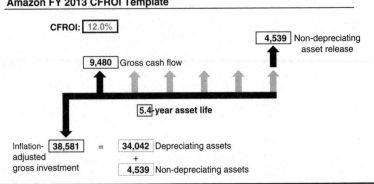

Amazon FY 2013 CFROI Template

CFROI: 12.0%

4,539 Non-depreciating asset release

9,480 Gross cash flow

5.4-year asset life

Inflation-adjusted gross investment 38,581 = 34,042 Depreciating assets + 4,539 Non-depreciating assets

Gross investment is comprised of two key elements: depreciating assets and non-depreciating assets.

Depreciating assets are principally plant and equipment which wear out over time and have different economic lives associated with each type of fixed asset. For Amazon, buildings are assumed to have a useful life of 40 years while networking equipment and software have a useful life ranging between two and five years. We assume depreciating assets fully depreciate and have no salvage value. Gains and losses from the disposal of fixed assets are accounted for on the income statement. Depreciating assets also include capitalized R&D, capitalized operating leases, and intangible operating assets with an identifiable useful life. Treatment of depreciating assets should reflect the economics of the firm that is being analyzed.[7]

Non-depreciating assets are comprised of working capital, land, and financial assets:

- Monetary assets such as cash, accounts receivable, and accounts payable;
- Inventory, which is a required factor of production and sales;
- Land, which does not depreciate and needs to be separated from the property, plant, and equipment account;
- Long-term financial investments which are relevant to the company's operations

These assets do not depreciate and can be converted to cash when a project or business winds down. Gains or losses associated with appreciation or spoilage flow through the income statement as operating or extraordinary items. Beware of firms that repeatedly mark down inventory and other assets, and record those adjustments as extraordinary losses.

---

[7] The sale of used cars is an integral part of a rental car business, and gains from selling used rental cars should be included in the operating income. Rental cars present an intriguing asset classification dilemma. Although rental cars are in essence depreciating assets, because their trade is integral to a rental car's business, we recommend treating rental cars as inventory marked to their net value. Depreciation would be treated as an operating expense as would the gains or losses from selling the cars well before their useful lives have expired. This approach can be applied to other asset rental businesses such as Atlas Copco.

If it's a regular occurrence, then it's probably due to operating inefficiency and should be included in the profitability assessment. Just because non-depreciating assets are recoverable does not mean that they are free. There is an opportunity cost and time value of holding them to sustain operations.

Depreciating Assets

The first step when calculating gross investment is to separate depreciating and non-depreciating assets.

The basic adjustments are as follows:

> Depreciating Assets:
> Inflation-adjusted gross plant
> + Construction in progress
> + Capitalized operating leases
> + Capitalized research and development
> + Capitalized exploration expense
> + Operating intangibles with identifiable lives
> = Inflation-adjusted depreciating assets (IADA)

We will outline the general adjustments for each component of the inflation-adjusted depreciating assets (IADA) before presenting the specific adjustments for Amazon. We then present the general components and Amazon adjustments for non-depreciating assets before showing the calculation of gross investment and moving systematically through each of the other CFROI inputs.

Inflation-Adjusted Gross Plant. Gross plant and equipment can be found in the fixed assets account, which typically resides in the notes of a company's annual report (we will refer to *plant and equipment* as *plant*). When calculating the inflation-adjusted gross plant, the first step is to remove any non-depreciating items such as land. Construction-in-progress (CIP) should also be removed since it is not yet being utilized and its inclusion will affect the asset life estimate and CFROI calculation. The reason for removing these items is twofold. First, gross plant and the depreciation expense are used to calculate asset life. Including CIP and non-depreciating assets in gross plant would distort the asset life calculation. Second, our goal is to separate depreciating from non-depreciating assets because non-depreciating assets are treated as an asset release, or salvage value, in the CFROI calculation.

We begin with gross plant, which is net fixed assets plus accumulated depreciation. Net fixed assets are typically referred to as net property, plant and equipment (PP&E) on the balance sheet. HOLT's adjustments to gross plant are:

> Inflation-adjusted gross plant:
> Gross plant (net fixed assets + accumulated depreciation)
> − Land and improvements
> − Construction in progress
> + Cumulative gross plant recaptured
> + Asset impairments
> + Inflation adjustment
> − Revaluations of plant
> = Inflation-adjusted gross plant

Let's begin with Amazon's reported gross property and equipment, which can be found on page 48 of the 2013 annual report under note 3 (Exhibit 3.4).

The total adjusted gross plant needs to be calculated before carrying out the asset life and inflation-adjustment calculations (Exhibit 3.5). Construction-in-progress is clearly identified under note 3. Unfortunately, land and buildings are not separated from each other. We will assume that most of the cost is in buildings and set the cost value of land to zero (from note 3 on page 48).

"In December 2012, we acquired our corporate headquarters for $1.2 billion consisting of land and 11 buildings that were previously

EXHIBIT 3.4 Amazon's reported gross property and equipment in 2013.

Amazon FY2013

Gross Property & Equipment	Amount ($m)	Source
Land & buildings	4,584	Note 3
+ Equipment & internal-use software	9,274	" "
+ Other corporate assets	231	" "
+ Construction in progress	720	" "
= Gross Property & Equipment	14,809	" "

EXHIBIT 3.5 Adjusted gross plant for Amazon in 2013.

Amazon FY2013

Adjusted Gross Plant	Amount ($m)	Source
Gross Property & Equipment	14,809	Note 3
− Land & improvements	0	" "
− Construction in progress	720	" "
= Adjusted Gross Plant	14,089	Calculated

accounted for as financing leases. The acquired building assets will be depreciated over their estimated useful lives of 40 years. We also acquired three city blocks of land for the expansion of our corporate headquarters for approximately $210 million."

The average gross plant asset life can be calculated by dividing adjusted gross plant by the annual depreciation charge, which was $2.5bn in 2013. From page 48, note 3:

"Depreciation expense on property and equipment was $2.5 billion, $1.7 billion, and $1.0 billion, which includes amortization of property and equipment acquired under capital lease obligations of $826 million, $510 million, and $335 million in 2013, 2012, and 2011."

$$Gross\ plant\ asset\ life = \frac{\$14.089bn}{\$2.460bn} = 5.7\ years$$

The gross plant asset lives were 5.6 years in 2011 and 5.7 years in 2012. HOLT uses a three-year median asset life to smooth distortions that might occur. The three-year median asset life is 5.7 years.

Inflation Adjustment. CFROI is an inflation-adjusted measure of financial performance. The inflation adjustment restates historical asset costs on the balance sheet to current purchasing units, that is, yesterday's dollars are restated in today's dollars.

Critics might argue that the inflation adjustment does not reflect the true cost of the asset today and insist that assets should be stated at "fair value."[8] For example, computers have declined in price over the years and are more powerful. Thus, a critic might point out that the inflation-adjusted cost of the computer reflects neither its fair value nor its replacement value. The CFROI calculation is not trying to estimate the fair value investment necessary to replace the assets as of today. It is attempting to estimate the investment made in past periods in terms of current purchasing units. For example, assume the firm purchased a computer for $2,000 in 2010. In 2013, a computer of equivalent functionality might cost $1,500 and be more powerful. However, the firm invested $2,000 of investors' funds in 2010. If the computer is still serving its function, the firm is not going to dispose of the 2010 computer and invest $1,500 of 2013 dollars for a new computer. The CFROI calculation simply reflects the current dollar value of the 2010 investment in 2013 dollars.

With respect to financial assets or equity investments held by industrial companies, these are not generally operating assets and there is often a market for these assets or an objective way to value them. In the HOLT CFROI framework, financial assets are stated at their fair value and removed from gross investment for the CFROI calculation. They are added back as non-operating investments when valuing the firm.

Calculation of the Inflation Adjustment. Because assets are acquired at different points in time and at different units of purchasing power, an adjustment is necessary to restate these assets in current dollar value. To achieve this goal, it is necessary to "de-layer" the asset base (Exhibit 3.6).

---

[8] The discussion of fair value relates solely to tangible fixed assets in this context and does not include financial assets.

EXHIBIT 3.6 Asset de-layering example.

	Year-4	Year-3	Year-2	Year-1	Year-0	Sum
Nominal growth rate	22.4%	22.4%	22.4%	22.4%	22.4%	
Asset layers (capex)	320	392	480	588	719	2,500
Inflation	2%	2%	2%	2%	2%	
Inflation adjustment	26	24	19	12	0	82
Inflation-adjusted gross plant	347	416	500	599	719	2,582
Inflation adjustment factor						*1.033*

There are four inputs in the de-layering calculation: asset life, historical cost, historical growth rate, and a GDP deflator time series. A company with long-lived assets that is growing slowly will have a larger inflation adjustment since its assets are older. A brand-new manufacturing plant requires no inflation adjustment while a thirty-year-old power station requires a significant adjustment.

We can approximate the annual capex and total subsequent inflation adjustment using our old friend from Chapter 1, the growing annuity equation:

$$Gross\ Plant_N = \frac{Capex_1}{g_{nom}}[(1 + g_{nom})^N - 1]$$

Imagine a firm that reports gross plant of $2,500 with a five-year life. To estimate the current dollar value of those five layers of investments, each investment layer must receive a distinct inflation adjustment. Assume the firm has grown its gross plant at a nominal average rate of 22.4% over the past five years and that annual inflation averaged 2% over this period. This translates into an average real annual growth rate of 20%. For simplicity, we assume all investment occurs at the end of the year (as opposed to the beginning of year or an average of beginning and ending values).

The first asset layer from four years ago equals $320, and is calculated by delayering the reported gross plant of $2,500 into an initial capex.[9]

---

[9] The $320 capex can be thought of as replacement capex for the oldest asset layer still being used in operation. The next year's capex will be one year newer, and so on. The oldest asset layer will have the largest inflation adjustment (the opposite will occur during periods of deflation).

$$Capex_1 = \frac{Gross\ Plant_N \times g_{nom}}{[(1 + g_{nom})^N - 1]} = \frac{\$2,500 \times 0.224}{[(1 + 0.224)^N - 1]} = \$320$$

Now that we know the initial asset layer, we simply grow it by 22.4% for each of the next four years to arrive at a gross plant of $2,500, for example, $Capex_2 = \$320 \times (1 + 0.224) = \$392$ in historical cost. You can check the result by adding the five capex values, which total to $2,500.

To bring the asset layers into current purchasing units, we need to inflation adjust for the number of years the asset has been in use. For example, the nominal capex of $320 made four years ago equals $347 in inflation-adjusted terms, leaving $26 as the inflation adjustment.

$$Capex_1\,(inflation\ adjusted) = \$320 \times (1 + 0.02)^4 = \$347$$

The inflation adjustments are depicted in Exhibit 3.7.

Calculation details are shown in Exhibit 3.6. Because we assumed that capex is made at the end of the year, there is no inflation adjustment for the most recent financial year.

A reported gross plant of $2,500 with 20% annual historical real growth and 2% yearly inflation results in the five asset layers represented

EXHIBIT 3.7 Estimated capital expenditure and the corresponding inflation adjustments to restate cumulative investment in current dollars.

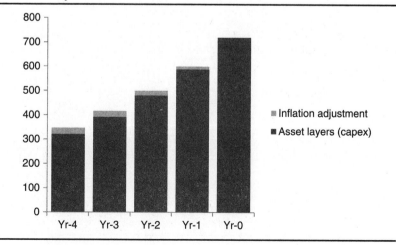

in Exhibit 3.6. The inflation adjustment factor shows that the reported gross plant receives the equivalent of a 3.3% inflation adjustment, which highlights the cumulative effect of inflation on aging assets. Finally, since growth rates for most companies are volatile from year-to-year, due to both organic and acquisitive growth, an average organic growth rate is used.

Because of acquisitions and disposals, it is easier to de-layer the assets than to try and track them through changes in the reported balance sheet, particularly since many acquisitions are of non-publicly traded companies so there is no disclosure of the gross assets acquired. We will further discuss acquisitions under gross plant recaptured.

Asset-light or short asset life firms may have relatively small inflation adjustments. If you don't have access to the HOLT software, which automatically inflation-adjusts the assets, you may decide to ignore the inflation adjustment. However, be aware that unless all the cash flows and assets used in the CFROI calculation are restated into equivalent units of purchasing power, CFROI is no longer reliably comparable across regions or time. In firms with long-lived assets, the inflation adjustment can reflect a large percentage of the gross investment base.

Exhibit 3.8 shows the impact of inflation on assets aged from 5 to 20 years and with inflation rates of 1%, 3%, and 5%. While an inflation rate

EXHIBIT 3.8 Impact of inflation on the oldest asset layer.

Years	Inflation Rate	Inflation Factor
5	1.0%	5.1%
	3.0%	15.9%
	5.0%	27.6%
10	1.0%	10.5%
	3.0%	34.4%
	5.0%	62.9%
15	1.0%	16.1%
	3.0%	55.8%
	5.0%	107.9%
20	1.0%	22.0%
	3.0%	80.6%
	5.0%	165.3%

EXHIBIT 3.9 Amazon's inflation-adjusted gross plant in 2013.

Amazon FY2013

Inflation-Adjusted Gross Plant	Amount	Source
Gross plant life	5.73	Calculated
Historical growth rate of gross plant	28%	HOLT
Inflation-adjustment ($m)	424	HOLT
+ Adjusted gross plant ($m)	14,089	Calculated
= Inflation-adjusted Gross Plant ($m)	14,513	Calculated

of 3% on a five-year old asset generates a 16% inflation adjustment, that same 3% inflation rate on a 20-year old asset is over 80%! Firms with long asset lives and low growth rates receive significant inflation adjustments.

Amazon has been undergoing tremendous growth and its assets depreciate rapidly, which limits the inflation adjustment (Exhibit 3.9).

The inflation adjustment of $424m for Amazon reflects the impact of estimated capex and individual GDP deflators over 5.7 years. You should employ an historical growth rate that is appropriate for the firm in question. Unusual growth rates such as those caused by acquisitions or asset disposals should be removed so they do not distort the re-layering process.

Capitalized Operating Leases. Whether it is planes, trains, or automobiles, leasing assets is big business and continues to grow (Exhibit 3.10). Approximately 90% of U.S. companies lease equipment. Of the more than $2 trillion spent by U.S. companies in 2016 on productive assets, 10% of these assets were procured through operating lease contracts.[10]

A lease is a contract between a lessee, who makes payments for the right to use an asset, and a lessor, who owns the asset and receives payments for lending an asset. Leases come in a wide assortment of sizes and colors. In a perfect market, the cost of leasing an asset is equivalent to the cost of borrowing to purchase the asset, and creates no value, that is, the NPV is zero.

---

[10]Credit Suisse HOLT. This amount includes aggregate expenditures on capital equipment, maintenance, and replacement of existing equipment, other investment in depreciating and non-depreciating assets, operating leases, and investment in R&D.

EXHIBIT 3.10 **Asset type as a percentage of total inflation-adjusted corporate assets for U.S. industrial/service firms.**

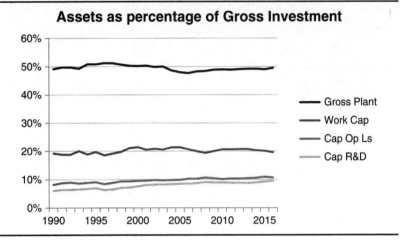

Assets as percentage of Gross Investment

So why do companies lease assets? It must be due to market imperfections with accounting, tax, and legal consequences. For accounting purposes, there are two types of leases:

- An operating lease in which the rental expense is treated as a periodic operating expense
- A capital or finance lease in which the asset is treated as a purchase

For accounting purposes, operating leases do not infer ownership and therefore neither the asset nor the liability for the leased asset appears on the balance sheet. Operating lease details are disclosed in the footnotes. Capital leases must be included on the balance sheet and have depreciation and interest expenses associated with them that run through the income statement. Firms often use operating leases to keep liabilities off the balance sheet and maintain a lower debt leverage, which is sometimes an explicit requirement of existing covenants.

This is yet another example where firms can engage in accounting obfuscation. If the lease classification has no direct impact on cash flow, then it should not affect the firm's value (remember the Law of

Conservation of Value from Chapter 1). Sophisticated investors see through this sleight-of-hand. Other suspect reasons for leasing include avoiding capital expenditure controls and preserving capital. On the flipside, leases can have value as options when flexibility is essential or tax advantages benefit shareholders.

Regardless of whether a company accounts for a lease as a capital or an operating item, the use of a lease is fundamentally a financing decision and a liability for the company. If the firm did not need the asset, it would not expend funds whether through cash, debt, or leasing. All operating leases are capitalized onto the balance sheet and treated as operating assets and liabilities for the CFROI calculation and equity valuation.

The inputs for capitalizing leases are: lease expense, asset life, and nominal cost of debt for the lease. The cost of financing is often available in the footnotes. If a company has secured, publicly traded debt, the rate on that debt is a good proxy for the lease debt rate. For companies that do not have publicly traded debt, information on secured bank loans, or an estimate of the approximate rating of the company if it has traded debt, will work. For example, if you believe a company would be A-rated, use an A-rated corporate bond debt rate. Because we are interested in the gross amount of the capitalized lease, the life used should not be the life of the lease contract but rather the total useful life of the asset being leased. A good proxy is to assume that leased assets mimic purchased plant and equipment, and to use the gross plant life if details about the lease are unavailable.

Exhibit 3.11 presents an example of a capitalized lease calculation given a nominal cost of debt of 5%, an asset life of 10 years, and an annual lease

EXHIBIT 3.11 Capitalizing operating leases using the Excel PV function.

Stylized example of how HOLT capitalizes operating leases	
Capitalizing Operating Leases	**Amount**
Nominal cost of debt, % (i)	5.0%
Asset life, years (n)	10
Rental expense, $m (pmt)	100
Capitalized operating leases, $m (pv)	772

EXHIBIT 3.12 Amazon's capitalized operating leases in 2013.

Amazon FY2013

Capitalized Leases	Amount	Source
Asset life	6.0	Calculated
Nominal cost of debt	4.63%	HOLT
Rental expense ($m)	· 759	Note 8
Capitalized operating leases ($m)	3,899	Calculated

expense of $100m. The letters in parentheses reflect Microsoft Excel inputs for the PV function. In this example, a capitalized operating lease asset of $772m is added to the gross asset base. It is important to bear in mind that CFROI is based on **gross** investment, thus this calculation estimates the **gross** value of operating leases and may look unfamiliar.

The HOLT framework employs the average yield on a 5-year, A-rated corporate bond when capitalizing operating leases, which was 4.63% in the United States at the end of 2013.[11] HOLT assumes the asset life for operating leases equals the gross plant life, and rounds the number up to the closest integer, which is 6 years for Amazon. From page 55 of the annual report under note 8, Amazon's rental expense in 2013 was $759m:

> "We have entered into non-cancellable operating, capital, and financing leases for equipment and office, fulfillment center, and data center facilities. Rental expense under operating lease agreements was $759 million, $561 million, and $381 million in 2013, 2012, and 2011."

We can call upon the Excel PV function (Exhibit 3.12) or apply the growing annuity equation to calculate the gross value of capitalized operating leases. We will include this amount in the gross investment and add back the rental expense to net income:

$$Capitalized\ Operating\ Leases = \frac{Rental\ expense}{r_d} \times \left[1 - \frac{1}{(1 + r_d)^N} \right]$$

$$Capitalized\ Operating\ Leases = \frac{\$759m}{0.0463} \times \left[1 - \frac{1}{(1.0463)^6} \right] = \$3.899bn$$

---

[11] To limit year-to-year distortions, the average yield on a five-year note is averaged over three years.

Capitalized Research and Development. Research and development (R&D) is an investment by a firm to generate future cash flows. Regardless of the accounting rules that vary by region to expense or capitalize R&D, like capex, it should be capitalized to capture the full economic impact on operating returns and valuation. If R&D expenditure is not valuable, the firm will experience a growing asset base with no concurrent increase in profitability from the R&D investment, resulting in declining CFROI.

A primary issue for capitalizing R&D is deciding how many years of R&D expenditure to capitalize. In concept, you should capitalize the asset for as many years as the investment is projected to generate future cash flows. Consistent with this view, companies with long-lived investments or long patent protection periods such as pharmaceutical companies should capitalize longer periods of R&D expense. Technology companies should use shorter R&D lives since technological innovation typically results in accelerated obsolescence. The HOLT software automatically capitalizes R&D based on the firm's industry, but when material, you should select appropriate R&D lives based on your analysis.

The capitalization procedure is straightforward. Simply take the R&D expense for each period for which R&D is capitalized, multiply it by the inflation factor for that period, and sum the inflation-adjusted R&D layers. Exhibit 3.13 presents an example for capitalizing R&D expense with a five-year R&D life. In this example, a capitalized R&D asset of $610 is added to the balance sheet. Please note that because CFROI requires **gross** investment, the aim of this calculation is to estimate the **gross** capitalized R&D.

EXHIBIT 3.13 Capitalized R&D calculation.

Year	R&D Expense	Inflation Rate	Inflation Factor	Inflation Adj R&D
−4	100	2.70%	1.11	111
−3	110	2.70%	1.08	119
−2	115	2.70%	1.05	121
−1	125	2.70%	1.03	128
−0	130	2.70%	1.00	130
Infl adj	580			610

Determining Amazon's R&D investment is not as simple as it is for most companies. Amazon does not disclose a specific line-item called "research and development expense." Instead, Amazon reports an operating expense called "technology and content" (T&C). This item is essentially research and development primarily related to Amazon's on-going investment in web-based services (AWS).

Regarding this particular expense, Amazon's 2013 Annual Report states, "We seek to efficiently invest in several areas of technology and content such as web services, expansion of new and existing product categories and offerings, and initiatives to expand our ecosystem of digital products and services, as well as in technology infrastructure to enhance the customer experience and improve our process efficiencies."[12] This expense meets HOLT's threshold for being considered R&D: It is an investment in critical assets and IP having an expected life beyond the current year and from which future earnings are expected to be derived.

Amazon's specific lack of disclosure on research and development means that HOLT has to carefully estimate this expense. Instead of assuming that the entire T&C expenditure is R&D, HOLT recognizes a portion of T&C as depreciation. This amount is determined as follows:

$4,584m of Land and buildings
+ $231m of Other corporate assets
= $4,815m of Total T&C depreciable assets / 5-year asset life
= $963m of T&C related depreciation

Subtracting $963 from T&C results in an estimated research and development expense of $5,602 for FY2013.

$$R\&D \; expense = \$6,565m - \$963m = \$5,602m$$

As Exhibit 3.14 shows, a total of $14.910bn in capitalized R&D is added to Amazon's depreciating assets.

---

[12] Source: Amazon 2013 Annual Report, 18.

EXHIBIT 3.14 Amazon's capitalized R&D in 2013.

Amazon FY2013

Capitalized R&D	Amount	Inflation Factor	Adjusted Amount
Asset life (years)	5		
R&D expense 2009 ($m)	1,086	1.0690	1,161
R&D expense 2010 ($m)	1,513	1.0562	1,598
R&D expense 2011 ($m)	2,495	1.0349	2,582
R&D expense 2012 ($m)	3,903	1.0161	3,966
R&D expense 2013 ($m)	5,602	1.0000	5,602
Capitalized R&D ($m)			14,910

Gross Plant Recaptured

Gross plant recaptured represents gross plant that was written off as impaired after an acquisition. Because Amazon did not have any gross plant recaptured, we will skip this topic here and provide an exploration of the adjustment in the appendix.

Total Depreciating Assets

After completing all the adjustments to gross plant, then construction-in-progress, capitalized leases, capitalized R&D, and gross plant recaptured are added back to arrive at total inflation-adjusted depreciating assets, the first input for gross investment (Exhibits 3.15 and 3.16).

EXHIBIT 3.15 Amazon's inflation-adjusted depreciating assets in 2013.

Amazon FY2013

Inflation-Adjusted Depreciating Assets	Amount ($m)	Source
Inflation-adjusted gross plant	14,513	Calculated
+ Construction-in-progress	720	Note 5
+ Capitalized operating leases	3,899	Calculated
+ Capitalized research & development	14,910	Calculated
+ Capitalized exploration expense	0	N/A
+ Intangibles included in depreciating assets	0	N/A
= Inflation-adjusted depreciating assets	34,042	Calculated

EXHIBIT 3.16 Amazon's CFROI calculation template: depreciating assets.

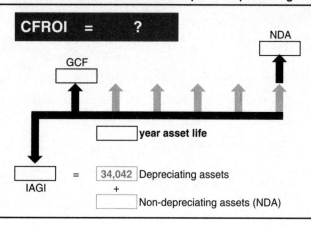

Non-Depreciating Assets

Non-depreciating assets include working capital and other non-depreciating items such as land. They can be converted to cash and represent the salvage value at the end of a project. Working capital, which includes operating cash, accounts receivable (AR) and accounts payable (AP), is the capital that is needed to run a business on a day-to-day basis. Any reduction in working capital generates positive free cash flow that the firm can distribute to shareholders. There is a value trade-off between too little and too much working capital. Most companies can't afford to lose business due to stock-outs or highly restrictive trade credit policies. Each industry has its own nuances, which need to be assessed.

A common approach is to calculate and track a firm's cash cycle (CC), which is the time from when the company pays cash to purchase inventory to when it receives cash from the sale of that inventory. Note the emphasis on cash paid and received.

$$CC\ (days) = AR\ (days) + Inventory\ (days) - AP\ (days)$$

The operating cycle (OC) is the time from ordering inventory to collecting the cash from the sale of the inventory.

$$OC\ (days) = AR\ (days) + Inventory\ (days)$$

Inventory management is a crucial driver for many industries. There is a benefit to reducing the carrying costs of inventory and eliminating spoilage and inefficient processes. Because excessive inventory consumes cash and effort, the introduction of effective inventory management can immediately increase firm value. Just-in-time (JIT) and Lean Management are two popular and related approaches to eliminating non-value-adding processes and acquiring inventory just-in-time for use. Efficient fulfillment is crucial to Amazon's success:[13]

> "Through our Kaizen program, named for the Japanese term 'change for the better,' employees work in small teams to streamline processes and reduce defects and waste."

Conceptually, non-depreciating assets include:

Non-depreciating assets:

Current monetary assets
− Current non-debt monetary liabilities
+ Inflation-adjusted inventories
+ Inflation-adjusted land
+ Other non-depreciating assets
+ Non-depreciating intangible assets
= Non-depreciating assets

Current Monetary Assets (Current Assets Less Inventory). The CFROI calculation does not net cash and cash-equivalents against debt. While management can certainly use cash to pay down debt, increase dividends, or buy back shares, there is no guarantee that they will do so. Thus, the CFROI calculation holds management responsible for this low return asset they keep on the balance sheet. We assume that all cash is operating cash.

Holding cash has a tax disadvantage due to the double taxation of corporate interest income on cash and marketable securities. Cash is simply

---

[13]Jeff Bezos, "2013 Letter to Shareholders," Amazon.com 2013 Annual Report.

negative debt, and the tax shield is negative for cash. What is the present value of a constant pile of cash held forever? It is the value of the after-tax interest income discounted at its interest rate. The NPV represents the net loss in value of holding the cash.

$$NPV = -Cash_0 + \frac{Cash_0 \times r_i \times (1 - \tau_c)}{r_i} = -Cash_0 \times \tau_c$$

If the firm pays no taxes, then there is no value loss. A corporate tax rate of 35% means that excess cash held into perpetuity has a market value equal to 65% of the cash's balance sheet value. It's no wonder activist shareholders put pressure on companies to "give 'em back" their money.

Companies hold cash for operational, strategic, and survival reasons. There is a clear cost to holding cash, so a firm's reasons need to be assessed. All excess cash should be distributed to shareholders via dividends or share repurchases, so shareholders can invest that cash elsewhere.

Many analysts adjust forecast cash levels to those necessary for maintaining operations. The remaining cash is considered "excess" and is forecast to be distributed to capital providers or netted against debt. For analytical purposes, it may be useful to adjust historical periods by removing excess cash from CFROI to better assess the true operating returns of the company, that is, not influenced by the low return on cash. Firms with lofty growth opportunities tend to hold a high level of cash, which might be treated as excess cash by an analyst. Risky firms may also hold a high level of cash, but this should not be regarded as excess cash in most cases.

Accounts receivable is effectively a loan from the firm to its customers and generally taken at book value unless the analyst has a contrary opinion regarding the amount that will ultimately be collected.

Most of Amazon's current assets can be observed directly on the balance sheet. Accounts receivable totaling $3.0bn can be found in note 1 on page 44 of the 2013 annual report. The balance sheet indicates "Accounts receivable, net and other" of $4.767bn, thus "Other current assets" must total $1.767bn:

"Included in 'Accounts receivable, net and other' on our consolidated balance sheets are amounts primarily related to vendor and customer receivables. As of December 31, 2013 and 2012, vendor receivables, net, were $1.3 billion and $1.1 billion, and customer receivables, net, were $1.7 billion and $1.5 billion."

Current Non-Debt Liabilities. Non-debt monetary liabilities are current liabilities excluding items that carry an interest rate such as the current portion due on long-term debt, which is commonly listed as on the balance sheet as "short-term debt." Although accounts payable are often viewed as interest-free loans to the firm, this does not mean they are free. Discounts are often offered if a firm pays before an agreed number of days after invoicing, which implies that the funding is not free. The greater the relative discount, the greater the loss in not taking advantage of it. A firm should choose to fund itself with accounts payable only if it is the cheapest source of funding. For valuation purposes, all interest-bearing liabilities are treated as debt and subtracted from the firm value to arrive at the equity value.

Amazon has lumped short-term debt obligations into its "Accrued expenses and other" line shown in "Current Liabilities" on the balance sheet (Exhibit 3.17). Interest-bearing current liabilities must be removed from the operating current liabilities and added to debt. The current portions of the three debt obligations can be found in notes 6 ("Long-term debt") and 7 ("Other long-term liabilities") on pages 53 and 54 of the 2013 annual report.

Inventory Inflation Adjustment. If inventory is accounted for using the Last In, First Out (LIFO) method, the LIFO reserve will be added to the inventory to reflect more accurately the cost in current dollars of the items in inventory. We will further discuss the LIFO reserve under the gross cash flow section. If inventory is treated as First In, First Out (FIFO), then no adjustment to inventory on the balance sheet is necessary. The economic and book values of inventory should be similar. Amazon uses the FIFO method according to page 43 of their 2013 annual report:

EXHIBIT 3.17 Amazon's adjusted current liabilities in 2013.

Amazon FY2013 − Current Liabilities	Amount ($m)	Source
Accounts payable	15,133	Balance sheet
+ Accrued expenses and other	7,671	" "
− Current portion of long-term debt	(1,736)	Note 6
− Current portion of capital leases	(955)	Note 7
− Current portion of financing leases	(28)	Note 7
+ Unearned revenue	1,159	Balance sheet
= Current liabilities	21,244	Calculated

"Inventories, consisting of products available for sale, are primarily accounted for using the FIFO method, and are valued at the lower of cost or market value. This valuation requires us to make judgments, based on currently-available information, about the likely method of disposition, such as through sales to individual customers, returns to product vendors, or liquidations, and expected recoverable values of each disposition category."

These three items make up the adjusted net working capital, which totaled $3.381bn at the end of 2013 (Exhibit 3.18). Net working capital is simply current assets minus current liabilities.

Inflation-Adjusted Land. Since land is a non-depreciating asset, it is removed from gross plant and added to non-depreciating assets. However, like gross plant, land should also be inflation-adjusted as its value typically appreciates over time. Unfortunately, land is often only disclosed as part of "land and buildings." In such cases, the "land and buildings" account remains in depreciating assets, unless an estimate can be made of the percentage land represents in the account.

Other Tangible and Intangible Assets. Since no information is generally available regarding the age or depreciability of these assets, they are treated as non-depreciating assets. If such information is available, these assets should be placed in the categories where they belong. Other tangible assets include "other assets," which should exclude any deferred charges, and operating "long-term investments" at their cost value. If the investments

EXHIBIT 3.18 Amazon's adjusted net working capital in 2013.

Amazon FY2013

Current Assets	Amount ($m)	Source
Cash and cash equivalents	8,658	Balance sheet
+ Marketable securities	3,789	" "
+ Accounts receivable	3,000	Note 1
− Financial subsidiary receivable	0	N/A
+ Inventories	7,411	Balance sheet
+ LIFO adjustment	0	N/A
+ Other current assets	1,767	Calculated
= Adj. Current assets	24,625	Calculated
− Current Liabilities	**Amount ($m)**	**Source**
Accounts payable	15,133	Balance sheet
+ Accrued expenses and other	7,671	" "
− Current portion of long-term debt	(1,736)	Note 6
− Current portion of capital leases	(955)	Note 7
− Current portion of financing leases	(28)	Note 7
+ Unearned revenue	1,159	Balance sheet
= Adj. Current liabilities	21,244	Calculated
= **Net Working Capital**	**3,381**	Calculated

are non-operating, then they should be removed from the non-depreciating assets and the market value of the investments should be added to the value of the operating assets at the end of the valuation process. Pension assets and post-retirement assets should be excluded from non-depreciating assets and accounted for at the end of the valuation process.

With more and more companies in possession of intellectual property and assets such as patents, brands, databases, and electronic spectrum, additional research is needed into the costs, returns, and asset lives of these intangible assets, which function as operating assets. Some of these assets, such as patents or trademarks, have legal protection for a finite period. The period of protection is akin to a depreciation or amortization life and such assets should be treated as depreciating. However, other intangible assets are in a true sense non-depreciating. An obvious example is radio spectrum. Radio spectrum does not wear out and although governments generally grant spectrum for a limited period, it is rare that a company has its spectrum license revoked. Acquisition goodwill and acquired intangibles are excluded from operating assets in the HOLT framework. Acquisition goodwill is treated as a sunk cost. Acquired intangibles, unless specifically identifiable as operating assets, are also treated as non-operating.

Another example of a non-depreciating asset might be classic films or songs. The cost of producing a James Dean movie or a Beatles album bears no relation to the value of such assets today. Even if the original cost had been capitalized, it would have been fully depreciated long ago. Thus, if a reliable value (usually related to a sale) can be placed on these assets, one might consider them non-depreciating. The digitization of music and film makes this non-depreciating argument ring even louder. Songs that were popular generations ago are readily available at the click of a mouse on sites such as iTunes, and it costs next to nothing to store them.

In Amazon's case, it lumps these items into "Other assets" located in note 1 on page 45 of the 2013 annual report:

> "Included in 'Other assets' on our consolidated balance sheets are amounts primarily related to acquired intangible assets, net of amortization; digital video content, net of amortization; long-term deferred tax assets; certain equity investments; marketable securities restricted for longer than one year, the majority of which are attributable to collateralization of bank guarantees and debt related to our international operations; and intellectual property rights, net of amortization."

Item 7A on page 32 states that "Other assets" includes $127m of equity investments, which are equity investments in private companies. This item should be excluded from Amazon's operating assets. The "Other assets" line also includes "Acquired intangibles" of $645m which are described in note 4 on page 51 of the 2013 annual report. There are lives listed for each item, so they could be treated as depreciating intangibles. Because they were acquired, we will follow the HOLT framework and treat them as non-operating assets (Exhibit 3.19).

Non-depreciating assets are the second input of the gross investment calculation and an input for the CFROI calculation (Exhibit 3.20).

The inflation-adjusted gross investment is simply the sum of the depreciating assets and non-depreciating assets (Exhibits 3.21 and 3.22).

EXHIBIT 3.19 Amazon's non-depreciating assets in 2013.

Amazon FY2013

Non-Depreciating Assets	Amount ($m)	Source
Net working capital	3,381	Calculated
+ Long-term investments at cost	0	N/A
+ Other assets	1,930	Balance sheet
– Acquired intangibles, net	(645)	Note 4
– Equity investments	(127)	Item 7A
– Pension & post-retirement assets	0	N/A
+ Non-depreciating intangible assets	0	N/A
= Non-depreciating assets	4,539	Calculated

EXHIBIT 3.20 CFROI calculation template: non-depreciating assets.

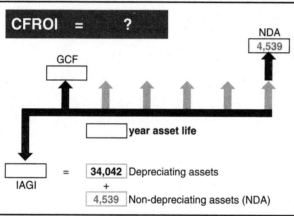

EXHIBIT 3.21 Amazon's gross investment in 2013.

Amazon FY2013

Inflation-Adjusted Gross Investment	Amount ($m)	Source
Inflation-adjusted depreciating assets	34,042	Calculated
Non-depreciating assets	4,539	Calculated
Inflation-adjusted gross investment	38,581	Calculated

Asset Life

Since CFROI is equivalent to the weighted-average return on all of a firm's projects, an essential part of the CFROI calculation is asset life. There are up to five inputs into the overall asset life calculation: adjusted gross plant life,

EXHIBIT 3.22 **CFROI calculation template: inflation-adjusted gross investment.**

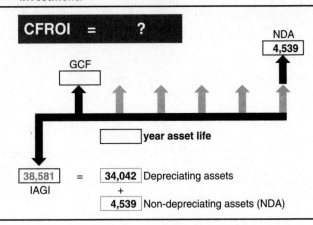

capitalized lease life, capitalized R&D life, capitalized exploration expense life for resource companies, and operating intangible assets life. The first three are generally the most important.

Gross Plant Asset Life

The asset life for gross plant is simply:

$$Asset\ Life = \frac{(Adjusted\ Gross\ Plant + Gross\ Plant\ Recaptured)}{Depreciation}$$

For companies that have made acquisitions, the depreciation expense represents a blend of gross plant purchased to support operations and acquired gross plant. Thus, it is necessary to include both adjusted gross plant and gross plant recaptured in the numerator. As discussed earlier, land is excluded from this calculation because it is a non-depreciating asset and construction-in-process is excluded because it is not yet a working asset and therefore does not have an associated depreciation charge. Finally, to avoid unusual asset lives since the depreciation expense may reflect a partial year, a three-year median life is used.

We showed earlier that the gross plant life for Amazon is 5.7 years. This might seem short in the face of a 40-year useful life for buildings, but the asset base is dominated by short-life items that require constant replacement such as internal-use software (2 years), servers (3 years), and networking equipment (5 years) which are spelled out in note 1 on page 44 of the 2013 annual report. The overall asset life is a harmonic average which weights it toward short-life assets, that is, networking equipment with a 5-year life needs to be replaced 8 times in a building with a 40-year life:

> "Property and equipment are stated at cost less accumulated depreciation. Property includes buildings and land that we own, along with property we have acquired under build-to-suit, financing, and capital lease arrangements. Equipment includes assets such as furniture and fixtures, heavy equipment, servers and networking equipment, and internal-use software and website development. Depreciation is recorded on a straight-line basis over the estimated useful lives of the assets (generally the lesser of 40 years or the remaining life of the underlying building, two years for assets such as internal-use software, three years for our servers, five years for networking equipment, five years for furniture and fixtures, and ten years for heavy equipment). Depreciation expense is classified within the corresponding operating expense categories on our consolidated statements of operations."

Life of Capitalized Operating Leases

Leased assets generally consist of a similar asset mix as capital assets. If the leased assets have a different known asset life than that of gross plant, it should be used.

Capitalized R&D Life

The capitalized R&D project life is the same as the number of years R&D is capitalized. In a world of full disclosure, the project life for each R&D investment would be known, and a harmonic average R&D life for each firm could be estimated. The HOLT framework capitalizes R&D based on the firm's industry, but you should select appropriate R&D lives based on your analysis (Exhibit 3.23).

Calculating the Life of Depreciating Assets

When calculating a firm's asset life, a harmonic mean of the five asset classes (depreciating plant & equipment, capitalized operating leases, capitalized

EXHIBIT 3.23 Estimated R&D life by Industry used by HOLT to capitalize R&D expenses.

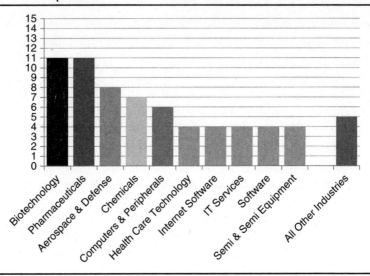

EXHIBIT 3.24 Calculating asset life.

	a	b	c	d	e	f	g
Asset	Life	Historical Cost	Implied Depreciation	Asset Life	Asset Life-Cycle Investment	Weighting	Harmonic Mean
Fixed assets	12	5,000	417	1.0	5,000	32%	3.9
Capitalized leases	8	3,000	375	1.5	4,500	29%	2.3
Capitalized R&D	4	2,000	500	3.0	6,000	39%	1.5
Total		10,000	1,292		15,500		7.7
Harmonic mean			7.7				

R&D, operating intangibles, and other depreciating assets having variable life) is used. A weighted-average life does not properly account for the life of each asset class. Exhibit 3.24 demonstrates two methods for calculating asset life. For the purposes of this example, we have assumed that capitalized leases have a different life than fixed assets.

Method 1 (for Physicists and Engineers). Implied depreciation (column c): Calculate the implied depreciation based on asset life and historical cost (column b/column a).

Asset life-cycle (column d): Calculate the asset life-cycle. To understand the concept of the asset life-cycle, consider two assets, one with a six-year life and one with a three-year life. During the six-year life of the first asset, there will be two three-year life assets used. Conceptually, the three-year asset will cycle through twice during a single cycle of the six-year asset. To calculate the asset life-cycle, take the maximum life of all the assets in column a, and divide that by the life of the specific asset in question. For example, the maximum life is 12 years for fixed assets. The asset life-cycle for capitalized leases is 1.5 given their eight-year life. One-and-a-half capitalized lease assets are used during the life of the fixed asset.

Asset life-cycle investment (column e): Calculate the asset life-cycle investment (column d * column b). For example, for every 12 years of $5,000 investment in fixed assets; three cycles of capitalized R&D at $2,000 are invested for a total capitalized R&D investment of $6,000.

Weighting (column f): Calculate the weighted-average of column e, the average asset life-cycle investment for each asset.

Harmonic mean (column g): Calculate the mean. The weighting (column f) multiplied by life (column a).

Total: Sum column g to arrive at the asset life.

Method 2 (Quick and Easy). Alternatively, it is possible to skip the calculations in columns d through g and calculate project life via implied depreciation. Simply take the sum of the historical costs (column b) and divide by the implied depreciation (column c) to arrive at the same answer. Columns d through g provide an alternate means to explain the concept of asset life-cycles (Exhibit 3.24).

When calculating asset lives for companies that report using an accelerated depreciation method, you should refer to the footnotes for the asset lives of the various asset categories. From the footnote information, an implied depreciation and project life can be calculated. Relying on accelerated depreciation to calculate project life will result in an artificially low life and an overestimated CFROI in early years and a high life and underestimated CFROI in later years. For Japanese industrial companies, where accelerated depreciation is the norm, the HOLT framework assigns lives based on industry-specific global medians.

The life for Amazon's gross plant and equipment is 5.7 years. We've assumed the same life for capitalizing Amazon's operating leases. Amazon is assumed to have a five-year life for R&D in the HOLT framework. The asset life for Amazon's 2013 CFROI calculation is 5.4 years (Exhibit 3.25).

Based on the harmonic mean of the asset lives, we can input a project life of 5.4 years into Amazon's CFROI template (Exhibit 3.26).

Gross Cash Flow

Gross cash flow (GCF) estimates the gross after-tax cash flow generated from the firm's operating assets and represents the final input of the CFROI

EXHIBIT 3.25 Amazon's asset life in 2013 based on the implied depreciation method.

Amazon FY2013 Asset Life	Amount ($m)	Life (years)	Implied Depr $m
Adjusted gross plant	14,089	5.7	2,460
Capitalized operating leases	3,899	6.0	650
Capitalized R&D	14,910	5.0	2,982
Total	32,898	5.40	6,092

EXHIBIT 3.26 CFROI calculation template: project life.

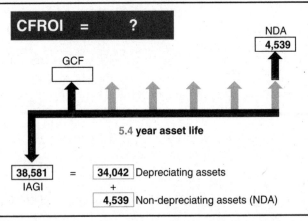

94

calculation. GCF can be calculated top-down from the revenue line or bottom-up from the net income line. All items that have been capitalized and included in the investment base must have their associated expense added back to net income. This makes it possible to compare the return on capital of firms that lease assets to peers who purchase assets.

Let's step through the key adjustments for Amazon and calculate its 2013 gross cash flow.

Gross cash flow:

Net Income
+ Depreciation & amortization
+ Interest expense
+ Rental expense
+ R&D expense
+ Total exploration expense
+ Monetary holding gain (loss)
+ FIFO profits
+ Net pension cash flow adjustment
+ Stock compensation expense (after-tax)
+ Minority interest expense
− Equity investment income
− Special items (after-tax)
= Inflation-adjusted gross cash flow

Net Income after Tax

Amazon reported a net income of $274m in 2013 on its consolidated statements of operations, that is, P&L statement. Amazon's return on average equity was a paltry 3.1%! How can a company trade at such a significant premium to its book value since its public listing when it only reports an ROE of 3.1% almost 20 years after its founding?! Accounting doesn't supply a plausible measure of Amazon's success. Let's see what happens when we finish with the economic adjustments.

$$ROE = \frac{\$274m}{0.5 \times (\$8,192m + \$9,746m)} = 3.1\%$$

Unlike general textbook approaches where an adjustment for taxes is undertaken to reflect the operating return on the unlevered firm, CFROI makes no such adjustment in arriving at gross cash flow. Instead of hiding the interest tax shield for debt in a nebulous weighted-average cost of capital (WACC), it is forecast and valued as a cash flow.[14]

When using a WACC, the cash savings from the interest tax shield are reflected in a tax-advantaged cost of debt, which is part of the discount rate. This approach, though popular and technically feasible, shrouds the cash savings and its sustainability. CFROI recognizes the tax advantage of debt in the gross cash flow and calculates a pre-tax weighted-average cost of capital that tends to rise (rather than fall) as debt rises. In other words, the tax savings from debt are recognized in the gross cash flow (the numerator of the CFROI equation) while the riskiness of debt is recognized through a rising cost of capital (the denominator) when performing the DCF analysis.

A word needs to be said about the use of book versus cash taxes. While many practitioners advocate the use of cash taxes when calculating performance metrics, HOLT uses book taxes to calculate CFROI. Most important and often overlooked is the fact that book taxes equal cash taxes over the long run. Differences are temporary and owed to timing. A key benefit of using book taxes is better tracking of a firm's economics: Book taxes are dependent on the activities and earnings reported within the income statement for each fiscal period. Cash taxes paid often contain the reversals and effects from transactions that are several years old, for example, use of net operating losses and tax incentives. Book taxes within the CFROI framework provide investors with the following advantages:

- Today's performance measurement isn't impacted by yesterday's tax games.
- CFROI variability is minimized by removing timing differences in taxes paid.

---

[14]The HOLT framework is an adjusted present value (APV) technique. In an APV model, unlevered cash flows and interest tax shields are discounted at a constant unlevered cost of capital if market leverage is assumed to remain stable.

- The starting point for forecasted returns can be more accurately assessed as an extension of past performance.

When calculating free cash flows as part of a valuation exercise, HOLT takes into account cash taxes paid since there is value to deferring the payment of taxes.

Depreciation and Amortization

Depreciation and amortization are added back to net income since they are simply bookkeeping entries and non-cash items. Depreciation and amortization represent the periodic expensing (under the matching principle) of an asset that has already been paid for. We disclosed earlier that Amazon's depreciation charge was $2.5bn in 2013. Note 4 on page 52 of the annual report indicates that amortization was $168m in 2013:

> "Amortization expense for acquired intangibles was $168 million, $163 million, and $149 million in 2013, 2012, and 2011."

Interest Expense

Interest expense is added back to net income since this amount represents the required return to debt investors and we are interested in measuring the return to *all* capital providers. The interest tax shield from debt remains in net income to reflect the tax advantage to cash flow from debt financing. As debt increases, the firm's risk increases, and this is recognized in part through a leverage risk factor in the company's discount rate. If financial distress is a distinct possibility, then the present value of the expected financial distress costs should be included in the valuation. This can be accomplished via scenario analysis and probabilistic modeling. The worst-case scenario will be the firm going bankrupt, and the best case will be survival as a profitable going concern. Trade-off theory suggests a balance between the tax shield benefit of debt and the cost of financial distress, for example, having to drop prices to retain customers and pay cash for inventory.

$$Firm\ value = Unlevered\ value + PV\ (Tax\ shield)$$

$$-PV\ (Financial\ distress\ costs)$$

Amazon reported an interest expense of $141m in 2013 on its income statement. Because cash is treated as an operating asset, we do not subtract interest income from net income. If cash is netted off against debt, then the interest income should be subtracted from net income.

Rental Expense

Whether they appear on the balance sheet or not, leases are liabilities and the leased assets are necessary for operations. Since rental expense is an asset financing expense and an integral component of the firm's operations, HOLT adds it back to net income and capitalizes it on the balance sheet as described in detail in the gross investment section. For valuation purposes, the debt value of capitalized leases is added to debt as a debt-equivalent and subtracted from the firm value to arrive at the equity value. This approach neatly treats the operating lease as though it had been purchased with debt. The tax advantage of expensing operating leases is treated similarly to interest expenses. It remains in the numerator as a cash flow benefit.

Research and Development Expense

The R&D expense is added back to net income since it is an investment that is expected to generate future cash flow. Whether a company succeeds or fails in an R&D endeavor is irrelevant for the purpose of evaluation. R&D represents capital invested in a project with an uncertain payoff. Firms with highly successful R&D initiatives will demonstrate higher "batting averages" compared to firms with less successful R&D efforts.

Companies should not be penalized for committing R&D funding to projects with positive expected NPVs. Amazon invests billions in improving its technology so that it can enhance its competitive moat and capture new and adjacent markets. Drug development is an excellent example since R&D investment occurs years before positive commercial cash flow is produced. A successful pharmaceutical company that chopped its R&D budget to increase this year's earnings would take a massive hit to its share price. This is an instance where short-term earnings and long-term value creation are at odds. Economics beats accounting every time the expense is perceived to be value enhancing. This helps to explain why Amazon with its pitiful ROE track record continues to trade at a premium to its accounting book value.

R&D is capitalized on the balance sheet as described in the gross investment section of this chapter. Amazon spent $5.602bn on R&D in 2013. This value is almost 20× greater than net income! Amazon has invested and continues to invest in its future.

Net Monetary Asset Holding Gain

The net monetary asset holding gain or loss simply reflects the impact of inflation on monetary assets during the year. If monetary assets exceed liabilities, then there will be a charge for the loss of value due to inflation. The beginning-of-year net monetary assets need to be calculated and multiplied by the GDP deflator. Inventory and short-term debt should not be included in the monetary assets and liabilities. Low inflation in many of today's industrialized countries results in a minor monetary holding adjustment.

$$Monetary\ holding\ gain = -(Monetary\ assets - Monetary\ liabilities)$$
$$\times\ GDP\ deflator$$

In Amazon's case, monetary liabilities exceed assets, and there is a gain since the firm is being funded in part by its short-term creditors (Exhibit 3.27).

FIFO Profits

In a period of rising inflation, firms using the FIFO method to quantify inventory report more accurate balance sheet accounts but less accurate cost of goods sold. HOLT's FIFO profit adjustment reduces the gross cash flow by the estimated increase in COGS not captured by the FIFO inventory method.

The benefit of FIFO inventory accounting is that it more accurately captures the replacement cost of inventory on the balance sheet in an inflationary environment. The newest assets remain on the balance sheet while

EXHIBIT 3.27 Amazon's net monetary holding gain in 2013.

Amazon FY2013 Net Monetary Asset Holding Gain	Amount ($m)	Source
Cash and cash equivalents	8,084	Balance sheet
+ Marketable securities	3,364	" "
+ Accounts receivable, net and other	3,817	" "
− Accounts payable	(13,318)	" "
− Other current liabilities ex debt	(4,550)	" "
= Net monetary assets for FY2012	(2,603)	Calculated
x −Percent change in GDP deflator	−1.61%	HOLT
= Monetary holding gain	42	Calculated

the oldest assets (first in) are sold (first out) and expensed as cost of goods sold on the income statement. The LIFO method more accurately captures the economic cost of inventory sold since the (last in) inventory is marked to the most recent market value. The mismatch in revenue and cost for FIFO inventory requires an economic adjustment to the gross cash flow calculation. The FIFO profits calculation is:

$$FIFO\ Profits = Inventory \times \%\ Change\ in\ PPI$$

The beginning-of-year inventory balance should be used. HOLT utilizes the Producer Price Index to broadly quantify the change in inventory purchasing power, but analysts with a more accurate assessment of inventory price changes should use their estimates.

This example assumes that all inventory is FIFO but can be adjusted proportionally. If all inventory is accounted for using LIFO, there are no FIFO profits and no adjustment is necessary to the gross cash flow. Most firms follow the FIFO method, thus overstating their operating profit. Amazon's inventory at the beginning of 2013 was $6.031bn (Exhibit 3.28).

Stock Compensation Expense

Stock compensation comes in a variety of forms including stock options, restricted shares, and stock appreciation rights. For firms that use stock compensation to reward employees, stock comp is treated as an ordinary expense in the determination of a firm's periodic net income.

EXHIBIT 3.28 Amazon's FIFO profits in 2013.

Amazon FY2013 FIFO Profits	Amount ($m)	Source
FIFO Inventory for FY2012	6,031	Balance sheet
x % Change in PPI	0.62%	HOLT
= FIFO profits	−37	Calculated

Stock compensation related to R&D investment is treated by HOLT as an R&D expenditure. This incentivized compensation is still aimed at developing future technologies, products, or services useful in deriving future cash flows. Therefore, it is also capitalized onto the balance sheet in the same manner as non-stock-based R&D. In contrast, vested stock options (that are in the money and exercisable) are treated as a debt-equivalent which reduces the equity value of shareholders.

The note underneath Amazon's 2013 income statement on page 36 indicates stock-based compensation for Fulfillment ($294m), Marketing ($88m), Technology and content ($603m), and General and administrative ($149m). The grand total is $1.134bn. The Technology and content portion is attributable to R&D investment, and this amount is added to R&D expense. R&D-related stock based compensation is treated the same as R&D in the determination of gross cash flow and capitalized R&D (see the technique described under "Capitalized research and development" found on page 79). The remaining stock-based compensation items (Fulfillment, Marketing, and G&A) sum to $531m and will have already been deducted from the firm's revenues, and thus require no further treatment.

Pension Expense

Net income includes an ethereal accounting pension gain or loss that is the combination of pension service costs (e.g., the pension wage), pension interest costs, expected return on pension plan assets, and pension actuarial gains and losses. HOLT's pension adjustment removes these charges except for the service cost, which is the true periodic economic cost of a pension plan. Pension expense can be found in the footnotes and is net of service cost and pension cost. Pension debt is added to debt-equivalents for valuation purposes. However, in the case of a pension surplus, this is not added to the value of the company, since these funds belong to the pension holders.

Minority Interest

Minority interest represents the portion of earnings in a non–wholly owned, consolidated subsidiary attributable to the minority owners. Minority interest is added back to net income since we are interested in the return to all capital providers. Minority interest for Amazon was zero.

Special Items

Special items are added back to net income (reversed) since CFROI is attempting to capture the *normalized* cash return on invested assets. Examples of special items include goodwill impairments, asset write-downs, large gains from the sale of a business, material FX or hedging gains/losses, restructuring charges, and tax settlements. The special item must first be tax adjusted to account for the impact on cash flow before it is added back. No material special items were reported for Amazon (Exhibit 3.29).

EXHIBIT 3.29 Amazon's gross cash flow in 2013.

Amazon FY2013		
Gross Cash Flow	**Amount ($m)**	**Source**
Net income	274	P&L
+ Depreciation	2,460	Note 3
+ Amortization	168	Note 4
+ Interest expense	141	P&L
+ R&D expense	5,602	Calculated
+ Rental expense	759	Note 8
+ Stock-compensation expense	0	Calculated
+ Net pension adjustment	0	N/A
+ Minority interest expense	0	P&L
+ Monetary holding gain	42	Calculated
− Special items (after tax)	0	N/A
− Equity investment income	71	P&L
− FIFO profits	(37)	Calculated
Gross cash flow	9,480	Calculated

EXHIBIT 3.30 Amazon's gross cash flow in 2013 based on a top-down approach.

Amazon FY2013

Gross Cash Flow	Amount ($m)	Source
Total net sales	74,452	P&L
− Total operating expenses	(73,593)	" "
Income from operations	859	" "
+ Depreciation	2,460	Note 3
+ Amortization	168	Note 4
EBITDA	3,487	Calculated
+ R&D	4,999	Calculated
+ Stock compensation expense	603	Calculated
+ Rental expense	759	Note 8
HOLT operating profit	9,848	Calculated
+ Interest income	38	P&L
+ Other income	(250)	P&L
− Taxes paid	(161)	P&L
+ Monetary holding gain	42	Calculated
− FIFO profits	(37)	Calculated
Gross cash flow	9,480	Calculated

EXHIBIT 3.31 Amazon's CFROI inputs and calculation.

Amazon FY2013

CFROI Calculation	Amount	Units
Asset life (nper)	5.4	Years
GCF (pmt)	9,480	$m
IAGI (pv)	38,581	$m
NDA (fv)	4,539	$m
CFROI = RATE (nper, pmt, −pv, fv)	12.0%	Percent

We took a bottom-up approach beginning with net income to calculate Amazon's gross cash flow. If you prefer a top-down approach, you can begin with revenue, work through to EBITDA and then make the same economic adjustments. The values for gross cash flow are the same (Exhibit 3.30).

CFROI Calculation for Amazon

Well done, we now have all the inputs for the CFROI calculation (Exhibit 3.31).

EXHIBIT 3.32 Amazon's Relative Wealth Chart as of April 30, 2014, indicates a prolonged period of value creation and growth. Shareholders have been handsomely rewarded.

Relative Wealth Chart
Internet & Direct Marketing Retail
Market Cap: 139.9 USD

Price: 304.13 (Apr 30, 2014)
Warranted Price: 345.06 USD (13%)

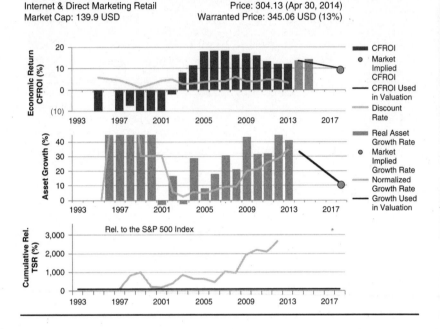

Amazon earned a CFROI of 12% in 2013. Is this result good or bad? Comparing Amazon's CFROI against its December 2013 real discount rate of 3.5% (as calculated by HOLT and discussed in further detail below), we see that Amazon has a positive spread of 8.5% above its cost of capital. This return would place Amazon well within the top quintile of global industrial returns.[15] Amazon has been creating positive shareholder value since 2003 and is expected to continue generating a CFROI that exceeds its cost of capital (Exhibit 3.32).

The HOLT Relative Wealth Chart is the first port of call for fund managers who wish to quickly assess a firm in HOLT Lens. We will return to reading Relative Wealth Charts later in the book but provide an overview now.

---

[15] Analysis based on the HOLT database of over 20,000 company returns.

UNDERSTANDING THE RELATIVE WEALTH CHART

The Relative Wealth Chart is composed of three panels. The top panel shows Amazon's historical CFROI and its real market-implied cost of capital. Amazon has been beating its cost of capital since 2003. CFROI has been fading since 2007. Consensus IBES earnings estimates are translated into expected CFROI for the next two years and provide investors with a strong link to near-term profit expectations. "Market-implied CFROI" (the Green Dot) and the "CFROI used in valuation" forecast in Exhibit 3.32 are similar for Amazon.[16]

The middle panel shows Amazon's real (inflation-adjusted) asset growth. The "Normalized growth rate" is an estimate of the firm's potential for organic growth. It is based on the cash generated by the company less the cash distributed back to capital providers. The normalized growth rate is likewise a measure of real growth. Amazon has aggressively grown its business.

The bottom panel shows the total shareholder performance of Amazon stock relative to the S&P 500 index. Amazon has created impressive wealth for its long-term shareholders and demonstrates a remarkable record of beating market expectations.[17]

In the HOLT framework, CFROI represents the weighted-average internal rate of return (IRR) on the investments that comprise the firm. In a sense, we are viewing the firm as a single project, however, the firm is assumed to be ongoing. We are simply measuring management's ability to generate returns on the assets currently in place. We've succeeded in filling the boxes for Amazon's 2013 CFROI calculation template (Exhibit 3.33). Are you ready to give it a try?

---

[16] HOLT's CFROI forecast is often referred to as the "default" forecast, or "default" CFROI. The implication here is not that the firm is nearing bankruptcy, but rather that the HOLT forecast CFROI is the expected value of firm profitability in HOLT Lens, i.e., the default. The "Green Dot" is the circled dot for "Market-implied CFROI" in the printed version. It is a green dot in HOLT Lens.

[17] HOLT often uses the terms "market-implied" or "market expectations." In this case, the term "market" refers to the average or consensus expectation of investors.

EXHIBIT 3.33 Amazon's 2013 CFROI calculation.

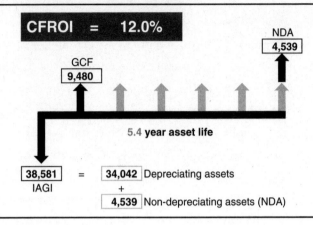

A COMMENT ON GOODWILL

Goodwill is the amount in excess of book value paid for an acquisition. The goodwill may reflect the value of a brand or a sustainable competitive advantage. It could also reflect an anticipation of future synergies or the hubris of the acquirer. You may have noticed that there is no place in the CFROI calculation for goodwill, yet it is on the books and it does reflect an expenditure of shareholder funds. How does CFROI hold management accountable for goodwill?

CFROI is designed to measure the economic profitability of the operating business: the cash generated against the cash invested. While goodwill is certainly an expenditure of shareholder funds, it is not recognized as an operating asset. Management can improve the return on operating assets. Managers can improve margins by cutting costs, or improve asset efficiency by generating more revenue from operating assets. However, management can do nothing to make goodwill more efficient. It is a sunk cost and has no bearing on future operations. Because it represents a premium over the book value of the assets, it can only be a drag on the operating returns of the business. This does not mean that senior executives and corporate boards should not be held responsible for acquisition goodwill.

Senior management should be answerable for the goodwill they acquire. However, though they cannot change the "efficiency" of goodwill, they can change the efficiency or profitability of the operating business. CFROI as a measure of the operating return of the business is a performance measure that operating managers can influence. To judge senior management's ability to acquire businesses and hold them accountable for the cumulative goodwill from acquisitions, a transaction CFROI can be calculated.

$$Transaction\ CFROI = CFROI \times \frac{IAGI}{IAGI + Cumulative\ goodwill}$$

The transaction CFROI represents the dilution of operating returns due to goodwill. The greater the amount of goodwill, the greater the dilution and the lower the transaction CFROI. Investors should be worried when the transaction CFROI is at or below a firm's cost of capital. A strict rule that Bob Hendricks followed was to avoid investing in companies where the transaction CFROI was below the cost of capital.[18]

This is not the case with Roper Technologies and management's extraordinary ability to acquire and integrate the companies they purchase. The HOLT Relative Wealth Chart indicates that Roper has a panache for growing by acquisition, a feat that most firms are unable to replicate as successfully. When goodwill is taken into account, Roper's transaction CFROI has maintained a steady 11% over the past decade. Roper squeezes exceptional performance out of its operating assets. Its CFROI has been improving since 2004 and its 2014 CFROI was 41%, which places it in the top 1 percentile of global industrials! Relative shareholder performance has also been excellent (Exhibit 3.34).

In Chapter 6, we'll show how the transaction CFROI and transaction HOLT Economic Profit can be used to dissect changes in shareholder value due to acquisitions.

---

[18] Bob Hendricks was one of the founders of HOLT, the "H" in HOLT, and a mentor to countless investors.

EXHIBIT 3.34 Roper Technologies Relative Wealth Chart as of June 16, 2015, indicates that it grows by acquisition. Although goodwill dilutes Roper's performance, its transaction CFROI has remained above its cost of capital. Shareholders have been handsomely rewarded.

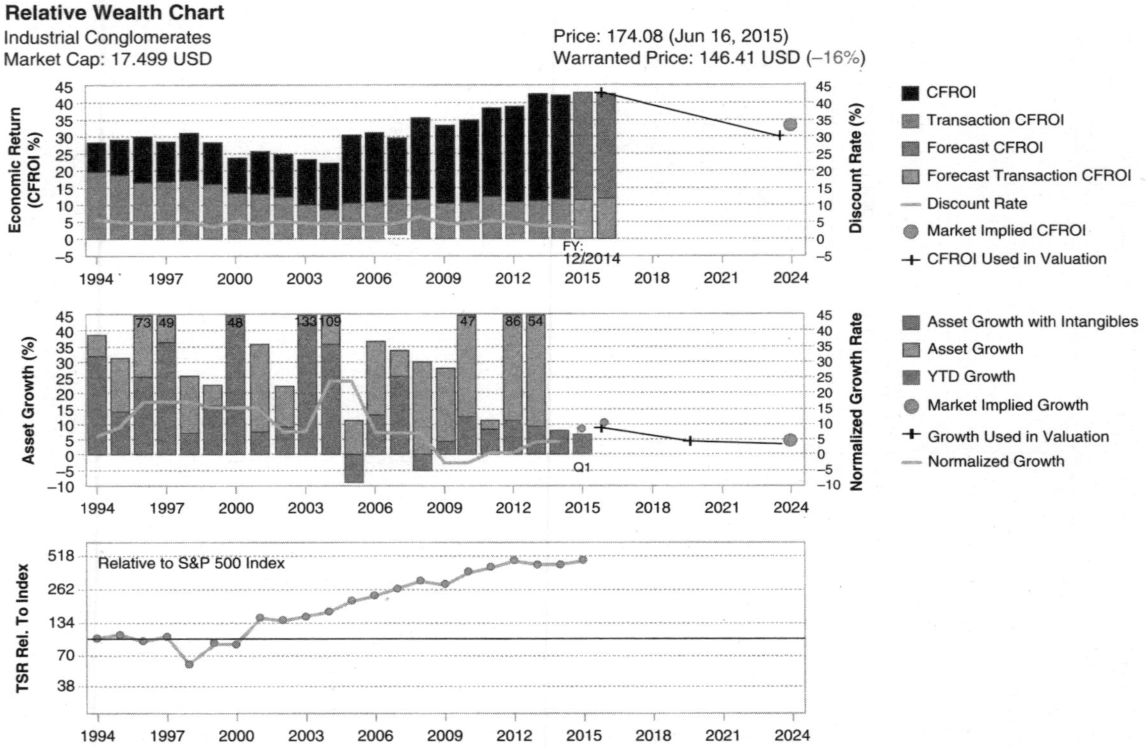
Relative Wealth Chart
Industrial Conglomerates
Market Cap: 17.499 USD
Price: 174.08 (Jun 16, 2015)
Warranted Price: 146.41 USD (−16%)
Economic Return (CFROI %)
Discount Rate (%)
FY: 12/2014
CFROI
Transaction CFROI
Forecast CFROI
Forecast Transaction CFROI
Discount Rate
Market Implied CFROI
CFROI Used in Valuation
Asset Growth (%)
Normalized Growth Rate
73
49
48
133
109
47
86
54
Q1
Asset Growth with Intangibles
Asset Growth
YTD Growth
Market Implied Growth
Growth Used in Valuation
Normalized Growth
TSR Rel. To Index
Relative to S&P 500 Index
518
262
134
70
38
1994
1997
2000
2003
2006
2009
2012
2015
2018
2021
2024

CHAPTER APPENDIX: GROSS PLANT RECAPTURED

Companies make acquisitions which leave room to distort asset registers. Under purchase accounting rules, net assets of the acquired firm are booked at fair value, which differs from the historical cost of the acquired assets. Since the CFROI calculation relies on historical cost gross investment (the capital providers' funds originally invested), an estimate of that historical cost is needed. Unfortunately, the original gross investment of the acquired company is rarely available if it was a private transaction, or is buried in the transaction disclosure documents.

When information is disclosed about the assets acquired, a good estimate of the historical cost can be made and the difference between fair value and the historical cost can be added back to the gross plant and inflation adjusted. However, lacking such information, we must make a gross plant recaptured estimate. Gross plant recaptured is the difference between the fixed assets reported after the acquisition and the value of the fixed assets prior to the acquisition. Gross plant recaptured relies on the net plant to gross plant ratio of the acquiring company. Exhibit 3.35 presents an example of the gross plant recaptured estimate when data relating to the historical cost of the acquired assets is not disclosed.

In this example, Company A acquires Company B. Company B was privately held so the true balance sheet has not been disclosed. We do know that pre-acquisition, publicly traded Company A had $1,000 in gross plant and $500 in net assets resulting in a net plant to gross plant ratio of 50%. Company A, as reported post acquisition, has $1,200 in gross plant and $700 in net assets for a net plant to gross plant ratio of 58%. To restore the ratio to 50% (the best guess we have), requires a gross plant recaptured of $200. While we have correctly estimated gross plant, we have underestimated accumulated depreciation and overestimated the ratio. The final column in Exhibit 3.35 reflects the true undisclosed gross investment. Finally, the gross plant recaptured is inflation adjusted based on the asset life of the acquiring company. No gross plant recaptured was reported in Amazon's annual report.

EXHIBIT 3.35 **Estimating gross plant recaptured.**

	Company A	buys	Company B (not disclosed)	As reported post acquisition Company A	The true post acquisition balance sheet
Gross plant	1,000		400	1,200	1,400
Accumulated depr	500		300	500	800
Net plant	**500**		**100**	**700**	**600**
Fair value adjustment (assume = net assets)			200		
Net plant/Gross plant ratio	50%		25%	58%	43%
[Net plant/[NP/GP ratio] =	700	divided by	50% =		
Less: reported gross plant				1,400	
Equal: gross plant recaptured				**1,200**	
				200	
Adjusted post acquisition Company A					
Gross plant as reported post acquisition				1,200	
Plus: Gross plant recaptured				200	
Equal: Adj GP recaptured				1,400	
Divided by net plant as reported post acquisition				700	
Equal: Adj NP/GP ratio				**50%**	

110

Section II

Discounted Cash Flow and Economic Profit Valuation

4

WHAT'S IT WORTH? VALUING THE FIRM

"The value of any stock, bond, or business today is determined by the cash inflows and outflows—discounted at an appropriate interest rate—that can be expected to occur during the remaining life of the asset."

—*The Theory of Investment Value*, John Burr Williams

KEY LEARNING POINTS

- We outline how to calculate and forecast free cash flow to the firm (FCFF), which is central to performing a discounted cash flow valuation.

- We show how to value the terminal period of a forecast. A fade factor can be easily incorporated, making it possible to test the sensitivity of a valuation to changes in the rate at which profitability decays.

- The calculation and utility of economic profit (EP) in assessing economic performance and valuing a firm is described. For a given forecast, discounted FCFF and EP valuations yield the same result. We value Air Liquide and demonstrate its sensitivity to profitability fade.

- We step through the calculation of FCFF in the HOLT framework, and show how it can be estimated from a CFROI and asset growth forecast.
- Different profitability and growth scenarios are valued for Amazon, indicating that it is expected to maintain high profitability *and* fast growth.
- Air Liquide is analyzed through the lens of the HOLT framework.

We have outlined how to calculate a firm's CFROI and analyze its historical operating performance. The next step is to calculate its intrinsic value based on profitability, growth, and cash flow forecasts. We will explore different discounted cash flow (DCF) approaches in this chapter and then apply our knowledge and estimate the value of companies using both the HOLT and conventional DCF frameworks.

The goal of a DCF forecast is to estimate the intrinsic value of a company and its sensitivity to changes in key drivers. By intrinsic value, we mean the present value of the firm's expected cash flows. Given the same forecast, we should obtain equivalent estimates of firm value from the various frameworks. But, as Yogi Berra quipped, "In theory, there is no difference between theory and practice. In practice, there is." Differences most often arise in assumptions about a firm's terminal value.

Let's begin by reviewing the conventional discounted cash flow valuation approaches.

A REVIEW OF CONVENTIONAL VALUATION APPROACHES

The Entity Free Cash Flow Approach

The most popular method for valuing companies is to determine the present value of future free cash flows to the firm (FCFF). FCFF is the free cash flow to all capital providers. It does not distinguish between debt and equity. Projected free cash flows are discounted at the firm's cost of capital r:

$$Firm\ value = PV(FCFF) = \sum_{n=1}^{N} \frac{FCFF_n}{(1 + r)^n}$$

Although the formula assumes the discount rate is constant, it will vary over time just as bond spot rates vary. The riskiness of future cash flows relative to the market might change too, causing the discount rate to change. For example, a biotech start-up will probably have a higher beta (systematic risk exposure) when it begins life and have a lower beta *if* it becomes a mature, successful pharmaceutical company.[1] The tools of decision analysis, such as decision trees, can help when confronted by these types of potential discontinuities.[2] Let's keep it simple for now and assume a constant discount rate. Because we are valuing long-term cash flows, the discount rate should reflect a long duration. Commonly, ten years is assumed to represent the long term.

Free cash flow to the firm is the total cash flow that remains after taxes are paid and investment requirements have been met. The term "free cash flow to the firm" is equivalent to the cash that would be available to shareholders if the company had no debt. This is a crucial point. When valuing a company or project (or even when measuring a firm's operational performance), it is best to keep operations and financing effects separate. Tax savings from debt or other financial subsidies can be accounted for in the cost of capital or valued separately. Disentangling financial choices from operations yields a clearer understanding of a firm's value.

---

[1] For those new to finance, beta is the covariance between a stock and the overall market. See William Sharpe's seminal introduction of CAPM to develop a solid understanding of this concept. William F. Sharpe, "Capital Asset Prices: A Theory of Market Equilibrium under Conditions of Risk," *The Journal of Finance* 19(3) (1964): 425–442.

[2] In this case, it would be best to use a decision tree for assessing the biotech start-up. The riskiest part is likely to be R&D followed by clinical testing. If R&D proves unfruitful, then you shut down the project. *If* development and clinical tests are successful, then the beta of the future commercial cash flows will likely be much lower; that is, *if* the drug is successful and unique, *then* doctors' and patients' decision to use the drug will not be very influenced by the stock market's gyrations and its beta will be lower. Different discount rates can be used for each branch of the probability tree. See Clemen and Reilly (2014) for more on decision analysis.

It is the potential value of the operating assets that is most important to operating managers. Their decisions on which projects to invest in, which assets to purchase, how the assets are deployed and maintained, and which products and services they support have the greatest impact on a company's value. Financial engineering is a secondary consideration and one where adding value is tenuous. We showed in Chapter 2 that when the effects of financing are eliminated from the measurement of operating performance, comparability across firms is greatly enhanced. When financing effects are likewise eliminated from the measurement of free cash flow, internal consistency is obtained between the performance metric and its related cash flow. For instance, it would make little sense to talk about a firm's ROE and then refer to its cost of capital or enterprise value in the same discussion. Instead, if ROE were the metric of choice, it would make sense to discuss the cost of equity and the firm's free cash flow to equity. For this reason, we will focus on free cash flow to all the firm's capital providers and return on capital. We need to define a few key terms to facilitate the discussion.

NOPAT = Net operating profit after tax

Capex = Capital expenditure (which might be either gross or net)

Gross Capex = net Capex + depreciation.

Δ Working capital = change in working capital.

Invested capital = net fixed assets + working capital.

Δ Invested capital = change in invested capital = net Capex + Δ working capital.

T_c = corporate tax rate (a firm's effective tax rate is often used, but it should be normalized so that it reflects the average tax rate expected over the long-term).

NOPAT equals the unlevered after-tax operating profit and can be derived from either a top-down approach (starting with sales) or bottom-up approach (starting with net income).[3]

$$NOPAT = EBIT \times (1 - T_c) = Net\ income + Interest\ paid \times (1 - T_c)$$

---

[3] This formulation is simplified. There are usually numerous adjustments that are necessary to equate top-down and bottom-up calculations of NOPAT, e.g., associate income and extraordinary items.

EBIT is earnings before interest and tax, or operating profit, and interest paid $\times T_c$ is the interest tax shield that corporations gain by deducting interest payments on debt from their taxable earnings. The interest tax shield is zero in a given year for each of these three situations: The corporate tax rate (T_c) is zero, interest payments are not tax-deductible, or the firm isn't generating enough operating profit to pay interest on its debts. The first two points can be related to Modigliani's and Miller's famous Propositions I and II where capital structure is irrelevant in perfect markets with no taxes, frictions, or market inefficiencies (this is not the world that lies outside university gates, but the conclusions remain highly instructive).[4]

In its simplest form, invested capital is the sum of net fixed assets and operating working capital (Exhibit 4.1). The distinction between operating and non-operating assets, for example, holdings in associates and their resulting income and costs on the Profit & Loss Statement (P&L), must be consistent. Because short-term debt is just the current amount due on the long-term interest-bearing debt, it is removed from working capital

EXHIBIT 4.1 Invested capital is the sum of operating working capital and net fixed assets.

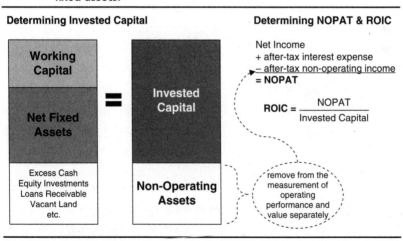

---

[4]F. Modigliani and M. Miller (1958), "The Cost of Capital, Corporation Finance and the Theory of Investment," *American Economic Review* 48(3): 261–297. Corporate finance textbooks cover the topic in detail. See, for example, the textbook *Principles of Corporate Finance* by Brealey, Myers, and Allen.

and added back to total long-term debt. Excess cash is often removed from working capital and subtracted from debt. That means that any interest earned and taxes paid on that excess cash should be excluded from NOPAT. Consistency is paramount.

This is the tip of the iceberg. If you wish to explore the adjustments and nuances of NOPAT and invested capital, please consult the textbooks written by Damodaran (2012) and Koller et al. (2010). Many of the adjustments they use are similar to those of HOLT with the caveat that HOLT measures the economic return on *gross* investment while the accounting in those textbooks measures the return on *net* assets.

Valuing the End of the Line

Most valuations start with the assumption that the firm will last forever. It would be unproductive to create forecasts that stretch to infinity. The most efficient approach is to split the forecast into a given number of years—ten, for example—and a terminal period that begins at the end of the tenth year. The detailed forecast is known as the forecast horizon, or the explicit period. The value of the terminal period is also known as continuing, horizon, residual, or ongoing value.

$$Firm\ value = \sum_{n=1}^{N} \frac{FCFF_n}{(1 + r)^n} + PV(Terminal\ period)$$

The easy way out is to forecast earnings in the eleventh year and multiply it by an EV/EBITDA or P/E ratio. We would advise against this slothfulness for all the reasons cited in Chapter 2. We recommend the following guidelines:

- The forecast horizon should be for as long as the firm is expected to maintain a competitive advantage with excess profitability or until its return on marginal investments is expected to occur at the cost of capital.
- Bullet one also holds true for the situation where a firm is generating returns below its cost of capital. This situation is unsustainable

and usually leads to industry consolidation, or bankruptcy for the worst performers. If liquidating a firm is worth more than allowing it to remain a going concern, then the firm should be wound down. Don't forget the NPV rule!

- Start-ups and turnarounds should be forecast until the firm hits a sustainable rate of profitability and asset growth cools to that of inflation or the general economy.

Exhibit 4.2 will help you decide how long an explicit forecast should be and what approach to take for estimating the terminal value.

The first thing we need is an equation relating FCFF, NOPAT, growth g in invested capital (IC), and return on invested capital (ROIC) (Exhibit 4.3).[5]

$$FCFF = NOPAT - \Delta IC = NOPAT(1 - g/ROIC) \qquad (4.1)$$

where $g/ROIC$ is the reinvestment rate, or plowback.

The lower ROIC is for a given growth rate, the lower the resulting FCFF. NOPAT only equals FCFF when growth is zero or ROIC is infinite. As in our earlier discussion about P/E and ROE in Chapter 2, ROIC is a measure of the *quality* of earnings to all capital providers. This equation tells us about the sign of FCFF. If $g >$ ROIC, then FCFF is negative irrespective of how well or poorly managed the firm is. If $g <$ ROIC, then FCFF is positive. The quickest way to boost cash flow is to stop growing. **A key takeaway is that the sign of FCFF tells us nothing about the quality of the company and its investments.**

A general expression can be written for the case where growth in the terminal period and the firm's ROIC remain constant. This equation arises from the growing perpetuity equation.

$$Terminal\ value_N = \frac{FCFF_{N+1}}{(r - g_\infty)} = \frac{NOPAT_{N+1}(1 - g_\infty/ROIC_\infty)}{(r - g_\infty)} \qquad (4.2)$$

---

[5]This derivation requires nothing more than a bit of algebra: $\Delta IC_i = g_i \times IC_{i-1} = NOPAT_i \times \frac{g_i}{ROIC_i}$ where $ROIC_i = \frac{NOPAT_i}{IC_{i-1}}$

EXHIBIT 4.2 Flowchart to determine how long an explicit forecast period should last and how best to estimate the terminal value. ROIIC is the return on incremental invested capital.

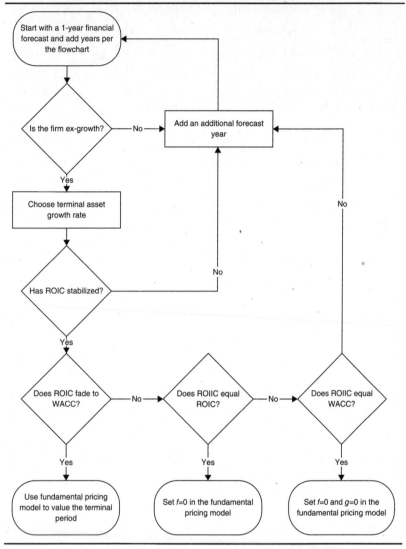

To remind you that the terminal period and its assumptions are forever, we use the subscript ∞. We have seen a mistaken form of this equation appear in more than a handful of actual valuation models.

$$Terminal\ value_N \neq \frac{NOPAT_{N+1}}{(r - g_\infty)}$$

EXHIBIT 4.3 Relationship between FCFF, NOPAT, and investment.

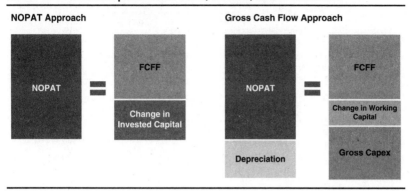

This is a fatal error unless the perpetual ROIC is approaching infinity. In other words, growth is not free unless a company can generate an infinite return on its investment. If you are auditing a valuation model that generates highly optimistic values, this is a mistake to check for immediately. The key point to remember is that NOPAT is not *free* cash flow except when growth is zero or ROIC is infinite; FCFF = NOPAT − ΔIC.

The perpetuity equation $NOPAT_{N+1}/r$ can be applied when the return on invested capital equals the cost of capital in year $N+1$ and is expected to remain at the cost of capital. The perpetuity relationship also holds true if the incremental return on future investments (ROIIC) equals the cost of capital, *and* the existing business at the end of year N maintains a constant NOPAT into perpetuity. The value of a firm does not change with growth if ROIC equals the cost of capital. You can prove this to yourself by substituting ROIC = r into equation 4.2.

For the case where existing assets will earn a perpetual ROIC that is expected to remain above the cost of capital but incremental investments are at the cost of capital, the terminal value can be written as a simple perpetuity:

$$Terminal\ value_N = \frac{NOPAT_{N+1}}{r}$$

Let's take a journey to France and value Air Liquide, which specializes in industrial gases. The firm has had stable margins and asset utilization over the past five years, so we'll assume that the forward drivers of firm value will be the past 5-year averages. The growth of sales is set to 5% in the explicit period and 2% in the terminal period; EBITDA margin is assumed to be 24.4%; the effective tax rate is 26%; operating working capital is set to 3.5% of sales; and net fixed asset turns are held constant at 1.16. A bare bone forecast and FCFF valuation is shown in Exhibit 4.4.

The weighted-average cost of capital (WACC) was set to 6%, which results in a DCF enterprise value of €47.4bn.[6] Air Liquide was trading at €100 per share at the ends of 2014 and 2015, which resulted in a market enterprise value of circa €44bn, in line with this valuation scenario.

A good check is to see whether a perpetual spread has been embedded in the terminal period. Air Liquide has averaged ROIC of 15% over the past five years (see ROIC in Exhibit 4.6), and is forecast to remain at 14.6% during the forecast period. It drops to 13.9% in the terminal period, which is an impressive 7.9% above WACC. The valuation will thus be sensitive to the terminal growth assumption, so let's set the terminal growth to zero and see what happens:

$$PV\,(Terminal\,period) = \frac{NOPAT_6}{r(1+r)^5} = \frac{2.451}{0.06(1.06)^5} = €30.5bn$$

Terminal value falls from €40.1bn to €30.5bn, and the intrinsic enterprise value drops to €37.7bn from €47.4bn for a decrease of almost €10bn from our base case simply by forecasting zero growth in the terminal period. Recall that the terminal value is insensitive to growth when ROIC equals the cost of capital. This underscores that not only is Air Liquide forecast to sustain a perpetual spread (ROIC $>$ r), but also to grow. Maintaining the present ROIC and investing in new projects that create value are crucial to Air Liquide's meeting the market's expectations.

Another approach to valuing Air Liquide might be to wind the ROIC down to the cost of capital during the explicit period by ramping down the EBITDA margin to reflect competitive pressures. Because Air Liquide is priced to earn operating returns above its cost of capital, this approach

---

[6]We discuss the cost of capital in Chapter 7. When valuing FCFF, the appropriate discount rate is the weighted average cost of capital (WACC).

EXHIBIT 4.4 Financial forecast and FCFF valuation of Air Liquide. The market enterprise value was circa €44bn as of December 31, 2014, and December 31, 2015.

Year	2009	2010	2011	2012	2013	2014	2015	2016	2017	2018	2019	2020	Terminal
			History						Explicit forecast				Terminal
Income statement													
Sales	11,976	13,488	14,457	15,326	15,225	15,358	16,126	16,932	17,779	18,668	19,601	19,993	
Cash costs	−9,047	−10,178	−10,949	−11,584	−11,468	−11,639	−12,191	−12,801	−13,441	−14,113	−14,818	−15,115	
EBITDA	2,929	3,310	3,508	3,742	3,757	3,719	3,935	4,131	4,338	4,555	4,783	4,878	
Depreciation	−959	−1,056	−1,086	−1,160	−1,145	−1,148	−1,209	−1,270	−1,333	−1,400	−1,470	−1,499	
EBITA	1,970	2,254	2,422	2,582	2,612	2,571	2,725	2,862	3,005	3,155	3,313	3,379	
Cash taxes	−484	−587	−643	−652	−690	−725	−709	−744	−781	−820	−861	−878	
NOPAT	1,486	1,667	1,779	1,930	1,922	1,846	2,017	2,118	2,223	2,335	2,451	2,500	
Balance sheet													
Working capital	198	387	432	1,100	322	357	564	593	622	653	686	700	
Net fixed assets	9,921	11,037	12,097	12,785	13,226	14,554	13,902	14,597	15,327	16,093	16,898	17,235	
Invested capital	10,119	11,424	12,529	13,885	13,548	14,911	14,466	15,189	15,949	16,746	17,584	17,935	
Operating cash flow													
NOPAT		1,667	1,779	1,930	1,922	1,846	2,017	2,118	2,223	2,335	2,451	2,500	2,322
Δ Invested Capital		−1,305	−1,105	−1,356	337	−1,363	445	−723	−759	−797	−837	−352	
Free cash flow		362	674	574	2,259	483	2,462	1,394	1,464	1,537	1,614	2,149	
PV of explicit FCF	7,216												
PV of terminal value	40,140												
Enterprise value	**47,356**												

would have to occur over a period that corresponds to the sustainability of their competitive advantages. If that period is infinity, then you can use the growing perpetuity equation.

Economic Profit Approach

Economic profit represents the profit of the firm less the opportunity cost of capital that investors require as compensation for funding the firm's assets and placing their wealth at risk.

The economic profit (EP) valuation approach should result in the same estimate of firm value for a given forecast, but it has the benefit of showing the economic profit created or lost each period.

Economic profit can be expressed either as NOPAT less a capital charge (the opportunity cost) or as the spread (ROIC − r) multiplied by the invested capital:

$$EP = NOPAT - Capital\ charge$$

$$Capital\ charge = r \times IC$$

$$EP = (ROIC - r) \times IC \tag{4.3}$$

If a firm's return on invested capital exceeds its cost of capital, then it is creating economic value. The more it can grow by investing in projects that exceed their cost of capital, the more value the firm will create for its shareholders. Firms that aren't meeting their cost of capital are destroying economic value. A firm that is meeting its cost of capital should trade at its book value, since economic profits will be zero. In this case, net assets will equal the present value of all future free cash flows. Exhibit 4.5 shows the value drivers and calculation of economic profit.

Economic profit is easier to comprehend and communicate than free cash flow. Economic profit combines size and return on invested capital and its opportunity cost into a single result. Too much focus on the size of earnings or earnings growth can lead to decisions that destroy value if

EXHIBIT 4.5 **Flowchart showing the calculation of economic profit and how its value drivers feed into it. Invested capital turns equal sales divided by invested capital. The DuPont relationship is $ROIC = EBIT\% \times (1 - T_c) \times$ Invested capital turns.**

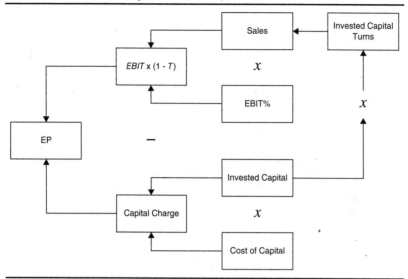

ROIC is less than the cost of capital. Conversely, an obsessive focus on earning a high ROIC on a low capital base may lead to missed opportunities if managers are rewarded for maintaining a high ROIC. Don't allow a myopic view to fool you; the NPV rule still prevails!

As before, we'll split the valuation into explicit and terminal periods:

$$Firm\ value = IC_0 + \sum_{n=1}^{N} \frac{EP_n}{(1 + r)^n} + PV(Terminal\ period)$$

The general expression for constant growth and ROIC in the terminal period is:

$$Terminal\ value_N = \frac{EP_{N+1}}{(r - g_\infty)} = \frac{NOPAT_{N+1} - r \times IC_N}{(r - g_\infty)}$$

$$= \frac{(ROIC_\infty - r) \times IC_N}{(r - g_\infty)} \tag{4.4}$$

This equation has some interesting properties. When ROIC equals the cost of capital, the terminal value is zero. No fuss or extra work required.

EXHIBIT 4.6 Financial forecast and EP valuation of Air Liquide. The market enterprise value was circa €44bn as of December 31, 2014, and December 31, 2015.

Year	2009	2010	2011	2012	2013	2014	2015	2016	2017	2018	2019	2020
			History						Explicit forecast			Terminal
Income statement												
Sales	11,976****	13,488	14,457	15,326	15,225	15,358	16,126	16,932	17,779	18,668	19,601	19,993
Cash costs	−9,047	−10,178	−10,949	−11,584	−11,468	−11,639	−12,191	−12,801	−13,441	−14,113	−14,818	−15,115
EBITDA	2,929	3,310	3,508	3,742	3,757	3,719	3,935	4,131	4,338	4,555	4,783	4,878
Depreciation	−959	−1,056	−1,086	−1,160	−1,145	−1,148	−1,209	−1,270	−1,333	−1,400	−1,470	−1,499
EBITA	1,970	2,254	2,422	2,582	2,612	2,571	2,725	2,862	3,005	3,155	3,313	3,379
Cash taxes	−484	−587	−643	−652	−690	−725	−709	−744	−781	−820	−861	−878
NOPAT	1,486	1,667	1,779	1,930	1,922	1,846	2,017	2,118	2,223	2,335	2,451	2,500
Balance sheet												
Working capital	198	387	432	1,100	322	357	564	593	622	653	686	700
Net fixed assets	9,921	11,037	12,097	12,785	13,226	14,554	13,902	14,597	15,327	16,093	16,898	17,235
Invested capital	10,119	11,424	12,529	13,885	13,548	14,911	14,466	15,189	15,949	16,746	17,584	17,935
Economic profit calculation												
ROIC		16.5%	15.6%	15.4%	13.8%	13.6%	13.5%	14.6%	14.6%	14.6%	14.6%	14.2%
NOPAT		1,667	1,779	1,930	1,922	1,846	2,017	2,118	2,223	2,335	2,451	2,500
Capital charge		−607	−685	−752	−833	−813	−895	−868	−911	−957	−1,005	−1,055
Economic profit		1,060	1,094	1,178	1,089	1,033	1,122	1,250	1,312	1,378	1,447	1,445
PV of EP	5,444						1,059	1,112	1,102	1,091	1,081	
Invested capital	14,911											
PV of terminal period	27,001											
Enterprise value	**47,356**											

EXHIBIT 4.7 Forecast scenarios and their valuations for Air Liquide. The market enterprise value was circa €44bn as of December 31, 2014, and December 31, 2015.

Scenario	Enterprise Value	Comment
1	€47.4 bn	Value creation continues and grows in the terminal period.
2	€37.7 bn	Growth is set to zero in the terminal period, but the core business sustains its profitability into perpetuity.
3	€20.4 bn	Value creation is limited to the explicit forecast period. EP is set to zero in the terminal period.
4	€14.9 bn	Book value of the firm; EP is set to zero in the explicit and terminal periods.

It's relatively easy to back into how much value must be created in the terminal period to match the market value of the firm. The economic profit valuation for Air Liquide is shown in Exhibit 4.6.

Whew, we calculated the same enterprise value as for our FCFF base case, €47.4bn. If the terminal growth is set to zero, the present value of the terminal period drops from €27bn to €17.4bn, resulting in an enterprise value of €37.7bn, which matches the FCFF valuation result. Here's where the advantages of the EP approach shine. If we assumed zero value creation in the terminal period, the enterprise value would bottom to €20.4bn (€14.91bn + €5.44bn). And if Air Liquide ceased creating value from 2015 onwards, its enterprise value would drop to its invested capital of €14.9bn. The results are summarized in Exhibit 4.7.

What Is Fade?

Fade is a concept with which HOLT clients are quite familiar. Fade is the rate at which profitability converges toward the long-term average level of profitability, which we assume is a firm's cost of capital. We discuss fade in profitability extensively in Chapter 9, and offer empirical evidence for its existence. For now, let's assume a general understanding of fade and show how it can be employed in valuing a firm.

An elegant manner of making the transition from a profitable or unprofitable state to a cost of capital (or normal) state is to utilize a fade factor f which is the rate at which ROIC converges to the cost of capital. In other words, it is the rate at which the economic profit spread decays to zero. A general expression can be derived where ROIC fades to r while the invested capital grows at g.

$$Terminal\ value_N$$

$$= \sum_{i=1}^{\infty} \frac{(1-f)^{i-1} \times (ROIC_{N+1} - r) \times IC_N \times (1 + g_\infty)^{i-1}}{(1+r)^i}$$

This might look like a dog's breakfast, but it is highly useful and has an interesting feature: **Fade is compound decay, which has the opposite sign of growth**.

The closed-form solution is simply that of a growing perpetuity. While the asset base grows *ad infinitum*, the economic spread fades into the sunset as ROIC converges toward the cost of capital:[7]

$$Terminal\ value_N = \frac{(ROIC_{N+1} - r) \times InvCap_N}{r - [(1-f) \times (1 + g_\infty) - 1]} \approx \frac{EP_{N+1}}{r - g_\infty + f} \quad (4.5)$$

This is a significant simplification and allows you to test how sensitive the valuation is to changes in the rate of decay in corporate profitability. The fade rate f can range from 0% (no fade) to 100% (immediate fade). This equation has a fascinating property: It is equivalent to calculating the terminal value of a growing EP stream that suddenly drops to zero after $1/f$ years. A fade rate of 10% would correspond to an expected competitive advantage period of 10 years, since $1/0.10 = 10$. Please see Chapter 5 for more detail on fade and CAP (competitive advantage period).

---

[7] The secret is to see that the spread (ROIC – r) is fading to zero at an exponential rate of f. By setting $(1-f)(1+g) = (1+x)$, the equation reduces to the form of a growing perpetuity and Bob's your uncle. Please see our report: Holland and Matthews, *Don't Suffer from a Terminal Flaw, Add Fade to your DCF*, Credit Suisse HOLT, June 2016. The term $[(1-f)(1+g) - 1]$ is approximately equal to $(g-f)$ when the cross-term ($f \times g$) is assumed to be negligible. This simplification makes the equation and its interpretation far more tractable.

Fade in Economic Profit Equation

If we put the pieces together, we can write the firm value as:

$$Firm\ value = IC_0 + \sum_{n=1}^{N} \frac{EP_n}{(1+r)^n} + \frac{EP_{N+1}}{(r - g_\infty + f)(1+r)^N} \qquad (4.6)$$

A valuation matrix for different combinations of fade and terminal growth is shown using this equation and the earlier Air Liquide forecast (Exhibits 4.8 and 4.9).

Growth and fade of 0% equate to the case of a simple perpetuity and generate the same enterprise value of €37.7bn (upper left corner of the table). The base case of 2% terminal growth results in the same value of €47.4bn. The benefit of including fade in the economic profit approach is that we can test how sensitive the valuation is to changes in profit persistence. Notice how quickly the value drops as fade increases! Just changing the fade from 0% to 5% causes the value to drop by a third. If the fade rate is increased to 10%, the average rate of profit decay for the average firm, total firm value drops by more than 40%.

EXHIBIT 4.8 Air Liquide's enterprise value (€m) for different combinations of terminal growth and fade. The market enterprise value was circa €44bn as of December 31, 2014, and December 31, 2015.

| | | Fade Rate | | | | | |
		0%	5%	10%	20%	50%	100%
	0%	37,745	29,841	26,877	24,369	22,219	21,340
Growth rate	1%	41,590	30,973	27,434	24,602	22,286	21,367
	2%	47,356	32,356	28,070	24,856	22,356	21,394

EXHIBIT 4.9 Air Liquide's enterprise value to book value for different combinations of terminal growth and fade.

| | | Fade Rate | | | | | |
		0%	5%	10%	20%	50%	100%
	0%	2.5	2.0	1.8	1.6	1.5	1.4
Growth rate	1%	2.8	2.1	1.8	1.6	1.5	1.4
	2%	3.2	2.2	1.9	1.7	1.5	1.4

Can Air Liquide sustain its present profitability for so far into the future? Are its competitive advantages this strong? Fade is an empirical reality and a crucial component of value; it is a feature that a fundamental analyst must think long and hard about. You are allowed to turn off your Bloomberg terminal and turn on your mind for this one. If you're wondering about Warren Buffett, he likes firms that he expects will experience little or no fade in their core business: Dairy Queen, See's Chocolate, Coca Cola, Gillette, Heinz, and Kraft. The value of these firms is about far more than next quarter's or next year's earnings.

Exhibit 4.10 summarizes the EP and FCFF valuation techniques. You should obtain equal valuations for a given forecast.

HOLT APPROACH TO FCFF VALUATION

The HOLT framework accommodates both the FCFF and the EP approaches to estimating firm value. We will use Amazon to demonstrate the HOLT FCFF adjustments and valuation. Let's begin by defining operating free cash flow and step through the adjustments.

Nominal Gross Cash Flow

The nominal gross cash flow (GCF) is the gross cash flow produced by the firm less tax due on current profits. Gross cash flow reverses the non-cash depreciation expense. In our conventional example, gross cash flow equals NOPAT plus depreciation. Because the gross cash flow in the CFROI calculation is inflation-adjusted and based on book taxes, we need to reverse the inflation adjustment and take into account the actual cash tax that is paid.

$$Nominal\ GCF = GCF - Monetary\ holding\ gain$$

$$+ \Delta\ Deferred\ tax + Special\ items\ (after\ tax)$$

EXHIBIT 4.10 Flowchart for the EP and FCFF valuation approaches: EP is on the left-hand side and FCFF is on the right-hand side. The valuations should be equivalent for a given forecast.

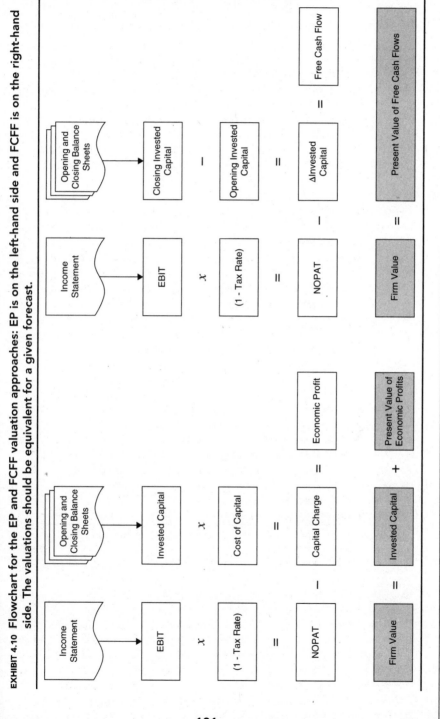

131

We calculated the first two items for Amazon in Chapter 3. No special items were reported in 2013. The change in deferred tax accounts for timing differences in taxes paid can usually be found on the balance sheet. Long-term deferred tax liabilities can be found in Note 7 on page 54 of Amazon's 2013 annual report.

$$\Delta\ Deferred\ tax\ (2013) = \$571m - \$476m = \$95m$$

$$Nominal\ GCF(2013) = \$9,480m - \$42m + \$95m = \$9,533m$$

Total Investment

Total investment consists of four components:

- Change in working capital
- Change in long-term assets
- R&D investment
- Change in capitalized operating leases

The changes in specific working capital items are presented in Exhibit 4.11. Most of these items can be pulled directly from Amazon's 2013 balance sheet.

Since cash is used to purchase assets, an increase in assets results in a decrease in cash. Accounts receivable and other current assets were split in

EXHIBIT 4.11 Change in working capital calculation for Amazon in 2013.

Amazon.com ($m) Change in Working Capital ($m)	Balance Sheet Items		
	2012	2013	Change
Accounts receivable	2,600	3,000	400
Other current assets	1,217	1,767	550
Operating cash	11,448	12,447	999
Inventories	6,031	7,411	1,380
- Accounts payable	(13,318)	(15,133)	(1,815)
- Other current liabilities	(4,550)	(6,111)	(1,561)
- Income taxes payable	0	0	0
= Working capital	3,428	3,381	(47)

Amazon's financial report. Note 1 on page 44 of the 2013 annual report indicates that vendor and customer receivables were $3.0bn in 2013 and $2.6bn in 2012. Because HOLT assumes that cash and marketable securities are operating assets, they are included as working capital items. Most analysts subtract excess cash and marketable securities from debt and exclude them from working capital. Management is held responsible for all cash it retains under the HOLT approach. However you decide to treat cash, make sure it remains consistent. If you decide to keep cash as part of working capital, interest earned on cash should remain in the free cash flow forecast and cash should not be deducted from total debt when estimating the intrinsic price per share (this would be double-counting).

An increase in current liabilities is equivalent to an increase in cash from operating activities. Creditors are providing funding for the business. Because interest-bearing short-term debt is the current portion due on long-term debt, it should be excluded from current liabilities, that is, it is not working capital; it is debt financing.[8] In Amazon's case, short-term debts of $1.736bn in 2013 and $1.134bn in 2012 were excluded from other current liabilities (see notes 6 and 7 on pages 53 to 54 of the 2013 annual report). The change in working capital was −$47m. Working capital decreased. This is the same as saying that net cash due to changes in working capital was a positive $47m, since creditors have increased their funding of Amazon's operations.

The investment in long-term assets is essentially the change in long-term net assets plus depreciation and amortization. The items for Amazon are in Exhibit 4.12.

Adjustments for the first three items were explored in Chapter 3. The net capex in property plant and equipment (PP&E) is simply the difference between the net PP&E values for fiscal years 2013 and 2012. To obtain gross capex, the depreciation charge of $2.46bn must be added to the $3.889bn change in net PP&E for a total of $6.349bn. Other long-term assets had to be adjusted for equity investments and intangible assets (see Chapter 3 for details). We also must account for cash spent on acquisitions.

---

[8]Interest-bearing current debt is the portion of long-term debt that is currently due.

EXHIBIT 4.12 Change in long-term assets calculation for Amazon in 2013.

Amazon.com ($m) Change in Long-Term Assets ($m)	2013	Balance Sheet items		
		2012	2013	Change
Net PP&E	3,889	7,060	10,949	3,889
Depreciation	2,460			
Other long-term assets	376	782	1,158	376
Goodwill	103	2,552	2,655	103
Non-goodwill intangibles	(80)	725	645	(80)
Amortization of intangibles	168			
Change in long-term assets	**6,916**			

Amazon reported its acquisition goodwill and acquired intangible assets in note 4 of the 2013 annual report (see pages 51–52 for the specific items of interest). The net change in goodwill and intangible assets was $23m, that is, $103m + (−$80m). The gross expenditure on goodwill and intangible assets is the net change plus amortization, which equaled $191m in 2013. Amazon spent a grand total of $6.916bn on long-term assets in 2013.

Because HOLT capitalizes the research and development expense, for the purposes of calculating cash flow we need to treat any money spent on research as an investment. Amazon reported an expense of $6.565bn under "Technology and content" on its 2013 income statement. In Chapter 3, we showed that a portion of this reported R&D expense was already included in Amazon's depreciation. Amazon's net R&D expense summed to $5.602bn.

We also showed how to capitalize operating leases in Chapter 3 and estimated a total of $3.899bn for Amazon at the end of 2013. For the purposes of calculating cash flow, we need to determine the total investment (gross change) in capitalized operating leases. Since we are mimicking the effect of having bought the assets, similar to measuring the change in net fixed assets, we need to determine the related depreciation charge in order to arrive at an estimated gross investment for operating leases. In this case, depreciation will exactly equal the replacement charge, since we are imputing these values.

Investment in capitalized operating leases

$$= \Delta Capitalized\ operating\ leases + Retirement$$

Calculation of retirement requires an estimate of the past growth rate of the firm's depreciating assets and the economic life of the leased assets. We showed how the delayering of assets works in Chapter 3, and once again employ the growing annuity equation.

$$Retirement = \frac{Capitalized\ operating\ leases \times g_{Historical}}{(1 + g_{Historical})((1 + g_{Historical})^N - 1)}$$

The historical real asset growth of depreciating assets for Amazon was 27.6% according to HOLT, and the economic asset life is 5.7 years, which we round up to 6 years.[9] The retirement of capitalized operating leases that needs to be replaced is $254m.

$$Retirement(2013) = \frac{\$3.899bn \times 0.276}{(1 + 0.276)((1 + 0.276)^6 - 1)} = \$254m$$

Amazon spent $561m in 2012 on operating leases, which amounts to an equivalent $2.760bn in capitalized operating lease assets. The change in capitalized operating lease assets is thus $1.139bn, and the total equivalent investment in capitalized operating leases in 2013 is $1.393bn.

Investment in capitalized operating leases

$$= (3.899 - 2.760) + 0.254 = \$1.393bn$$

On the funding side, this amount results in an increase in debt-equivalents since we assume that the operating leases are funded entirely by debt.

The total investment in operating assets can now be tallied (Exhibit 4.13).

We have all the inputs to calculate Amazon's free cash flow in 2013:

$$FCFF = Nominal\ GCF - Total\ Investment$$

$$= \$9.533bn - \$13.864bn = -\$4.331bn$$

Amazon invested over $13bn to grow its business, which resulted in a net cash flow of minus $4.331 billion. Amazon is not afraid of investing

---

[9]Because gross investment is in current dollars and inflation-adjusted, real rates need to be employed for delayering calculations.

EXHIBIT 4.13 Total investment tally for Amazon in 2013.

Amazon.com ($m)	
Total Investment ($m)	**2013**
Change in working capital	(47)
Change in long-term assets	6,916
R&D investment	5,602
Change in capitalized operating leases	1,393
Total investment	**13,864**

EXHIBIT 4.14 Amazon has a long history of investing more cash than it generates from its operations.

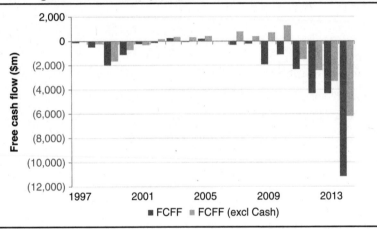

more cash than it generates from its operations, which it achieves by issuing equity or debt or selling non-operating assets (Exhibit 4.14). Shareholders don't seem to mind judging from Amazon's share price performance over the years.

Debt and Equivalents

After calculating the firm's enterprise value, we need to determine the total liabilities of the firm and subtract it from the enterprise value to compute the equity value and stock price. The fundamental accounting rule states:

$$Assets = Liabilities + Equity$$

And, therefore:

$$Equity = Assets - Liabilities$$

It is tempting to use Amazon's book debt as our estimate of total liabilities, but remember, we capitalized operating leases since we determined these were long-term investments and not short-term expenses. Since leases are a financing option, we assume that operating leases are funded with 100% debt. We now need an estimate of the value of the debt related to capitalized operating leases. Recall the features of the operating lease, which in 2013 were:

- Asset life = 6
- Lease expense = $759m
- Nominal cost of debt = 4.63%
- 7-year average growth rate = 28%
- Capitalized operating lease = $3,899m

Given these values, we can de-layer the lease capital expenditure through time and estimate accumulated depreciation. Our estimate of capitalized operating lease debt is the net of gross operating leases and estimated accumulated depreciation.[10]

From Exhibit 4.15, Amazon's capitalized operating lease debt is $2,401m, which is equal to the capitalized operating lease asset of $3,899m less the accumulated depreciation of $1,498m. This technique assumes that the life and wear of the leased assets are like that of gross plant.

The final component of Amazon's long-term debt is found on the balance sheet. Other long-term liabilities amount to $1,681m and can be found on page 54 of the 2013 Annual 10-K. This amount includes $385m in construction liabilities, $457m in tax contingencies, and $839m in other.

---

[10] See HOLT NOTES: Capitalized Operating Leases for a succinct description.

EXHIBIT 4.15 Calculation of Amazon's 2013 net value of capitalized operating leases and its corresponding debt-equivalent. All values are in $m.

Lease Calculator

Lease expense	759
Lease life	6.0
Cost of debt	4.6%
Historical growth rate	28.0%
Capitalized operating lease	3,899
− Accumulated depreciation	(1,498)
= Capitalized op. lease debt	2,401

Year	Lease Pmt	Cap. Lease Value	Capex Equiv.	Accum. Deprec.
1	759	3,899	1,105	164
2	593	3,045	863	256
3	463	2,378	674	300
4	362	1,857	526	312
5	282	1,451	411	305
6	221	1,133	321	160
Total	2,679	13,763	3,899	1,498

Tally up total long-term debt results by adding interest-bearing debt, capitalized operating lease debt, and other long-term debt:

$$Total\ debt = \$6,917 + \$2,401 + \$1,681 = \$10,999\text{m}$$

We are ready to estimate Amazon's share price for different forecast scenarios.

Valuing Different Forecast Scenarios for Amazon in the HOLT Framework

What if we wish to approximate free cash flow by simply changing CFROI and asset growth? This is useful for projecting cash flows without the need for detailed future income statements and balance sheets, and particularly beneficial for valuing the terminal period. The key is to work in inflation-adjusted current dollars throughout the forecast.

$$FCFF = GCF - \Delta IAGI - Retirement$$

EXHIBIT 4.16 Illustration of how CFROI and asset growth drive the estimation of future free cash flows for Amazon.com.

Year	CFROI	Growth	IAGI	IADA	NDA	Retirement	GCF	Investment	FCFF
2013			38,581	34,042	4,539	3,093			
2014	12.0%	40.0%	54,013	47,659	6,355	3,946	13,272	19,378	(6,107)
2015	11.5%	31.3%	70,893	62,552	8,340	5,034	17,158	21,913	(4,755)
2016	11.0%	22.5%	86,843	76,626	10,217	6,421	20,701	22,372	(1,672)
2017	10.5%	13.8%	98,784	87,162	11,622	8,191	23,187	20,132	3,054
2018	10.0%	5.0%	103,724	91,521	12,203	10,450	23,969	15,389	8,580

Gross cash flow can be determined from CFROI, that is, GCF = PMT (CFROI, n, $-pv$, fv, 0), and this amount is adjusted for inflation. Total investment is approximated by taking the change in gross investment, also adjusted for inflation, and adding the cost of replacing worn-out assets.

Beginning from the 2013 results, let's estimate the forward FCFF assuming a CFROI of 12% in FY2014 fading to 10% in FY2018 (Exhibit 4.16). Asset growth is forecast to decline from 40% to 5% over this period.

Total investment is the sum of the change in IAGI and Retirement.[11] The estimated FCFF for FY2014 is −$6.107bn, which swings to $8.58bn in FY2018.

$$FCFF(2014) = GCF - \Delta IAGI - Retirement$$

$$= 13.3 - (54.0 - 38.6) - 3.9 = -\$6.1bn$$

As asset growth cools, the free cash flow switches from negative to strongly positive. The key for Amazon is to cut capex once marginal investments only earn their cost of capital, and to maintain profitability on its core assets. This is easier said than done. Firms like Amazon that manage this transition successfully evolve from Stars (high profitability and fast growth) to Cash Cows (high profitability and slow growth). Over-investment, poor management or disruption leads to Stars crashing to Dogs (low profitability and slow growth), and low valuation multiples.

---

[11] The PMT function in Excel can be employed for this calculation. Retirement = PMT (rate = historical real asset growth rate; nper = economic life; pv = 0; fv = capitalized operating leases) ÷ (1 + $g_{Historical}$).

Investors must be confident that a company can handle the transition from Star to Cash Cow, since it has a major influence on the value of the firm. When the focus changes from growth to tightly managing operations, management will need a new set of skills (and, quite possibly, the firm will need a new set of managers).

Amazon's assets grew by 50% in FY2014 net of inflation, while its CFROI dropped to 7.6%. Much of that growth was due to increasing the cash the company held from $12.4bn to $17.4bn, which diluted the CFROI.[12] Let's run the forecast for asset growth and CFROI beginning from FY2014. The assumptions about fade start in the terminal period: CFROI fades to 6% at a geometric rate of 10% while asset growth fades to 2.5%, also at a decay rate of 10%. The real discount rate was set to its FY2012 and FY2013 average level of 4.0% (Exhibit 4.17).[13]

This forecast and subsequent fade in CFROI and growth suggest that a price of $228 a share is justified. The actual price on April 30, 2014 was $304. The market was expecting Amazon to remain profitable *and* grow! Take note how the impressive CFROI results tell us a different tale from the depressing ROE history. The market wants Amazon to grow and invest, and doesn't view ROE as a plausible measure of Amazon's economic performance.

What if investments sour and CFROI fades from the FY2014 value of 7.6% to 6% while the other inputs remain the same (Exhibit 4.18)?

The sharp drop in profitability has a powerful impact on Amazon's intrinsic value suggesting that the shares are worth $155 rather than $304. Note that we haven't altered our forecast for growth, only CFROI, so it is imperative that Amazon maintain its profitability as it transitions to lower growth to sustain the current share price.

---

[12] Amazon increased its long-term debt from $5.2bn to $12.5bn in 2014. This resulted in a significant increase in Amazon's cash balance, which diluted the CFROI in 2014. This is an instance where excess cash should be removed from the operating asset base.

[13] We showed how to calculate retirement earlier in this chapter. An historical asset growth of 28% was assumed along with an asset life of 6 years. Note that only depreciating assets are retired, thus the calculation is based on IADA not IAGI.

EXHIBIT 4.17 This forecast assumes Amazon's CFROI fades from 12% to 10% while growth fades from 40% to 5%. The warranted share price of $228 is 25% below the April 30, 2014 share price of $304.

Sensitivity

Internet & Direct Marketing Retail
Market Cap: 139.9 USD

Price: 304.13 (Apr 30, 2014)
Warranted Price: 228.09 USD (−25%)

CFROI & Asset Growth Inputs

	2011	2012	2013	t + 1	t + 5
Economic Return (CFROI %)	13.2	12.0	12.0	12.0	10.0
Real Asset Growth %	32.2	44.4	40.9	40.0	5.0
Discount Rate	4.94	4.59	3.47	4.00	

Warranted Valuation

	Amount (MM)	Per Share
Total Economic Value	115,268	250.6
-Market Value of Debt & Equivalents	10,347	22.49
-Market Value of Minority Interest	0	0.00
Warranted Equity Value	104,922	**228.09**
Shares Outstanding	460	

downside
−25%

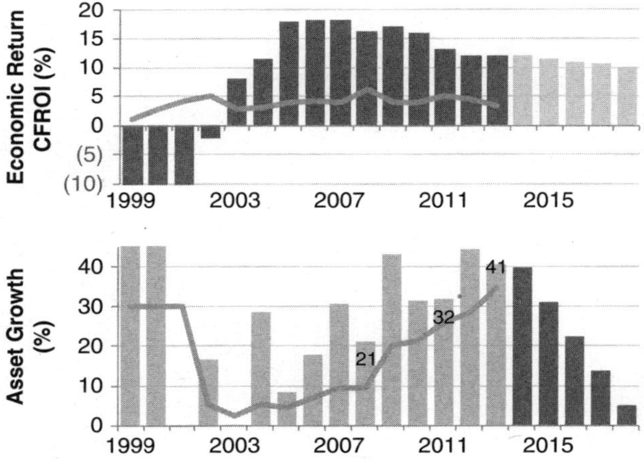

Economic Return CFROI (%)

Asset Growth (%)

EXHIBIT 4.18 This forecast assumes Amazon's CFROI fades from 7.6% to 6% while growth fades from 40% to 5%. The warranted share price drops to $155 for this pessimistic scenario.

Sensitivity

Internet & Direct Marketing Retail
Market Cap: 139.9 USD

Price: 304.13 (Apr 30, 2014)
Warranted Price: 155.08 USD (−49%)

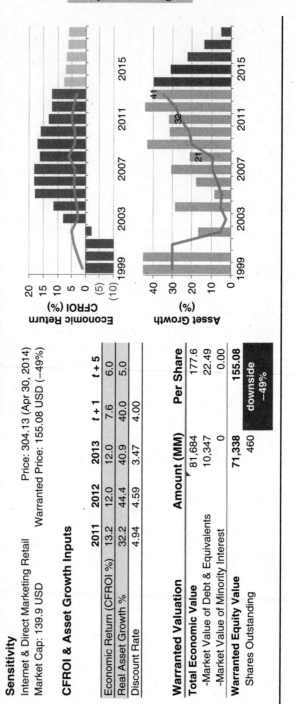

CFROI & Asset Growth Inputs

	2011	2012	2013	t + 1	t + 5
Economic Return (CFROI %)	13.2	12.0	12.0	7.6	6.0
Real Asset Growth %	32.2	44.4	40.9	40.0	5.0
Discount Rate	4.94	4.59	3.47	4.00	

Warranted Valuation

	Amount (MM)	Per Share
Total Economic Value	81,684	177.6
-Market Value of Debt & Equivalents	10,347	22.49
-Market Value of Minority Interest	0	0.00
Warranted Equity Value	**71,338**	**155.08**
Shares Outstanding	460	downside −49%

EXHIBIT 4.19 This forecast assumes Amazon's CFROI fades from 12% to 10% while growth fades from 20% to 5%. The warranted share price of $169 is 45% lower than the April 30, 2014, share price of $304.

Sensitivity

Internet & Direct Marketing Retail
Market Cap: 139.9 USD

Price: 304.13 (Apr 30, 2014)
Warranted Price: 168.67 USD (−45%)

CFROI & Asset Growth Inputs

	2011	2012	2013	t + 1	t + 5
Economic Return (CFROI %)	13.2	12.0	12.0	12.0	10.0
Real Asset Growth %	32.2	44.4	40.9	20.0	5.0
Discount Rate	4.94	4.59	3.47	4.00	

Warranted Valuation	Amount (MM)	Per Share
Total Economic Value	87,936	191.2
-Market Value of Debt & Equivalents	10,347	22.49
-Market Value of Minority Interest	0	0.00
Warranted Equity Value	77,589	168.67
Shares Outstanding	460	downside −45%

EXHIBIT 4.20 This forecast assumes Amazon's CFROI fades from 10% to 6% while growth fades from 20% to 5%. The warranted share price drops to $122 for this pessimistic scenario.

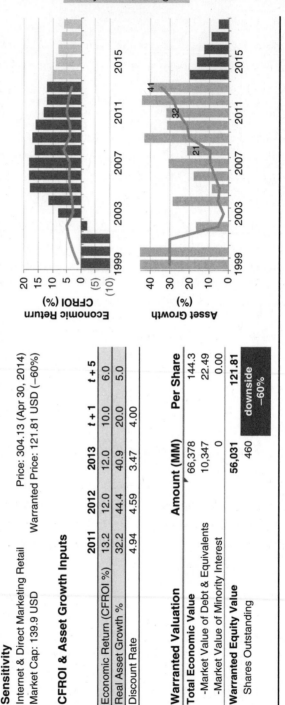

Sensitivity

Internet & Direct Marketing Retail   Price: 304.13 (Apr 30, 2014)
Market Cap: 139.9 USD   Warranted Price: 121.81 USD (−60%)

CFROI & Asset Growth Inputs

	2011	2012	2013	t + 1	t + 5
Economic Return (CFROI %)	13.2	12.0	12.0	10.0	6.0
Real Asset Growth %	32.2	44.4	40.9	20.0	5.0
Discount Rate	4.94	4.59	3.47	4.00	

Warranted Valuation	Amount (MM)	Per Share
Total Economic Value	66,378	144.3
–Market Value of Debt & Equivalents	10,347	22.49
–Market Value of Minority Interest	0	0.00
Warranted Equity Value	**56,031**	**121.81**
Shares Outstanding	460	

downside
−60%

Amazon grew its assets by 41% in 2013 and by 50% in 2014. That growth hasn't been matched by sales, which grew only 21.8% and 19.6%, respectively. Asset turns have dropped sharply since 2011. What if Amazon can grow at only 20% (similar to sales) fading to 5% (in real terms) over the next four years? For our next scenario, let's also assume that CFROI recovers to 12% and fades to 10% (Exhibit 4.19).

Chopping the growth leads to a significant drop in value. All things being equal, a cut in initial growth from 40% to 20% results in the warranted share price dropping from $228 to $169! Investors are clearly optimistic about Amazon's prospects since historically, less than 20% of companies sustain this level of growth for five years. What if the pessimistic growth scenario occurs and is accompanied by CFROI falling to 6% over five years (Exhibit 4.20)? The warranted share price will drop to $122 if the market views this scenario as likely.

Successful investment in research and development is crucial to building value for Amazon. An investor should study this in detail before betting on Amazon.

Valuing Air Liquide in HOLT Lens

Let's close the chapter by returning to France and Air Liquide. If we load the previous forecast into Lens and then allow the HOLT default fade settings to begin after the explicit period, the warranted value for Air Liquide equals €80 versus its price of €116 on June 2, 2015 (Exhibit 4.21). Air Liquide's historical CFROI has bobbed around the global average of 6%. Our forecast indicates that CFROI should remain at 6%.

The individual components of the valuation can be seen in Exhibit 4.22. The warranted enterprise value equals €39bn, which is close to our NOPAT perpetuity valuation of €38bn. To calculate the equity value, debt and debt-equivalents and minority interests must be subtracted from the enterprise value. The valuation is as of the end of the financial year, December 31, 2014. This value can be adjusted for the passage of time.

EXHIBIT 4.21 The explicit forecast for Air Liquide was loaded into the HOLT model to calculate its future CFROI, asset growth, and warranted value. A real of discount rate of 4.8% was assumed to be consistent with the earlier analysis. The warranted share price is €80 versus the June 2, 2015 share price of €116.

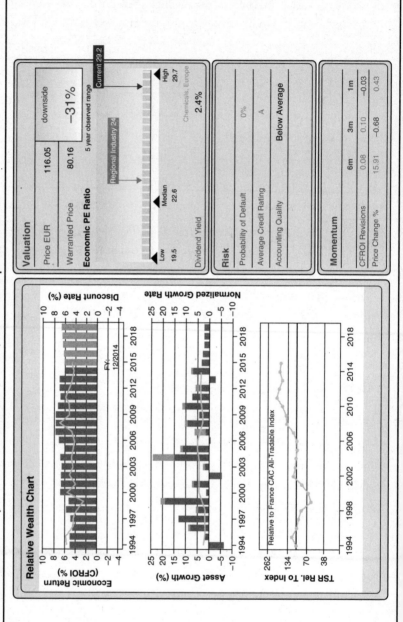

EXHIBIT 4.22 Valuation of Air Liquide based on a five-year forecast run through the HOLT model. The real discount rate was set to 4.8%.

Valuation Results	2015	02-Jun-15
PV of Existing Assets	38,265	
NPV of Future Investments	626	
+ Market Value of Investments	100	
Total Economic Value	**38,991**	
+ Share issuance	0	
- Debt & Equivalents	11,230	
- Minority Interests	676	
Warranted Market Cap.	**27,085**	
Shares Outstanding	345	
Warranted Share Price (EUR)	**78.51**	**80.15**
Closing Price	117.45	
% Upside	−33.2%	−31.8%

EXHIBIT 4.23 Valuation of Air Liquide based on a five-year forecast run through the HOLT model. The discount rate was set to the June 2015 market-implied discount rate of 3.3%.

Valuation Results	2015	03-Jun-15
PV of Existing Assets	46,099	
NPV of Future Investments	4,697	
+ Market Value of Investments	100	
Total Economic Value	**50,896**	
+ Share issuance	0	
− Debt & Equivalents	11,230	
− Minority Interests	966	
Warranted Market Cap.	**38,700**	
Shares Outstanding	345	
Warranted Share Price (EUR)	**112.17**	**113.33**
Closing Price	116.05	
% Upside	−3.3%	−2.3%

Why is the intrinsic share price so much less than the actual price? Despite the apparent plausibility of our forecast, it could be that it is too pessimistic and that future CFROI will exceed past levels. Another explanation is that risk appetite for equities is greater than our discount rate assumes. As we wrote this chapter, discount rates in the United States, Europe, and many other regions hadn't been this low since the dot.com bubble, which makes this line of reasoning less likely. Although a real discount rate of 4.8% is in line with Air Liquide's average discount rate over the past three years, the discount rate implied by the market today is 3.3%. At this low cost of capital, the warranted share price and actual price are nearly equivalent (Exhibit 4.23).

Market neutral investors should use discount rates set by the market when estimating share prices. Air Liquide's economic PE is currently at an all-time high of 29 relative to its 15-year median of 23 (Exhibit 4.24).

EXHIBIT 4.24 The historical default valuation for Air Liquide versus its actual price is shown in the top panel. The economic PE and VCR time series are in the second and third panel, respectively.

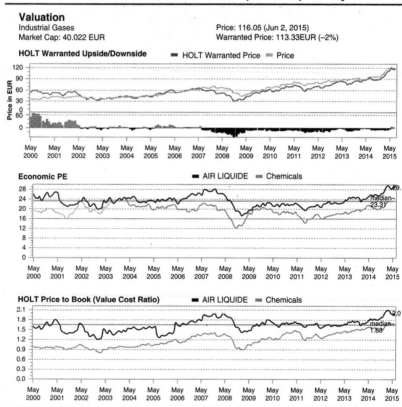

Interestingly, this equates to an economic yield of 3.4%, which is close to the equilibrating discount rate of 3.3% implied by the market.[14] Its value-to-cost ratio (VCR) is 2.0 versus an all-time high of 2.1 in March 2015 and a 15-year median of 1.6. Drawing from these important pieces of information, it doesn't appear that it is a case of Air Liquide looking relatively expensive but rather the market's appetite for risk is currently relatively greedy.

---

[14]Economic PE is defined as VCR/CFROI. Economic yield is simply the inverse of economic PE, CFROI/VCR. VCR equals market enterprise value divided by inflation-adjusted net assets.

5

QUANTIFYING THE VALUE AND RISK OF A COMPANY'S CAP

"In order to attain the impossible, one must attempt the absurd."

—Cervantes

KEY LEARNING POINTS

- A company's ability to create economic value for its stakeholders is intimately linked to building a sustainable competitive advantage for its products and services. When determining whether a company with superior profitability is a good investment, it is beneficial to know the length of the competitive advantage period (CAP) priced into the stock.

- A company's competitive advantage has two dimensions: the *magnitude* of the competitive advantage, which is represented by the spread between the return on capital and cost of capital;

and the *sustainability* of the competitive advantage or how long it is expected to last in years. The value driver corresponding to sustainability is the rate at which a company's profitability is expected to fade. A remarkably elegant insight is that its inverse is the competitive advantage period (CAP).

- We show that a fade rate can be incorporated into a Fundamental Pricing Model for performing back-of-the-envelope valuations and estimating terminal value in DCF analyses. The sensitivity of a company's valuation to changes in the competitive advantage period can be readily quantified by valuing the company at different fade rates.

- The material risk in owning a high quality firm isn't represented by how it co-varies with the market, that is, the stock's beta, but rather by any real or perceived changes to its competitive advantage. The recent cliff drop in the U.S. department store index is yet another example of this sustainability risk. We demonstrate how this risk can be quantified.

INTRODUCTION

A company's ability to create lasting economic value for its stakeholders is intimately linked to building a sustainable competitive advantage for its products and services.[1] A competitive advantage is exactly what it says on the tin: an advantage held by a firm that confers competitive benefit. A modern paragon is Apple with its iconic iPhone, which garnered legions of fans and spawned a cottage industry of related mobile apps and games. Apple holds a handful of competitive advantages, but two important ones are brand loyalty, which still might not have reached its zenith, and switching costs, which are non-trivial. Over the past decade, Apple's competitive advantage has been enormous and exceedingly valuable as reflected by the premium at which Apple's shares trade. As of August 2017, Apple is the

---

[1] According to Professor Jay Barney: "A firm is said to have a *sustained competitive advantage* when it is implementing a value creating strategy not simultaneously being implemented by any current or potential competitors *and* when these other firms are unable to duplicate the benefits of this strategy."

largest firm in the world and another 25% increase in its stock price will make it the first company in the world to attain a trillion dollar market cap.

A competitive advantage acts as a barrier that insulates the firm's profitability from the attacks of competitors. As Warren Buffett famously said, "In business, I look for economic castles protected by unbreachable moats." In Buffett's metaphor, the wider the moat, the greater the competitive advantage of the business. Excess profits on new products that are easy to reproduce and market do not last long since competitors will mimic them and drive profitability down to the industry average.

Investors pay handsomely for companies sporting attractive returns on capital and competitive advantages, which can come in the form of superior products, customer loyalty, brand value, first-rate business processes, patents, exceptional management, innovative R&D, network effects, switching costs, and proprietary know-how. This topic remains a major area of research in strategic management and organizational economics.

When assessing whether a company with superior profitability is also an attractive investment, it is beneficial to gauge the length of the competitive advantage period (CAP) priced into the stock.[2] The price-to-book multiple P/B is highly sensitive to changes in CAP for companies whose profitability exceeds the cost of capital. Unfortunately, most valuation models are ill-equipped to deal with competitive advantage and its decay as a value driver.

Two quantitative aspects of competitive advantage need to be defined:[3]

- The *magnitude* of competitive advantage, indicated by the percentage points of excess profitability or the spread between a company's return on capital and its cost of capital

---

[2]Warren Buffett wrote, "The key to investing is not assessing how much an industry is going to affect society, or how much it will grow, but rather determining the competitive advantage of any given company and, above all, the durability of that advantage." We will show how it can be quantified and how changes in CAP impact intrinsic value.

[3]M. J. Mauboussin and D. Callahan. "Measuring the Moat: Assessing the Magnitude and Sustainability of Value Creation." Credit Suisse Global Financial Strategies, July 22, 2013.

- The *sustainability* of competitive advantage, which is the number of years the competitive advantage and excess profitability can be maintained

We will show that a firm's intrinsic value can be linked to its CAP by introducing a profitability fade driver. The fade driver, which acts as a profitability attenuator, elegantly connects the magnitude of a firm's profitability to its anticipated sustainability. Our technique is particularly worthwhile for gauging the value of highly profitable companies that have stable growth. A major advantage of this approach is that you can quickly test the sensitivity of a firm's stock price to changes in its perceived CAP.

THE WORST INVESTMENT I EVER MADE

"Blockbuster turned out to be the worst investment I ever made. To this day I don't know what would have happened if we'd avoided the big blowup over Antioco's bonus and he'd continued growing Total Access. Things might have turned out differently."

—Carl Icahn[4]

The global movie and entertainment industry is worth about US$100 billion annually, making it an attractive hunting ground for companies that can build sustainable competitive advantages. Until the 1980s, movies were primarily shown in film theaters. The distribution of movies came under siege with the introduction of video cassettes and players. In 1986, home video sales outstripped revenues from theaters, forever changing the fundamental structure of the industry.

Blockbuster Video sat at the pinnacle of this revolution, dominating the movie rental industry throughout the 1990s and early 2000s with 9,000 retail locations around the world at its peak. Early investors in Blockbuster's stock were abundantly rewarded as its price increased 98× from

---

[4]John Antioco, "How I Did It: Blockbuster's Former CEO on Sparring with an Activist Shareholder," *Harvard Business Review*, April 2011.

1988 through 1993. A strategic merger between Viacom and Blockbuster with the intent to purchase Paramount Pictures all but guaranteed Blockbuster's fortunes as an influential actor in the movie and entertainment industry.

Prior to being acquired by Viacom in 1994 for $8.4 billion and de-listed, Blockbuster had an impressive cash flow return on investment (CFROI) of 14.8%, ranking it in the top 10% of profitability worldwide.[5] Investors were enthusiastic about the company's prospects. How long was Blockbuster's competitive advantage and this CFROI priced to last? We estimate Blockbuster was priced for a competitive advantage period (CAP) of more than 50 years. But before casually accepting this comment, stop and ask yourself: How many firms have continuously earned a return on investment above their cost of capital for 50 years? Few firms spring to mind.[6] The price Viacom paid for Blockbuster suggested they were betting on a long and lucrative life for their investment.

To nourish its prospects, Viacom appointed John Antioco, who had a successful history in retail, as the CEO of Blockbuster in June 1997. During the heat of the dot-com bubble, Viacom decided to part with most of its ownership. After Blockbuster's public offering in November 1999, it peaked at a market cap of $2.7 billion. Blockbuster's CFROI of 9.5% in 1999 was much lower than in the early 1990s but still above its inflation-adjusted cost of capital of 6.5%; that is, its magnitude of competitive advantage had significantly declined, but its sustainability was still expected to persist. Despite this downturn in profitability, we estimate that by the end of 1999, Blockbuster was priced for a 38-year competitive

---

[5] Credit Suisse HOLT. CFROI deciles for global non-financials from 1950-1994 were:

Percentile	10	20	30	40	50	60	70	80	90
CFROI	-4.8	0.6	2.7	4.1	5.3	6.6	8.0	10.0	13.3

[6] In the HOLT database, which contains almost 90,000 unique firms since 1950, only 94 companies have earned a CFROI above their cost of capital for 50 or more years.

advantage period, signaling investors' continued confidence in the firm's business model (Exhibit 5.1).[7]

In 2004, revenue peaked at $6 billion, but the share price had already begun sliding. CFROI slipped further to 8.8%, and the implied CAP plummeted to 5 years. Legendary activist investor Carl Icahn sniffed value and began building a stake in the company. It seemed like a favorable bet for Icahn, but he underestimated the speed at which Blockbuster's business model would be disrupted by Netflix and Redbox. CFROI fell to

EXHIBIT 5.1 Blockbuster's timeline:[8] The figures for 1994 are as of December 31, 1993, and those for 2010 are as of December 31, 2009.

Year	Event	Market Cap (US $mil)	Sales (US $mil)	CFROI (percent)	CAP (years)
1985	David Cook opens the first Blockbuster store in Dallas, Texas.				
1987	Blockbuster is sold for $18.5 million.	78	43	10.1%	
1992	Blockbuster owns the video rental market with over 2,800 stores worldwide.	3,576	1,200	17.6%	58
1994	Viacom buys Blockbuster for $8.4 billion.	7,576	2,227	14.8%	51
1999	Viacom takes Blockbuster public.	2,341	4,464	9.5%	38
2004	Blockbuster peaks in sales. Carl Icahn begins building a stake in the company.	1,752	6,053	8.8%	5
2007	CEO John Antioco leaves Blockbuster.	753	5,517	3.0%	
2010	Blockbuster files for bankruptcy.	130	4,062	4.2%	

---

[7]Investors were still paying for a long and prosperous future even though CFROI peaked at 18% in 1991 and had been evidently fading since the early nineties. There was a track record of overestimating Blockbuster's competitive advantage.

[8]Matt Phillips and Roberto A., "A Brief, Illustrated History of Blockbuster, Which Is Closing the Last of its U.S. Stores," *Quartz*, November 6, 2013. The financial figures were sourced from Credit Suisse HOLT.

3.5% in 2005, spelling the end of Blockbuster's competitive advantage. In fact, 2004 turned out to be the last year for Blockbuster that CFROI exceeded its cost of capital.

A firm that had once dominated investors' A-list had become a flop.

Where Did It Go Wrong?

A famous tale about Blockbuster's downfall is the meeting in 2000 between Reed Hastings, the founder of start-up Netflix, and Antioco at Blockbuster's headquarters in Dallas, Texas.[9] Hastings confidently walked into Blockbuster's boardroom and proposed that Netflix run Blockbuster's online business. After all, he argued, it's what Netflix was good at. His proposal was met with disbelief, and he was ushered out the door. In a cosmic twist of fate, Netflix went on and achieved extraordinary success and is now worth $61 billion.[10]

Why were Viacom, IPO investors, and then Carl Icahn so wrong about the magnitude and sustainability of Blockbuster's competitive advantage?

Disruption typically springs from technological innovation. This was true for Blockbuster, as Netflix capitalized on ever-improving data streaming technology, and Redbox neatly exploited the size and storage advantages of DVD over video, a seemingly small but consequential technological innovation that rendered Blockbuster's physical warehouses unnecessary. Disruption can also arise from deep-seated customer dissatisfaction. And, in this particular case, Blockbuster sowed the seeds of its own demise.

A component of Blockbuster's revenue was charging late fees on videos. These charges were despised by customers and proved to be its Achilles' heel. Netflix offered subscriptions to its customers, obviating the need for late fees, and did away with physical stores and their costly overhead and

---

[9]Greg Satell, "A Look Back at Why Blockbuster Really Failed and Why It Didn't Have To," *Forbes*, September 5, 2014.
[10]Another twist to the tale is that John Antioco bought Netflix's shares after he left in 2007 believing that a return of the old business model at Blockbuster would not be able to compete with the new business model of Netflix. Unfortunately, he sold his Netflix shares far too soon and missed superlative gains.

maintenance.[11] These innovations paved the way for disrupting Blockbuster. But it was the late fees that helped incentivize many customers to switch to Netflix or simply away from Blockbuster.

Although Netflix had become a threat by 2003, there was still time to turn around Blockbuster's fortunes. Antioco proposed that Blockbuster discontinue its late fees and launch Blockbuster Online, both strategically sound ideas. But after a profit-sapping start (CFROI dropped sharply to 3.5% in 2005), Carl Icahn and the board decided this strategy was too risky and Antioco was forced out in 2007. By 2010, Blockbuster crawled into bankruptcy.

Antioco contends that had the Blockbuster online strategy "not been essentially abandoned, Blockbuster Online would have 10 million subscribers today" and would be rivalling Netflix for the leadership position in the Internet downloading business.[11] Whether this would have played out or not, we'll never know. What is clear is this: Despite Icahn's history of successful activism, he failed to respond quickly enough to changes in the video rental industry and lost a ton of money on his worst investment ever.[12]

QUANTIFYING THE MAGNITUDE AND SUSTAINABILITY OF CAP

To have a competitive advantage, a company must sustainably generate a return on capital that exceeds its cost of capital, and the company must create more value than its average competitor.[13]

---

[11] John Antico, "How I Did It: Blockbuster's Former CEO on Sparring with an Activist Shareholder," *Harvard Business Review*, April 2011.

[12] Icahn reveals an uncanny ability to analyze his decisions in a dispassionate manner. "Maybe the board did make a mistake in picking Jim Keyes as Antioco's successor—Keyes knows retailing and did an excellent job with the stores, but he isn't a digital guy. I also think Antioco did a good job in executing on Blockbuster's Total Access program, which allowed customers to rent unlimited movies online and in stores. Over time it might have helped Blockbuster fend off Netflix. But Keyes felt the company couldn't afford to keep losing so much money, so we pulled the plug. To this day I don't know what would have happened if we'd avoided the big blowup over Antioco's bonus and he'd continued growing Total Access. Things might have turned out differently."

[13] Michael Mauboussin and Paul Johnson, "Competitive Advantage Period (CAP): The Neglected Value Driver," *Credit Suisse First Boston*, January 14, 1997.

EXHIBIT 5.2 The relationship between excess profits and CAP. Firms that earn a return above the cost of capital possess a competitive advantage. Colgate-Palmolive's excess profitability (CFROI above the cost of capital, shown in light filler) is large. For how long might this magnitude of profitability persist?

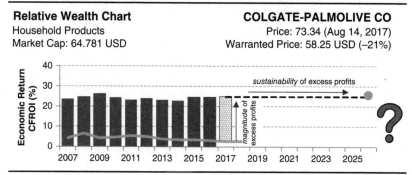

Relative Wealth Chart
Household Products
Market Cap: 64.781 USD

COLGATE-PALMOLIVE CO
Price: 73.34 (Aug 14, 2017)
Warranted Price: 58.25 USD (–21%)

A company is not creating economic value when its return on capital is equal to its cost of capital, and it is destroying value when the return on capital is below its cost of capital. Importantly, a competitive advantage that doesn't endure beyond a single year is hardly a competitive advantage at all. Sustainability is an essential component.

Colgate-Palmolive is a world leader in the production and distribution of household products, with popular brands including its namesake toothpaste, Irish Spring soap, Palmolive dishwashing detergent, Murphy Oil furniture soap, and its Mennen deodorant. The firm is highly profitable, earning CFROI well above its cost of capital. Exhibit 5.2 shows the key elements of a firm with indisputable competitive advantages: profitable and stable return on investment. Colgate's Green Dot highlights the confidence that investors have in the ability of the firm to sustain profits.[14]

Like Colgate, Blockbuster was beating its cost of capital in 2000 and had a substantial CAP embedded in its share price when Reed Hastings of nascent Netflix paid a visit. In hindsight, investors were too optimistic about Blockbuster's ability to protect its profitability and successfully

---

[14]See Chapter 11, Evaluating Market Expectations, for a full discussion of HOLT's Green Dot. The Green Dot in the printed book is the light gray dot with a circle outlining it.

adjust its business model to accommodate changing consumer preferences. Icahn's rejection of Antioco's plan to end late fees and invest heavily in online technology was the nail in the coffin that sealed Blockbuster's fate.

Michael Mauboussin and Paul Johnson wrote about CAP as the neglected value driver in 1997, and we continue to believe that the concept is important and remains the most overlooked component of valuation. The authors cited two main factors. "First, the vast majority of market participants attempt to understand valuation and subsequent stock price changes using an accounting-based formula, which generally defines value as a price/earnings multiple times earnings."[15]

Professor Damodaran of New York University found that 85% of the valuations in 550 equity research reports he perused were based on relative multiples.[16] Less than 10% of the research reports utilized a full discounted cash flow (DCF) valuation. And in a twist of irony, many of the DCF models used a relative multiple to estimate terminal value, thereby reintroducing a weakness that DCF valuations are intended to negate. This error is as alive today as it was in 1997, and we would agree with Professor Damodaran in calling this 2-stage approach just another form of relative valuation.

A fundamental issue with relative valuations is that all the value driver assumptions embedded in the multiple are hidden. Value drivers are explicit inputs in a DCF valuation and open to debate. This hidden aspect of relative valuation is particularly problematic for successful firms with high returns on capital. We can demonstrate this effect by testing the sensitivity of the price-to-book ratio P/B to changes in the number of years a firm maintains a constant return on equity above its cost of equity, that is, the *sustainability* of the competitive advantage. CAP clearly matters, particularly for firms earning high returns, that is, those with a high *magnitude* of competitive advantage!

---

[15] See Mauboussin and Johnson (1997).
[16] Aswath Damodaran, "Valuation Approaches and Metrics: A Survey of the Theory and Evidence," *Foundations and Trends® in Finance* 1(8) (2005): 693–784.

EXHIBIT 5.3 Price/Book versus forward spread for different CAPs (in years). A spread of 0% results in a P/B of 1 no matter what the CAP or growth in book equity is. The impact of CAP on P/B increases significantly as the spread increases, e.g., for a forward spread of 20%, P/B increases 67% from 1.8 to 3.0 if CAP is extended from 5 to 20 years. In this example, the cost of equity is 10%, constant growth in book equity is 5%, and forward spread equals ($ROE_1 - r_e$).

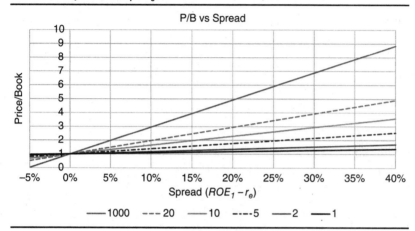

Price-to-book multiples are comprised of implicit assumptions about growth, spread, and CAP. These value drivers require thoughtful consideration and are better modelled as explicit inputs. As we demonstrate in Exhibit 5.3, the greater the magnitude of the economic spread and the greater its sustainability (CAP), the greater the P/B is. The risk of owning a high quality stock trading at a stretched P/B is that the competitive advantage period implied in its price might be overly optimistic. A fall in the expected CAP results in a steep drop in share price.[17]

The second explanation for a lack of focus on CAP given by Mauboussin and Johnson is that "most companies use a forecast period for strategic planning purposes (usually three to five years) that is substantially different

---

[17]Note that when P/B < 1.0, a firm is expected to earn a return on equity below its cost of equity, and destroy shareholder value. The amount of value destroyed decreases as the time to recover decreases. Intuitively, CAP is the expected recovery time when a firm's economic spread is negative. Our focus is on pricing the degree and sustainability of competitive advantage in this paper, but the mathematics work just as well for value destroyers.

from their CAP. As a result, investor communication is geared more toward internal company-based expectations rather than external market-based expectations."

Professors Baruch Lev and Feng Gu provide evidence in their book *The End of Accounting* that accounting figures have lost relevance in explaining value due in large part to the increasing importance of intangible assets.[18] For example, R&D is expensed on an income statement and lowers earnings. If R&D is an investment that helps create a sustainable competitive advantage and increases a firm's long-term value, then shareholders shouldn't mind receiving lower short-term earnings *today* if R&D investments are being made in positive net present value (NPV) projects for *tomorrow*. Lev and Gu argue that it is intangible assets that create sustainable competitive advantage, not physical assets. They build a strong case that corporations should provide investors a Strategic Resources & Consequences Report whose focus is on the creation, preservation, and deployment of a company's strategic assets to create value (Exhibit 5.4).[19] Until reporting improves, we are left with financial statements, short-term forecasts, and key performance indicators (KPIs) that are often not aligned with long-term value creation.

A final explanation for the inadequate focus on CAP as a value driver may be the lack of a simple method for expressing it in a valuation. We will show an intuitive way to understand CAP and to elegantly quantify changes in valuation for different levels of CAP. This application is crucial when valuing successful businesses with attractive returns on capital, and for quantifying the risk to those valuations for changes in CAP.

Why should you care about CAP? The key to successful investing in the stock market is to anticipate revisions in a company's expectations. If you understand the competitive advantage period implied in a company's share price, you can quantify the impact on the stock price and its price

---

[18] Baruch Lev and Feng Gu, *The End of Accounting and the Path Forward for Investors and Managers*, John Wiley & Sons, 2016.

[19] Lev and Gu state that "included in the preservation of strategic assets are efforts to slow down the obsolescence of these assets." We would model this slowing of obsolescence as a reduction in the rate of profitability's fade, which is synonymous with an extension of the firm's competitive advantage period.

EXHIBIT 5.4 Strategic Resources and Consequences Report proposed by Professors Lev and Gu. The information in squares is quantitative ($ denotes monetary value), and in circles is qualitative (narrative). Used with permission by the authors.

THE STRATEGIC RESOURCES & CONSEQUENCES REPORT

DEVELOPING RESOURCES	RESOURCE STOCKS	RESOURCE PRESERVATION	RESOURCE DEPLOYMENT	VALUE CREATED
R&D ($) Internal • Research • Development Acquired technology	**Patents & Trademarks** Quantity • Applied • Approved • Stock Patent attributes (quality)	*(Infringement)* Detection programs	**Patents** • Developed • Sold/licensed • Donated • Expired	**Value Created in Period ($)** Cash flows from operation Plus: • Expensed investments Minus: • Capital expenditure Minus: • Cost of equity capital
Customer Acquisition Costs ($)	**Customers** • Additions • Terminations • Total • Churn	*(Disruption)* Mitigation programs *(Resources)* Decay prevention	**Oil & Gas Rights** • % explored • % producing • % abandoned	

Oil & Gas Exploration ($)
 • Successful
 • Unsuccessful
 Rights acquisition
	Proven Oil & Gas Reserves ($)
	 • Exploration rights
	 • No. of rigs
		Knowledge Management
		 • No. of employees participating
			Alliances & Joint Ventures
			 • Investment in alliances ($)
			 • No. of alliance
			  – R&D
			  – Manufacturing
				Plus:

TV & Movie Content ($) • New • Sequels	**Brands** • Number • Market share • Brand value ($)	**Maintaining Workforce Quality** • In-house and external training ($) • Employee turnover	**Movie / TV Content** • No. streams to customers • Serialization • International	**Resources Value Changes ($)** • Lifetime value of customers • Value of oil & gas reserves • Brand value
Spectrum • Acquisition ($) • Broadband				

163

multiples if investors' expectations about the firm's competitive advantage period change.

THOUGHT EXPERIMENT: THE VALUATION OF CORE UNLIMITED

The conventional view on incorporating competitive advantage into a discounted cash flow valuation dates to Miller and Modigliani's 1961 classic paper, which was casually laid out in a footnote.[20] The authors broke the firm into an existing business and its future investments.

Firm Value = Value of Existing Business

+ Net Present Value of Future Investments

The existing business was valued as a stable perpetuity and the economic prospects of all future investments were placed in the second term. One of MM's brilliant insights was to note that the value of the second term is zero if future incremental returns equal the firm's cost of capital.[21] The net present value (NPV) of all future investments is zero under this condition.

The premium investors should be willing to pay for a company is related to:

- The magnitude of the firm's economic spread (the difference in percentage points between the return on invested capital ROIC and the cost of capital r)

---

[20] M.H. Miller and F. Modigliani. "Dividend Policy, Growth, and the Valuation of Shares," *The Journal of Business* 34(4) (October 1961): 411–433. MM didn't use the phrase "competitive advantage" in their description. They referred to the finite period available for "special investment opportunities." Their equation in our notation is $Value \cong \frac{NOPAT_1}{r} + \frac{(ROIC_1 - r) \times \Delta Invested\ Capital_1 \times CAP}{r(1+r)}$ where the first term is the value of the existing firm and the second term is the value of "special investment opportunities." This equation is only valid for short CAP. Amazingly, the description and derivation feature in a footnote of the paper.

[21] It is worthwhile quoting Miller and Modigliani, " ... a corporation does not become a "growth stock" with a high price-earnings ratio merely because its assets and earnings are growing over time. To enter the glamor category, it is also necessary that p*(t) > p (authors' note $ROIC_t$ > r in our formulation). For if p*(t) = p, then however large the growth in assets may be, the second term will be zero and the firm's price-earnings ratio would not rise above a humdrum 1/p (author's note 1/r in our formulation). **"The essence of 'growth,' in short, is not expansion, but the existence of opportunities to invest significant quantities of funds at higher than 'normal' rates of return."**

- The firm's growth rate
- The number of years T (sustainability) that investments can earn returns in excess of the cost of capital

The competitive advantage period under these conditions is generally defined as T years despite the hidden assumption that the existing business might have a constant ROIC above its cost of capital that is implicitly assumed to last forever.

As the case of Blockbuster illustrates, the operating returns on its core business decreased and became worthless to equity investors after its business model was disrupted by Netflix and Redbox. Today, Amazon is disrupting retail but so too did Sears and then JC Penney once upon a time. No firm's profits are immune from disruption. We are reminded of the Yogi Berra quote, "Even Napoleon had his Watergate."

Although MM's concept of splitting existing assets from future investments is elegant, its mathematical formulation is based on the absurd assumption that the existing assets will maintain a perpetual return on capital. The existing business is not immune to competitive pressures and if it has a high return on capital, it is far more likely that its margins and return on capital will decay over time than remain high and stable forever. When it comes to corporate profitability, reversion to the mean is a fact of life and it should be included as a value driver.[22] We have a neat solution.

Let's take the hypothetical case of Core Unlimited. Core is a mature, highly successful firm that has run out of investment opportunities. All strategies and incremental investments proposed to the CFO are determined to have an NPV of zero or less, so she behaves rationally and rejects them. Core's existing business has zero growth and pays out all the cash it generates to its capital providers. If Core can maintain its impressive return on capital, then its intrinsic value is a simple perpetuity, which also equals

---

[22] M. Mauboussin, D. Callahan, B. Matthews, and D. Holland, "How to Model Reversion to the Mean: Determining How Fast, and to What Mean, Results Revert," *Credit Suisse Global Financial Strategies*, September 2013.

the value of the existing business from MM's formulation.

$$Value = \frac{NOPAT_1}{r}$$

The forward price-to-earnings ratio equals the inverse of the cost of capital.[23] The value can be reformulated as a price-to-book ratio:

$$\frac{Value}{Invested\ Capital_0} = \frac{ROIC_\infty}{r}$$

If the perpetual return on invested capital $ROIC_\infty$ is greater than the cost of capital r, the firm will trade at a premium to book. The CAP of incremental investments might be zero, but the CAP of Core Unlimited's existing business is infinite.

Let's now assume that the spread over the cost of capital decays at a constant rate f towards zero, that is, economic equilibrium. In a previous report, we showed how to incorporate fade in profitability into a DCF valuation.[24] The intrinsic value of Core Unlimited can be written as:

$$Value = \frac{NOPAT_1 \left(1 + \frac{f}{ROIC_1}\right)}{(r+f)}$$

$NOPAT_1$: Forward net operating profit after tax. It will converge toward the capital charge $r\ x\ Invested\ Capital_0$ over time.

$ROIC_1$: Forward return on invested capital. It will decrease toward the cost of capital r over time.

r: Cost of capital which pulls $ROIC$ toward it with a gravitational force of f, that is, 0% represents zero gravity and 100% represents a competitive black hole which instantly eliminates all excess returns.

---

[23]ROIC = NOPAT / Invested Capital. When performing valuations, ROIC should be based on the beginning-of-year invested capital.
[24]D. Holland and B. Matthews, "Don't Suffer from a Terminal Flaw, Add Fade to your DCF: An Improved Method for Valuing Mature Companies and Estimating Terminal Value," *Credit Suisse HOLT*, June 2016.

EXHIBIT 5.5 A forward spread of 15% decays at different rates. A fade rate of 0% signifies no fade and a constant spread that lasts forever. A fade rate of 100% means instantaneous fade like a light being switched off.

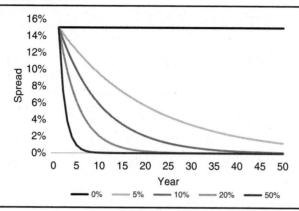

f: The exponential decay rate of $(ROIC_t - r)$ toward zero. It varies from 0%, where the spread remains constant forever and there is no decay in profitability, to 100%, where fade is instantaneous and the competitive advantage period is limited to the forward year (Exhibit 5.5).

We also showed in the same report that the expected competitive advantage period equals $1/f$. Does our formulation pass the sniff test?

- If there is no decay in profitability, f equals 0% and we arrive at MM's famous formulation. The CAP for Core Unlimited would be infinite, that is, $1/f = \infty$ if the return on invested capital exceeds the cost of capital.
- If $ROIC_1 = r$, then we also arrive at MM's simple perpetuity. Under this condition, fade has no meaning since the forward spread is already zero. The greater the spread, the more fade matters. It is an inconsequential value driver when operating returns are at or near the cost of capital.

- If the fade rate is 100%, then the equation simplifies to the opening invested capital plus the present value of one year of economic profit.[25] This is precisely the result we expect for one year of competitive advantage, that is, $1/f = 1$ year!

THE PROBABILITY OF PERMANENT DISRUPTION

The fade rate can also be interpreted as the probability of the economic spread (ROIC – r) irreversibly jumping to zero in any given year. **In other words, fade is also the probability of a successful firm's economic moat being permanently disrupted.** The expected CAP is simply the inverse of the fade rate (or the probability of permanent disruption):

$$Expected\ CAP = \frac{1}{f}$$

You might be surprised to discover that it is mathematically equivalent to think of excess profitability as exponentially decaying or as being abruptly and permanently disrupted. In the latter case, we would describe it as a sudden and irreversible loss of a firm's economic moat—in today's business parlance, we would define it as *permanent economic disruption*. If an explicit period of value creation is forecast followed by fade in the terminal value, then the total expected CAP is the length of the explicit forecast in years (that is, the forecast horizon H) plus $1/f$ (Exhibit 5.6).

$$Total\ E[CAP] = H + \frac{1}{f}$$

---

[25]After a bit of algebraic juggling and substitution of the equation for forward economic profit, $EP_1 = NOPAT_1 - r \times Invested\ Capital_0$, we obtain the expression $Value = Invested\ Capital_0 + \frac{EP_1}{(1+r)}$. If $ROIC_1$ equals r, then EP_1 is zero and there is no competitive advantage. Under this condition, the firm should trade at book, which is economically sensible. No value is being created when the return on capital equals the cost of capital. Note that economic profit can also be written as $EP_1 = (ROIC_1 - r) \times Invested\ Capital_0$ where the first term on the equation's right-hand side is the forward spread. If the spread is zero, EP is zero. If the spread is positive, the firm is creating value. If the spread is negative, which it can be for commodity industries with too much capacity, e.g., steel, airlines, and paper, then the firm is destroying value.

EXHIBIT 5.6 A forward spread of 15% fades toward 0% at a decay rate of 5%, that is, 5% of the spread is whittled away each year. This is equivalent to a constant spread of 15% collapsing to 0% in 20 years, that is, 1/f years.

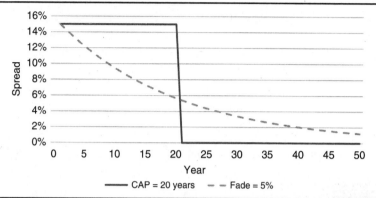

The competitive advantage period (CAP) is the number of years a firm's return on capital is expected to exceed its cost of capital due to the firm's sustainable competitive advantages. For a DCF model utilizing a fade rate, the total competitive advantage period in years is the explicit forecast period plus the inverse of the fade rate.

THE CHARACTERISTICS OF COMPETITIVE ADVANTAGE

From a value driver perspective, decay in profitability can be due to a decrease in asset turns: obtaining less revenue per unit of capital, or a decrease in profit margin, that is, a drop in operating margin (Exhibit 5.7).

Competitive advantage has two general aspects. Firms with economies of scale and superior operating efficiency often have a *production advantage*, which results in higher asset turns. Firms with strong brand names and loyal customers have pricing power and thus higher operating margins than their competitors. They have a *consumer advantage*. The most successful companies have both and generate attractive returns on capital (Exhibit 5.8).[26]

---

[26]For more on this topic, see M.J. Mauboussin and D. Callahan, "Measuring the Moat: Assessing the Magnitude and Sustainability of Value Creation," *Credit Suisse Global Financial Strategies,* July 22, 2013.

EXHIBIT 5.7 There are various profitability metrics which feature similar traits. Three popular measures of profitability are return on equity (ROE), return on invested capital (ROIC), and cash flow return on investment (CFROI). All measures of profitability can be split into two drivers whereby Profitability = Profit Margin x Asset Turns. Net profit margin is net income divided by sales. CFROI can also be expressed as a ratio, which we demonstrate in Chapter 6. The profitability margin for CFROI is net cash flow margin (NCF%) which equals gross cash flow (GCF) minus an economic depreciation divided by sales. Gross investment and gross cash flow are adjusted for inflation in the HOLT CFROI framework, which makes CFROI and its drivers comparable over time and across borders.

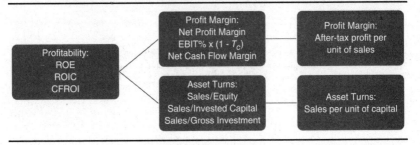

EXHIBIT 5.8 Profitability drivers and types of competitive advantage. Best-in-class firms possess a rare mix of above-average margins and asset efficiency. These firms enjoy both a consumer and production advantage.

When contemplating the competitive advantage period (CAP) for a value-creating company, it is critical to consider which advantages the firm has and how secure they are. It can be difficult to protect high operating margins when barriers to entry are low. Plotting asset turns versus profit

EXHIBIT 5.9 CFROI can be expressed as net cash margin multiplied by asset turns. In this example, we show the margins and turns for companies in the global auto parts industry along with CFROI isocurves of 3%, 6%, and 12%.[27] One of the star performers is Continental AG (CONG).

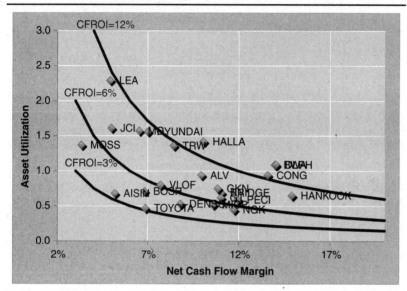

margin for competitors in an industry helps visualize relative strengths. Because these two terms are multiplicative, profitability isocurves can be drawn (Exhibit 5.9).

HOLT research has much to say about reversion to the mean. For instance, fade in corporate profitability is greater for higher growth firms than it is for lower growth businesses. This is true for both profitable and unprofitable companies. Profitable, higher-growth firms tend to reside in nascent industries, and the high profits quickly attract yield-hungry

---

[27] D.A. Holland and B. Matthews, "CFROI as a Ratio and DuPont Identity," *Credit Suisse HOLT*, August 2014. The data are from the CS HOLT database as of August 1, 2014. "Continental (CONG) sported an impressive CFROI of 13.2% in 2013, which was driven by one of the higher NCF margins in the industry, 13.6%. R&D is not an expense for Continental; it is a driver of value. Tire manufacturers Goodyear (GT) and Michelin (MICP) have lower margins and turns than Continental. Laggards on the 3% CFROI isoline include Aisin Seiki and Toyota Industries while stars above the 12% CFROI isoline include Borg Warner (BWA), Halla Visteon Climate Control (HALLA), Delphi Automotive (DLPH), and Continental."

competitors and capital. Unprofitable firms with high growth can generally be split into two groups: early lifecycle firms for whom quickly attaining profitability is essential for survival, and restructuring stage companies that often seek to work their way out of trouble through acquisitions or unhealthy expenditures. A clear consequence of high growth for all business models is amplified volatility.

On the other hand, HOLT research shows that stable profitability is a powerful predictor of future operating returns. In fact, last year's CFROI level is the single best predictor of next year's CFROI level. The decay in profitability will be largely driven by the firm's industry, its growth rate, and its size. Large firms tend to exhibit less fade than smaller ones. Large cap firms (with market capitalization in excess of 10 billion USD) typically lose just 5% of their excess return each year (the difference between CFROI and the long-term cost of capital of 6%), whereas firms below $250m fade at an average of 20% a year. Fade happens.

FADE IS A VALUE DRIVER

Firms can be valued by discounting future free cash flows to the firm (FCFF) or by discounting future economic profits (EP). The valuations will be the same for a given forecast when performed correctly (Exhibit 5.10).

THE FUNDAMENTAL PRICING MODEL

In our Core Unlimited example, we set future growth in assets to zero. We can relax that assumption and write a generalized pricing equation that includes growth in invested capital. Because this equation includes all the key drivers of corporate value used to effectively gauge a firm's intrinsic value, we term it the Fundamental Pricing Model.

The value of a firm with constant growth g and profitability spread declining to zero at a constant fade rate f equals:

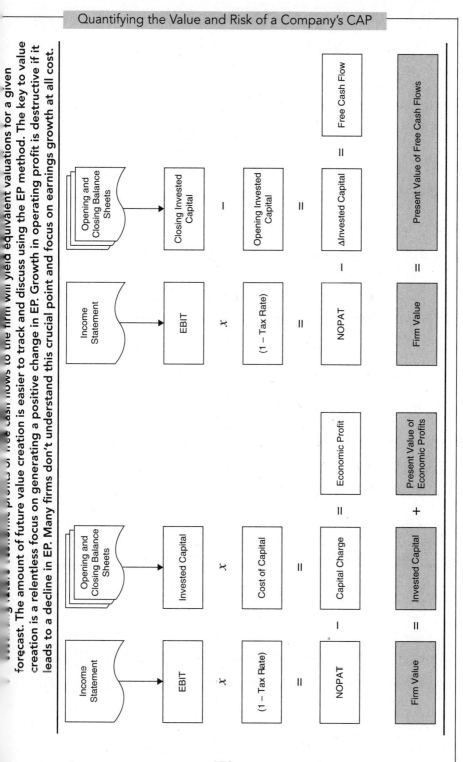

... generating future profits of free cash flows to the firm will yield equivalent valuations for a given forecast. The amount of future value creation is easier to track and discuss using the EP method. The key to value creation is a relentless focus on generating a positive change in EP. Growth in operating profit is destructive if it leads to a decline in EP. Many firms don't understand this crucial point and focus on earnings growth at all cost.

Fundamental Pricing Model (EP Method):

$$Value = Invested\ Capital_0 + \frac{EP_1}{(r - g + f)} \qquad (5.1)$$

Fundamental Pricing Model (FCFF Method):

$$Value = \frac{NOPAT_1 \left[1 - \frac{(g-f)}{ROIC_1}\right]}{(r - g + f)} \qquad (5.2)$$

Depending on your preference, you can use the equation of either method to value stable, mature firms as of today on the back of an envelope, or as a means of estimating the ex-growth terminal value in a DCF model after an explicit forecast period.[28] These are the only equations you need to know to value these types of companies.

The equations reduce to the well-known simple perpetuity if growth and fade are zero. The equations simplify to the widely-used growing perpetuity if only fade is zero. Remember that the expected CAP equals $1/f$. Thus, we can test the sensitivity of a valuation to changes in profitability fade rate and CAP. The impact will become more pronounced the wider the spread in profitability.

THE VALUE DRIVER TREE

The value drivers in the Fundamental Pricing Model can be represented in a value driver tree, which is useful when analyzing a company's levers and its opportunities for increasing its value. The four drivers are ROIC, invested capital growth, profitability fade rate, and the cost of capital (Exhibit 5.11).

ROIC

We described the relationship between ROIC and its main drivers, which are operating margin and asset turns. All things being equal, the greater ROIC, the greater a firm's intrinsic value.

---

[28] Please see the appendix for the mathematical relationships.

EXHIBIT 5.11 Value driver tree showing the key variables in our Fundamental Pricing Model.

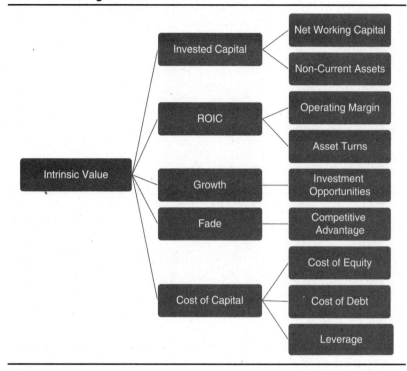

Investment Growth

Although many corporate executives think of all growth as beneficial, its suitability is contingent on the quality of investment opportunities available. Investment in strategies with positive expected NPVs should be pursued. Companies that cite revenue and earnings growth as KPIs are liable to grow at any cost and potentially guilty of destroying value.

Fade

For companies whose ROIC exceeds the cost of capital, the sustainability of the competitive advantage is a crucial consideration. The corresponding value driver is the fade rate, which is the speed at which profitability mean-reverts to the cost of capital, and which also equals the probability of permanent economic disruption. All things being equal, a slower rate of decay in profitability leads to higher future economic profits and a greater intrinsic value.

By rearranging the equation and solving for f, we can calculate the market-implied fade rate. The market-implied CAP is the number of years a company is priced to maintain its return on capital above its cost of capital. The inverse of fade is the market-implied CAP:

Market implied fade rate

$$= \frac{EP_1}{(Market\ Enterprise\ Value - Invested\ Capital_0)} + g - r$$

$$(5.3)$$

The difference between the market enterprise value and invested capital is the market premium, which is the NPV of all present and future projects. This is what investors pay for, not short-term earnings as the media might have you believe.

Let's calculate the market-implied fade rate and CAP for Blockbuster at the end of 1993 before it was acquired by Viacom. On December 31, 1993, the market enterprise value and inflation-adjusted invested capital were $8.96bn and $2.616bn, respectively; the economic profit was $0.261bn; and Blockbuster's real cost of capital was 4.76%. For the sake of illustration and simplicity, we'll assume the company was expected to grow its assets at a constant real growth rate of 2.5%; that is, we're assuming the company was ex-growth.

$$Market\ implied\ fade\ rate = \frac{0.261 \times 1.025}{(8.960 - 2.616)} + 0.025 - 0.0476 = 2.0\%$$

Blockbuster had a market-implied fade rate of 2.0%, which is equivalent to an expected CAP of 50 years. Its CFROI averaged a healthy 17% over the previous 5 years. Viacom paid a rich premium for Blockbuster and was expecting many decades of sustainable value creation. To illustrate the risk associated with a change in sustainable competitive advantage, we calculated the intrinsic enterprise value assuming a typical fade of 10%. The intrinsic value drops from $9bn to $4.8bn under this assumption, which is approximately equal to the enterprise value when Blockbuster reissued shares in 1999. Fades happens, and it happened to Blockbuster well before it went bust.

Cost of Capital

The final value driver in the fundamental pricing model is the cost of capital, which is the expected return or opportunity cost required by capital providers. It is driven by the systematic risk of the company relative to the market, leverage, and the market's appetite for risk per the equity risk premium and risk-free rate. It is the hurdle rate that the return on capital has to clear to create value.

INVESTMENT GROWTH IS A VALUE DRIVER

Revenue or earnings growth is the growth driver in most valuation models. Revenue is not a control variable and input but rather the output resulting from investments. The proper control variable and driver should be investment growth (Exhibit 5.12). This is a subtle and important difference between our Fundamental Pricing Model and other pricing models.

Our growth driver is the growth in invested capital whether the assets are tangible or intangible; for example, R&D and training expenses can be capitalized and shifted to the balance sheet as intangible assets. Because investment growth is our value driver, it is unnecessary for us to split the

EXHIBIT 5.12 Investment growth is the control variable and input while revenue and earnings are outputs.

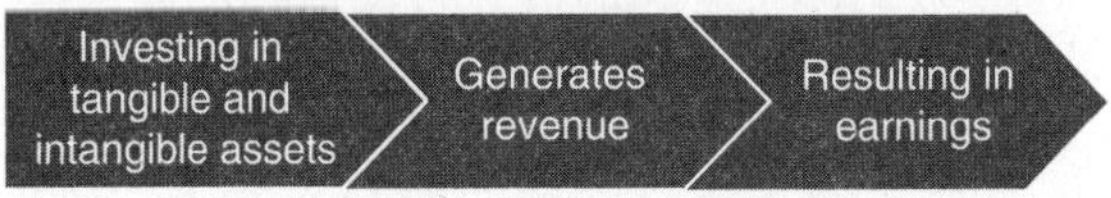

Investing in tangible and intangible assets → Generates revenue → Resulting in earnings

firm into separate existing and growth components.[29] We believe it is reasonable to assume that a mature firm manufacturing widgets can't grow at a rate greater than the risk-free rate in the terminal period. The real growth in widgets and investment won't exceed the real growth of the economy over the long run. However, the marginal profitability would be expected to drop. This reasoning is consistent with our Fundamental Pricing Model and investment growth as a value driver.

There is a great deal of confusion about earnings growth and its sources. The number all too often drives headlines. Earnings growth can result from growth due to investment or growth due to efficiency (Exhibit 5.13). Growth from efficiency gains is unsustainable. When these gains approach their limit, the related earnings growth will fall to zero. Growth from efficiency should be a central element in an explicit forecast. The return on incremental investment growth most likely decays for maturing firms since marginal customers find the products and services less valuable, which is in line with our pricing model.

APPLYING THE FUNDAMENTAL PRICING MODEL

We showed how the Fundamental Pricing Model could be used to estimate Blockbuster's CAP and intrinsic value at an average fade rate. We'll walk through another example to show the utility of our model and the sensitivity of value to changes in CAP.

On May 13, 2017, the *Financial Times* reported that "investors wiped $4.6bn from the market value of the U.S. department store sector in the space of two days, as concern mounted about sliding sales and the effects of

---

[29] In our formulation, investment growth exceeds operating profit growth when ROIC is greater than the cost of capital and fading toward it. In other words, the operating margin is being compressed, which is a realistic expectation. In closed-form equations utilizing a return on incremental invested capital ROIIC, the firm has to be split into an existing component where NOPAT and ROIC are constant into perpetuity, and all future investments occur at a constant perpetual ROIIC. The constant growth in this formulation, e.g., see McKinsey's *Valuation*, assumes NOPAT grows at a constant rate into perpetuity, which means that the growth in invested capital might be substantially more when ROIC > ROIIC. The growth in invested capital could be substantially more than the growth in NOPAT, which hardly seems realistic in a terminal period assumption. Also, if ROIIC > r, then the existing business and all future investments have CAPs of infinity, which strikes us as an absurd assumption.

EXHIBIT 5.13 Earnings growth, whether net income, NOPAT, or net cash flow, results from two sources: investment growth and efficiency growth. The latter results from improvements to operating margin and asset turns and is not sustainable growth. Investment growth in the terminal period should not exceed the risk-free rate. As the return on capital fades, the retention ratio will have to increase to fund sustainable steady-state growth.

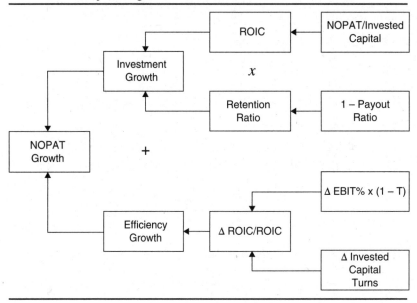

online competition." U.S. department stores suffered an astonishing fall in market value of over 16% in two days.[30] Who is responsible for this vaporization of equity value? Amazon is disrupting the industry. It is now the biggest online retailer in the world, and accounts for 5% of retail spending in the United States. It is presently the world's fifth most valuable company.[31]

One of the department stores affected by this plunge in valuation was Macy's. Let's calculate Macy's market-implied competitive advantage period before and after this industry disruption (Exhibit 5.14).

---

[30] Adam Samson, Mamta Badkar, and Nicole Bullock, "U.S. Retail Sector's Misery—In Charts," *Financial Times*, May 13, 2017.
[31] Reported in *The Economist* on March 25, 2017, in "Primed" on pp 24–26.

EXHIBIT 5.14 The HOLT relative wealth and economic profit charts for Macy's, a U.S. department store. Real asset growth has been less than zero for the past decade. The change in economic profit has been negative for the past two years due to a fall in CFROI. The stock has underperformed the S&P 500 since 2014.

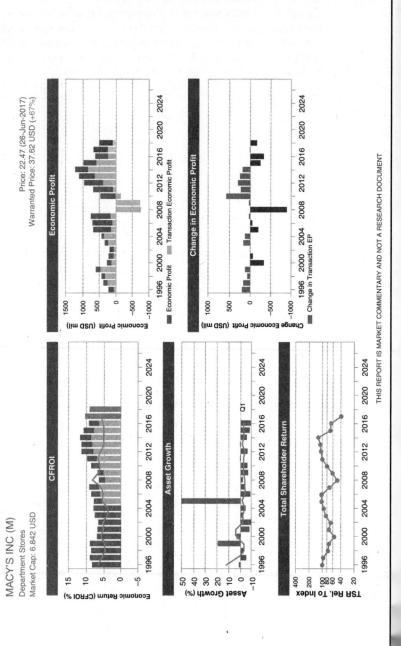

MACY'S INC (M)
Department Stores
Market Cap: 6.842 USD

Price: 22.47 (26-Jun-2017)
Warranted Price: 37.62 USD (+67%)

THIS REPORT IS MARKET COMMENTARY AND NOT A RESEARCH DOCUMENT

EXHIBIT 5.15 Share price sensitivity matrices on two different dates for Macy's. The fundamental pricing model was used to generate warranted (intrinsic) share prices for different combinations of the fade rate and the real asset growth rate. On June 26, 2017, Macy's stock price was $22.47, and on July 1, 2015, it was $63.48.

Macy's Intrinsic Stock Price versus Actual Stock Price of $22.47 (June 26, 2017): Warranted Share Price Sensitivity Analysis

		Fade Rate			
		0%	**5%**	**10%**	**20%**
	−1%	46.77	30.72	24.74	19.70
Growth rate	0%	54.31	32.84	25.76	20.11
	1%	65.69	35.45	26.92	20.55

Macy's Intrinsic Stock Price versus Actual Stock Price of $63.48 (July 1, 2015): Warranted Share Price Sensitivity Analysis

		Fade Rate			
		0%	**5%**	**10%**	**20%**
	−1%	76.64	47.39	36,67	27.71
Growth rate	0%	90.60	51.22	38.48	28.43
	1%	111.95	55.93	40.56	29.21

Macy's real asset growth has been flat or negative for the past decade, so we can consider it ex-growth. CFROI and economic profit have been trending south for the past two years. Let's use the Fundamental Pricing Model to calculate the intrinsic stock price for Macy's as of June 2017 and 2015 for different combinations of growth and CAP (Exhibit 5.15).[32] The inputs are shown in the Appendix.

Macy's economic profit has halved over the past two years from $1.254bn in January 2015 to $0.639bn in January 2017 while its share price has dropped 64%. Assuming a perpetual real growth of zero, Macy's market-implied fade rate increased from 2.6% to 14.5%; that is, the market-implied CAP dropped from 38 years to 7 years. Investors were highly optimistic about the sustainability of Macy's competitive advantage

---

[32] In the HOLT framework, the fundamental pricing model using HOLT EP is:

$$Enterprise\ Value = Economic\ Net\ Assets_0 + \frac{HOLT\ EP_1}{(DR-g+f)}.$$

The economic net assets equal the inflation-adjusted gross investment minus the accumulated economic depreciation. The HOLT discount rate DR and economic profit EP were taken from HOLT Lens. We flexed the real growth rate g and fade rate f. The inputs are shown in the Appendix.

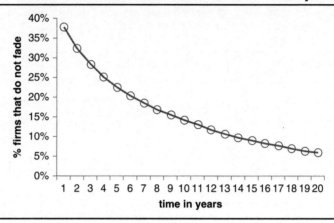

EXHIBIT 5.16 Percentage of firms with starting CFROI of 6% or higher that maintain or improve CFROI over time. Note that less than 5% of firms can sustain a level CFROI for more than 20 years.

Source: Credit Suisse HOLT. Global industrial/service firms, market capitalization +USD250m, 1950–2016.

and profitability two years ago. They are pessimistic about its sustainability today.

The matrices indicate how you can use the Fundamental Pricing Model to generate a highly insightful analysis of a stock's price sensitivity to changes in its fade and investment growth rates. Observe how sharply the intrinsic value falls as the fade rate increases. Also note how insensitive valuation is to growth when profitability fades quickly. On July 1, 2015, you had to believe that Macy's CFROI of 12% would not fade to consider it a value stock; that is, its share price of $63 implied a fade rate of between 0% and 5%, which suggests an almost impenetrable economic moat. Exhibit 5.16 shows that an assumption of zero fade is unrealistic. The chart even allows for intervening years of profit decline followed by CFROI improvement. But even under this relaxed assumption, few firms can maintain profitable CFROI.

As we like to say, "Fade happens!" By June 2017, investors realized that Macy's was not impervious to competitive threats and reassessed its long-term profit potential. Macy's share price of $23 now implied a much quicker fade rate of 10% to 20% in profitability.

If you had used the usual growing perpetuity assumption to value the terminal period for Blockbuster or Macy's, you might have overestimated the intrinsic value due to implicitly assuming the competitive advantage and CFROI would continue *ad infinitum*. Exhibit 5.15 shows an estimated price for Macy's of $90.60 from June 2015 assuming 0% growth and 0% fade, indicating more than 40% upside. How many investors were led astray by applying the classic growing perpetuity assumption to Macy's valuation and purchased the stock assuming it was trading at a discount?

This is a never-ending issue when using a growing perpetuity model to value successful companies beating their cost of capital. Our Fundamental Pricing Model with its fade value driver offers an elegant solution to this dilemma. **The material risk in owing a high quality firm isn't represented by how it co-varies with the market, that is, the stock's beta, but rather by changes in its competitive advantage.** The recent cliff drop in the U.S. department store index is yet another example of the risk associated with the *sustainability* of profits.

FINAL THOUGHTS FOR THE MOMENT

Although there is plenty of academic and HOLT research to suggest that corporate profitability reverts to the mean, it is impossible to prove that the mean is always the cost of capital. The assumption of mean-reversion to the cost of capital is grounded in neoclassical economic theory and reasonable over the long run. However, this assumption can be troublesome for entrenched and highly successful companies in defensive industries that possess valuable intangible assets. In these cases, we recommend using a sensitivity matrix to estimate the firm's intrinsic value at different profitability fade rates. Remember, a fade rate of zero is equivalent to the classic growing perpetuity assumption of conventional terminal period valuations. We offer you the opportunity to quickly flex that assumption and quantify the risk associated with it by using our pricing model. In the

HOLT framework, we recommend setting the final fade rate to 5% for firms judged to have significant and sustainable competitive advantage.

Exhibit 5.17 can help you determine how long the explicit forecast period should be and how to think about the valuation of the terminal period in your DCF analysis. The Fundamental Pricing Model can be used to perform back-of-the envelope valuations for stable companies that are ex-growth similar to our Macy's example.

CHAPTER APPENDIX

Valuation Mathematics

Valuations from the FCFF and EP methods are equal for a given forecast and inputs:

$$Enterprise\ Value = \sum_{n=1}^{\infty} \frac{FCFF_n}{(1+r)^n} = Invested\ Capital_0 + \sum_{n=1}^{\infty} \frac{EP_n}{(1+r)^n}$$

If we break the valuation into an explicit period of N years and a terminal period that begins in year $N+1$, the expressions can be written as:

FCFF Method

$$Enterprise\ Value = \sum_{n=1}^{N} \frac{FCFF_n}{(1+r)^n} + \frac{NOPAT_{N+1}\left[1 - \frac{(g-f-gf)}{ROIC_{N+1}}\right]}{(r-g+f+gf)(1+r)^N}$$

For low rates of growth and fade, the cross-term of $g \times f$ is negligible, and can be dropped to simplify the equation:

$$Enterprise\ Value = \sum_{n=1}^{N} \frac{FCFF_n}{(1+r)^n} + \frac{NOPAT_{N+1}\left[1 - \frac{(g-f)}{ROIC_{N+1}}\right]}{(r-g+f)(1+r)^N} \quad (5.4)$$

EXHIBIT 5.17 Flowchart to help determine how long the explicit forecast period should be for valuing a company. The flowchart also helps establish assumptions for estimating the terminal value. The Fundamental Pricing Model can be used to value relatively stable ex-growth firms on the back-of-an-envelope.

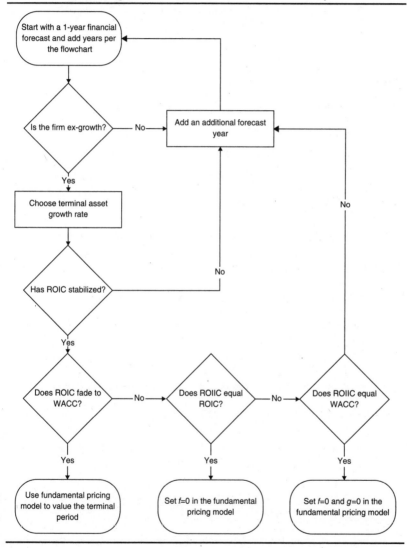

EP Method

$$Enterprise\ Value = Invested\ Capital_0$$

$$+ \sum_{n=1}^{N} \frac{EP_n}{(1+r)^n} + \frac{EP_{N+1}}{(r-g+f+gf)(1+r)^N}$$

Again, for low rates of growth and fade, the cross-term of $g \times f$ is negligible, and can be dropped to simplify the equation:

$$Enterprise\ Value = Invested\ Capital_0$$

$$+ \sum_{n=1}^{N} \frac{EP_n}{(1+r)^n} + \frac{EP_{N+1}}{(r-g+f)(1+r)^N} \tag{5.5}$$

We prefer the latter expression, which is intuitive and easy to remember.

Inputs for Valuing Macy's and Assessing Its Competitive Advantage Period

The inputs for performing the back-of-the-envelope valuation of Macy's and calculating the sensitivity table shown in Exhibit 5.15 are shown in Exhibit 5.18. We applied the EP form of our pricing model using HOLT inputs. In HOLT terms, the invested capital is the inflation-adjusted net assets, the economic profit is the HOLT EP, the cost of capital is the HOLT real discount rate, and asset growth is in real terms. Consistency is imperative.

$$Enterprise\ Value = Economic\ Net\ Assets_0 + \frac{EP_1}{(r-g+f)}$$

Debt must be subtracted from the enterprise value to calculate the intrinsic share price.

Macy's economic profit has halved over the past two years from $1.254bn in January 2015 to $0.639bn in January 2017 while its share price has dropped 64%. Assuming a perpetual real growth of zero, Macy's

EXHIBIT 5.18 The HOLT inputs for the back-of-the-envelope valuation of Macy's as of June 2015 (left-hand side) and June 2017 (right-hand side).

Macy's Back-of-the-Envelope Valuation			Macy's Back-of-the-Envelope Valuation		
Real growth rate	0.0%		Real growth rate	0.0%	
Fade rate	2.6%		Fade rate	14.5%	
Discount rate	4.8%		Discount rate	4.9%	
Today's share price (USD)	63.48		Today's share price (USD)	22.47	
Item	2014	2015	Item	2016	2017
EP ($mil)	1,254	1,254	EP ($'mil)	639	639
IAGI ($mil)	22,592		IAGI ($'mil)	19,221	
NDA ($mil)	5,939		NDA ($'mil)	4,878	
Investments ($mil)	–		Investments ($'mil)	–	
Debt ($mil)	11,309		Debt ($'mil)	9,932	
Minority Interests ($mil)	–		Minority Interests ($'mil)	–	
Valuation ($mil)			Valuation ($'mil)		
Economic Net Assets	15,931		Economic Net Assets	13,484	
PV of EP	16,997		PV of EP	3,280	
Operating Enterprise Value	32,928		Operating Enterprise Value	16,764	
Investments	–		Investments	–	
Debt	(11,309)		Debt	(9,932)	
Minority Interests	–		Minority Interests	–	
Equity Value	21,619		Equity Value	6,832	
Shares (mil)	340.57		Shares (mil)	304.06	
Share Price ($)	**63.48**		**Share Price ($)**	**22.47**	

market-implied fade rate increased from 2.6% to 14.5%; that is, the market-implied CAP dropped from 38 years to 7 years. Investors were highly optimistic about the sustainability of Macy's competitive advantage and profitability two years ago. They are pessimistic about its sustainability today.

A Detour Through the Twilight Zone: Making Sense of P/E

The Fundamental Pricing Model was used to generate Exhibit 5.3, and can be used to illustrate how meaningless P/E ratios can be:

$$\frac{P}{B_0} = \frac{[ROE_1 - g + f]}{(r_e - g + f)}$$

EXHIBIT 5.19 **The unbearable lightness and absurdity of P/E ratios. This example illustrates how confusing and unhelpful P/E ratios can be.**

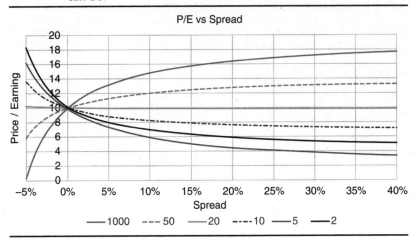

$$\frac{P}{E_1} = \frac{\left[1 - \frac{(g-f)}{ROE_1}\right]}{(r_e - g + f)}$$

All things being equal, an increase in forward ROE results in an increase in P/B and P/E. Growth in book equity only adds value and increases P/B if the forward ROE exceeds the cost of equity. A slower rate of fade for a value creating firm also results in an increase in the P/B. These results make intuitive sense. Now look at the behavior of P/E in Exhibit 5.19 and witness how it does your head in!

We don't know whether up is down or right is left when we calculate a fundamental P/E ratio as a function of forward spread and CAP. In this example, a company with a 5% spread and CAP of 5 years would trade at the same P/E of 8 as a company with a higher spread of 15% and a CAP of 10 years. Comparing these P/E ratios makes little sense. If the fade rate exceeds the growth in book equity, then the forward P/E ratio decreases as the spread increases. This result is unintuitive. It happens because the return on incremental investments is less than the cost of equity, but you would never know it unless you calculated the change in economic profit. The intuitive result of the P/E multiple expanding as forward spread increases only happens when the fade rate is less than the growth in book equity, e.g., the top two curves when CAP is 1,000 years (fade rate of 0.1%) and 50 years (fade rate of 2%). Note that the P/E remains constant when the spread is zero. Growth and fade are irrelevant for cost of capital businesses. In this example, the cost of equity is 10%, the perpetual growth in book equity is 5%, and forward spread equals $(ROE_1 - r_e)$.

If you assume P/E ratios are a sensible and intuitive valuation metric, think again. Use equations with explicit assumptions when estimating value, not P/E ratios.

6

HOLT ECONOMIC PROFIT

"Businesses logically are worth far more than net tangible assets when they can be expected to produce earnings on such assets considerably in excess of market rates of return. The capitalized value of this excess return is economic Goodwill."

—Warren Buffett, 1983

KEY LEARNING POINTS

- Unlike debt, which has an interest charge associated with it, there is no charge recorded on an income statement for shareholders' equity. Accounting earnings are not economic earnings.
- Economic profit represents the economic earnings of a firm. It equals the spread between return on capital and the cost of capital multiplied by the invested capital. Companies able to beat their cost of capital are value creators while those that fall short are value destroyers.

- The value of an asset equals the invested capital plus the present value of future economic profits. For a given forecast, the EP valuation and FCFF will be equal.
- HOLT economic profit improves upon the conventional EP since it accounts for asset life, asset mix, and inflation. We show how to calculate HOLT EP and use it to perform a valuation.
- EP can be split into operating and acquisition components. Total EP should preferably be greater than zero, but it is more important that the *change* in EP is positive.
- Change in EP can be split into margin, growth, goodwill, and market risk components. You can identify how EP is evolving, and study trade-offs such as growth versus margin compression.
- Amazon and Danaher are used as examples to illustrate the calculations and application of HOLT EP.

The usual approach to valuing a firm is to calculate the present value (PV) of its future free cash flows. An alternative approach is to calculate the PV of its economic profits (EP). We have already introduced the conventional definition of EP. We will focus on the HOLT Economic Profit (HOLT EP) framework in this chapter.

Economic profit represents the economic earnings of a firm. EP is proportional to the spread between a company's return on capital and cost of capital. If a firm earns its cost of capital, EP is zero. Growth based on investments that are below their cost of capital destroys economic value, and these strategies should be rejected. Investment into positive spread strategies creates economic value and should be encouraged.

We will demonstrate how HOLT EP is calculated and can be used to analyze company performance and value the firm. This approach applies all the advantages of the HOLT framework to the measurement of economic profit: asset mix, asset life, inflation, and accounting distortions are handled identically, making HOLT EP a first-class economic measure.

By splitting EP into operating and acquisition goodwill components, absolute value creation can be assessed. Insights can be gained from analyzing change in EP, which can be decomposed into three parts: change in economic spread, growth, and change in goodwill. Amazon is an excellent example of a firm whose increase in EP due to growth has more than compensated the loss in EP due to declining CFROI. Amazon is used as an example throughout this chapter.

Corporate boards and investors should insist on positive change in EP. A brief case study at the end of this chapter using Danaher Corporation illustrates how EP and change in EP can be used to analyze an acquisitive company.

INTRODUCTION

The usual approach to valuing a firm is to calculate the present value of its future free cash flows to the firm's capital providers (FCFF). A highly informative alternative is to calculate the present value of the firm's economic profits and add it to the firm's invested capital.

Although technically correct, the FCFF method has nothing to say about the *quality* of the cash flow. Is a high level of free cash flow a good or bad thing? The answer depends on whether the company is forsaking value-creating opportunities to report higher cash flow. Rational investors prefer reinvestment in positive NPV projects rather than receiving dividends given a choice.

A company should invest its capital and available cash flow into strategies that exceed their cost of capital. If value-creating opportunities are unavailable, the firm should maximize cash flow and return it to shareholders via dividends or share buybacks. As a rule of thumb, free cash flow will be negative when asset growth, g, is greater than the return on capital:

$$\text{Cash flow rules: if } g > \text{CFROI, then FCFF} < 0$$

Value-destroying firms often make the mistake of expanding their operations to report earnings growth. They think Wall Street wants earnings growth at any cost. This misunderstanding can lead to expensive corporate mistakes. Earnings are an accounting value, and cash flow is an economic one. These profit measures are frequently conflated.

EXHIBIT 6.1 Assessing growth options.

Cash from Operations	Growth Option	Decision
If CFROI > g, then FCFF > 0	Are projects available that exceed their cost of capital?	**Yes** – invest cash flow and raise additional capital if necessary. **No** – return the cash flow to capital providers.
If CFROI < g, then FCFF < 0	Are projects available that exceed their cost of capital?	**Yes** – raise additional capital **No** – don't grow and consider downsizing if the firm is destroying value.

It is the *quality* of earnings that should inform a firm's growth strategy (Exhibit 6.1).

The quickest way to generate cash flow is to stop growing. Exhibit 6.1 indicates that this is suboptimal if a firm has strategies available which exceed their cost of capital. This choke-growth turnaround rule is only warranted for value destroyers whose return on capital isn't meeting the cost of capital (typically, subpar companies in mature industries that might benefit from consolidation). For them, it is wise to remember humorist Will Rogers' adage on the first law of holes: If you find yourself in a hole, stop digging.

On the flip side, potential value creation is squandered when CFOs don't do their job of investing available cash flow and raising capital to finance strategies expected to beat their cost of capital. Negative cash flow is acceptable if project returns are expected to exceed their cost of capital and generate positive net present value (NPV) for the firm. To do otherwise is to leave money on the table. Rational shareholders prefer more value to less and the aim of the firm is to create the greatest possible NPV from its portfolio of present and future investments. Accounting earnings should never be confused with economic value.

Can the concept of value creation be communicated more comprehensively? All capital providers expect compensation. There is a charge on debt which appears on the income statement as interest expense. Operating profit must cover interest charges and debt-equivalent charges such as operating lease expenses. If not, net income will be negative.

But what about equity? There is no charge for equity on the income statement, so it appears to have no cost to the untrained eye. Economists know that there is an opportunity cost for providing equity, which should reflect the investment's riskiness. A residual income would subtract a charge on the equity at the opportunity cost of equity from net income. The residual income is an economic profit, which differs profoundly in concept and absolute value from accounting profit. The equity charge is simply the cost of equity multiplied by the equity. The more equity required to support earnings, the greater the economic charge and lower the residual income.

When analyzing the operating performance and value of industrial and service companies, it is beneficial to separate the firm's operating and financing decisions, and to value the firm with respect to all capital providers. Financial structure is a secondary consideration in the capital budgeting process. Of primary concern is the intelligent allocation of capital and resources with the aim that all capital provided will create positive NPV. As Weingartner notes, "Capital budgeting represents in some respects the central problem of the firm. The complexity of the problem derives from the fact that any set of actions taken today has consequences at later times, and the opportunities available at later dates are related to decisions being implemented currently."

The opportunity cost for the firm's capital, which is a weighted-average of its cost of equity and debt, is the cost of capital. Value creation can be communicated by calculating economic profit and discounting future economic profits to their present value. Valuations from the FCFF and EP methods should yield equivalent results for an identical forecast.

Another benefit of economic profit is that it connects project economics and corporate valuation. The present value of a firm's economic profits is equal to the total NPV of its existing and future investments!

$$Firm\ value - Invested\ capital = \sum_{n=1}^{\infty} \frac{EP_n}{(1+r)^n} = \sum_{p=1}^{P} NPV_p$$

The invested capital is the net asset value of the firm, and the starting point for a firm's existing projects and value creation. Distant economic

EXHIBIT 6.2 The value drivers for change in economic profit are diagrammed in the flowchart. Investment growth comes from investing in positive NPV projects, and efficiency growth comes from improving operating margins and asset turns. Key performance indicators and incentives should be aligned with increasing economic profit.

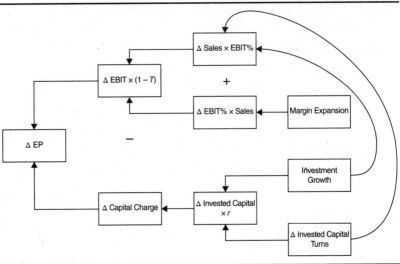

profits are generated from projects that have yet to be imagined. A relentless focus on building a sustainable competitive advantage and investing in positive NPV projects results in increasing economic profit and the firm's valuation. A firm's key performance indicators (KPIs) and incentives should be based on increasing economic profit, whether by investment in positive NPV strategies or efficiency improvements (Exhibit 6.2).

CALCULATING CFROI AS A RATIO

CFROI is a single period measure of a firm's weighted-average IRR on its existing businesses and projects. CFROI can be expressed as a ratio, which equals the result from the familiar RATE function in Microsoft Excel.[1]

$$CFROI = RATE\,(Life,\ GCF,\ -IAGI,\ NDA) = \frac{(GCF - ARC)}{IAGI} \quad (6.1)$$

---

[1] We show the full proof and outline the advantages of CFROI as a ratio in the report: D.A. Holland and B.A. Matthews, "CFROI as a Ratio and Du Pont Identity," *Credit Suisse HOLT,* August 2014.

The HOLT variables were covered in Chapter 3: *Life* is the weighted-average useful life of the depreciating assets, *GCF* is gross cash flow, *IAGI* is inflation-adjusted gross investment, and *NDA* represents non-depreciating assets. Calculating CFROI as a ratio requires the introduction of an economic depreciation variable, the asset recovery charge (ARC).

$$ARC = PMT \, (RATE, Life, \, 0, \, -IADA) = \frac{RATE \times IADA}{[(1 + RATE)^{Life} - 1]} \quad (6.2)$$

ARC is a depreciation annuity that represents the sinking fund charge of recovering the inflation-adjusted depreciating assets (IADA) over the asset life. A lower recovery rate translates into a higher asset recovery charge.

A can of worms has now been opened. What is the rate at which the depreciating assets are recovered? In a CFROI ratio calculation, there is an implicit assumption that ARC is recovered at a rate equal to the CFROI.

Economists would argue that the sinking fund depreciation should be calculated at the firm's cost of capital (or discount rate DR) since by definition it represents the risk-adjusted opportunity cost of the capital provided.

$$ARC@DR = PMT \, (DR, \, Life, \, 0, \, -IADA) = \frac{DR \times IADA}{[(1 + DR)^{Life} - 1]}$$

We have maintained that a project's NPV and the present value of its economic profits are equal. The calculation of HOLT economic profit is greatly simplified if an adjusted CFROI is defined where ARC is calculated at the firm's cost of capital. To distinguish between traditional IRR, where the asset recovery charge is imputed at the IRR, and economic return on investment (EROI), we introduce economic depreciation.

Economic depreciation (ED) equals:

$$ED = PMT \, (DR, \, Life, \, 0, \, -IADA) = \frac{DR \times IADA}{[(1 + DR)^{Life} - 1]} \quad (6.3)$$

ED is simply ARC calculated at the discount rate.

EXHIBIT 6.3 **Comparison of two mutually exclusive projects with the same IRR but different asset compositions. Which would you choose?**

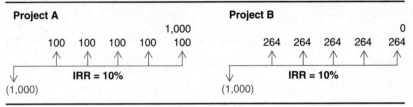

Economic ROI Calculation

$$EROI = \frac{(GCF - ED)}{IAGI} \qquad (6.4)$$

CFROI and economic return on investment (EROI) are equivalent when CFROI equals the discount rate. They are always equivalent if the asset base is comprised entirely of non-depreciating assets, for example, net working capital and land. EROI will be less than CFROI when CFROI is greater than the discount rate; that is, the sinking fund depreciation decreases as CFROI increases. EROI will be greater than CFROI when CFROI is less than the discount rate; that is, the sinking fund depreciation increases as CFROI decreases.

Why is EROI important? Because it is an economic measure aligned with the calculation of EP and NPV. We illustrate its significance by contrasting two mutually exclusive projects (Exhibit 6.3). Investment in Project A consists only of non-depreciating assets; for example, production is outsourced, while the investment in Project B is solely in depreciating assets; for example, in-house production.

Both projects have an IRR and CFROI of 10%, and would appear equally attractive to investment decision makers. NPV tells another tale (Exhibit 6.4)! If a 6% cost of capital is assumed, the NPV of Project A is 50% higher than that of Project B, making it the clear winner in a capital budgeting exercise. In fact, Project B's cash flow would have to increase to 277 and its IRR to 12% for the NPV of the projects to be equivalent at 168. IRR is not aligned with the NPV rule in this example.

EXHIBIT 6.4 Calculation of the NPV for the two mutually exclusive projects. Project A is the clear winner when NPV is considered. Never forget the golden rule.

Year:	0	1	2	3	4	5
Project A	(1,000)	100	100	100	100	1,100
Project B	(1,000)	264	264	264	264	264
IRR_A	10%	NPV_A, where DR = 6%			$168	
IRR_B	10%	NPV_B, where DR = 6%			$111	

Internal rate of return is a popular and treasured metric since it does not require an *external* cost of capital and all the squabbling that accompanies its quantification. NPV is a superior metric for assessing value but requires an explicit risk-adjusted discount rate.

Calculation of EROI is perfectly aligned with NPV in this example. Project A has an EROI of 10% while Project B has an EROI of 8.6%. Project A is preferable using NPV or EROI.

We can further illustrate differences between CFROI and EROI by varying the ratio of GCF to gross investment (IAGI) and NDA% for a typical company. The straight lines represent CFROI and the dashed lines represent EROI for GCF/IAGI ratios of 5%, 10%, and 20%. (GCF/IAGI is sometimes used as an ROA proxy, but it is a poor return on assets substitute.)

First, note how CFROI and EROI equal the return GCF/IAGI when all the assets are non-depreciating. The discrepancy between CFROI and EROI grows as the relative amount of depreciating assets increases. The asset replacement charge causes this discrepancy. Investors must recover the cost of the depreciating assets whereas non-depreciating assets are fully recovered at the project's conclusion. This is the basic distinction between earning a return *on* investment and recovering the principal invested, that is, return *of* investment. In the CFROI calculation, when CFROI is greater than the discount rate, the replacement charge decreases as CFROI increases. This is not the case for the EROI, where depreciating assets are funded *at the discount rate* (Exhibit 6.5).

EXHIBIT 6.5 **EROI and CFROI are compared as a function of non-depreciating asset intensity.**

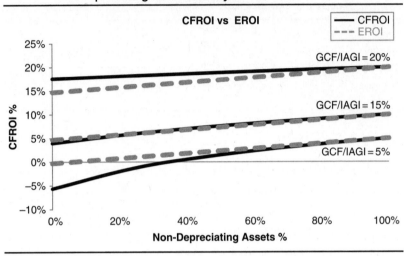

A benefit of EROI is that it compresses returns toward the discount rate and has lower overall variance than CFROI for companies with a high percentage of fixed assets. Note how there is very little difference between CFROI and EROI when they are near the discount rate, which was assumed to be 6%. This example also illustrates why it is vital to consider asset composition when measuring corporate profitability.

Let's conclude this section by calculating EROI for Amazon. ED is calculated at Amazon's 2013 average real discount rate of 4.0%, which results in a charge of $5.768bn and an EROI of 9.6% versus a CFROI of 12%:

$$ED\ (2013) = PMT\ (4.0\%,\ 5.4\ \text{years},\ 0,\ -\$34.042bn) = \$5.768bn$$

$$EROI(2013) = \frac{(\$9.480bn - \$5.768bn)}{\$38.581bn} = 9.6\%$$

HOLT ECONOMIC PROFIT

Economic profit (EP) is the amount of value a firm creates over a specified period, typically annual. It is proportional to the spread between a company's return on capital and cost of capital. If a firm is meeting its cost

EXHIBIT 6.6 The equivalence of NPV and the present value of EP is demonstrated for two projects.

Equivalence of NPV and the PV of EP

DCF Analysis—Projects A & B

	0	1	2	3	4	5	IRR	DR	NPV
Project A—cash flows	(1,000)	100	100	100	100	1,100	10.0%	6.0%	168
Project B—cash flows	(1,000)	264	264	264	264	264	10.0%	6.0%	111

Economic Profit Analysis— Project A

GCF		100	100	100	100	100			
$- ED_{@DR}$		0	0	0	0	0			
Economic Cash Flow		100	100	100	100	100			
/ IAGI		1,000	1,000	1,000	1,000	1,000			
= EROI		10.0%	10.0%	10.0%	10.0%	10.0%			
Economic Spread (EROI − DR)		4.0%	4.0%	4.0%	4.0%	4.0%			**PV**
Economic Profit (Spread × IAGI)		40	40	40	40	40			168

Economic Profit Analysis—Project B

GCF		264	264	264	264	264			
$- ED_{@DR}$		177	177	177	177	177			
Economic Cash Flow		86	86	86	86	86			
/ IAGI		1,000	1,000	1,000	1,000	1,000			
= EROI		8.6%	8.6%	8.6%	8.6%	8.6%			
Economic Spread (EROI − DR)		2.6%	2.6%	2.6%	2.6%	2.6%			**PV**
Economic Profit (Spread × IAGI)		26	26	26	26	26			111

of capital, its EP is zero. Growth into strategies below the cost of capital destroys shareholder value, and these strategies should be rejected. Growth at the cost of capital is value neutral. For every dollar invested, a dollar is returned for a NPV of zero. The HOLT EP is simply the economic spread multiplied by assets if EROI is specified as the return on capital:

$$EP = (EROI - DR) \times IAGI \qquad (6.5)$$

Use of EROI leads to equivalent valuations for the FCFF and EP approaches. We demonstrate that the NPV and present value of economic profits are equivalent for the previous Project A and B example (Exhibit 6.6).

This simple example demonstrates several key points. First, the present value of future EP streams equals the NPV of each project's cash flows. The EROI for Project A is equivalent to IRR and CFROI since the assets are 100% non-depreciating. The NPV of 168 is equivalent to the present value of Project A's economic profit stream, assuming a discount rate of 6%. The EROI for Project B is lower than the IRR and CFROI, indicating that this project is not as attractive as Project A. Another key point is that EROI is rank-order aligned with the lower NPV of 111, which is equivalent to the present value of Project B's economic profits.

Another way of stating EP is economic cash flow (ECF) minus a capital charge (DR × IAGI). ECF is an after-tax operating profit less an economic depreciation charge.

$$EP = GCF - ED - DR \times IAGI = ECF - Capital\ Charge$$

The inflation-adjusted capital charge is the opportunity cost of using the assets, equal to the assets multiplied by the discount rate. This charge is analogous to the capital charge of invested capital multiplied by WACC in conventional approaches. A firm can increase its economic profit by attaining greater productivity out of its assets; for example, improved working capital management leads to a decrease in assets and the capital charge. It can improve profitability by improving ECF margin and/or asset turns (Exhibit 6.7).

Amazon's EP in 2013 was $2.154bn, which is the amount by which ECF exceeded the capital charge:

$$EP(2013) = (9.6\% - 4.0\%) \times \$38.581bn = \$2.154bn$$

What Is the Connection Between EP and Value?

The level of economic profit and its sustainability are integral to a company's intrinsic value. We established that the present value of a project's EP and its NPV are equivalent. The value of a firm equals the present value

EXHIBIT 6.7 Diagram outlining the calculation of HOLT EP.

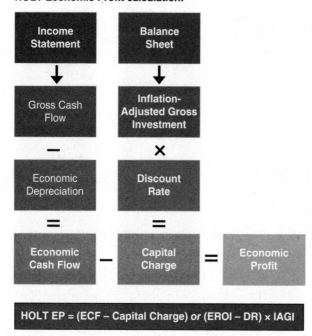

HOLT EP = (ECF – Capital Charge) *or* (EROI – DR) × IAGI

of its future EP streams and its inflation-adjusted economic net asset value (ENA) (Exhibit 6.8).[2] ENA equals IAGI minus the accumulated economic depreciation, and is a measure of a firm's inflation-adjusted book value:

$$Value = ENA_0 + \sum_{i=1}^{N} \frac{EP_i}{(1 + DR)^i}$$

If a firm is forecast to generate cost of capital returns, its EP will be zero, and the firm should trade at its book value. The enterprise book value is the current-dollar net assets. Firms unable to meet their cost of capital will trade at a discount to their book value, and those able to beat their cost of capital will trade at a premium.

---

[2]In practice, economic profit is often based on average assets. The HOLT framework uses the end-of-year assets. In a valuation, the beginning-of-year asset base must be used.

EXHIBIT 6.8 Diagram outlining the calculation of HOLT EP and FCFF.

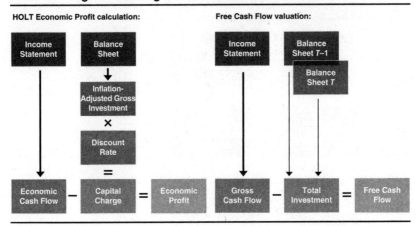

Growth and sustainability as value drivers are crystal clear in the EP framework. Firms able to grow EP via investment, margin expansion, and/or asset productivity will increase shareholder value. Firms able to sustain value-creating returns longer into the future and withstand the gravitational pull of fade will generate more shareholder value. A crucial performance measure, which we will investigate shortly, is the change in economic profit (ΔEP).

THE POWER OF SIMPLICITY: SPREAD, FADE, AND GROWTH IN AN EP FRAMEWORK

The importance of economic spread and fade can be readily shown. Consider a firm whose assets are growing at a rate g but whose profitability is fading at a rate f towards the cost of capital DR. An analytical solution exists for firm value:[3]

$$Firm\ value \cong ENA_0 \times \left(\frac{EROI_1 - g + f}{DR - g + f} \right)$$

The impact of profitability and fade can now be evaluated. Quicker fade accelerates value depletion! The table below, which assumes a real discount

---

[3]The exact equation is $Firm\ value = IAGI_0 \times \left(\frac{EROI_1 - g + f}{DR - g + f} \right) - Accumulated\ Economic\ Depreciation$

EXHIBIT 6.9 The HOLT price-to-book ratio for different combinations of fade and EROI.

Estimated HOLT Price-to-Book

		EROI (1)				
		0%	3%	6%	12%	24%
	1%	−0.20	0.40	1.00	2.20	4.60
	5%	0.33	0.67	1.00	1.67	3.00
Fade Rate %	10%	0.57	0.79	1.00	1.43	2.29
	25%	0.79	0.90	1.00	1.21	1.62
	50%	0.89	0.94	1.00	1.11	1.33
	100%	0.94	0.97	1.00	1.06	1.17

rate of 6% and real growth of 2%, shows the multiple of intrinsic enterprise value to ENA_0, which is the HOLT price-to-book ratio (HOLT P/B). It is analogous to Tobin's Q ratio. When the forward CFROI is equal to the discount rate, the P/B remains constant at 1.0. Fade doesn't matter, growth doesn't create value, and the firm is worth its inflation-adjusted net asset value.

The inverse of the fade rate is a measure of the expected competitive advantage period (CAP). A value-destroying firm with an EROI of 3% should trade at a P/B of 0.67 if it expects 20 years (5% fade rate) to recover to its cost of capital, and a significantly higher P/B of 0.94 if it only expects 2 years (50% fade rate) to recover. A stellar value-creating firm with an EROI of 24% should trade at a P/B of 3.0 if its expected CAP is 20 years versus a significantly lower P/B of 1.3 for an expected CAP of 2 years. Fade happens, and its impact can be enormous (Exhibit 6.9).

USING ECONOMIC PROFIT TO MEASURE THE VALUE OF ACQUISITIONS

Thus far, we have focused on understanding the economics of operating assets. Economic profit analysis is also helpful in understanding the value of acquisitions.

Acquisition goodwill, which HOLT treats as a non-operating intangible asset, can be factored into the analysis of economic profit and change in economic profit. The cumulative goodwill should be used since any premium paid represents a wealth transfer from the acquiring firm to target shareholders and is an unrecoverable cost, or penalty, to the acquiring firm's equity investors. The penalty for control, however, isn't indefinite if change in EP becomes the focus, since ΔEP negates sunk costs such as goodwill. Let's begin with EP.

$$Capital\ Charge\ on\ Goodwill = DR \times Cumulative\ Goodwill$$

$$Transaction\ EP = Operations\ EP + Goodwill\ EP$$
$$= (EROI - DR) \times IAGI - DR \times GW$$

(6.6)

The transaction EP includes operating EP and goodwill EP.[4] The transaction EP for Amazon in 2013 was $2.018bn after a relatively small goodwill charge of $137m on a cumulative goodwill total of $3.384bn.

$$Transaction\ EP(2013) = (9.6\% - 4.0\%) \times \$38.581bn - 4.0\%$$
$$\times \$3.384bn = \$2.018bn$$

Amazon's EP performance over the past decade is specified in Exhibit 6.10. Operating EP swamps any charges due to goodwill. The exponential increase in Total EP from $59m at the end of 2003 to $2.0bn in 2013 is extraordinary, highlighting 10 years of double-digit

EXHIBIT 6.10 **A table and chart showing Amazon's operating EP and transaction EP from 2004 to 2013.**

EP Outputs	2003	2004	2005	2006	2007	2008	2009	2010	2011	2012	2013
EP (Operations)	69	210	400	468	644	617	957	1,272	1,171	1,397	2,154
EP (Goodwill)	−10	−8	−10	−13	−16	−36	−97	−79	−120	−161	−137
Total EP	59	202	390	455	628	581	860	1,193	1,050	1,237	2,018

---

[4]Acquired intangibles are treated as a goodwill equivalent in HOLT.

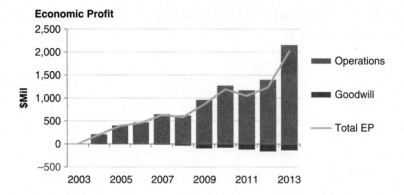

Economic Profit

compounding value (CAGR = 42%). What is the market expecting now and will this trajectory continue?

A transaction EROI that incorporates acquisition goodwill can be defined, which allows another way of stating the transaction EP:

$$Transaction\ EROI = \frac{ECF}{IAGI + GW} \tag{6.7}$$

and, rearranging

$$Transaction\ EP = (Transaction\ EROI - DR) \times (IAGI + GW)$$

Amazon's transaction EROI in 2013 was 8.8%, indicating that Amazon remains a value-creating business if acquisition goodwill is taken into account:

$$Transaction\ EROI(2013) = \frac{(\$9.480 - \$5.768bn)}{(\$38.581 + \$3.384bn)} = 8.8\%$$

The higher the premium paid for an acquisition, the greater the capital charge. Economic profit can help judge whether the charge on goodwill is being offset by growth in operating EP. This can be achieved by splitting the change in economic profit into its spread, growth, and goodwill components.

DECOMPOSING VALUE CREATION INTO DELTA EP COMPONENTS

A firm can increase its intrinsic value by generating a positive change in economic profit. ΔEP is a crucial measure of corporate performance and value creation. Annual changes in EP should be calculated and cumulative totals tallied. Bonuses of executives, division managers, project leaders, and employees can be based on cumulative ΔEP over a 3- to 5-year period if shareholders want each level of the firm to be focused on value creation. Operationally, increases in spread and growth in value-creating businesses are the two major routes to achieving this goal. If acquisitions are the strategy guiding growth, then the charge on additional goodwill can be compared to the ΔEP generated from the acquired assets. If the premium paid is too high, then the economic charge on that premium will surpass the additional economic profit generated from the larger asset base.

The change in EP can be calculated for any two periods but is generally calculated on an annual basis:

$$\Delta EP_{i+1} = (EROI_{i+1} - DR_{i+1}) \times IAGI_{i+1} - (EROI_i - DR_i) \times IAGI_i$$

For Amazon, the operating ΔEP in 2013 was $757m:

$$\Delta EP(2013) = (9.6\% - 4.0\%) \times \$38{,}581m - (10.0\% - 4.8\%)$$
$$\times \$26{,}950m = \$757m$$

Amazon created $757m more in economic profit in 2013 than in 2012 despite its EROI dropping from 10% to 9.6%. Some of this increase was due to the higher risk appetite of markets; that is, the average discount rate dropped from 4.8% to 4.0%, but most of it was due to the enormous growth in assets, which was an astonishing 43% in nominal terms. Tremendous insight comes from decomposing the sources of value creation. Let's see how to separate change in EP due to economic spread expansion from that due to growth.

The ΔEP equation can be rewritten as the expression:

$$\Delta EP_{i+1} = \underbrace{(\Delta EROI_{i+1} - \Delta DR_{i+1}) \times IAGI_i}$$

Value creation from expansion in economic spread

$$+ \underbrace{(EROI_{i+1} - DR_{i+1}) \times \Delta IAGI_{i+1}}$$

Value creation from growth and reinvestment

There are two terms that comprise the change in operating EP. The first is the improvement in EP due to economic spread expansion. The expansion comes from improvement in EROI and change in the discount rate.[5] The second term is change in EP due to growth and re-investment. If growth is zero, then this term is zero. If the spread is positive, then growth creates value.

The beginning-of-year asset growth rate, g, can be used to restate the equation in an explicit manner.

$$\Delta EP_{i+1} = [(\Delta EROI_{i+1} - \Delta DR_{i+1}) + (EROI_{i+1} - DR_{i+1}) \times g] \times IAGI_i$$

It is worthwhile dwelling on the economic spread component for a moment. The change in EROI is related to the operating performance of the firm. Change in EROI has a directly proportional impact on change in EP. Because HOLT employs a forward-looking, market-implied discount rate, the change in discount rate is related to market risk appetite and the firm's non-diversifiable risk. The firm has some say over the latter, for example, via its leverage and credit risk, but cannot control the former. This can prove unsettling since change in value is a function of the firm's operating performance and market whims. The HOLT Lens product splits these effects. Corporate managers and executive remuneration committees might find it preferable to settle on an absolute discount rate that remains constant to reduce the effect of market vagaries.

---

[5] In the HOLT Lens product, the change in EP due to change in the discount rate is separated from the change in EP due to change in EROI. The former is termed the "change in EP due to market risk" and equals $\Delta DR \times IAGI$.

Change in EP due to EROI and discount rate changes (change in economic spread):

$$\Delta EP_1(spread) = (EROI_1 - EROI_0 - DR_1 + DR_0) \times \frac{IAGI_1}{1+g} \quad (6.8)$$

The change in EP due to spread compression was \$108m in 2013 for Amazon:

$$\Delta EP_{2013}(spread) = (9.6\% - 10.0\% - 4.0\% + 4.8\%)$$

$$\times \frac{\$38,581m}{1 + 43.2\%} = \$108m$$

Amazon increased its economic profit in 2013 due to an improvement in spread—even though EROI declined. The overall increase was due to a decline in the discount rate.

What did growth contribute?

Change in EP due to growth:

$$\Delta EP_1(growth) = (EROI_1 - DR_1) \times \frac{g \times IAGI_1}{1+g} \quad (6.9)$$

Note that the measures can be normalized by dividing by IAGI, ENA, or sales. Normalization by sales results in economic profit and ΔEP margins, which are particularly insightful for asset-light companies.

How much additional value did Amazon's growth in 2013 generate?

$$\Delta EP_{2013}(growth) = (9.6\% - 4.0\%) \times \frac{0.432 \times \$38,581m}{1 + 0.432} = \$649m$$

Amazon created tremendous value by growing its business rather than maintaining a higher level of overall profitability. The operating ΔEP was \$757m in 2013, that is, \$108m + 649m. How much of the growth came from acquiring assets?

WHAT ABOUT GOODWILL?

The previous analysis is based on operating returns and does not account for goodwill that may have been paid to acquire assets. Fortunately, the mathematics remains the same if we substitute Transaction EROI for EROI and IAGI plus Goodwill for Invested Capital in the equations:

$$Tr\, EP_i = (Tr\, EROI_i - DR_i) \times (IAGI_i + GW_i)$$

A highly insightful adjustment is to separate the effect of goodwill from operations:

$$Tr\, EP_i = (EROI_i - DR_i) \times IAGI_i - DR_i \times GW_i$$

The contribution of operations and goodwill to EP can now be easily calculated. The change in EP can also include an acquisition component.

$$\Delta Tr\, EP_{i+1} = [(\Delta EROI_{i+1} - \Delta DR_{i+1}) + (EROI_{i+1} - DR_{i+1}) \times g]$$
$$\times IAGI_i - DR_{i+1} \times \Delta GW_{i+1}$$

The goodwill term assumes that the discount rate remains constant at times i and $i+1$ to simplify the math. Goodwill is a sunk cost. If there is no change in the cumulative goodwill, then there is no change in value due to past acquisitions. Thus we avoid penalizing future value creation for past acquisitions. This is not the case when looking at absolute EP, which has sunk costs anchored to it.

Change in EP due to M&A goodwill:

$$\Delta Tr\, EP_1(M\&A) = -DR_1 \times \Delta GW_1 \qquad (6.10)$$

There was no material change in goodwill for Amazon in 2013, thus the charge due to change in goodwill is zero.

Amazon is not averse to acquisitions. The years 2009, 2011, and 2012 are noteworthy. But the charges in these years due to increases in goodwill were drowned by increases in operating EP. Despite Amazon's EROI falling since 2007, it has been generating impressive improvements in economic profit (Exhibit 6.11). Investors want more economic profit, even if it means lower profitability. The aim is maximizing the present value of all future economic profit streams.

EXHIBIT 6.11 Amazon's economic profit and change in economic profit components.

Change in EP Outputs	2003	2004	2005	2006	2007	2008	2009	2010	2011	2012	2013
Due to change in EP spread	90	148	−17	10	−145	47	−2	−404	−220	107	
Due to growth	51	42	84	166	119	293	317	303	447	649	
Operating change in EP	**141**	**190**	**68**	**176**	**−26**	**340**	**314**	**−101**	**227**	**756**	
Due to Goodwill	−1	−1	−2	−2	−16	−61	−4	−31	−32	−1	
Total Change in EP	140	190	66	174	−42	229	310	−132	195	756	

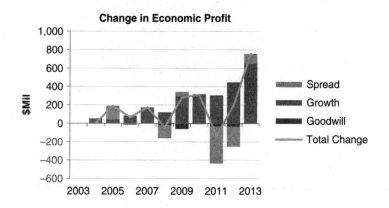

Change in EP (ΔEP) is the metric of choice in judging how well managers are performing as stewards of invested capital. It should be a key metric in value-based incentive programs. It has the advantage that value lost from sunk costs is negated; that is, if the sunk cost doesn't change, then change in its capital charge is zero. **Investors prefer a positive change in value creation, irrespective of whether the firm is a value destroyer or value creator.** The principle of value additivity informs us that any improvement in economic profit is an improvement in the firm's NPV and intrinsic value. Multi-year ΔEP accounts that get amortized on a rolling basis are highly suitable for incentivizing company managers.

Case Study: Danaher Corporation

Danaher is an American industrial company with a long track record of acquiring firms and successfully integrating them. Danaher has created

EXHIBIT 6.12 Danaher's EROI and value driver performance from 2003 to 2013.

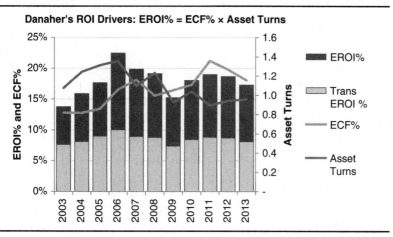

Danaher's ROI Drivers: EROI% = ECF% × Asset Turns

EXHIBIT 6.13 Danaher's EROI and transaction EROI from 2003 to 2013.

CFROI Outputs	2003	2004	2005	2006	2007	2008	2009	2010	2011	2012	2013
EROI	13.8%	15.9%	17.6%	22.5%	199%	19.2%	15.2%	180%	19.0%	18.7%	17.3%
Transaction EROI	7.7%	8.1%	9.0%	10.0%	9.0%	8.8%	7.4%	8.5%	8.9%	8.7%	8.1%

tremendous value for its shareholders and sports an impressive CFROI (Exhibit 6.12).

We begin by looking at Danaher's operating EROI and its DuPont drivers.

Danaher has maintained a remarkable operating return of greater than 15% for the past decade. Asset turns declined from their peak in 2006 and have been relatively steady at 1.0 for the past five years ($1 of sales is generated from every $1 of inflation-adjusted gross assets). The lower asset utilization has been compensated for by improving profitability, ECF%.

Exhibit 6.13 indicates that Danaher knows how to manage operating assets. However, nothing can be said about its ability to make value additive acquisitions. We can get a clue from the transaction EROI.

EXHIBIT 6.14 Danaher's economic profit from 2003 to 2013.

EP Outputs	2003	2004	2005	2006	2007	2008	2009	2010	2011	2012	2013
EP (Operations)	476	684	844	1,295	1,547	1,387	1,155	1,716	2,504	2,552	2,526
EP (Goodwill)	−161	−186	−219	−363	−548	−689	−725	−650	−1,046	−1,212	−1,044
Total EP	315	498	625	932	999	699	430	1,066	1,458	1,339	1,483

EXHIBIT 6.15 Danaher's economic profit from operations and after acquisition goodwill has been accounted for from 2003 to 2013.

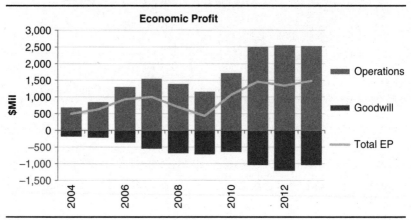

The transaction EROI, which has remained above Danaher's cost of capital for the past decade, is about half of the operating EROI due to acquisition goodwill. Danaher is creating value through its acquisition strategy, but unfortunately, we have no feel for the magnitude and timing of value creation. The next step is to calculate the absolute economic profit for each year and to split it into operating EP and goodwill EP (Exhibit 6.14).

Cumulative goodwill grew from $3.9bn at the end of 2003 to $22.5bn in 2013, a 474% increase! Danaher is not averse to paying a premium for control of other firms. The increasing charge on goodwill can be seen. But once it gains control, does Danaher convert its capital paid into shareholder value? Danaher was able to generate more economic profit from the operating assets than what it paid. Total EP grew from $315m at the end of 2003 to nearly $1.5bn in 2013. Of most interest is the change in economic profit and where it is coming from.

EXHIBIT 6.16 Danaher's annual change in EP split into its components.

Change in EP Outputs	2003	2004	2005	2006	2007	2008	2009	2010	2011	2012	2013
Due to change in EP spread	132	84	270	−207	−193	−401	475		55	−137	−98
Due to growth	76	76	180	458	34	169	86	733	185	73
Operating change in EP	**208**	**10**	**451**	**251**	**−159**	**−232**	**561**	**787**	**48**	**−25**
Due to Goodwill	−48	−20	−122	−156	0	−40	−71	−315	−81	−21
Total Change in EP	161	140	329	96	−159	−272	490	472	−33	−47

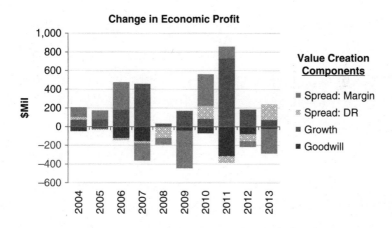

The effects of spread, growth, and goodwill are calculated. Danaher was increasing economic profit and intrinsic value until the global financial crisis of 2008/9. Significant acquisitions were made in 2006, 2007, and 2008; look at the change in EP due to goodwill line (Exhibit 6.16). The increase in EP due to growth more than compensated for the loss due to goodwill. It is interesting to note that the increase in EP due to growth in 2007 compensated for an increase in the goodwill charge *and* a drop in spread.

EROI dropped to 15.2% in 2009 because of the global slowdown. The 2009 change in EP due to spread compression was a loss of $403m.

Significant acquisitions were again made in 2011 and 2012. The change in EP due to growth in 2011 far exceeded the loss due to goodwill.

Except for 2009, the 5-year cumulative change in EP has been positive.

Danaher's managers can take a bow for generating excellent operating returns and consistently creating value through acquisitions. Few firms can so effectively integrate acquisitions and expand shareholder value.

7

RISK, REWARD, AND THE HOLT DISCOUNT RATE

"Assets are bundles of factors, each of which defines a set of bad times for the average investor. Over the long run, investors exposed to factors earn high returns. But there is risk. There are superior returns to factors, on average, because during bad times they can underperform—sometimes dramatically. Factor premiums also result from the behavior of investors that is not arbitraged away."

—Andrew Ang[1]

KEY LEARNING POINTS

- Risk is the potential for loss and has two sources: systematic and unsystematic. Systematic risk is market risk and cannot be diversified away. Unsystematic risk is idiosyncratic and can be diversified away by owning a portfolio of assets. Investors should not expect to be rewarded for unsystematic risk.

---

[1] Andrew Ang, *Asset Management: A Systematic Approach to Factor Investing*, Oxford University Press, 2014.

- The long-run inflation-adjusted return on U.S. equities has been circa 6% versus 2% for U.S. Treasury bonds. Equity investors expect a greater return due to more risk. The equity risk premium (ERP) is the difference between equities and government bonds, and varies with risk appetite. The long-run geometric and average ERPs for the world are 3.2% and 4.4%, respectively. The valuation of future cash flows should use an arithmetic ERP when estimating the cost of equity.

- HOLT calculates a forward-looking cost of capital and adjusts it with firm-specific risk factors. It is a total system approach to valuation because the discount rate is tuned to future cash flow assumptions. The discount rate level indicates the market's appetite for risk. Bearish markets result in higher market-implied discount rates while bullish markets result in lower market-implied discount rates.

- HOLT's discount rate is a cost of *capital*, not a cost of *equity*. It is a measure of total firm risk. HOLT's discount rate is equivalent to an unlevered cost of equity (as though the firm had no debt). HOLT's discount rate is a weighted-average cost of capital, but it does not embed the tax savings from debt into the cost of debt. Savings from the tax deductibility of interest are embedded in the forecast net cash receipts. The HOLT valuation model is an adjusted present value (APV) model.

- The market-implied discount rate is a random walk process. Any sign of mean-reversion is drowned in volatility.

RISK, RETURN, AND DIVERSIFICATION

Periods of braking economic growth, racing inflation, and exploding volatility spell bad times for most investors. These occasions are made worse by psychological suffering. Most asset owners feel the pain of bad times more acutely than they do the elation of good times—the amplification is over 2× according to Daniel Kahneman, who was awarded the Nobel Memorial Prize for his groundbreaking work with Amos Tversky on the psychology of judgment and decision-making. This asymmetric reaction helps explain why investors are risk averse.[2] Losses are more painful than gains are pleasurable, and investors expect a premium for bearing risk. How should that risk premium be assessed and applied in valuing assets? Can risk be moderated and returns enhanced?

Holding a diversified portfolio lessens the severity of hard times because some assets perform better than others, and company-specific risks tend to cancel—one company is successful in its pre-clinical R&D tests to develop a new drug while another fails in an unrelated effort. A perpetual challenge for asset and risk managers is to identify specific risk factors and relate them to the risk premiums they can earn or the potential losses they can avoid. If you cannot associate a specific risk with a specific risk premium, it is most likely diversifiable within a broad portfolio. If you accept that the intrinsic value of an asset is the present value of its future cash flows, then we can identify where and how risks should be considered:

$$Value = \sum_{n=1}^{N} \frac{E(FCFF_n)}{(1 + r)^n}$$

Cash flow risks should be modeled and captured in the expected free cash flow forecast, $E(FCFF_n)$, where $E(\dots)$ signifies *expected*. Systematic risks are captured in the expected return or discount rate r used to calculate the present value of those expected cash flows.

Let's take a simple example to illustrate the key points. You have an opportunity to win $1,000, which is payable in one year, or nothing. The odds are favorable: If a random number generator yields a value greater than the golden mean, 0.618, then you lose; if less, you win.[3] The expected cash

---

[2] Daniel Kahneman, *Thinking, Fast and Slow*, Penguin Books, 2011.
[3] The golden ratio (1.618 …) is considered the most aesthetic of irrational numbers and appears everywhere, including technical analysis. It was known to the ancient Greeks and called *de divina proportione* by Renaissance Italians. Amongst its properties, is $x = 1 / (1 + x)$ where x is the golden ratio conjugate (0.618 …). Technical analysts should be aware that the ratio of two consecutive numbers from the Fibonacci sequence converges towards the golden ratio.

flow one year forward is simply:

$$E(FCFF_1) = 0.618 \times 1{,}000 + (1 - 0.618) \times 0 = \$618$$

What is its present value? The outcome from a random number generator is unrelated to macroeconomic variables such as inflation, GDP growth, or unemployment. Importantly, the outcome is unrelated to changes in stock market indices (unless you believe both are controlled by the stars). Because of this bet's random outcome, the appropriate discount rate would be the risk-free rate, which represents the pure interest rate, or the *price of time*.[4] If the one-year Treasury bill is 2%, the present value would be:

$$Value = \sum_{n=1}^{N} \frac{E(FCFF_n)}{(1 + r)^n} = \frac{\$618}{(1 + 0.02)} = \$605.88$$

How much would you pay for this bet today? The answer is dependent on your risk tolerance. A risk-neutral investor would be willing to pay up to $605.88, at which point the NPV is zero.

Does this mean that casinos should be valued at the risk-free discount rate? The probability distributions for games of chance are known, but the number of people visiting the casino and the size of their bets is related to the state of the overall economy. The expected cash flows and their riskiness for a casino require an expected return greater than the risk-free rate, and more in line with the stock market returns of consumer discretionary companies. Stock market investors are more likely to spin roulette wheels in Baden Baden when markets are up, and sink into its Roman baths when they are down.

The discount rate is an integral part of any discounted cash flow (DCF) valuation. In this chapter, we introduce the HOLT fundamental risk factor approach to estimating discount rates for valuing equities, and show how the HOLT risk model corresponds to modern financial theory.

---

[4]Sharpe referred to this as the "price of time." William F. Sharpe, "Capital Asset Prices: A Theory of Market Equilibrium under Conditions of Risk," *The Journal of Finance* 19(3) (September 1964): 425–442.

What Is Risk?

A simple definition of risk is "probable loss." Lack of certainty implies an expectation about different possible outcomes. The probability of loss can be high or low. When the possibility of loss is high, risk is high, and vice versa. The *probability* of loss (as opposed to *certainty*) suggests that gains are also possible. Potential gains are the reward for taking risk.

In finance, a chief concern is how investment returns deviate from the expected return. If you purchase a U.S. Treasury bill and hold it to maturity, you'll obtain the yield at which you purchased it with risk-free certainty. The same cannot be said for stocks. Investors demand an expected return appropriate for the magnitude and probability of loss. Common estimates of risk include *standard deviation* (volatility), *correlation,* and *beta.* Asymmetric properties can be described by *skewness* and *kurtosis* (colloquially known as "fat tails" when large).

In Exhibit 7.1, the average rate of return on equities after inflation over time is close to 6%, 2% for bonds, and 1% for U.S. Treasury bills. There are significant deviations in these real rates of return over the last 100 years, indicating that investors do not always get what they expect. The *y*-axis is plotted on a logarithmic scale, so that vertical changes represent equal percentage changes, regardless of the starting base value.

Treasury bills show the least volatility and equities the highest. In accordance with our definition of risk as "probable loss," equities have delivered the highest real return over time and Treasuries the lowest. Based on a long-term view, we might anticipate that the inflation-adjusted (real) return on equities over the next 100 years will continue to be 6%, and 2% for Treasury bonds. If long-term inflation averages 2%, equity investors can anticipate an average nominal rate of 8% if the future mirrors the past. The risk premium for equities relative to bonds is circa 4%.

A popular misunderstanding is that a relationship exists between stock price volatility and return for individual stocks, but this mistakenly assumes all risk should be factored into the expected return. Risk can be divided into two components: *systematic* and *unsystematic.*

EXHIBIT 7.1 Annual returns to Treasuries, Bonds, and Equities, 1900–2016.

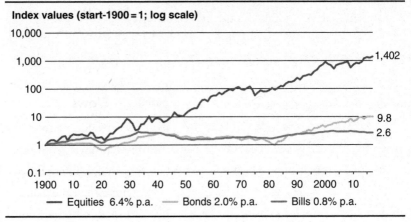

Index values (start-1900 = 1; log scale)

Source: Copyright © 2017 Dimson, Marsh, and Staunton, *2017 Credit Suisse Global Investment Returns Yearbook.*

Systematic risk is a *common* risk inherent to the entire stock market and is non-diversifiable. Systematic risk can be mitigated by investing *across* different asset classes. An incoming tide lifts all boats (or sinks them if it happens to be a tsunami). Systematic risk is also known as *market* risk. Unsystematic risk, also referred to as *unique, residual, company-specific,* or *idiosyncratic* risk, is diversifiable. Investors can eliminate it by owning a portfolio of imperfectly correlated stocks and should not expect to be compensated for holding company-specific risk. Idiosyncratic risks are diversified in a large portfolio while common risks are not. Thus, stock price volatility is not an appropriate measure of risk and expected return for a security. Around 50% of the typical stock's volatility is diversifiable![5]

The notion that some risks are diversifiable is so important that it bears mentioning again: Within the context of a diversified portfolio, investors should not expect to be compensated for bearing diversifiable risk.

---

[5]This can be mathematically demonstrated. Given any measure of stock volatility, σ, a diversified portfolio with n companies and assumed correlation, r, across stocks within the portfolio will have a portfolio volatility: $v_p = \sqrt{\frac{1}{n}\sigma^2 + \left(1 - \frac{1}{n}\right)r\sigma^2}$. Thus, a diversified portfolio of 30 stocks having company volatility of 50% and correlation of 25% has portfolio volatility of 26%.

Corporations making acquisitions with the aim of diversifying risk on behalf of their shareholders are not doing them a favor. The corporation should return any excess capital to shareholders via dividends or share repurchases, and let them diversify their risk according to their needs.

How Do Corporate Managers Discount Cash Flows to Present Value?

Calculation of the present value of a firm's future cash flows requires an appropriate discount rate, also known as the cost of capital. Modern finance splits the discount rate into time and risk components. The time value of money is discounted at a risk-free rate, which is assumed to be the appropriate term U.S. Treasury when the U.S. dollar is the currency of interest. It should be borne in mind that riskier countries carry a sovereign risk premium in their "risk-free" rates; for example, the difference between German and Italian euro bonds represents the risk premium investors expect for buying bonds issued by Italy instead of Germany.

The capital asset pricing model (CAPM) is the simplest and best-known approach for discounting risk. Surveys indicate that it is used by almost 75% of financial managers in U.S. corporations.[6]

$$r_e = r_f + \beta \times ERP \tag{7.1}$$

The cost of equity r_e equals the risk-free rate r_f (time-component) plus a stock-specific risk premium where β is a measure of how a stock co-varies with the market, and ERP is the equity risk premium.

How Should Investors Think about Risk When Discounting Cash Flows?

The equity risk premium acts as a reward to counter the losses that occur when economic or geopolitical disaster strikes. Because equities are perpetual securities, they are highly sensitive to long-run risk

---

[6]J.R. Graham and C.R. Harvey, "The Theory and Practice of Corporate Finance: Evidence from the Field," *Journal of Financial Economics* 60 (2001): 187–243.

and the ERP rewards investors for their exposure to risk over the long-run.

Portfolio theory and general investment experience indicate a wonderful property of idiosyncratic risk: It can be diversified away! Individual stocks typically have annual share price volatilities of 25% to 50%, yet the S&P 500 index has only averaged a volatility of 20% per annum over the last century. How can this be when the overwhelming majority of stocks have annual volatility above 20%? Why are individual stocks more volatile than stock markets?

A key insight from portfolio theory is that uncorrelated company-specific risk cancels when an investor holds a large collection of stocks, such as the S&P 500. The remaining risk is systematic and varies with the market. If a company's stock is as risky as the market, then its beta β is one, which means that, on average, a 1% increase or drop in the market leads to a 1% increase or drop in the stock price. Companies that are highly sensitive to macroeconomic developments such as energy stocks or capital equipment manufacturers have betas greater than one while those that are less sensitive to market movements, such as food retailers, have betas less than one. The riskiness of a diversified portfolio of stocks is a function of the market capitalization weighted-average beta of the individual betas and independent of idiosyncratic risks. Fully diversified portfolios maximize return for a given level of risk. This is an extraordinary result and explains why it is foolish not to diversify one's holdings.

To demonstrate this effect, let's assume that we can invest in equal weights of individual stocks, each with a volatility of 40%. If the price movements of all the stocks are perfectly correlated, then the portfolio will always have a volatility of 40% (see Corr=1 in Exhibit 7.2). This would be tantamount to owning a portfolio of oil drillers and calling it a diversified portfolio. Their fortunes will be highly correlated to energy prices, and you would be exposed to a single risk factor.

The volatility of a portfolio of stocks that move independently of each other would drop dramatically as stocks were added to the portfolio. The volatility is halved from 40% to 18% by simply increasing the portfolio

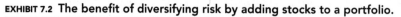

EXHIBIT 7.2 The benefit of diversifying risk by adding stocks to a portfolio.

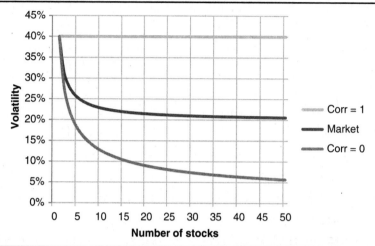

from one to five bets (see Corr=0 in Exhibit 7.2). If it were increased to 10 and then 50 stocks, the volatility would drop to 13% and then 6%. Eventually, the volatility will converge toward zero for a portfolio of uncorrelated bets, thus investors should only expect a risk-free return on investments that are uncorrelated to the market. It would be incorrect for corporate managers to include a premium for idiosyncratic risk in the discount rate when evaluating such an investment.[7] If the diversifiable risk of an investment were compensated with an additional risk premium, then the corporate manager (or investor) could buy the investment, earn the additional premium, and simultaneously diversify with other projects and eliminate the risk. By doing so, he could earn an additional premium without taking on additional risk. This opportunity to earn something for nothing would quickly be exploited and eliminated by investors. The "no arbitrage" principle at work in competitive markets virtually guarantees that such opportunities will not arise, or are short-lived.

The price movements of individual large cap stocks tend to move with the market and co-vary with a correlation of around 25%. The market

---

[7]Within a portfolio, diversification reduces volatility, but only up to a point (and not zero). That is because all stocks share some amount of risk—systematic risk—related to the market as a whole, and this risk cannot be eliminated through diversification.

scenario in Exhibit 7.2 indicates that the volatility of this portfolio converges towards 20% as more stocks are added. Unsurprisingly, the volatility of the S&P 500 has averaged 20% over the long run. Volatility drops from 40% to 21% by holding a portfolio of 30 stocks. Skeptics should heed Mark Twain's advice, "Put all your eggs in one basket—and watch that basket!"

The key takeaway is that the risk premium for *diversifiable risk* is zero. Investors should not expect to be compensated for holding project—or company-specific risk. This point is too often forgotten when evaluating investments. The addition of arbitrary risk premiums by corporate managers or investors to augment hurdle rates might turn value-creating projects into value-destroying projects that get rejected. It can also lead to fallacious forecasts meant to counter unjustifiably high hurdle rates, thus subverting the entire capital allocation exercise. Money is often left on the table in these situations.

HOW LARGE IS THE EQUITY RISK PREMIUM (ERP)?

This is one of the huge questions that keep financial researchers busy. Unfortunately, there is no single number or simple answer. Berk and DeMarzo (2014) reference several sources that indicate an expected range of 3% to 5% over long-term government bonds based on recent historical numbers. They cite the same future equity risk premium range based on fundamental forward-looking approaches using the dividend discount model. In markets experiencing financial repression, it might be safer to assume an ERP towards the 5% end of this range. McKinsey presents arguments and evidence for an ERP of 4.5% to 5.5%.[8] The global authorities on long-run market performance are Professors Dimson, Marsh, and Staunton (DMS) of the London Business School who publish an annual yearbook of global investment returns.[9] Equity risk premiums

---

[8] See Koller, Goedhart, and Wessels (2010).

[9] Elroy Dimson, Paul Marsh, and Mike Staunton, *Credit Suisse Global Investment Returns Yearbook 2017*, Credit Suisse Research Institute, 2017. The original work can be found in Elroy Dimson, Paul Marsh, and Mike Staunton, *Triumph of the Optimists: 101 Years of Global Investment Returns*, Princeton University Press, 2002.

EXHIBIT 7.3 **The worldwide geometric and arithmetic premiums relative to bonds since 1900. Dimson, Marsh, and Staunton.**

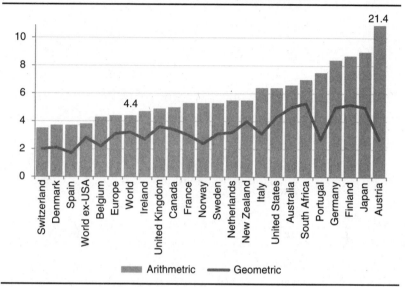

Source: *2017 Credit Suisse Global Investment Returns Yearbook.*

relative to bonds since 1900 for numerous countries and the world are shown in Exhibit 7.3.

The geometric (compound) and arithmetic risk premiums for the United States from 1900 to 2016 are 4.3% and 6.4% relative to bonds. The United States has been an economic success, and reliance on its historical performance suffers from success bias. For example, Argentina and the United States had similar size economies at the turn of the twentieth century, but have diverged significantly since then. There is also survivor bias. What if we considered Russian shares purchased before the Russian revolution or Chinese stocks owned before 1949? Will the United States be as successful in the next century as in the previous one and surprise on the upside? A better estimate of ERP might be the DMS world risk premiums of 3.2% and 4.4% relative to bonds.[10]

---

[10]Our first puzzle should have been whether to measure the ERP versus Treasury bills or bonds. The cleaner method would be the spread over bills since bonds include a duration premium. Because we are interested in discounting cash flows many years forward, we will focus on spread over bonds. Most corporate valuation textbooks follow this convention.

SHOULD I USE THE ARITHMETIC OR GEOMETRIC AVERAGE?

The next riddle to solve is whether the arithmetic or geometric mean should be used in discounting future cash flows. Corporate finance books argue for the use of an arithmetic average for discounting *future* expected cash flows.[11] The compound return is a better description of *historical* performance. Damodaran (2013) argues for the use of geometric returns but suggests that a forward-looking estimate of the ERP is best.

In our experience, which only dates to the 1990s, the use of an ERP of 6% or more when discounting future cash flows leads to disappointment. Most stocks would have looked—and still look—too expensive if an ERP of 6% or more is assumed. Before the financial meltdown began in 2008, we recommended an ERP of 4% to those who calculated the cost of capital by the CAPM method. In today's world of quantitative easing and low real bond yields, we would err toward an ERP of 5%. We'll have more to say when we show the forward-looking ERP calculated for U.S. stocks based on the HOLT approach.

OTHER RISK FACTORS TO CONSIDER

There is no controversy about the benefits of diversification in modern finance. However, the CAPM model has been pilloried by financial researchers who have uncovered numerous anomalies:[12]

- Small caps have historically outperformed large caps. This size anomaly has diminished and many researchers now consider it to be nonexistent.

---

[11] See Berk and DeMarzo (2014) or Brealey, Myers, and Allen (2014). Assume that an asset with a value of 100 has an equal probability of increasing 20% to a value of 120 or decreasing 20% to a value of 80. The most likely result is 100, i.e., $0.5 \times 120 + 0.5 \times 80 = 100$, for an expected return of 0%. The geometric return over many observations would be $100 \times 0.8 \times 1.2 = 96$ for an annual compound return of -2%, i.e., $0.960^{0.5} - 1 = -2\%$. The compound average will always be less than arithmetic average, on the order of $0.5 \times$ variance of returns. In our example, compound return $= 0\% - 0.5 \times 0.20^2 = -2\%$.

[12] See Andrew Ang's excellent book *Asset Management* (2014) for more on these anomalies and the subject of factor risks.

- Value stocks with low price-to-book (P/B) ratios have outperformed growth stocks with high P/B ratios. This value anomaly suggests a value-growth premium.
- Although today's stock price should be independent of past price movements, there is evidence of a momentum effect where stocks that have exhibited relative price outperformance over the past 6 to 12 months tend to do better than those that have underperformed. This momentum anomaly suggests a momentum premium.
- Companies with low beta and low volatility have done relatively better vis-à-vis CAPM predictions than riskier high beta and high volatility stocks. This is called the "low risk anomaly."

The first two effects are factors captured in the Fama-French three-factor model:[13]

$$E(r_i) = r_f + \beta_{i,MKT} \times E(r_m - r_f) + \beta_{i,SMB} \times E(SMB)$$
$$+ \beta_{i,HML} \times E(HML)$$

A company's expected return is related to its sensitivity to market movements (MKT); its sensitivity to the performance spread between small caps and big caps (SMB); and its sensitivity to the spread between value and growth stocks (HML).[14] More recent variations are the Fama-French-Carhart (FFC) factor model, which includes a one-year price momentum factor, and most recently a five-factor model from Fama and French that includes a quality factor.

---

[13] E. F. Fama and K. R. French, "Common Risk Factors in the Returns on Stocks and Bonds," *Journal of Financial Economics* 33(3).

[14] The three-factor model is a special case of the more general arbitrage pricing theory (APT) introduced by Stephen Ross. APT does not specify what the factors are but simply that a stock's return depends on a set of macroeconomic factors and idiosyncratic noise. The expected risk premium for a stock is related to the expected risk premium for each factor multiplied by the stock's sensitivity to each of the factors. For more on the three-factor model, see E. F. Fama and K. R. French, "Size and Book-to-Market in Earnings and Returns," *Journal of Finance* 50 (1995): 131–155. Note that SMB means small minus big stocks and HML means high minus low book-to-market, which is the inverse of P/B.

The low-risk anomaly is one that Warren Buffett has intuitively preached over the years:

> "We simply attempt to be fearful when others are greedy and to be greedy only when others are fearful."

When market indices are dropping, volatility is rising. Risk increases as measured by higher volatility, for example, leaps in the VIX, otherwise known as the "fear index." When risk is high, risk premiums are high and prices are low. In terms of fundamental valuation, these are times of low risk and opportunities to buy! Stated another way, as share prices drop, leverage increases, which necessitates a higher cost of equity and greater expected return.

Surveys have indicated that most corporations rely on CAPM to calculate the cost of capital, and this approach is still recommended by many modern books on finance and corporate valuation. It is simple and relatively reliable if industry betas are used as guides, and future risks are expected to be like recent history. Logic dictates that errors in estimating future cash flows are likely to have a greater impact on valuation than discrepancies in the cost of capital.

Investors require a risk premium for taking on risk, but their concern should be with the risks that they cannot eliminate by diversification. Only systematic risk is rewarded. The key takeaway for corporate managers is that they should not be overly concerned about diversifiable risk, which their shareholders can eliminate in their portfolios. Brealey, Myers, and Allen (2014) put it very well:

> "Don't be fooled by diversifiable risk. Diversifiable risks do not affect asset betas or the cost of capital, but the possibility of bad outcomes should be incorporated in the cash flow forecasts. Also be careful not to offset worries about a project's future performance by adding a fudge factor to the discount rate. Fudge factors don't work, and they may seriously undervalue long-lived projects."

Fudge factors manifest themselves in hurdle rates that are often significantly higher than a market-related cost of capital. Brealey et al. make clear that idiosyncratic risk should be incorporated in cash flow forecasts. Corporate managers should not avoid market risk due to higher perceived idiosyncratic risk; this is a common mistake.

INTRODUCTION TO THE HOLT APPROACH OF ESTIMATING A FIRM'S DISCOUNT RATE

"The development of a forward-looking, or market-derived discount rate, was rooted in a total system approach to valuation. The approach emphasizes the connections among the components of the valuation model. Changes in one component necessarily impact other components."

—Bartley J. Madden[15]

HOLT employs a "total system approach" to measuring and forecasting corporate returns, growth rates, risk, and valuation. Within this system, CFROI is measured as a real rate of return, adjusted for inflation and other distortive effects. This increases comparability across time, countries, industries, and peers, which makes CFROI a more useful performance metric than nominal accounting return figures. Because CFROI is persistent, historical CFROI levels serve as a benchmark against which current and expected operating returns can be compared. Since CFROI is a real rate of return, it is directly comparable to a real cost of capital.

HOLT's total system approach is agnostic: Near-term estimates of consensus earnings are converted to CFROI and linked to empirically derived medium- and long-term CFROI and growth outcomes. The extensive history of HOLT-adjusted data offers an unsurpassed source for measuring the long-term expected yield and growth rate, and for providing meaningful empirical benchmarks. Within this total system approach, the discount rate acts as the calibrating mechanism, tuning current price to empirical CFROI and growth trends. This method results in a self consistent discovery of the prevailing risk appetite.

---

[15] David Holland and Tom Larsen, *Beyond Earnings: A User's Guide to Excess Return Models and the HOLT CFROI® Framework*, John Wiley & Sons 2008.

EXHIBIT 7.4 **The HOLT Pricing Puzzle. Solving for the discount rate that equates future free cash flows to current enterprise value results in a firm-specific clearing rate, or a market-implied cost of capital.**

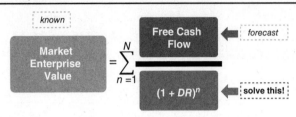

The HOLT discount rate is a practical measure of asset risk. It captures key elements of the capital providers' required return on capital, which are influenced by investors' tax rates, inflation expectations, business risk, and competing yields from alternative securities. It is an after-tax, real, forward-looking, or *expected* rate of return.[16]

HOLT's measure of risk is determined in a three-step process. First, a clearing rate is determined that equates the present value of company-specific future cash flows to current market enterprise value, as shown in the Pricing Puzzle in Exhibit 7.4. A firm's forecast free cash flows are based on HOLT's empirically derived fade algorithms, which are tuned to a company's competitive life cycle position.[17] The discount rate estimation is analogous to a bond's yield-to-maturity calculation where future cash flows are interest and principal payments, and the present value is the bond's price.

Next, a base market rate is derived. The base rate is applicable to all firms for a given period and equals the average clearing rate for the sample. Because the sample for most markets is based on a country or region, the base rate represents the country or region average unlevered cost of capital

---

[16]The HOLT discount rate is after corporate but before investor taxes. However, investors seek a target real return net of personal taxes. The market-implied discount rate is affected by expected inflation and personal tax rates, which can change and impact the discount rate. Taxes matter. Personal tax rates qualify as a long-run risk for investors, e.g., what would the effect on share prices be if capital gains tax rates were raised to the level of income tax rates?

[17]See chapter 8 on the Competitive Life-Cycle and chapter 9 on CFROI fade.

prior to adjustments for size and leverage.[18] The base rate is determined by regressing the company clearing rates for each region against the chief explanatory variables.

The final step is to adjust a firm's cost of capital per the prevailing market sentiment toward leverage and size, which act as risk factors. In concert with the base rate (a), size (S) and leverage (L) characterize a firm's expected asset return:[19]

$$Discount\ rate = a + b_1 L + b_2 ln(S)$$

These steps can be summarized:

- Determine a firm's company-specific clearing rate, i.e., its implied cost of capital.
- Measure the average required cost of capital across all firms in a region, i.e., base *systematic risk.*
- Measure a firm's additional systematic risk exposure to size and credit-worthiness, i.e., leverage.

Leverage is the firm's market leverage and includes off balance sheet items such as capitalized operating leases and net pension liabilities in the total debt tally, which increase a firm's riskiness. A simple application of the Merton model is used to estimate the market value of the debt. Size is the firm's market capitalization. Average coefficients are calculated for each region from the regression.[20]

The HOLT discount rate (DR) is a measure of relative risk, not absolute. It is an agnostic, market-neutral gauge of contemporaneous risk appetite. Within HOLT's total system approach, the HOLT discount rate ensures that 50% of stocks appear attractive and 50% expensive at any time. Company-specific discount rates are updated weekly.

---

[18] HOLT adjusts the base rate so that it reflects the risk associated with the global standard firm (GSF) which has $5 billion in market capitalization as of December 31, 2000, and 25% market leverage. The GSF DR is comparable across all countries.

[19] Firms with no debt (leverage=0) and size $1 billion inherit the intercept term only, which is the basis for the market base rate. It can be readily shifted.

[20] Factor models generally use historical risk factor premiums and historical beta coefficients specific to the company of interest. The HOLT discount rate is forward looking and uses contemporaneous variables.

EXHIBIT 7.5 **The global standard firm (GSF) discount rate for U.S. Industrial and Service companies.**

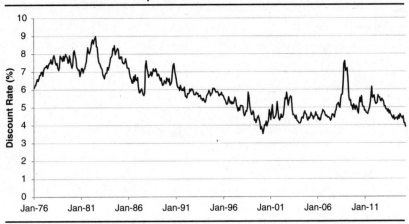

The discount rate time-series for a U.S. firm of standard size and leverage is shown in Exhibit 7.5. We describe its dynamic behavior later in the chapter. Suffice to say it is persistent over short intervals but highly volatile, which is also consistent with other contemporaneous equity risk signals. Risk averse, highly volatile periods are marked by leaps in the discount rate. Note the peak after the Lehman Brothers bankruptcy in September 2008. At the time of writing (April 2015), the U.S. discount is at a level that was only lower during the dot.com bubble.

HOLT routinely tests different risk factors for statistical importance. Most factors can be attributed to one of four groups, including: credit quality, relative price level, asset size level, and price volatility. None of these variables as either stand-alone or in combination have been as parsimonious and effective as the present two-factor model. What are possible explanations for these two factors?

When interest payments are tax deductible, a company can increase its value by taking on debt. Firm risk and the possibility of default increases with leverage, placing equity holders at greater risk. Too much of a good thing can be bad. Market leverage is associated with credit quality and the possibility of financial distress. As market

EXHIBIT 7.6 **Market leverage differential for U.S. Industrial/Service firms.**

capitalization shrinks, leverage increases. Although we would ideally model financial distress in the expected cash flows, this is difficult to accomplish on a systematic basis. The measurement of the market-implied discount rate for a highly risky firm would increase to compensate for the negative value of financial distress that we are unable to capture.

Market leverage is also relevant to quality and growth, which undoubtedly feed into this factor as hidden variables. Firms experiencing strong growth tend to have lower leverage. Stars that are growing with attractive CFROI trade at large price-to-book ratios, which lowers the market leverage relative to book leverage. Value stocks trade at lower price-to-book multiples and are associated with higher leverage, which results in a higher discount rate.[21] The discount rates for low and high leverage U.S. firms are shown in Exhibit 7.6.

Note the striking spread that occurred during the dot-com bubble. Low leverage stocks (growth) traded at a significantly lower market-implied discount rate than high leverage stocks (value). Value investors felt severe pain

---

[21] We are investigating fundamental factors to uncover what might be hidden variables. See our report for theoretical support: D.A. Holland and B.A. Matthews, *An Economic Foundation for Profitability and Its Fade as Quality Risk Factors*. Credit Suisse HOLT, April 2016.

EXHIBIT 7.7 Size differential for U.S. Industrial/Service firms.

relative to day traders in the run-up to the bubble popping but were then rewarded for their fortitude.

Firm size tends to be inversely related to risk. Larger firms typically display less risk than smaller ones, due partially to higher liquidity and quality. We would find a higher representation of high-quality firms and companies trading at premium multiples amongst the large cap universe. These can act as hidden variables in this factor. Results for the United States are shown in Exhibit 7.7 and indicate that the spread has oscillated around zero since 2004. Although the size factor appears diminished for the United States, this is not the case for many of the emerging markets we follow.

Investor preference for large or small cap firms, or for higher or lower levered stocks, waxes and wanes, at times creating periods where the factors are statistically insignificant. Even when these explanatory factors are not significant, insight is gained by comparing the prevailing signal against its historical levels and the levels of other regions.

The dominant historical trend is that the expected risk of larger firms is less than smaller firms, and lower levered firms have generally been less risky than higher levered ones. HOLT's discount rate charts are updated weekly in HOLT Lens for all regions. Routine monitoring can help quantify and track potential risk anomalies.

RELATING THE HOLT DISCOUNT RATE AND FRAMEWORK TO CAPM AND APV

"In practice, users of DCF valuation models often import a CAPM/beta discount rate which is independent of the method used to forecast NCRs. Biases are unrecognized, and the notion of a total valuation system is ignored. In contrast, HOLT's total system approach derives firm-specific discount rates consistent with specified procedures for assigning fade rates for future CFROIs and sustainable growth rates that drive the NCR stream."

—Bartley J. Madden[22]

HOLT's discount rate is a *forward-looking*, expected return on assets, which sidesteps a significant weakness of CAPM. Beta estimates the *historical* covariance between a company and the market index, and uses this measure as a proxy of future covariance. However, as shown in financial studies, historical covariance is not necessarily representative of a stock's future performance relative to its market index.[23] Our experience shows that differences between a stock's historical beta and its market-implied beta underscore that investors often anticipate meaningful changes in how a stock is likely to behave relative to its past. Our research on competitive life-cycle transitions reinforces this view. When investor expectations in these cases are borne out, the value of CAPM is further tarnished.

For many firms, beta is a reasonable predictor of a stock's relative riskiness, but more broadly, beta may expose investors to meaningful error in the determination of current risk since a firm's prospects may have altered considerably or are likely to alter, or statistical noise may have affected the historical estimate of beta. HOLT's method of risk measurement identifies the market's consensus perception of *anticipated* asset risk as opposed to *historical* asset risk. Instead of using historical beta to predict a stock's (forward) relative risk, HOLT imputes an expected return by measuring the

---

[22] Bartley J. Madden, *CFROI Valuation: A Total System Approach to Valuing the Firm,* Butterworth Heinemann (1999).
[23] See Andrew Ang (2014).

average return anticipated across all stocks. Firm-specific adjustments for exposure to the size and leverage factors serve to further refine this estimate.

Another weakness of CAPM is the reliance on a historical average of the ERP. Mr. Market's risk appetite can change suddenly from euphoria to panic. Changes in risk appetite feed directly into the equity risk premium that the market demands. Skittish markets associated with scared investors and greater market volatility demand a higher risk premium. Overheated markets associated with high multiples, potential bubbles, and low volatility revel with a lower risk premium. The HOLT discount rate is forward-looking and market neutral. It "tells it like it is" and acts as a highly useful meter of the market's prevailing risk appetite.

What Type of Discount Rate Is the HOLT Cost of Capital?

The HOLT framework is a self-consistent system. The discount rate is tuned to market prices and cash flow projections, and there is no need to parachute in an exogenous cost of capital which is disconnected from these elements. The HOLT discount rate is relative to the market's present risk state and not absolute. The more accurate the predictions of future expected cash flows, the better the estimate of average expected returns.

Because HOLT includes tax savings from interest paid in gross cash flow, HOLT's discount rate is equivalent to an asset's pre-tax weighted-average cost of capital. HOLT's discount rate represents the required return to all capital providers. If the risk of the tax shield is the same as the risk of the firm, then the cost of capital is equivalent to the unlevered cost of equity.[24]

Please don't get confused. The asset cost of capital is not equal to conventional after-tax WACC, which buries the tax shield in the discount rate.[25] HOLT's discount rate is a weighted-average cost of capital that *excludes* the

---

[24]This condition holds if the firm maintains a target leverage ratio. In other words, the level of debt fluctuates with the firm's market value. In this case, the firm's tax savings would vary with its free cash flows and should be discounted at the same discount rate. Asset beta would be used to calculate the cost of capital from CAPM.

[25]WACC reduces the cost of debt by a factor of (1 − Tax rate) so that the value of the tax shield, whose associated cash flows have been removed from NOPAT, can be estimated. This is achieved via the discount rate.

tax shield term from the cost of debt (the tax shield is valued in the cash flows). Note below that the $(1 - T_c)$ term is missing in HOLT's discount rate:

$$WACC = \frac{D}{EV}(1 - T_C)r_d + \frac{E}{EV}r_e \tag{7.2}$$

$$DR = r_u = \frac{D}{EV}r_d + \frac{E}{EV}r_e \tag{7.3}$$

To keep matters straight, we will denote the HOLT discount rate as DR. When leverage is present and corporate tax exceeds zero, WACC < DR.

Valuation Method Equivalence

To demonstrate that HOLT's discount rate can be related to traditional measures of risk, let's take a simple example where a firm generates a perpetual EBIT of \$100m and net income of \$70m.[26] Earnings are paid out as a dividend, and leverage is constant (Exhibit 7.8).

We can value the constant free cash flow to equity holders of the firm by simply dividing net income by the cost of equity of 10%.

$$Equity\ value = \frac{Net\ income}{r_e} = \frac{\$63m}{0.10} = \$630m$$

When using WACC, the appropriate cash flow is the cash to equity and debt holders (FCFF). FCFF is equivalent to the free cash flow for the unlevered firm. However, FCFF excludes the tax savings associated with debt. To capture the value of this benefit, the discount rate is reduced by $(1 - T_c)$, where T_c is the corporate tax rate. This allows the tax benefit to be valued via the discounting mechanism since tax benefits are not included in cash flow.

$$WACC = \frac{D}{EV}(1 - T_C)r_d + \frac{E}{EV}r_e$$
$$= \frac{200}{830}(1 - 0.30) \times 5\% + \frac{630}{830} \times 10\% = 8.43\%$$

---

[26] For simplicity, we will assume inflation is zero in this example. Thus traditional WACC becomes a real rate of return comparable to HOLT's real discount rate.

EXHIBIT 7.8 The equivalence of valuation for different cost of capital perspectives is demonstrated.

Key Inputs		WACC Valuation		HOLT Method		EQUITY Method	
Cost of debt	5.0%	$DR\ USED = WACC$	8.43%	$DR\ USED = r_U$	8.80%	$DR\ USED = r_e$	10.0%
Cost of equity	10.0%						
Tax rate	30.0%	EBIT	100	EBIT	100	EBIT	100
Debt	200	Interest Expense	10	Interest Expense	10	Interest Expense	10
Market Cap	630	Taxes	27	Tax on EBIT	27	Taxes	27
Market EV	830	Net Income	63	Net Income	63	Net Income	63
		Free Cash Flow to the Firm		**Capital Cash Flows**		**Free Cash Flow to the Firm**	
		Net Income	63	Net Income	63	Net Income	63
		+ Interest Expense	10	+ Interest Expense	10		
		− Tax Shield	3				
		FCFF	70	CCF	73	FCFE	63
		WACC	8.43%	Unlevered Cost of Equity	8.80%	Cost of Equity	10.00%
		Enterprise Value	830	**Enterprise Value**	830	**Enterprise Value**	830

If the firm were unlevered, its net income would be $70m. This is equivalent to the net operating profit after tax (NOPAT) to all capital providers.

$$Enterprise\ value = \frac{\$70m}{0.0843} = \$830m$$

The equity value is simply enterprise value minus debt, which is the same result as valuing the free cash flow to equity providers.

$$Equity\ value = \$830m - \$200m = \$630m$$

The adjusted present value (APV) approach also values the firm to all capital providers based on the unlevered free cash flows. Instead of including the tax shield in the discount rate, tax savings are valued separately as a stream of tax shields. The value of the unlevered operating business (V_U) and the value of the tax shields are separate items.

$$Enterprise\ value = APV = V_U + PV(Interest\ tax\ shields) \qquad (7.4)$$

$$r_u = \frac{D}{EV}r_d + \frac{E}{EV}r_e = \frac{200}{830} \times 5\% + \frac{630}{830} \times 10\% = 8.80\%$$

If the firm were all-equity financed, its cost of equity would be 8.8% and its net income would be $70m. The unlevered value is $796m. The annual tax shield is $3m, which is discounted at the unlevered cost of capital and has a value of $34m.

$$Enterprise\ value = \frac{\$70m}{0.0880} + \frac{\$3m}{0.0880} = \$830m$$

The APV approach yields the same result as the first two methods. It has several advantages:

- The value of the unlevered firm and its tax shields are separate and identifiable items. Operating managers can focus on creating more economic value from their assets while financial managers can identify benign and value-enhancing levels of debt.

- The asset cost of capital is constant. All cash flows are identified and valued on their own merit. If a firm is expected to experience financial distress, it can be modeled in the numerator. Also, if a firm is changing its capital structure, it is easier to use the APV approach. Private equity investments and highly leveraged acquisitions should utilize the APV approach.

It would be incorrect to use the levered cost of equity as the discount rate in the APV approach. It needs to be unlevered since cash flows are unlevered. The risk to equity holders manifests itself as a greater sensitivity in the intrinsic equity value to changes in cash flow or their riskiness. If debt is increased, any variance in the enterprise value will be magnified after subtracting the higher debt level to calculate the equity value. In other words, the equity cash flows are levered.

The asset or unlevered cost of capital is the expected return *all* investors will earn holding the firm's assets, and is related to the costs of equity and debt, and their weighted averages.

$$r_U = \frac{E}{E + D} r_E + \frac{D}{E + D} r_D$$

The beta of an asset is the weighted-average of the betas of its components.

$$\beta_A = \beta_U = \frac{E}{E + D} \beta_E + \frac{D}{E + D} \beta_D$$

Industry asset betas can be used to estimate the levered cost of equity for firms and their projects.[27]

$$\beta_E = \beta_U - \frac{D}{E}(\beta_U - \beta_D) \tag{7.5}$$

The HOLT discount rate most closely resembles the discount rate used in an APV approach. It is equivalent to the *asset* cost of capital. HOLT includes the tax shield in its estimate of total free cash flow since it is a

---

[27] For investment grade companies, the beta for debt is very low and generally assumed to be zero. This is not the case for risky firms with sub-investment grade status. An APV approach is more sensible than the traditional FCF/WACC approach for such risky firms. Industry betas can be found on Professor Damodaran's website, http://pages.stern.nyu.edu/~adamodar/.

real cash benefit that accrues to the firm (the government is subsidizing the use of debt, after all). HOLT's DCF approach is thus an APV method that includes the tax shield in the free cash flow to capital providers. In this example, the free cash flow would include the net income of $63m plus the interest paid of $10m for a total of $73m. The discount rate is the unlevered cost of capital of 8.8% for an enterprise value of $830m. All the valuation approaches yield the same result.

$$Enterprise\ value = \frac{\$73m}{0.088} = \$830m$$

Capital Cash Flows

We need to get highly technical for a moment. The combination of unlevered cash flows and interest tax shields is referred to as capital cash flows (CCF):

$$CCF_i = FCFF_i + Interest\ tax\ shield_i$$

This valuation approach is called the *CCF* or *compressed APV* method,[28] and is the correct technical description for the HOLT valuation approach, which implicitly assumes that tax shields and cash flows have similar risk; that is, if the value of the firm drops, it will reduce its debt level and the interest tax shield will be lower. If a firm maintains constant debt, or has a fixed debt plan, then the tax shields should be discounted at the cost of debt since they have lower risk than the firm's cash flows; that is, they don't fluctuate since they are fixed.

Cost of Capital and Its Relationship to Debt

The theoretical relationship between the various costs of capital and leverage is shown in Exhibit 7.9.[29] *Note that the unlevered cost of equity (r_U) is*

---

[28] S. Kaplan and R. Ruback, "The Valuation of Cash Flow Forecasts: An Empirical Analysis," *Journal of Finance* 50 (1995): 1059–1093; and R. Ruback, "Capital Cash Flows: A Simple Approach to Valuing Risky Cash Flows," *Financial Management* 31 (2002): 85–103.

[29] We are assuming that the riskiness of the firm's cash flows does not change by increasing leverage. In other words, the firm is generating sufficient cash flow to meet all of its obligations. Reality might be

EXHIBIT 7.9 The relationship between the various costs of capital. The asset or unlevered cost of capital is constant and equals the expected cost of debt when leverage approaches 100%. WACC is the after-tax cost of capital and equals the after-tax expected cost of debt when leverage approaches 100%.

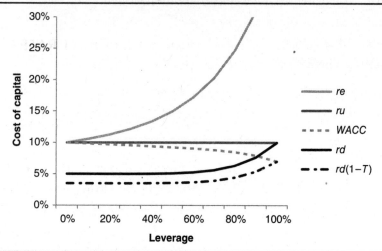

constant for a firm of given asset volatility. The *expected* cost of debt increases until it equals the unlevered cost of equity at 100% leverage. The riskiness of the firm's cash flows hasn't changed, just its owners. The levered cost of equity increases rapidly with increasing leverage. WACC falls since it contains the benefit of the interest tax shield and equals the after-tax *expected* cost of debt at 100% leverage.

We can hear the echo of shaking heads. A common mistake is to assume a firm's marginal cost of debt or yield-to-maturity (YTM) on its debt is the *expected* cost of debt. This assumption is valid for investment grade debt but fails when debt gets riskier. If you buy a junk bond with a 25% yield, do you *expect* a 25% return? The answer is clearly "nein" since there is a high probability of default.

$$r_D = (1 - \textit{Probability of default \%}) \times \textit{YTM}$$

$$+ (\textit{Probability of default \%}) \times \textit{Recovery yield}$$

---

different particularly if suppliers and customers were scared by the higher leverage and played hardball with prices, contracts, and payment schedules. Financial distress increases the sensitivity of the firm's value to market risk, thus necessitating a higher cost of capital.

The *expected* return on debt depends on the probability of default and value that can be recovered in the event of default. If the probability of default is negligible, then r_D equals *YTM*. The cost of capital relationships meets the requirements of Modigliani and Miller.

CHAPTER APPENDIX: DO EQUITY DISCOUNT RATES MEAN REVERT?[30]

"The future ain't what it used to be."

—Yogi Berra

Mean reversion is a natural phenomenon that provides contrarian investors with a powerful rationale for making and justifying their investment choices. Well-behaved macro signals are highly prized but elusive. Investors often ask us if changes in the cost of capital for equity markets can be predicted, and if the likelihood and magnitude of those changes can be quantified. They would like to know if there is an equilibrium or mean-reverting level for the cost of capital and, if so, how quickly does it revert?

Exhibit 7.10 reveals multi-year trends that can be associated with economic developments in the United States and spikes that can be associated with specific market and macroeconomic events. Spikes indicate bouts of market panic and risk aversion. The large spike in late 2008 highlights the widespread panic of the credit crisis. Conversely, the extraordinary risk appetite preceding the dotcom bubble which peaked in 2000, and accompanying the commodity cycle during the mid-2000s, is associated with very low discount rates during these periods.

As a general rule of thumb for developed economies, a discount rate below 5% indicates that investors might be too euphoric and above 7% that investors might be too pessimistic. It is clear from Exhibit 7.10 that the market can remain relatively cheap or expensive for many years at a

---

[30] This section, which was originally published in the *Credit Suisse Global Investment Returns Yearbook 2015*, was written by David Holland, Bryant Matthews, and Pratyasha Rath.

EXHIBIT 7.10 Monthly time-series of the weighted-average real discount rate for U.S. Industrial and Service companies (1976 to present).

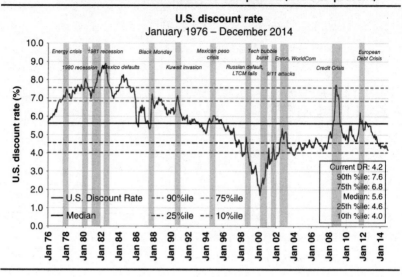

U.S. discount rate
January 1976 – December 2014

time. As John Maynard Keynes is credited saying, "Markets can remain irrational a lot longer than you and I can remain solvent."

What are the latest discount rates for key equity markets?

The market-implied discount rates for key equity markets are calculated on a weekly basis and used by our clients to obtain a relative sense of value and risk appetite in each market. As a general rule, when the discount rate exceeds or falls below its 75th or 25th percentile, the market has entered either pessimistic or optimistic territory. This can help fund managers decide which markets to gain exposure to, and which to avoid.

Market-implied discount rates as of January 2015 are graphed as triangles from lowest to highest in Exhibit 7.11. Indonesia, China, and Switzerland have the lowest discount rates (risk on), while Russia, Argentina, and Italy have the highest (risk off). The blue vertical bars indicate the interquartile range for each country over the past decade. The black line is the 10-year median. These are useful for relative observations. Ten countries are trading in their bottom quartile (risk on), while only Russia is trading in its top quartile (risk off). Fifteen countries out of 23 are at or below their

EXHIBIT 7.11 Market-implied discount rates for Industrial and Service firms in key equity markets.

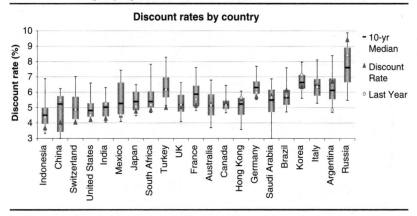

Source: Credit Suisse HOLT as of 10 January 2015.

10-year medians. While this chart gives us an excellent bird's eye view of regional risk appetite, it does not indicate if and how quickly mean reversion occurs.

General Observations about Annual Changes in the U.S. Discount Rate

Let us assume the discount rate is mean-reverting. This suggests a rounded discount rate of 6% for U.S. industrial and service companies. Using this rate today in a discounted cash flow model would show that most U.S. stocks are expensive. Due to the highly auto-correlated nature of the discount rate, the best guess for next month's discount rate is not the mean-reverting level, but rather the most recent observation. Fund managers are paid to be in the market, so using the most recent market-implied discount rate is rational, but care should be taken.

Because of the importance of the discount rate in determining value, it is beneficial to understand whether it is mean-reverting or random walk. If it is mean-reverting, what is the level and rate of mean reversion? (There is no need to pick stocks when you know which way the discount rate is heading.) A great place to start is to understand how the discount rate

EXHIBIT 7.12 Behavior of U.S. discount rate and 12-month changes in DR since 1976.

Percentile	p(10%)	p(25%)	p(50%)	p(75%)	p(90%)
U.S. Discount Rate	4.0%	4.6%	5.7%	6.9%	7.6%
12-m change in DR (all)	−1.1%	−0.6%	0.0%	0.5%	1.0%
12-m change in DR if DR < 5%	−0.9%	−0.4%	0.2%	0.7%	1.3%
12-m change in DR if DR > 7%	−1.7%	−1.0%	−0.1%	0.3%	1.0%

has changed over 12-month periods. This information can be used to construct probability trees comprised of worst, base, and best-case scenarios. Summary statistics since 1976 are shown in Exhibit 7.12.

Since 1976, the median U.S. discount rate has been 5.6% with dramatic swings. The discount rate was below 4.0% for 10% of the time and over 7.6% for 10% of the time. These outer values could be used to quantify best and worst cases, but that would ignore the fact that the best indicator of next month's discount rate is this month's discount rate.

To take advantage of this property, we calculated the 12-month change in discount rate since 1976. The median change is minus ten basis points. This suggests that in one year the discount rate will essentially be the same as today. The discount rate dropped by 110 basis points or more 10% of the time and increased by 100 basis points or more 10% of the time. A general rule of thumb is to use the 10th, 50th, and 90th percentiles for the worst, base, and best cases when constructing probability trees. Thus a change of ±100 basis points in the discount rate over the next 12 months is a perfectly sensible assumption for worst (+100 basis points) and best (−100 basis points) cases.

Is the likely change in the discount rate different when the market is euphoric or highly pessimistic? Exhibit 7.13 shows the 12-month percentage point change when the starting discount rate is less than 5% (euphoric market) and when it is greater than 7% (pessimistic market). Note the asymmetry in changes, particularly for pessimistic markets. Significant drops in discount rate have been more likely for pessimistic markets. This asymmetry suggests that mean reversion might be at work when the discount rate wags its tail.

How Does the Monthly Change in the U.S. Discount Rate Behave?

To better understand the discount rate's behavior, it is helpful to look at the distribution of monthly changes, shown in the Exhibit 7.13 overleaf. The median monthly change is a negligible –1 basis point with a 10th percentile change of –26 basis points or less, and a 90th percentile change of 26 basis points or more. The standard deviation is 24.6 basis points, which annualizes to 85 basis points.

As is so often the case for financial data, the observations indicate more bunching in the center and fatter tails (leptokurtosis) than that predicted by a normal distribution (red line).

In summary, the best guess for next month's discount rate is this month's value with a 10% chance it could drop by 26 basis points or more (best-case scenario for those anticipating an increase in risk appetite) and a 10% chance it could increase by 26 basis points or more (worst-case scenario for those anticipating an increase in risk appetite).

EXHIBIT 7.13 Distribution of one-month changes in the U.S. discount rate since 1976.

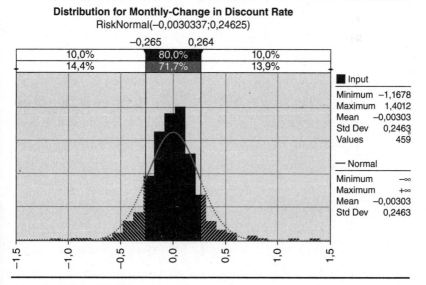

Distribution for Monthly-Change in Discount Rate
RiskNormal(–0,0030337;0,24625)

	–0,265	0,264	
10,0%	80,0%		10,0%
14,4%	71,7%		13,9%

■ Input

Minimum	–1,1678
Maximum	1,4012
Mean	–0,00303
Std Dev	0,2463
Values	459

— Normal

Minimum	–∞
Maximum	+∞
Mean	–0,00303
Std Dev	0,2463

Source: Credit Suisse HOLT data and analysis.

EXHIBIT 7.14 A plot of the U.S. discount rate versus its value in the preceding month since 1976.

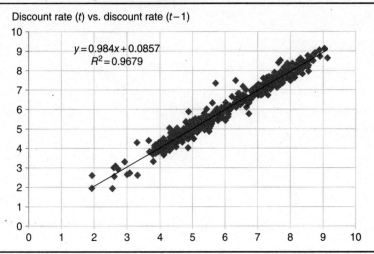

Discount rate (t) vs. discount rate ($t-1$)

$$y = 0.984x + 0.0857$$
$$R^2 = 0.9679$$

Source: Credit Suisse HOLT data and analysis.

Does the Discount Rate Mean-Revert?

We tested for this by plotting the discount rate versus its value one month earlier. Random walk behavior is indicated by a slope of one and mean reversion results in a slope less than one. The results are shown in Exhibit 7.14.

The slope of 0.986 and correlation coefficient of 0.985 give a weak indication of mean reversion (and a strong display of the auto-correlation). The mean-reverting point for this sample is 5.6%, which means that 98.5% of the spread between today's discount rate and the mean-reverting level is expected to remain in one month's time with a standard deviation of 0.25%. If today's discount rate were 4.20%, then next month's most likely value would be 4.22% plus or minus 0.25%. The volatility and noise of 0.25% swamps any possible mean reversion and signal of 0.02%. If anything is clear, it is that noise dominates signal! This makes the discount rate behavior appear random and muddies the identification of a clear mean-reverting level. **For all intents and purposes, the monthly change in discount rate is a random walk process.**

EXHIBIT 7.15 Probabilistic evolution of the April 21, 2014, U.S. discount rate of 4.3% as a function of months forward.

		Months forward					
		1	3	6	12	24	36	60
Cumulative	10%	4.0%	3.8%	3.7%	3.5%	3.3%	3.1%	2.9%
Probability	25%	4.2%	4.1%	4.0%	4.0%	4.0%	4.0%	4.0%
	50%	4.3%	4.4%	4.4%	4.6%	4.8%	5.0%	5.3%
	75%	4.5%	4.7%	4.9%	5.2%	5.6%	6.0%	6.6%
	90%	4.6%	4.9%	5.2%	5.7%	6.4%	6.9%	7.7%

Since HOLT's discount rate is a measure of aggregate risk appetite, and stock price changes are characterized as random walk, it makes sense that HOLT's discount rate approximates a random walk process. The apparent nonexistence of mean reversion should not be dismissed by those whose investment horizons are secular; that is, just because the discount rate seems far too high or low does not mean it will not persist at stretched values. Forward estimates of the discount rate can be generated by incorporating an error term in a simple predictive model. The probability of a given level can be determined, where t is in months, $DR(0)$ is today's discount rate, and $LTDR$ is the long-term discount rate.

$$DR_t = DR_{LT} + 0.985_t \times [DR_0 - DR_{LT}] + e_t$$

The U.S. discount rate on January 10, 2015, was 4.2%, which places it firmly in the lower quartile of historical observations. The above equation can be used to generate a probability table for the evolution of today's discount rate. The top row in Exhibit 7.15 indicates the number of months forward and the left-hand column indicates the cumulative probability of achieving a discount rate at or below the value indicated. Note how the median slowly drifts toward an assumed mean-reverting point of 6% as time rolls on. Looking one month ahead, the most likely U.S. discount rate is 4.2% with a 10% chance of being 3.9% or lower, and a 10% chance of being 4.5% or higher. Looking 12 months ahead, the expected discount rate is 4.5% with a 10% probability of being 3.4% or less (which is deep bull territory), and a 10% probability of being 5.6% or higher (which is tantamount to full mean reversion). The market is a noisy system!

How Do Changes in the Discount Rate Manifest in the Equity Risk Premium?

The market-implied equity risk premium (ERP) can be estimated from the weighted-average discount rate. The results for U.S. industrial and service firms are charted in Exhibit 7.16. Investors are risk averse and demand a premium for the riskiness of equity yields relative to safe "risk-free" yields on government bonds. The median market-implied ERP since 1976 is 4.5%, which is in line with the historical ERP of 4.2% from 1928 to 2012 that Mauboussin and Callahan report, and the 4.5% reported by Dimson, Marsh, and Staunton from 1963 to 2012 (all values are relative to U.S. Treasury bonds).

The market-implied ERP is highly volatile, reflecting the vicissitudes of the market's risk appetite for equities. An ERP of 0% suggests risk-neutral behavior and a value less than 0%, which accompanied the dotcom bubble, implies aggressive risk-seeking behavior. The high level of ERP since the credit crisis has been amplified by depressed yields on risk-free treasuries due to quantitative easing and fears of slower growth. Today's ERP of 4.8% is in line with the median. An increase in the risk-free rate due to an ending of quantitative easing would likely reduce the ERP.

EXHIBIT 7.16 Time series of the market-implied ERP for U.S. Industrial and Service companies.

The Bitter Truth about Mean Reversion

"Predictions are hazardous, especially about the future."

—Danish proverb

Expectations of reversion to the mean drive many investments. Well-behaved macro signals are highly prized but elusive. By assuming the stock market is in aggregate fairly priced, Credit Suisse HOLT determines a market-implied discount rate and then uses this to value individual stocks. For investors who have to be invested in equities, or believe the market is approximately right in the aggregate, it is sensible to take a market-neutral approach and use the most current market-implied discount rate when valuing stocks.

Asset allocators and strategists, however, need to take a view on the attractiveness of markets, and can use market-implied discount rates as a signal. Their job is difficult. Any hints of mean reversion in the market-implied discount rate and ERP are swamped by volatility, suggesting that macro predictions based on imminent mean reversion are precarious at best. For all intents and purposes, monthly changes in the discount rate and ERP are random walk. The market can remain seemingly irrational for long periods, debunking naïve arguments for near-term mean reversion.

We'll end this chapter with advice from Andrew Ang (2014):

> "Active investors spend a lot of effort trying to forecast equity returns. But the consensus view in financial theory is that, while equity risk premiums vary over time, movements are hard to predict. Thus, I advise most investors not to time the market, and this is behind my advice to rebalance back to constant weights or exposures."

Stock-pickers should use a forward-looking, market-neutral discount rate when valuing stocks.

Section III

Value Driver Forecasting

8

THE COMPETITIVE LIFE-CYCLE OF CORPORATE EVOLUTION

"One general law, leading to the advancement of all organic beings, namely, multiply, vary, let the strongest live and the weakest die."

—Charles Darwin, *The Origin of Species*

Elwood: It's 106 miles to Chicago, we got a full tank of gas, half a pack of cigarettes, it's dark, and we're wearing sunglasses.

Jake: Hit it!

—The Blues Brothers

KEY LEARNING POINTS

- A competitive life-cycle framework can help investors think critically about the challenges a firm will confront as it develops and quantify its probability of success.

- Four states of development can be described by profitability and expected growth:
  - Question Mark (low profitability and high growth)
  - Star (high profitability and high growth)
  - Cash Cow (high profitability and low growth)
  - Dog (low profitability and low growth)
- New firms typically start as Question Marks; less than 13% become Stars.
- Cash Cows exhibit the highest profit persistence and lowest CFROI volatility. An elite subgroup of Cash Cows and Stars are unusually persistent. HOLT calls these stocks eCAPs, which is a badge of honor that signifies impressive competitive advantage.
- Dogs have the largest variability in future CFROI. Most Dogs fail to fix their business.
- Companies "exit" at all points. By exit, we mean the corporate entity ceases to exist as a stand-alone enterprise. Only 50% of companies survive as a listed entity for 10 years. Most companies are acquired or merge as they age; about 2% go bankrupt every year. Other firms de-list from their exchange, are privatized, and a few simply cease operations.

INTRODUCTION

In 1886, an illicit scheme was underway in the United States that involved a handful of wholesalers shipping finished goods to merchants who had not ordered them. The wholesalers offered to discount the goods below the cost to the merchant to send them back. Retailers typically bought the goods instead of dealing with the hassle of shipping them back, and then tried to sell them for a profit.

One retailer refused to take possession of a shipment of pocket watches, and so it sat at the local railroad station. Richard Warren Sears, a railway station agent for the Minneapolis & St. Louis Railroad, saw an opportunity to sell the watches to railroad passengers, colleagues, and nearby farmers. Sales were surprisingly vigorous, and he was soon hawking other items. Within six months, he moved to Minneapolis and started the R.W. Sears Watch Company. One year later, he established new headquarters in Chicago. To further enhance sales, he developed a mail-order catalogue to showcase his expanding product list. Sales exploded and the catalogue grew to 500 pages. Within just a few years, Sears had a customer base that exceeded 300,000 people, an enviable number even by today's standards.

At first blush, it might be easy to dismiss the innovation of Sears's early twentieth-century business model. Bear in mind that Sears was perhaps the first businessman to see the full potential of the mail-order catalogue as an appealing medium for consumption. From the comfort of one's home, after a hard day's work, customers could relax and browse the Sears catalogue and discover new items that excited the imagination or search for basic household staples. Items could be price-compared to substitutes without pressure from an aggressive salesman. A little research and the quality of one item could be distinguished from a close substitute.

This revolution in shopping was facilitated by an advanced intercontinental shipping network. Goods previously restricted to a region, or that might have taken a year to deliver, were increasingly accessible. In the United States, the rail system had by then fully spanned the U.S. continent, connecting rural America to major shipping ports. The final component in this shopping revolution was a postal service that conveniently placed purchased goods on one's doorstep.[1] Richard Sears understood the power of this network and shrewdly connected the dots.

Although it is challenging to gather clear insight into the economics of the early Sears business model, we highlight return on equity as indicated by the *Moody's Manual of Investments* for the years 1912–1920 (Exhibit 8.1). ROE hovers close to 17%. This is a high rate of return during this period.

---

[1] The story of Sears is well catalogued (pun intended). A few interesting books include: *Sears Homes of Illinois* by Rosemary Thornton (2010), *Richard Warren Sears, Icon of Inspiration: Fable and Fact about the Founder and Spiritual Genius of Sears, Roebuck & Company* by Frederick Asher (1997), *Catalogues and Counters: A History of Sears, Roebuck and Company* by John E. Jeuck (1950). The Sears website offers a brief history of the firm: http://www.searsarchives.com/history/history1886.htm.

EXHIBIT 8.1 Sears's ROE and prevailing cost of equity, 1912–1920.

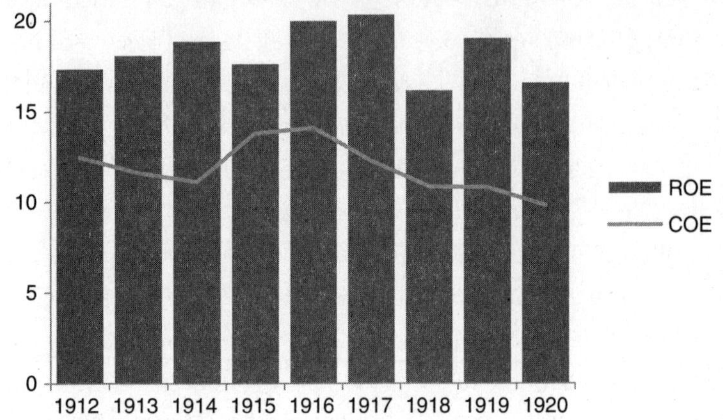

Source: Moody's Investment Manual.

The story of Sears is no less innovative than that of Apple or Tesla. Like Apple with its iPhone and iPad, Sears tapped into a previously unidentified need that brought about a transformation in consumer preference. Sears became a retail juggernaut and the largest firm of its kind in the world. In 1916, the company generated more than $137 million in annual revenue. When adjusted for inflation to 2017 dollar value, this translates into approximately $3 billion. The bulk of sales were through mail-order!

Is there a modern firm that fits this profile? Amazon springs to mind. Like Richard Sears in the century before, Jeff Bezos perceived how recent technological advances could benefit consumers. The explosion in home computer sales offered a gateway to the Internet, and the Internet, in Bezos's mind, was the ultimate portal for shopping.

Amazon sells a vast array of products online. It is not encumbered by brick and mortar. It harnesses the postal service, FedEx, UPS, trucking companies, airlines, railroads, and shipping companies—every viable means of moving goods from one location to customers. Customer orders soar at ever-increasing speed from their fingertips to Amazon's computer servers. The firm has cobbled together a network of merchants and suppliers to rival the number of rivets on railcars used to ship its goods. Amazon's catalogue isn't printed; it is painted by pixels on a monitor. And if printed, it would surely exceed thousands of pages. Amazon is the Sears of today!

Sears is the storyline of start-ups that beat the odds to become a Star and then waltz into old age.[2] High growth and impressive profitability are followed by maturity and decline. Beginning on day one, there is no guarantee of success or survival. Even for firms that become wildly successful, disruption is always just around the corner. The basic theme of innovation/disruption has been played out since the first company was invented, and it is as true of the plucky East India Company and Sears as it will be for Amazon, Google, or Facebook.

No matter how successful or innovative a firm is, competitors will emerge and chip away at profits. It might have seemed incomprehensible in 1915 that a competitor could upend the Sears success story. It would take a bit of time, but by 1950, JC Penney had ousted Sears from its perch as the most profitable large retailer in the United States.

For investors who can't imagine Apple or Amazon losing their place as two of the most profitable firms in the modern era, bear in mind that after topping Sears, JC Penney was itself toppled. The era of massive brick-and-mortar department stores serving as anchors to malls where legions of consumers flocked throughout the week came to a close, but Sears and JC Penney plodded forward with their outmoded business strategy.

Sears paints a vivid picture of a company transitioning through all the key phases of the competitive life-cycle. The pursuit of profit requires continual adaptation and innovation to prosper. Few firms become Stars, and those that survive for any length of time will decline. The best-managed firms (or the luckiest) may prosper for decades, but most will become average. A handful will undergo renewal, experiencing corporate rebirth. Regardless of a firm's current advantages, the cycle of innovation/disruption endures. Competition makes earning profits difficult. Competition spells fade.

---

[2] Sears warned investors in March 2017 that "substantial doubt exists related to the company's ability to continue as a going concern."

WHAT IS FADE?

Corporate profitability does not persist indefinitely. Instead, empirical evidence shows that profitability converges toward the average as a company matures. This tendency is called "reversion to the mean," and it is visible over time, across industries and countries (see Chapter 9).

Fade is the *speed* at which profitability reverts to the mean. There are some impediments to fade. Size matters, for instance. Often, large firms sustain profitability longer than smaller ones. This is certainly due to competitive advantages, of which some result from significant size and scale. Still, the end result appears to be inescapable. There are exceptions, firms that defy gravity and earn outsized profits for long stretches of time, but such events are rare and never permanent.[3] As a general rule for competitive markets, reversion to the mean in profitability is inevitable.

HOLT calls the process of reversion to the mean "fade," and a large body of academic research is available on the topic under its academic heading of "profit persistence." A crucial point is that although fade can happen suddenly (comprehensive disruption) or take decades, profitability tends to decay at a reliable rate. Investors can use knowledge of fade to improve their forecasts and estimates of corporate value.

To begin incorporating fade into forecasts, we need to understand how a firm's profitability is likely to change in future periods. The competitive life-cycle is a useful tool that can help us think more critically about fade.

THE COMPETITIVE LIFE-CYCLE

The hallmark of a well-functioning competitive market is that excess profits are difficult to earn and sustain. When competition is unfettered, there is a strong incentive to maximize profits through innovation. Innovation brings about disruption, and disruption flushes obsolescence and waste from the system. In a nutshell, competition brings about change.

---

[3] Rare events should be modeled as low-probability occurrences. Forecast optimism is a well-known cognitive bias and should be restrained.

EXHIBIT 8.2 A stylized view of the competitive life-cycle.

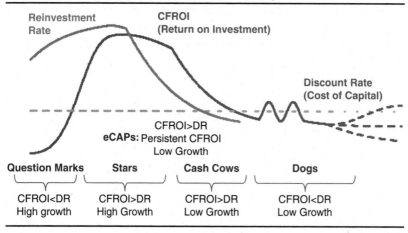

Because competition challenges the status quo, forecasting the level of and the changes in corporate profitability is difficult. The competitive life-cycle is an intuitive framework for thinking about the connection between a firm's track-record of success and its stock price (Exhibit 8.2). It is also helpful for considering where a firm will likely transition next.

The framework describes the pattern of economic return on capital and the rate at which a firm reinvests as it successfully transitions from startup to star. For the most successful firms, the combination of high return on investment and continued growth telegraphs a sizeable opportunity for profit. As rivals enter the market, profitability erodes and declines toward the cost of capital and growth falters, trending toward the average growth rate of the economy. This process can be sudden or take decades.

The competitive life-cycle framework can be divided into four appealing states that describe corporate evolution: early development, star, maturity, and decline.[4] Firms with buoyant growth expectations but low profitability

---

[4]Note that we use the word "state" instead of "stage" to describe life-cycle evolution. Our motivation is to steer clear of any implication that firms evolve linearly and—assuming survival—without fail from one development state to another.

are known as Question Marks. Their aim is to become Stars, which are companies with high growth expectations and attractive profitability. The cash generative Cash Cow phase of the life-cycle occurs when growth diminishes but profitability remains high. Businesses with low growth and poor profitability are Dogs.

For readers interested in gaining a high-level perspective on the phases of the life-cycle, we offer a brief overview below. Readers familiar with the competitive life-cycle may wish to jump straight to the next chapter, which focuses on profit persistence, or fade.

Determining a Firm's Life-Cycle Position

A firm's position in the life-cycle is easily discovered by its CFROI level and *expected* growth rate (Exhibit 8.3). The life-cycle can also be mapped to a matrix with its quadrants being: Question Marks, Stars, Cash Cows, and Dogs. Stocks with above-average expected growth are Question Marks and Stars, and stocks with below-average growth are Dogs and Cash Cows. Highly profitable firms are either Stars or Cash Cows.

Note importantly, that we do not assume firms evolve chronologically through the life-cycle. There is no evidence to support such a claim. Instead, corporations transition from one state to any other. Transition depends upon competitive success or failure, not age.

EXHIBIT 8.3 An adaptation of the Boston Consulting Group product matrix to identify firms by their position in the competitive life-cycle.

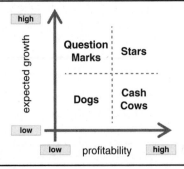

QUESTION MARKS (EARLY LIFE-CYCLE)

An early life-cycle firm is characterized by high innovation. As the firm successfully commercializes its service or product, its incremental return on capital improves. High growth rates and elevated price multiples coupled with low profits are the distinctive plumage that sets these firms apart from those occupying later states. These firms are "Question Marks" because *expectations* for profitability are high but *actual* profitability is low. Will these firms succeed and become Stars?

For highly innovative firms, growth commonly exceeds the return on capital (CFROI). When $g >$ CFROI, external financing is necessary to fund expansion and meet demand for products and services.[5] Start-ups typically use little if any debt, rarely pay dividends, and issue equity to fund growth.

Two examples of early life-cycle companies are Q2 Holdings (QTWO), a U.S. provider of secure cloud-based virtual banking solutions and Applied Genetic Technologies (AGTC), a clinical-stage biotechnology firm that develops gene therapy products to treat patients with eye disorders. Both firms are relative newcomers, have grown rapidly, and—as of December 2016—are still unprofitable. Investor expectations are sky high.

QTWO has a market capitalization of nearly $1 billion. Though annual sales have expanded at a brisk clip, averaging over 30%, revenue only recently passed $100 million. QTWO trades at a price-to-sales (P/S) ratio of 10, an extraordinarily high valuation multiple considering that the average P/S ratio of Star is 2.0! CFROI has been below 0% for the four years ending in 2015, and its HOLT price-to-book ratio exceeds 6 (the average HOLT P/B in the USA is close to 1.5). Investors are ebullient about this firm's prospects.

AGTC has a market capitalization of $296 million versus sales of $2.4 million. Its price-to-sales ratio exceeds 10. CFROI was below 0% each year from 2012 to 2015. Sales doubled in 2015, and the prior three year's sales

---

[5] Sustainable growth rate (SGR) is the rate at which a company can grow without external financing, or rather, from cash from operations. A useful rule of thumb for gauging a firm's growth potential is that CFROI = SGR when a firm is at or near steady state.

growth averaged nearly 70%, so the firm is experiencing an encouraging upswing. Despite this, investors have become increasingly skeptical about AGTC's prospects, and its HOLT P/B ratio has withered from a high of nearly 5.0 June 2014 to a low of 1.5 by December 2016.

A fascinating example of an early life-cycle firm is Sage Therapeutics. As of financial year 2015, Sage had not yet produced a single dollar in revenue but trades at a market capitalization in excess of $1 billion! From its own annual filing, the firm confirms its early life-cycle status: "Given our stage of development, we have **not yet established a commercial organization or distribution capabilities**, nor have we entered into any partnership or co-promotion arrangements with an established pharmaceutical company. We are concentrating our internal efforts on CNS [central nervous system] disorders where we believe we can efficiently commercialize our products, if approved, on our own." Without having earned a single dollar in sales, Sage is the ultimate expression of a start-up firm trading at a lofty multiple. We wish Sage and her investors luck!

These examples underscore our point that investors price stocks based on perceptions of future profit. Expected cash flow, not earnings, is the essential ingredient. But investors in Question Marks are exposed to considerable risk. What happens if sales and profits fail to materialize?

This begs an important question about firm evolution: How often do early life-cycle firms succeed? What percentage of start-ups transition to Stars? More broadly, how often do firms transition between life-cycle states?

Statistically, just one in eight Question Marks becomes a Star.[6] When it happens, shareholder gains can be enormous (one of our colleagues likes to say "the positive convexity on success is massive"). We are pointing out this *potential* for massive gain to be fair-minded, but the reality is that most early life-cycle companies do not become Stars, and so the odds of winning as an investor in this segment of the life-cycle are low.

But don't think that seven out of eight early life-cycle companies fail; instead, most remain in the early life-cycle phase or bypass the quadrant of Stars to land face first on planet Earth.

---

[6]Authors' research findings at Credit Suisse HOLT.

Competition is relentless. For Sage Therapeutics, the odds of being bought at a discount or folding up shop are high unless the firm demonstrates clinical success and commercializes its R&D.

In nascent markets, a firm with early sales leadership can forego current profits in exchange for greater market penetration. The aim is to gain a long-term leadership advantage. Tesla is a prime example. With a market capitalization greater than $34 billion as of December 2016, sales growth has averaged over 100% a year since 2011. Despite this, Tesla has earned a CFROI above its cost of capital just once, in 2013. Reported profit is low, but expectations for profits are high, and so the firm trades at a HOLT P/B multiple above 5.0 (remember, the average is close to 1.5).

But rest assured, Tesla is no longer just a fledgling start-up. With more than $4 billion in revenue in 2015, it has demonstrated that is a viable car maker. Tesla is an interesting case study of a firm choosing not to maximize its current profits so that it can more deeply penetrate and redefine its industry. Tesla is disrupting the status quo.

Examples of early life-cycle firms that became Stars are Google and Facebook. Regeneron Pharmaceuticals—a biotechnology firm that languished for as many as 15 years with subpar operating returns—is a good example that age isn't what determines a company's life-cycle position. NXP Semiconductors, founded in 2006 and which now trades at +$32b in market capitalization, has also made the transition from start-up to Star. LinkedIn is a fine example of a start-up leaping to stardom by joining together its business and social nexus.

Stars

Stars are headline stocks. CFROI is above the cost of capital, and growth is high. Flip on any financial news channel, and chances are that the bulk of discussion will center on these celebrity corporations.

A Star sets the price at which its product or service sells. (Stars are price-setters.) They typically possess budding or bulked-up competitive advantages that help to insulate profitability. Facebook's vast network advantage springs to mind. This network links together over a billion people with shared access to real-time information and idea exchange. Microsoft Office is another example and has reigned supreme in its market segment for nearly two decades.

The allure of healthy profits and stratospheric growth rates motivates firms to enter and compete against the Star. Over time, intense rivalry and marginal customers will cause profitability to drop. Stars may become price takers or surrender pricing power to fuel growth. Amazon is a classic example of a stock with rock-star status that has sacrificed profitability to attain greater market penetration: From 2010 through 2014, EBITDA margins were squeezed by nearly 1.5 percentage points. At the same time, sales grew at a torrid rate of 30% each year. Amazon's high growth rate more than offset the decline in its margins and resulted in record economic profits.

As an industry matures, excess incremental profits from a Star's core offering become increasingly difficult to earn. After all, there are only so many consumers. At some point, profitability peaks and incremental profits decline. The process of decay can be sudden or might take decades. Recall how Netflix and Redbox upended Blockbuster over a relatively short time. In 2000, Blockbuster dominated the video rental industry. It controlled a staggering 75% of U.S. home video rental revenue. CFROI was a hefty 10% and Blockbuster was the envy of its peers. Netflix founder Reed Hastings flew to Dallas, Texas, to see Blockbuster CEO John Antioco to propose a partnership. The pitch was that Blockbuster would promote Netflix within its stores, and Netflix would manage Blockbuster's online strategy. Antioco laughed Hastings out of the room. Blockbuster was the heavyweight champ; there was no way Antioco was going to share the crown with a wannabe start-up.

But here's where things can go wrong for an incumbent firm: When it stops innovating, stops thinking about how it might be disrupted by technologies that will make its customers' lives better, or when it starts harvesting profits at the expense of customer satisfaction and loyalty ($5.00 late fees?!), profits will fall. Within 10 years of the

Hastings/Antioco meeting, Blockbuster went bankrupt while sales soared for Netflix, eventually surpassing Blockbuster's peak revenue and using just half the capital! In time, Netflix would be worth 10× Blockbuster's highest market cap, and little red boxes would become as common as gas stations and ATMs while Blockbuster video stores vanished into memory.

Motorola offers another striking lesson. It dominated mobile phone sales from the first commercially available mobile phone in 1983 (which sold for over $3,000) up to 1997. Motorola's R&D and technology were unrivaled. By the mid-nineties, Motorola appeared unassailable.

Investing heavily in its Iridium network (a secure, private communications satellite system), it failed to anticipate the shift to digital technology. At the same time, its greed for profits exceeded its common sense, and Motorola alienated its client base by refusing to sell its StarTAC phone to carriers who did not source at least three-fourths of their mobile phones from Motorola.

In contrast, Nokia, a relative newcomer in the mobile phone industry, introduced the largest number of new product innovations between 1995 and 1997, aggressively challenging Motorola's market position. There were no strings attached, no ploys to manipulate retailers to offer Nokia phones at the expense of competitive products. In 1998, the seemingly impossible happened: Nokia surpassed Motorola in mobile phone unit sales and by 2002 controlled one-third of the global handset market. This is one call that ended badly for Motorola.

As a final example, consider Eastman Kodak. Kodak's demise took decades to play out. In the early part of the twentieth century, Kodak introduced a commercial camera that revolutionized the photographic industry. Prior to this, photography was an art limited to professionals. The cost of photographic equipment had previously been beyond the reach of the common man. With the introduction of its Brownie camera, however, taking pictures soon became a treasured opportunity to capture rare moments with family and friends. Some experts consider this the most important camera ever manufactured, because it was produced so cheaply that even non-professionals could afford it.[7] Kodak's innovation altered society.

But, where is Kodak today? As early as 1974, Kodak had a rare opportunity to invest in digital technology. An internal engineer named Mark Sasson developed the first digital camera. It was bulky and unwieldy, hardly the camera to replace existing products. Still, the technology offered staggering potential. Sasson had a glimpse of this potential and presented his ideas to Kodak's board. He was told that Kodak would not sell the digital camera, because doing so would eat away at existing Kodak profits derived from its highly profitable film and flash cubes.[8] Kodak failed to focus on how its core business could be disrupted.

Summarizing this Kodak moment, we see that the firm suppressed a wonderful innovation. It did eventually resurface the digital idea, but by then, it was too late, and Kodak lost a valuable opportunity for first-mover advantage and a chance to rejuvenate its business model. What do we see now? Barely twenty years ago (1996), Kodak's market capitalization exceeded $26 billion, but today, Kodak's value has withered below $700 million and the firm is merely a ghost of its former self.[9] It's a picture-perfect example of disruption and the unyielding effect of competition.

Cash Cows

A Cash Cow earns CFROI above or near its cost of capital but typically grows below its sustainable growth rate. Growth rates for sales, assets, earnings, and dividends are approximately the same and generally consistent with the rate of growth in GDP or less. Cash Cows are mature companies that pay dividends and aggressively use debt to minimize taxes and maximize returns to shareholders. Examples of mature Cash Cows include Walmart, Pfizer, Comcast, Intel, Bayer AG, Safran, Tata Motors, and Foot Locker to name a few. These

---

[7] www.brownie-camera.com/5.shtml.
[8] lens.blogs.nytimes.com/2015/08/12/kodaks-first-digital-moment/.
[9] Kodak filed for bankruptcy protection in January of 2012 and emerged out of bankruptcy in 2013 after selling assets and patents, and reorganizing its business.

companies typify maturity: They are large, efficiently scaled, and generally profitable businesses.

A wonderful subgroup of companies can be found within the Star and Cash Cow phases. These firms are known as "eCAPs" within HOLT, and they are best treated as a distinct group. Here's why: These businesses are highly profitable, have low expectations for future growth, and tend to earn durable excess profits. The trait that most distinguishes eCAPs is the persistence of their excess profits. In fact, eCAP is an acronym that stands for **E**mpirical **C**ompetitive **A**dvantage **P**eriod. eCAPs are firms that have demonstrated above-average and enduring profitability.

eCAP firms typically own top-shelf brands for which consumers pay a premium. A successful brand can act as a moat that protects a firm's profits. eCAPs are (or were) Stars that adeptly cultivated brand value. eCAPs, like Stars, are price setters.[10]

Competitive advantages are valuable. According to Professor Bruce Greenwald, the types of competitive advantage are demand, supply, and/or economies of scale.[11] If a firm's market share is stable and profitability is high, it is no doubt enjoying those advantages. When measured by potency, production advantages are the weakest barrier to entry. (A production advantage means a firm can produce its goods or services more efficiently and effectively than its competitors.) The strongest barrier against competitors is when economies of scale are coupled with customer captivity. Enduring examples of eCAPs with scale and strong customer loyalty include the tobacco companies Altria and RJ Reynolds (tobacco users are very reluctant to switch brands, and even when they do, they tend to use another brand from the same company) and Coca-Cola.

In contrast to these examples, the only sustainable competitive advantage in a commodity-based industry is efficiency. The steel industry has been savaged since the credit crisis of 2008. On average, stock prices have fallen 50% from 2007 highs. The average efficiency ratio

---

[10] Due to the uniqueness of their offering, price setters can establish the price at which their product or service sells and maximize expected profits at a lower output level than price takers.

[11] Bruce C. Greenwald and Judd Kahn, *Competition Demystified: A Radically Simplified Approach to Business Strategy*. Penguin Group, 2005.

EXHIBIT 8.4 Asset efficiency.

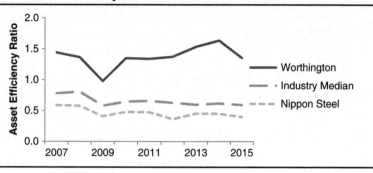

(sales/gross investment) for steel companies is just slightly over 0.60. In contrast, Worthington Industries, a value-added steel processing and metals products firm, demonstrates better asset utilization than peers, and has even managed to lift efficiency a bit higher over the past few years (Exhibit 8.4). In the Steel Works, Blast Furnaces (including Coke Ovens), and Rolling Mills segment, Nippon Steel has seen its market capitalization fall by 60% since the end of 2007, even as asset efficiency degraded and CFROI dropped from 4% to negative 1.5% (Exhibit 8.5). Nucor, a U.S. peer, and the Dutch company Arcelormittal also saw CFROI plummet from above 15% to close to zero by 2009. Worthington management has worked hard to lift CFROI back toward 6%. Nucor's market cap is flat since 2007, and up 25% from the 2009 CFROI low.

EXHIBIT 8.5 Stock price performance.

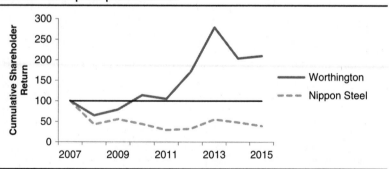

EXHIBIT 8.6 **CFROI drivers and competitive advantage. Image shows that best-in-class firms possess a rare mix of above-average margins and asset efficiency. These firms enjoy both a consumer and production advantage.**

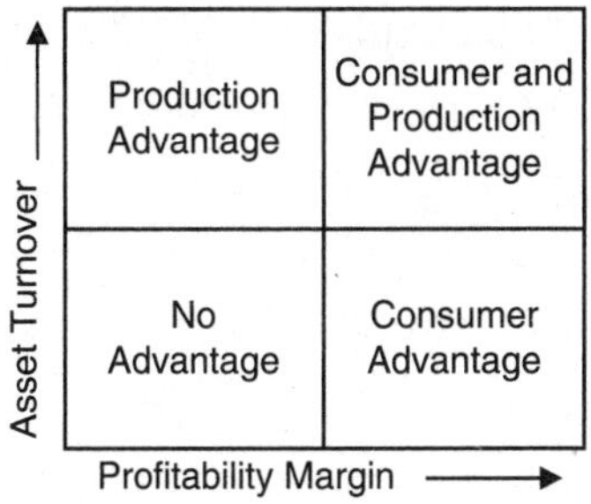

Exhibit 8.6 summarizes the types of advantages firms with superior asset utilization and profitability have.[12] Few firms possess both a consumer and a production advantage, and nearly all of them are eCAPs.

As a firm matures, it may earn a great deal of cash but lack opportunities to grow organically. In modern times, firms have repurchased shares to distribute profits back to shareholders. (Historically, dividends have been treated like ordinary income and taxed at a higher rate than capital gains; stock buybacks have been a tax-efficient form of capital distribution and, more cynically, of boosting EPS and executive bonuses.) Since 2005, for instance, Microsoft has repurchased more than $140 billion in stock versus issuance of $25 billion and taken its debt/equity ratio from 0% to above 50%.

Mature firms are generally price takers. The rate of decay in profitability is twice as high as it is for eCAPs. In industries that lack competitive advantages, the key to survival is efficiency. Only the very best operators can prosper in such industries. Examples include Exxon, the world's most successful integrated oil & gas energy firm, and BHP Billiton, a skilled operator in the highly volatile mining industry. Both firms have seen operating profitability rise from below cost of capital to lofty peaks and fall again as underlying commodity prices tanked.

---

[12] Michael J. Mauboussin and Dan Callahan, "Calculating Return on Invested Capital: How to Determine ROIC and Address Common Issues," 15. Published by Credit Suisse.

Dogs (Turnarounds or Restructuring)

The final phase of the life-cycle describes unprofitable mature firms. As a company evolves, the organization can become increasingly complex, challenging management and its organizational structure in novel ways. Previously innovative firms can become bureaucratic where marginal choices are dictated by subcommittee. These firms have likely lost the plot that meeting customer needs with novel or cost-effective solutions is the key to longevity and prosperity. Such firms reside in the Dogs quadrant where CFROI is below the cost of capital and growth is sputtering. Dividends are a larger portion of capital payments, and can become difficult to sustain as profitability erodes. In many cases, management is reluctant to cut the dividend since that would signal the trouble that the company is in. High debt coupled with a year of poor profitability can ruin the firm if appropriate steps are not taken.

In 2000, Castle A.M., a specialty metals and plastics distributor, vigorously debated cutting its dividend. A decline in profitability brought on by a fall in steel prices placed the firm in a precarious position. It began borrowing debt to fund its common dividend so that management could hoard what remained of its small cash pile to support the firm's daily operating activities. This is not a good position in which to be. An existential crisis loomed and many firms have come to a premature end by failing to adhere to the principles of value creation.

Castle made the brave choice. On May 2, 2001, the board announced a significant cut in the quarterly dividend from 19.5 cents to 12.5 cents. Another cut would soon be necessary, and the fourth quarter dividend was slashed even further to six cents per share. Before the year was over, the dividend was suspended. The 2001 annual report notes the decision of the board as follows:

> "In order to build a stronger equity base, the Company has made significant and sustainable reductions in its operating expense base. These structural changes will increase profitability once the economy begins to recover ... Finally, dividends have been suspended in order

to maintain working capital compliance and minimize any further reduction in stockholder's equity."

The language of the report shows Castle was dangerously close to defaulting on its debt, in which case the firm would likely no longer exist. Management was wrong to allow the firm's financial condition to deteriorate so egregiously, but at the eleventh hour they made the hard, but correct, choice to fix the business and slash the dividend.

Conventional finance theory states that the market reacts poorly to dividend cuts and favorably to its increase. This is termed the "signaling effect," and the implication from a cut is that the firm no longer has favorable growth opportunities. For Castle, the conventional view was wrong. Investors were not hoodwinked by the machinations of corporate managers to fund common dividends with an increasingly onerous debt obligation. Nor were they fooled by the grim outlook for U.S. steel companies in the face of improving international competition and guttering commodity prices.

On the day that the dividend cut was announced, the share price leapt 3.3%. Eliminating the dividend freed the company from an unnecessary and burdensome obligation it could not afford, and signaled that the firm was serious about getting its house in order. Shareholders applauded the changes. Management must never forget that ultimately, rational investors prefer more wealth to less and that destructive policies that focus on window dressing will be penalized by investors. Smart choices will be rewarded.

In this phase, it is vital for managers to stop trying to grow out of trouble. Tough decisions are required. Unsustainable dividends must be cut or eliminated. As cash flow declines, oppressive debt obligations need to be corrected, perhaps by selling assets. Management must jettison unprofitable projects and renew focus on operational excellence. Industry consolidation may be necessary to purge excess capacity and restore profitability.

It is no exaggeration that successfully navigating this phase is a matter of corporate life and death. Few managers succeed in turning an unprofitable Dog around. We found that *30% of turnaround efforts lead to improved*

CFROI, but less than 10% of firms are capable of sustaining the improvement. These are grim odds. Dogs that fail to compete effectively are ultimately ground into the dust of history.

Final Remarks on the Competitive Life-Cycle

"The value of a company selling a trendy product, such as television shopping, depends on the profitability of the product, the product lifecycle, competitive barriers, and the ability of the company to replicate its current success."

—Seth Klarman of Baupost

Corporations evolve in myriad ways. Common traits characterize a firm's position in the competitive life-cycle. These traits can be helpful in understanding many of the key challenges a firm will face in its pursuit of profits.

The working assumption of analysts should be that a firm is more likely to become average than stellar. Some firms are extraordinary and will become Stars, but they are rare. Competition is relentless. Most are already fading toward average. Understanding the pace at which a firm will tend toward average should be the principle focus of consideration. Fade differs by life-cycle position, as we will see in the next chapter. Firms that survive long enough will eventually earn little better than average profitability.

Honeywell is an interesting contrast to the story of Sears. Exhibit 8.7 displays the CFROI for Honeywell since 1950. Markers circles show the life-cycle position of Honeywell over time. In the early 1960s, Honeywell had high growth expectations embedded in its stock price and CFROI accelerated off the 1958 low. Honeywell entered a Question Mark phase as investor excitement gained momentum. Would the firm become a Star with CFROI climbing well-above average coupled with several years of bountiful growth?

Many investors priced the stock with this expectation, but Honeywell disappointed. CFROI peaked in 1964, but by then investors had already

EXHIBIT 8.7 Honeywell International and its different life-cycle states.

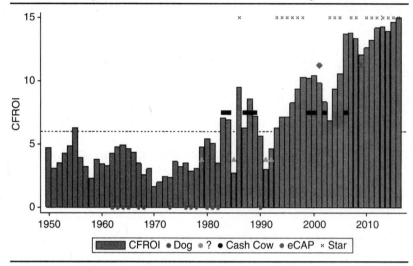

lost confidence and re-priced the stock to remain a Dog for years to come. Dogs typically do not quickly reverse their fortunes. Honeywell floundered until the 1980s, twenty years of lackluster performance. Improving CFROI throughout the seventies and eighties slowly lifted its status from Dog toward Cash Cow. Investors started to wonder: Could management stabilize operational performance above the cost of capital and remain profitable? Were better prospects on the horizon? Was Honeywell destined for the stars? The stock price inched higher.

Honeywell is a wonderful example of a mature company (HON traces its roots back to 1885) that reinvigorated itself.

Regardless of a firm's current life-cycle position, it can transition to any other state. Exhibit 8.8 provides the empirical evidence. The vertical axis represents a firm's starting life-cycle position, and the horizontal axis is its position five years later.

Note how few Question Marks become a Star or eCAP over any five-year horizon (but it does happen). The odds of becoming a Star are roughly 1-in-8. Stars disperse and scatter to every group. eCAPs are resilient, and nearly 80% remain in position or move favorably to Star. Dogs are similarly

EXHIBIT 8.8 Life-cycle transition probabilities. The y-axis is a firm's starting position; the x-axis is its ending position five years later.

	?	Star	eCAP	Cow	Dog	Exit%
?	32%	13%	3%	21%	31%	40%
Star	12%	29%	26%	17%	16%	32%
eCAP	4%	16%	63%	11%	6%	30%
Cash Cow	10%	13%	12%	30%	35%	38%
Dog	13%	7%	2%	18%	59%	39%

Source: Credit Suisse, HOLT. 1990–2015, minimum market capitalization $250m.

EXHIBIT 8.9 Life-cycle transition annualized shareholder return. The y-axis is the firm's starting position, the x-axis is its ending position five years later.

	?	Star	eCAP	Cow	Dog
?	−5%	10%	−7%	−6%	−15%
Star	−9%	6%	55	−10%	−21%
eCAP	−8%	2%	3%	−11%	−19%
Cash Cow	−2%	14%	10%	0%	−10%
Dog	3%	21%	7%	5%	−10%

Source: Credit Suisse, HOLT. 1990–2015, minimum market capitalization $250m.

persistent but with a negative consequence, and few Dogs sustain lasting improvement.

Transitioning from a Dog or Cash Cow to an eCAP or Star is infrequent, but possible. Over any five-year interval, about 7% of Dogs transition to Stars and 2% to eCAPs, giving investors odds of about 1-in-10 of hitting a long ball with such an investment.

But the payoff for correctly anticipating a transition can be enormous (Exhibit 8.9). Stocks that went from Dog to Cash Cow, eCAP, or Star outperformed their benchmark index by an average 9% each year! Using the life-cycle framework to think about a firm's transition possibilities can reap big dividends when investors get it right.

ESSENTIAL FACTS ABOUT THE COMPETITIVE LIFE-CYCLE

The competitive life-cycle framework is a useful tool for thinking in a principled and probabilistic way about a firm's profitability and growth challenges. Key traits describe a firm's life-cycle position and help quantify the odds of its next transition.

- Corporate persistence and its variation differ by life-cycle state.
- Only 1-in-8 (13%) of Question Marks become a Star. eCAPs and Cash Cows (eCAPs are primarily a subgroup of Cash Cows) exhibit the highest persistence and lowest volatility in CFROI compared to other life-cycle states.
- Dogs demonstrate the largest variability in future CFROI. This is intuitive as many of these firms are grappling for survival. Even though future CFROI ranges widely, most Dogs are ultimately unable to fix their businesses.
- Question Marks have the next highest average fade and volatility in future profitability. Cash Cows are in a state of slow profit decline whereas Question Marks are often priced for big success. Still, transitioning to Star is rare.
- Companies "exit" at all points. By exit, we mean the corporate entity ceases to exist *as a stand-alone enterprise*. Just half of companies survive as a listed entity for 10 years. Most companies are acquired or merge as they age; about 2% go bankrupt every year. Other firms de-list from their exchange or are privatized, and a few simply cease operations.

Exhibit 8.10 summarizes key traits of corporations at different life-cycle states.

By count, mature firms make up the largest group of traded stocks, making up roughly 50%. This group includes Dogs (14%), Cash Cows (32%), and close to one-half of eCAPs. Question Marks comprise 26% of traded stocks, followed by Stars at 19% (Exhibit 8.11).

Based on market capitalization, Stars make up an impressive 42% of aggregate size even though they represent 19% of stocks by count. eCAPs represent less than 10% of all firms but make up a sizeable 20% of aggregate market capitalization, more than double their influence by count.

EXHIBIT 8.10 General features of competitive life-cycle states.

State 1	State 2	State 3	State 4	State 5
Start-up / Question Marks	Star	eCAPs	Cash Cow	Dogs
CFROI < r	CFROI > r	CFROI > r	CFROI ~ r	CFROI < r
g > CFROI	g ~ CFROI	g < CFROI	g < CFROI	g < CFROI
P/B high	P/B high	P/B high	P/B high	P/B low
Low			low	
no debt	no or low debt	low - med debt	med-high debt	high debt
no dividend	no or low dividend	high dividend	high dividend	dividend

EXHIBIT 8.11 Percent of publicly traded firms by life-cycle state.

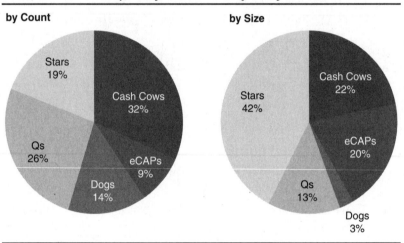

Not surprisingly, Dogs represent a withering 3% of aggregate size. Total market capitalization for all mature firms sums to roughly 45% (eCAPs, Cash Cows, and Dogs). The remaining 13% of aggregate market capitalization are Question Marks.

9

THE PERSISTENCE OF CORPORATE PROFITABILITY

There is no more important proposition in economic theory than that, under competition, the rate of return on investment tends toward equality in all industries.

—George Stigler

KEY LEARNING POINTS

- Fade is the rate at which corporate profitability trends towards the mean.
- Fade is the complement of persistence ($f = 1 - \rho$).
- On average, firms lose 10% of their excess return per year.
- Highly persistent firms fade at half the rate of an average firm. Many of these firms are classified as eCAPs (a subgroup of Stars and Cash Cows).

- Firms in highly cyclical industries often fade at a rate of more than 10% per year.
- By competitive life-cycle state, Cash Cows are the most persistently profitable, while Dogs are the most persistently unprofitable.

LONG-TERM REAL RETURN ON INVESTMENT

We have laid the groundwork for measuring corporate performance and recognizing that metrics have their strengths and weaknesses. Return on equity (ROE) is simple to calculate but susceptible to misrepresentation and manipulation. Return on invested capital (ROIC) is a better measure of profitability but still vulnerable to accounting distortions. CFROI takes more effort to calculate but better reflects a firm's true economic performance.

Superior metrics require considerable attention to maintain because accounting standards are not intended to mirror economic reality; are not globally aligned; are vulnerable to corporate influence; and standards change over time.[1] Professors Lev and Gu demonstrate that accounting measures now have a far lower statistical relationship to market prices than before the information age rocketed to dominance. They state that, "The 1980s saw the emergence and steep rise in the economic role of intangible (intellectual) assets."[2]

We have shown the steps that HOLT takes to ensure that CFROI remains an unrivaled measure of corporate performance. A significant amount of energy is expended each year so that CFROI is measured in an economically consistent manner across companies, sectors, regions,

---

[1] We recall well the rancorous debates over accounting issues such as whether to eliminate pooling-of-interests, treatment of operating leases, executive compensation and stock option expense, and how best to account for pension obligations, among others (remember when options could be back-dated?). An interesting book on this topic is *Called to Account: Financial Frauds that Shaped the Accounting Profession* by Paul M. Clikeman, Professor of Accounting at University of Richmond, published by Rutledge, 2013.

[2] Baruch Lev and Feng Gu, *The End of Accounting and the Path Forward for Investors and Managers.* John Wiley & Sons, 2016.

and time. Given a reliable metric, we now turn to the topic of fade, or reversion to the mean, in corporate profitability.

THE LONG-TERM REAL REQUIRED RATE OF RETURN

Exhibit 9.1 shows the median and size-weighted annual CFROI for global industrial and service firms from 1950 to 2015. Firms outside the United States are generally not available in the HOLT database before 1985 (aside from ADRs), so the history of CFROI from 1950 to 1985 is predominantly that of corporate United States, but increasingly global thereafter.

The median CFROI across all years is 6%. This is considered by HOLT to be the long-term mean-reverting CFROI level. Unsurprisingly, this level coincides with the long-term real rate of return earned by equities as indicated by Dimson, Marsh, and Staunton in their exhaustive study (see Exhibit 7.1 in Chapter 7) on long-run rates of return.

Global aggregate CFROI, shown as bars, is asset-weighted and represents the average return to the largest firms. Note the lower

EXHIBIT 9.1 Size-weighted CFROI for Global & USA Industrial / Service Firms, $250 million minimum market cap 1950–2015.

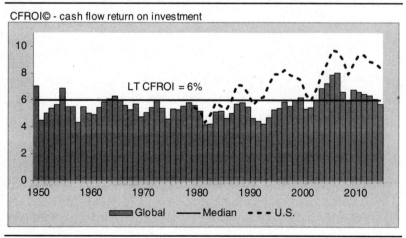

Source: Credit Suisse HOLT.

return to large global firms during the years 1965 to 1995. This pattern reverses thereafter, and over the most recent twenty years, size is associated with earning and sustaining profits. The shift away from asset-intensive manufacturing in many developed economies and the attractive profitability of asset-light firms (companies with significant intangibles), such as Microsoft, Oracle, Apple, Google, Johnson & Johnson, Pfizer, and Amgen, help to explain the boost in CFROI.

Beginning in 2003, CFROI significantly improved above its long-term level, peaking at 8.2% in 2007 for global equities and 10% for the United States. This spike in CFROI captures the feverish pace of economic activity and animal spirits that pushed the global economy to its frothy peak right before the credit crisis of 2008. Since then, global CFROI has declined, supporting the tendency to revert to the mean. CFROI for U.S. companies remains elevated.

Hidden behind the data plot in Exhibit 9.1 is an interesting dynamic: Every year, there is a constant reshuffling of winners and losers within each industry as veterans and new entrants compete for profits. This shuffling makes it unclear how the average rate of return evolves for *aging* firms since we only see the average. This distinction is important because we now wish to understand how CFROI tends to behave as a company matures. Is it random walk, improving, or deteriorating in an unpredictable fashion depending on the fortunes of the company? Or, is there a general pattern that lends itself to prediction?

In Exhibit 9.2, we created two portfolios based on a company's CFROI rank and placed the top 20% of firms in the highest CFROI portfolio and the bottom 20% in the lowest CFROI portfolio. Beginning in 1980, we tracked the median CFROI of each portfolio over time. These portfolios represent aging firms. For both profitable and unprofitable groups, CFROI converges toward 6%. This process is known as "reversion to the mean."

This phenomenon isn't limited to just 1980. We could pick any year, and the results would be similar: Firms with high CFROI *tend* to earn

EXHIBIT 9.2 Median CFROI of High and Low CFROI portfolios over time.

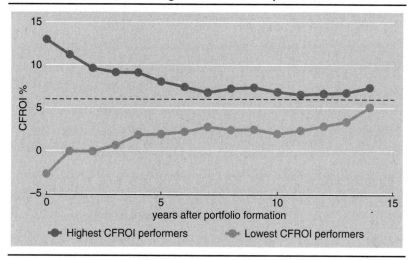

Source: Credit Suisse HOLT. Global non-financials, $250 million minimum market capitalization. CFROI ranked and grouped in 1980, subsequent performance is median CFROI by group.

lower future CFROI, and firms with low CFROI *tend* to earn higher future CFROI. Regardless of starting profitability, CFROI *tends* to converge toward 6% over time.

It is true that there are always exceptions. These exceptions are what make predicting corporate performance exciting. Some companies like LVMH, the luxury goods powerhouse, display unusual profit persistence. But enduring profit makers make up less than 5% of all publicly traded firms. Most firms revert to the mean.

Is mean-reversion in CFROI a result of random behavior (in any given year, a few firms win and then next year's winners are shuffled again), or is this process explained by something other than chance? Exhibit 9.2 does not provide proof of mean-reversion; it only hints at its possible existence in the data. In the chapter on the competitive life-cycle, we stressed that companies can transition from their current state to any life-cycle state over time. Is there a detectable pattern that can help us make better predictions? We require convincing evidence.

MEASURING PERSISTENCE

Transition Matrices as a Means of Quantifying Fade

An intuitive approach for testing persistence in corporate profitability is to examine the transition rates of firms moving from one performance category to another over some time interval. Let's develop a simple test and place companies into quartiles (four rank-based groups) based on their starting CFROI level. In which quartile are firms after four years?

If firms do not move between quartiles, then persistence is high: Companies that make money will continue to make money. Conversely, if firms frequently change quartiles, then persistence is low: Companies that make money, as well as companies that don't, will become average performers with age.[3]

In Exhibit 9.3, CFROI quartiles are determined by a firm's sector-relative rank. The vertical axis (y-axis) shows the starting CFROI quartile, and a firm's ending quartile (after four years) is located by moving horizontally. The highest CFROI companies are in Q4, which represents the top 25% of CFROI earners from each sector. If corporate performance is random, then regardless of a firm's CFROI rank at the start, it will wander into any of the four quartiles with a probability of 25%.

What is the relative rank after four years for the lowest quartile (Q1)? 56% of Q1 firms remained in the bottom quartile after four years, more

EXHIBIT 9.3 Transition Probability % Global Industrial/Service Firms, 1985–2013.

		Q1: --	Q2: -	Q3: +	Q4: ++
quartile, *t*+0	Q1: --	**56**	27	11	6
	Q2: -	28	**40**	23	8
	Q3: +	13	28	**39**	20
	Q4: ++	9	12	28	**51**
		-------------- quartile, *t*+4 --------------			

Source: Credit Suisse HOLT. Global non-financials, $250 million minimum market capitalization.

---

[3] This does not necessarily imply mean-reversion, where return on investment tends to converge toward an average level. Instead, in the case where return on investment is random, a firm's performance over time equals the average. The property of mean-reversion is met under certain conditions, defined hereafter.

than twice the amount expected if CFROI was random. On the other hand, 44% (100% − 56%) of these firms transitioned into higher quartiles. We would have expected 75% of these firms to have transitioned into higher performance quartiles if CFROI was random. Only 17% of bottom quartile firms transition to being above average performers over four years.

Firms with high CFROI behaved similarly, though transitions occurred with slightly greater frequency: 51% remained in the highest CFROI quartile after four years; 49% fell in relative rank. This higher probability of transition may hint that competition between profitable businesses is more aggressive than it is for unprofitable firms. In the previous chapter, we saw that Dogs (firms with CFROI and growth below average) remain stuck in the mud. Note that 21% of top quartile performers fall to below average over four years.

The transition matrix offers further evidence that CFROI is persistent and not random.

Industry Persistence: Does Industry Matter?

"A truly great business must have an enduring 'moat' that protects excellent returns on invested capital. The dynamics of capitalism guarantee that competitors will repeatedly assault any business 'castle' that is earning high returns … Our criterion of 'enduring' causes us to rule out companies in industries prone to rapid and continuous change. Though capitalism's 'creative destruction' is highly beneficial for society, it precludes investment certainty. A moat that must be continuously rebuilt will eventually be no moat at all."[4]

—Warren Buffett

Return on capital and its persistence vary by industry. For example, the median CFROI for Food, Beverage, and Tobacco (FBT) from 1985 to 2015 was 7.6% compared with a median CFROI of 4.2% for Energy. The

---

[4]www.businessinsider.com/warren-buffetts-4-investing-principles-2016-1.

average firm in FBT earns a CFROI equal to that of a top-tier Energy company. Although return on capital for FBT is stable, CFROI for Energy is cyclical. FBT is a defensive industry and its companies have considerable competitive advantages and economic moats. The time-series charts in Exhibits 9.4 and 9.5 show that meaningful differences can exist in both the level and variation of CFROI at the industry level.

How often do firms within an industry transition between performance quartiles? Exhibit 9.6 shows that there is a 70% probability of a top-performing FBT firm remaining in the top quartile after four years, and only a 9% chance (3% + 6% = 9%) of it transitioning to a below-average company. In contrast, Energy firms, which have significantly higher variation in CFROI, show lower persistence (Exhibit 9.6). Only 41% of top-performing Energy firms remain in the top quartile of industry performance after four years.

The high rate of persistence for FBT companies hints at strong barriers to entry that keep new competitors out and existing competitors locked in place. Energy's lower persistence suggests greater dynamism, intense

EXHIBIT 9.4 Time-series of CFROI for global Food, Beverage, and Tobacco, $250 million minimum market capitalization, 1985–2015.

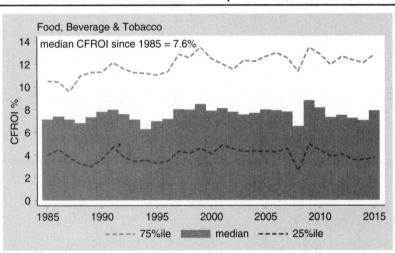

Source: Credit Suisse HOLT.

EXHIBIT 9.5 Time-series of CFROI for global Energy, $250 million minimum market capitalization, 1985–2015.

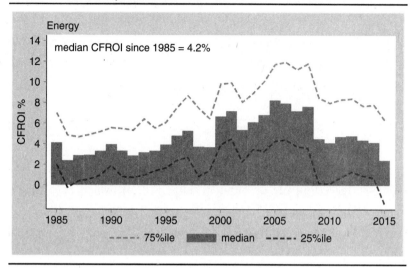

Source: Credit Suisse HOLT.

EXHIBIT 9.6 CFROI transition matrix for Food, Beverage, and Tobacco.

		Q1: −−	Q2: −	Q3: +	Q4: ++
quartile, *t*+0	Q1: −−	73	20	6	2
	Q2: −	23	47	24	5
	Q3: +	8	24	45	23
	Q4: ++	3	6	21	70

-------------- quartile, *t*+4 --------------

Source: Credit Suisse HOLT, min size $250m, 1985–2015.

EXHIBIT 9.7 CFROI transition matrix for energy.

		Q1: −−	Q2: −	Q3: +	Q4: ++
quartile, *t*+0	Q1: −−	43	29	17	11
	Q2: −	22	36	30	12
	Q3: +	12	29	37	22
	Q4: ++	11	20	28	41

-------------- quartile, *t*+4 --------------

Source: Credit Suisse HOLT, min size $250m, 1985–2015.

competition, and significantly lower switching costs to customers for choosing a different brand. In commodity sectors, it is crucial to be the best operator and to possess production advantages. For most people, the nearest gas station will do just fine, but switching between consumer brands is rare, for example, Coca Cola versus Pepsi, and even when it happens, consumers tend to quickly revert to their preferred brand.

Did you notice that all the transition matrices indicate that companies with above-average CFROI are more likely to earn lower *future* CFROI? In Exhibit 9.3, firms with above-average CFROI in Q3 had a 41% probability of transitioning to a lower quartile after four years versus a 20% probability of becoming a top quartile performer. Even highly persistent Q3 firms in the FBT sector show a 32% probability of declining to a lower quartile after four years as compared to a 23% probability of improving relative performance. What you are seeing is reversion to the mean in corporate profitability, not random chance. Corporate profitability is sticky (persistent) but tends to deteriorate for above-average companies.

Reversion to the Mean

The empirical evidence is mounting that corporate profitability reverts to the mean. High levels of profitability are more likely to fall toward the mean than increase and vice versa. Reversion to the mean does not require a cause for investors to put it to work as a predictive tool. It is a statistical fact of life and can be utilized to make better forecasts.

In econometrics, the workhorse empirical model of mean reversion analysis is the first-order autoregressive model, denoted AR(1). An autoregressive process is one in which the current value of a variable, x, depends upon the values that the variable took in previous periods, plus an error term:

$$x_t = \alpha + \beta x_{t-1} + e_t$$

where e_t is a random error term with an expected value of zero, and α is a constant equal to the intercept. An AR(1) model relies on serial correlation.

Correlation measures the strength of the relationship between two variables. It is a scaled measure bounded between -1 and $+1$, which makes it easy to interpret. When association is perfect and positive, correlation is $+1.0$. When the association is perfect and negative, correlation is -1.0. An example of a perfect positive relationship is if students retained their same relative rank over two consecutive terms. A negative correlation would see the rank reverse with the best students becoming the worst. If the best students retain top positions over many terms, then the ranking is highly *persistent*. Reversion to the mean occurs for any linear process where correlation is between 0 and 1.[5] We want to stress that correlation does not imply causation.

Substituting CFROI into equation (9.1) produces:

$$CFROI_{i,t} = \alpha_i + \beta \times CFROI_{i,t-1} + e_t \qquad (9.1)$$

Equation (9.1) states that the CFROI of company i at time t is a function of its most recent CFROI at time $t - 1$ plus a random error term, e, with expected value of zero. The intercept is related to the mean, which is the level of mean reversion.[6]

Exhibit 9.8 shows the correlation (rho or ρ) between 2011 and 2012 CFROI for Industrial and Service firms in the United States (we could have picked any year; the results will be similar). The correlation equals 0.90, suggesting a very strong and positive relationship, but also indicating reversion to the mean. Notice that the slope β from Equation 9.1 is 0.88. This value is derived from linear regression and is almost identical to the correlation because annual CFROI variance is stable.

Hereafter, we refer to beta as the CFROI **persistence factor**, and denote it as ρ.

For CFROI, the persistence factor should be interpreted in the same way as correlation. A value of 1.0 indicates perfect persistence, $\rho=0$ describes randomness, and ρ between 0 and 1 indicates reversion to the mean.[7] Note that ρ should not exceed $+1$ or fall below -1. A persistence factor of -1 is generally unrealistic, and would indicate a situation where CFROI cycles above and below its mean.

---

[5] It will also occur when correlation is between -1.0 and 0, but every other time period will oscillate between positive and negative values. We will exclude this possibility for simplicity.

[6] For the AR(1) equation, the mean equals $\bar{x} = \alpha/(1 - \beta)$.

[7] To be precise, a slope of 1.0 would be an indication of a random walk process where your best guess is the last observation and then it wanders with a random error term.

EXHIBIT 9.8 Scatter plot of CFROI persistence for U.S. Industrial and Service Firms.

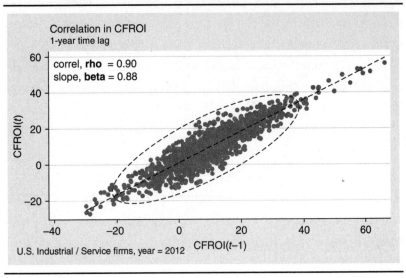

Source: Credit Suisse HOLT.

An interesting property of an AR(1) model is that the rate of decay, or $(1 - \rho)$, is geometric and compounds over time.[8] Thus, a firm with a one year persistence factor of 0.9 will likely retain 90% of its previous excess return. After two years, 81% of the excess return remains $(0.9^2 = 0.81)$. **The complement of persistence, $(1 - \rho)$, is the fade rate, f, or the speed of reversion to the mean.**

Competitive Advantage and Its Effect on Fade

How does fade affect corporate profitability? A stylized example of a firm with a starting CFROI of 20% and different levels of profit persistence is shown in Exhibit 9.9. The average CFROI is assumed to be the long-term global average of 6%. A high fade rate indicates faster reversion to the mean; a low fade rate indicates slower reversion.

As persistence rises, the fade rate decreases, which extends a firm's period of competitive advantage. A 90% persistence rate means that a

---

[8] In discrete space, decay is geometric; in continuous space, it is exponential.

EXHIBIT 9.9 Stylized example of excess return half-life.

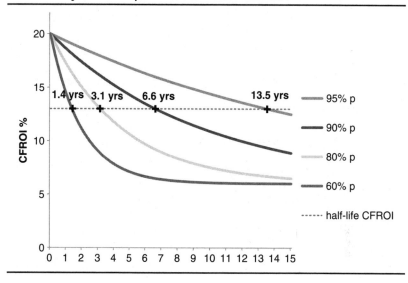

firm will likely lose 10% (1 − ρ) of its excess profitability each year as CFROI converges toward the long-term average. After 10 years, a firm enjoying 90% persistence will still earn excess profits. On the other hand, a firm with profit persistence of 60% will shed 40% of excess profit each year, and will earn little more than a CFROI of 6% after just four years.

Fade is a powerful and intuitive way to understand if a firm possesses a competitive advantage and for how long it is likely to persist. Scientists refer to *half-life* to describe exponentially decaying phenomena. For instance, a piece of uranium 238 will be only half uranium after 4.5 billion years of radioactive decay, the approximate age of the earth. During that time, the uranium atoms turn into atoms of other materials, such as thorium. If you wish to know how long it will take for a highly profitable firm to lose half of its excess return when its fade rate is 10%, then use this formula:

$$T_{0.5} = \frac{-0.693}{ln(\rho)}$$

EXHIBIT 9.10 Empirical fade in CFROI.

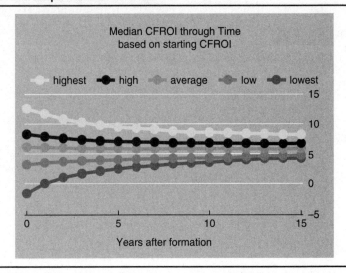

Source: Credit Suisse HOLT.

where $T_{0.5}$ is the half-life in years, and ρ is the persistence rate.[9] For the profitable firm with a 90% persistence factor, it will take 6.6 years to lose half of its excess profitability.

Highly persistent companies with strong competitive advantages tend to fade at or below 5% per year, while a typical firm fades at approximately 10%. Firms in cyclical industries like Energy and Materials might fade at 20% or more per year.

Exhibit 9.10 helps to visualize the tendency of corporate performance to revert to the mean. The data are not restricted to a single starting year, as in the scatter plot of Exhibit 9.8 but rather represent the average rate of decay in CFROI for portfolios of high, medium, and low CFROI firms over time.

The transition matrices show that CFROI migration is not a random process. Our autoregressive test confirms this point. While chance plays

---

[9]Exponential decay is a continuous process which can be described by the equation $(x(t) - \bar{x}) = (x(0) - \bar{x})e^{-ft}$. The first term is the spread at time t and the second is the beginning spread. The natural log of 0.5 is -0.693. We will compound in discrete space. In exponential space, $T_{0.5} = -\dfrac{\ln(0.5)}{f}$

an undeniable role, the steady march of corporate profitability toward 6% over the long haul highlights the challenge of maintaining excess profits and stresses how urgent it is that poor performers improve.

Industry CFROI Persistence

Exhibit 9.11 shows median annual CFROI persistence rates by industry group and provides further evidence that profitability mean-reverts, and that the rate of persistence can vary significantly by industry.

Firms in the industry groups, Household & Personal Products, Food Beverage & Tobacco, and Consumer Services show the strongest average annual persistence, whereas firms in the industry groups Semiconductors, Energy, and Diversified Financial Services reveal the least persistence. Lower persistence (higher fade) is an indication of a lack of pricing power and competitive barriers.

EXHIBIT 9.11 Median annual CFROI persistence by U.S. Industry Groups. Global Industrial/Service firms, $250 million minimum market capitalization, 1985–2015.

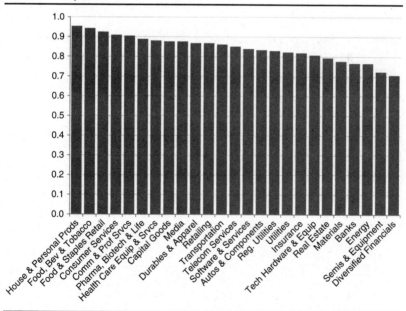

Source: Credit Suisse HOLT.

Does CFROI Persistence Vary over Time?

As a final consideration, let's explore whether CFROI persistence varies over time. Our research indicates that highly persistent industries will likely remain highly persistent despite economic ups and downs.

For instance, global firms selling Food, Beverage, and Tobacco products show strong correlation between annual CFROI. Except during a few periods, average correlation since 1985 has been 0.94 (Exhibit 9.12).

On the other hand, the returns from Energy companies are vulnerable to many different forces, such as volatile commodity prices, abrupt changes in what people want to buy, how the industry is regulated, geopolitical and resource luck, government policy in different countries, and even environmental disaster (BP's Gulf oil spill). Firms subject to these forces are price takers, not price setters, and CFROI persistence will be low. The only way such a company can enjoy a competitive advantage is to be more efficient than the rest of the industry. Look for the most efficient operators in commodity industries and where competitors have limited consumer advantages.

EXHIBIT 9.12 Annual CFROI correlation for Food, Beverage, & Tobacco versus Energy, $250 million minimum market capitalization, 1985–2015.

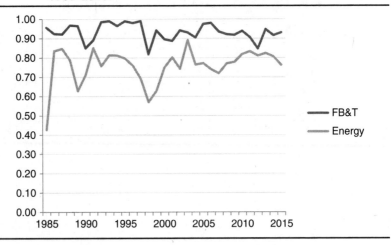

Source: Credit Suisse HOLT.

The waxing and waning of annual CFROI persistence indicates that companies are subject to exogenous (external) forces, the most notable being the overall economic cycle. The HOLT framework treats such shocks as temporary. By ignoring the temporary boosts and declines in annual CFROI persistence, HOLT effectively "looks through" the transient shock. The implication is that the shock is unpredictable. Can the shock be anticipated? Probably not. On the other hand, if you have a strong view, and expect—for instance for the Energy sector—that CFROI will be severely depressed for an extended period, the speed of profit mean-reversion can be dampened (that is, unprofitable CFROI can be forecast to persist for a longer period). This type of thoughtful deliberation is superior to one that slaps a multiple on a terminal forecast.

PUTTING IT ALL TOGETHER: DEVELOPING A MEAN-REVERTING FORECAST MODEL

HOLT measures persistence as the rate of decay in excess profitability (or the difference between current profitability and the long-term mean of 6%). We assume that all firms converge over a forecast horizon toward 6% at a pace that depends on their specific rate of persistence.

By subtracting the mean CFROI from both sides, we rewrite equation 9.1 as:

$$x_{t+1} = \rho(x_t - \bar{x}) + \bar{x} + \varepsilon_{t+1} \qquad (9.2)$$

where:

x_t	=	current CFROI
$\bar{x}$	=	mean-reverting level or long-run industry average CFROI
ρ	=	persistence factor
ε_{t+1}	=	random shock to CFROI at $t+1$

The term ρ equals the persistence factor and $\bar{x}$ equals the mean-reverting or average value of x.

EXHIBIT 9.13 Annual CFROI persistence and the long-term CFROI by Industry Group. Global industrial/service firms, $250 million minimum market capitalization, 1985–2015.

Industry Group	ρ	LT CFROI %	CFROI ($t+0$) %	E[CFROI ($t+4$)] %
House & Personal Prods	0.95	11.6	20	18.5
Food, Bev & Tobacco	0.94	7.9	20	17.5
Food & Staples Retail	0.92	8.0	20	16.8
Consumer Services	0.91	7.6	20	16.1
Comm & Prof Srvcs	0.90	10.5	20	16.9
Pharma, Biotech & Life	0.89	6.4	20	14.9
Health Care Equip & Srvc	0.88	10.1	20	16.0
Capital Goods	0.88	6.3	20	14.4
Media	0.88	9.8	20	15.8
Durables & Apparel	0.87	7.7	20	14.7
Retailing	0.87	8.5	20	15.0
Transportation	0.86	5.0	20	13.3
Telecom Services	0.85	5.6	20	13.2
Software & Services	0.84	10.6	20	15.3
Autos & Components	0.83	5.1	20	12.3
Reg. Utilities	0.83	2.9	20	11.0
Utilities	0.82	4.0	20	11.3
Insurance	0.82	7.7	20	13.3
Tech Hardware & Equip	0.81	6.6	20	12.3
Real Estate	0.79	4.7	20	10.8
Materials	0.78	4.6	20	10.2
Banks	0.77	9.0	20	12.8
Energy	0.77	4.9	20	10.1
Semis & Equipment	0.72	5.9	20	9.8
Diversified Financials	0.71	8.8	20	11.6

Source: Credit Suisse HOLT.

CFROI persistence factors are shown in Exhibit 9.13 by industry group for global equities. We added an additional category for regulated Utilities. Industries are sorted by their persistence from strongest to weakest. Persistence is measured over a four-year period, which allows us to forecast for five years given a forward $t+1$ estimate. The long-term historical median CFROI for each industry is shown.

Given the industry persistence rates and mean-reverting CFROI levels shown in Exhibit 9.13, we are now ready to apply the concept of mean reversion to forecasts of corporate profitability. We will assume that the expected CFROI for each industry will equal the historical average.[10]

---

[10] In the HOLT framework, it is conservatively assumed that all companies fade to 6% in the long run and not to their industry averages.

First, let's consider the case of a Household & Personal Products (HPP) firm. The median CFROI in this industry is 11.6%. Annual CFROI persistence is quite strong at 0.95, which translates into an annual fade rate of 5%. A firm in HPP that earns a CFROI of 20% is expected to fade over the next four years in the following manner:

$$CFROI_{t+n} = \rho^n(CFROI_t - \overline{CFROI}) + \overline{CFROI} + \varepsilon_{t+n}$$

$$CFROI_4 = 0.95^4 \times (20 - 11.6) + 11.6 = 18.5\%$$

A highly profitable Energy firm is expected to fade like this:

$$CFROI_4 = 0.77^4 \times (20 - 4.9) + 4.9 = 10.1\%$$

The HPP firm is expected to fade from 20% to 18.5% whereas the Energy firm is expected to fade from 20% to 10.1%. The Energy firm reverts to average profitability much faster than the HPP firm. Energy firms' profits are influenced by commodity prices and macroeconomic fluctuations, suggesting that randomness and luck play a more influential role in this industry. HPP firms are more defensive and many possess exceptional and durable brands that insulate sales and profits during economic downturns. Warren Buffett put it best:[11]

> "A business that constantly encounters major change also encounters many chances for major error. Furthermore, economic terrain that is forever shifting violently is ground on which it is difficult to build a fortress-like business franchise. Such a franchise is usually the key to sustained high returns."

Because HOLT forecasts CFROI over a five-year period, an adjustment is necessary to forecast over longer horizons. This can be accomplished by *bootstrapping* annual persistence, as follows:

$$CFROI_t = \rho^t(CFROI_0 - \overline{CFROI}) + \overline{CFROI} \qquad (9.3)$$

---

[11] James O'Loughlin, *The Real Warren Buffett: Managing Capital, Leading People*, Nicholas Brealey, 2004.

EXHIBIT 9.14 Example of fading CFROI using industry inputs.

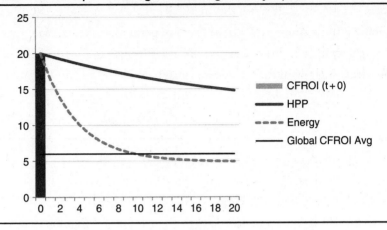

For a 20-year forecast, we would expect CFROI to fade as follows for a HPP firm:

$$CFROI_{20} = 0.95^{20}(20 - 11.5) + 11.5 = 14.8\%$$

compared with the Energy firm:

$$CFROI_{20} = 0.77^{20}(20 - 4.9) + 4.9 = 4.9\%$$

It is likely that a highly profitable HPP firm will maintain much of its profitability, while an Energy firm starting at the same CFROI will quickly revert to its industry mean. The HPP firm requires a longer forecast horizon to eliminate excess profits. Exhibit 9.14 highlights the expected fade in CFROI for these two examples.

CONCLUSION

Persistence in corporate profitability is an empirical fact. A trove of academic research reinforces this view. Largely overlooked by academia is the practical application of persistence research to forecasts of corporate profitability, an endeavor that HOLT has been actively leading for over forty years. The concept of persistence is intuitively grasped by HOLT clients as "fade."

Fade is the mathematical complement of persistence. The average firm's profitability decays toward its mean-reverting level at about 10% per year. This decay rate, or fade, is the *speed* at which excess profitability declines.

Companies with exceptional brands in defensive industries reveal stronger persistence in CFROI and often fade at half the speed of the average company. Some of these firms maintain high levels of profitability for decades and are priced to maintain it for many more decades. Highly stable and profitable companies comprise less than 5% of all equities, and are heavily concentrated amongst the largest companies in the world. When it comes to persistence, size matters. If you are convinced that a firm has built and can maintain a sustainable competitive advantage, then a fade rate of 5% is appropriate.

On the other hand, highly cyclical firms like those in the Energy and Materials industries, are generally quite volatile and fade faster than most other firms. Fade for these companies can exceed 20% a year, which means that profitability should not be expected to persist beyond a handful of years.

Given the empirical evidence of fade, a simple but major improvement to forecasting is to tamp down potential bias by adopting the logic (and evidence) of reversion to the mean. Adopting fade is using an outside view to make a better prediction.[12] Unbiased forecasts of corporate profitability can be developed with confidence using the information provided in this chapter. Short and long-term forecasts can be developed by bootstrapping. Let's not forget the wry, but astute, observation of Professor Bruce Greenwald speaking on the topic of competitive dynamics to help guide us all in making better predictions: "In the long run, everything is a toaster."

---

[12]Michael J. Mauboussin, *Think Twice: Harnessing the Power of Counterintuition*, Harvard Business Press, 2009.

10

FORECASTING GROWTH

"Insufficient facts always invite danger."

—Spock, *Star Trek*, season 1, episode 24 ("Space Seed," 1968)

KEY LEARNING POINTS

- High growth rates for sales, assets, and earnings are short-lived and rarely persist.
- On average, few firms sustain exceptional growth beyond five years.
- Lacking any other information, the most reasonable estimate of asset growth net of inflation is 5%.
- The long-term asset growth rate after inflation has been approximately 2.5%.
- The probability of maintaining a given growth rate or higher for different lengths of time is shown and available to check growth rate assumptions.

High growth rates are the holy grail of zealous investors. That's because extraordinary growth can vastly improve a company's (and investor's) fortunes. Backtests with perfect knowledge demonstrate that companies with the highest growth had better total shareholder performance than lower growth firms. This potential persuades many investors to pay large premiums for high-growth stocks, but few firms actually deliver on these expectations.[1] The brutal reality is that, whereas CFROI is persistent over a five- to ten-year window, growth is not.

Let's consider the attraction of a growth stock by looking at Apple in late 2007, a few months before the global credit crisis rocked the world. Stock prices were flying high, and investors were optimistic about global growth. Apple was undergoing a mesmerizing transformation. With Steve Jobs back at the helm, the firm had heaved its corporate body out of the trenches. From a low of −6% in 2001, CFROI had risen to 15% by the end of 2006. The degree of CFROI improvement was unanticipated, and investors reaped huge rewards. Market capitalization rose from $7.7 billion at the end of 2001 to $172 billion in just six years, a 68% annual compound rate of return. Investors were ecstatic, and they had every right to be. Apple's turnaround was nearly unprecedented.[2]

Given this virtuoso performance by Apple, by the end of 2007 it might have seemed almost reasonable if investors had priced in sustained growth rates above 30% for years to come. But that wasn't the case at all.

Let's recreate the pricing dynamics embedded in Apple's stock price as of December 2007. If we credit investors with nearly perfect foresight in anticipating Apple's CFROI over the ensuing five years (we will show that CFROI is easier to predict than growth), what growth rate was necessary to equate the prevailing stock price of December 2007 with the present value of the forecast cash flows?

The answer is shown in the middle panel of Exhibit 10.1, which reveals a dashed line forecast growth rate of 31% falling to 8% by 2012. The hashed

---

[1] Bryant Matthews and David A. Holland, *Quantifying Growth Expectations* (2014); *Prepared for Chance: Forecasting Corporate Growth* (2015). Both articles published by Credit Suisse HOLT.
[2] Bryant Matthews and David A. Holland, *Terminal Success: Lessons from History's Titans*, Credit Suisse HOLT, 2012.

EXHIBIT 10.1 Apple's Relative Wealth Chart from 2006 through 2015. Assuming investors accurately anticipated Apple's CFROI would improve to 24% over the next five years (forecast date December 2007), then growth was clearly under estimated. Sustained hyper-growth is highly unusual and hugely rewarding for positive spread businesses. Attributing the rise in share price over this period to unexpected growth, then growth multiplied Apple's value by 2.5×.

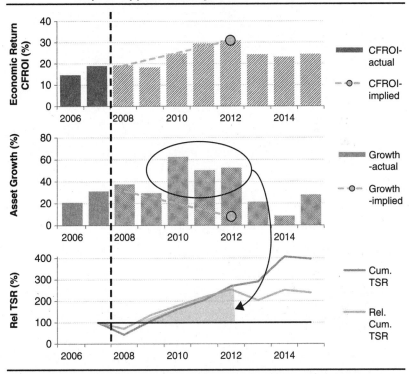

bars represent Apple's achieved growth rate, and the area of the dashed bars above the hashed line (circled) can be thought of as the *unanticipated* growth rate that Apple achieved, thereby besting market expectations. But investors are quick to absorb new information, and as early as 2009 were re-ratcheting their anticipation of what Apple could achieve and pushing its share price higher. It should be evident that the strong price gains in Apple's stock over the next few years far exceeded the performance of a firm whose future CFROI and growth rates had been correctly anticipated.

The lesson from this bite-sized Apple example is that sizzling growth is not only exciting, but that for profitable firms and greedy investors, it can be transformative. In Apple's case, investors did not price in sky-high growth rates. Nevertheless, the extraordinary achievement of Apple and similar firms persuades some investors, perhaps, that high growth is more attainable than it really is. Behavioralists might attribute it to the availability bias. (The probabilities of airline accidents, shark attacks, and spectacular share price appreciation are overestimated after corresponding news is reported.)

The empirical evidence has a lot to say about the persistence (or lack thereof) of corporate growth. Rather than being a drawback, this information can be used to make better predictions. Let's use the skills acquired from the last chapter to understand the persistence of corporate growth.

MEDIAN REAL ASSET GROWTH RATE

Since 1950, corporations listed on major exchanges have grown their asset base each year by an average of 5% net of inflation. This level is not representative of the average organic growth rate of older, mature companies. The data on corporate growth is riddled with acquisitions which skews the measurement of organic growth. Also, new firms enter the data set each year having higher average growth. The effect of these two influences makes it difficult to gain clear insight into the distribution of organic growth. This is a critical point because a firm's forecast cash flows should be based on organic growth unless the cost of acquisitions is deducted.[3] We have witnessed many forecasts that assume an acquisitive firm can continue to grow at the same rate but without any recognition of the cost of future acquisitions. As we've pointed out throughout the book, growth is not free.

---

[3]It is generally foolhardy to model an acquisitive future by mixing potential acquisitions with an existing business. In an efficient market, we would expect the NPV of an acquisition to be zero. The reality is that the NPV is usually negative for acquirers. The best way to model an acquisitive firm is value its existing business with organic growth and to add the NPV of future potential acquisitions. Never forget the NPV rule.

EXHIBIT 10.2 Median real asset growth rate (RAGR). Global non-financials, no size restriction.

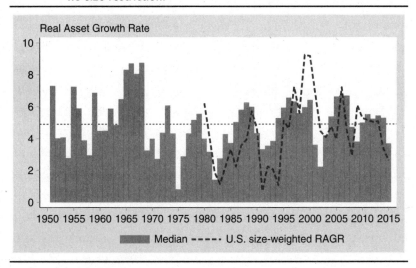

Source: Credit Suisse HOLT.

Adjusting for acquisition effects to better measure organic growth is challenging but not impossible.[4] We estimate that organic growth tends to average around 4% to 5%, real, for firms having a market cap of $250 million or more. (Firms below this size displayed lower average growth.)

Our first key insight is that, lacking any other information, the most reasonable estimate of asset growth net of inflation is 5%, which coincides well with Exhibit 10.2.

THE AVERAGE GROWTH RATE AS COMPANIES MATURE

What happens to corporate growth as firms mature? Do they "tend" toward a real asset growth rate of 5%?

---

[4]The authors have conducted two studies that attempt to measure organic growth. In the first study, conducted in 2004, all firms with unusual spikes in sales growth, goodwill, or assets (or, alternatively, debt or equity) were examined for acquisitive effects and removed from the sample. In another study conducted in 2007, firms were linked by acquisition from data supplied by MergerStat and removed from the sample. In both cases, average "organic" growth was 5% after inflation (real).

To answer this, we collected new entrants and examined the median growth rate for this group over time. Firms just entering the public record tend to grow at high rates: the average freshman experienced real asset growth averaging 16% in its first public year, but this level quickly converges toward 5%. Beyond 10 years, the average growth rate reverts toward 2.5%, and this process is generally complete within the next 10 years.[5]

Exhibit 10.3 motivates several observations. First, twenty years is a long time for any company to survive as a stand-alone entity. Most firms survive for less than ten years before being privatized or merged with another firm. Second, to remain alive for twenty years is likely due to the fact that the firm has competent managers and is a capable competitor. It is reasonable to expect that the growth rate of these firms is biased upward, reflecting both *survivorship* and *success* biases. Third, it is unreasonable to assume that sales and assets will grow at different rates over any long forecast horizon. To do so implies steadily increasing or decreasing asset efficiency, whereas our research on asset utilization shows that assets and sales tend to co-vary together; and over long time horizons, asset utilization approximates the average of the

EXHIBIT 10.3 Five-Year Median Forward Real Growth Rate by Firm Age.

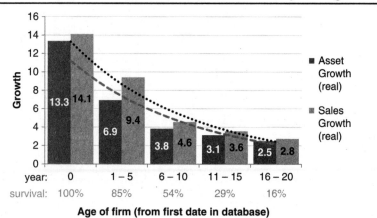

---

[5]The cross-sectional average is 5% and the longitudinal average is 2.5%. In the HOLT model, asset growth fades to 2.5% after the explicit forecast ends. Bear in mind that we cannot rid the data of a possible success bias.

firm's industry.[6] For this reason, we are comforted to see both assets and sales converging toward a similar rate of growth. Finally, note that growth rates do not immediately converge toward the long-term level of 2.5%. By year ten, the average firm is growing close to 4% to 5%. A two-stage process is evident for most companies in which growth first converges toward 5%, and then toward 2.5% for veterans. A difference of 2% to 3% in growth for a profitable company over a ten or twenty-year forecast horizon can lead to a material difference in estimated value. If you do not have an informed view, we recommend using a medium-term real growth rate of 5%, and 2.5% as the terminal growth rate.[7] Stable Cash Cows and eCAPs, for whom growth has tapered, can be forecast using 2.5% throughout the forecast horizon.

IS CORPORATE GROWTH MEAN-REVERTING?

We've now come to the meat of the chapter. Is corporate growth a mean-reverting process, or is growth simply a random outcome? The tendency of maturing companies to grow closer to 2.5% over time is an interesting observation but does not in any way empirically validate reversion to the mean in corporate growth.

To test for mean-reversion, we first examine our helpful transition matrices to get a sense of how growth behaves (Exhibit 10.4).

Recall that for any random process in which values are rank-ordered and grouped by quartile, there will be a 25% probability of shifting into any other quartile over time. In Exhibit 10.4, we do not see a random process. Instead, both sales and asset growth reveal that they are "sticky" or persistent over a one year gap but nearly random after four years. Persistence is not nearly as high as it is for CFROI.

In the top left transition matrix of Exhibit 10.4, a firm in the highest quartile of asset growth (Q4) has a 40% probability of remaining in the top quartile after one year and a 66% probability of maintaining above average

---

[6] Bryant Matthews and David A. Holland, *The Anatomy of CFROI Fade: The Persistence of Profitability Margin and Asset Turns*, November 2015, Credit Suisse HOLT.
[7] The assumptions regarding cost of capital and terminal growth should be consistent. In a conventional DCF model using CAPM, the terminal growth rate should not exceed the long-term risk-free rate. Also, the rates must be consistently stated in real or nominal space.

EXHIBIT 10.4 Inflation-adjusted asset growth and sales growth transition matrices.

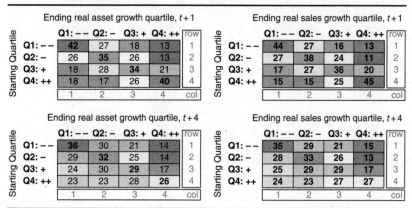

Ending real asset growth quartile, $t+1$

Starting Quartile	Q1: − −	Q2: −	Q3: +	Q4: ++	row
Q1: − −	42	27	18	13	1
Q2: −	26	35	26	13	2
Q3: +	18	28	34	21	3
Q4: ++	18	17	26	40	4
	1	2	3	4	col

Ending real sales growth quartile, $t+1$

Starting Quartile	Q1: − −	Q2: −	Q3: +	Q4: ++	row
Q1: − −	44	27	16	13	1
Q2: −	27	38	24	11	2
Q3: +	17	27	36	20	3
Q4: ++	15	15	25	45	4
	1	2	3	4	col

Ending real asset growth quartile, $t+4$

Starting Quartile	Q1: − −	Q2: −	Q3: +	Q4: ++	row
Q1: − −	36	30	21	14	1
Q2: −	29	32	25	14	2
Q3: +	24	30	29	17	3
Q4: ++	23	23	28	26	4
	1	2	3	4	col

Ending real sales growth quartile, $t+4$

Starting Quartile	Q1: − −	Q2: −	Q3: +	Q4: ++	row
Q1: − −	35	29	21	15	1
Q2: −	28	33	26	13	2
Q3: +	25	29	29	17	3
Q4: ++	24	23	27	27	4
	1	2	3	4	col

Source: Credit Suisse HOLT.

growth. Similar persistence is observed for the lowest growth firms. Clearly, growth rates are not random, and persist for at least one year.

The bottom transition matrix shows that, however strong or weak a company's growth is, it is unlikely to sustain such growth over a four-year horizon. Instead, growth rates devolve into a random process after only a few years. This means that estimating above or below average growth beyond five years is empirically difficult to justify. Amazon's phenomenal growth is an exception to the rule.

The growth transition matrices indicate that growth is not random, but rather weakly persistent. What does our empirical workhorse model of mean-reversion show?

Recall that the AR(1) model measures the autocorrelation between a variable with lags of itself. Assuming growth is best modeled as a linear process, a correlation signal of 1.0 reveals perfect persistence, correlation of −1.0 perfect negative persistence, and correlation of 0.0 represents random association. Correlation between zero and 1.0 indicates reversion to the mean. We once again chose 2012 to visualize the strength of association for our measure of interest, in this case asset growth (Exhibit 10.5).

Autocorrelation of 0.31 indicates weak association and fast reversion to the mean. 69% of excess growth was lost over a period of one year. The low

EXHIBIT 10.5 One-year correlation in Real Asset Growth.

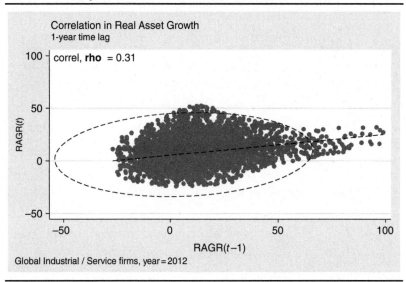

Source: Credit Suisse, HOLT. Global Industrial/Service companies, $250 million minimum market capitalization.

correlation reveals that growth rates are difficult to predict. This observation is just as applicable for sales growth as it is for asset growth. Also note the circle on the scatter plot is not centered as it was for CFROI. That's because growth rates are positively skewed.

In Chapter 9, we introduced half-life to describe exponentially decaying phenomena. A company with a persistence factor of 90% (fade =10%) reveals a half-life of 6.6 years, the time it takes on average to lose 50% of excess profitability. Growth rates are nowhere near as persistent as profits. A typical firm will lose half of its excess growth in just one year,

$$T_{0.5} = \frac{-0.693}{ln(0.31)} = 0.60 \; years,$$

and 99% of excess growth is eliminated within four years. This is consistent with the insights gained from the transition matrices showing the relationship between growth at time t and four years later.

311

THE SUSTAINABILITY OF GROWTH

Because growth rates show little persistence, and a five-year forecast horizon is a common feature of most DCF models, we examine the sustainability of growth over five-year planning horizons. Do any detectable signals emerge?

Exhibit 10.6 shows the percentage of firms that sustained growth above a given level for 1, 3, 5, and 10 years. You can use this cumulative probability table as a guide to gauge a company's likelihood of exceeding a target rate of growth.

Column 1 shows a level of growth, g. The "≥50%" row shows the percentage of firms that sustained growth at or above 50% for the indicated time, t, in years.

Columns 2, 3, and 4 show the compound effect of growth g. For example, 50% growth compounded five years equals 7.6 ($1.5^5 = 7.6$). Sales of 1,000 compounded at this rate will have grown to 7,600.

Columns 5 to 12 show the percentage of firms that sustained growth g for the indicated interval. Less than 1% of firms sustain annual growth of 50% or more for five years.

Let's examine the 15% growth row. Some investors like to look for stocks that can double over the next five years. The table shows that 24% of global

EXHIBIT 10.6 Global Industrial/Service firms, $250 million minimum market cap, 1980–2015.

g	Compound Size Increase			Median Real Asset Growth > g				Median Real Sales Growth > g			
	$t=3$	$t=5$	$t=10$	1 yr	3 yr	5 yr	10 yr	1 yr	3 yr	5 yr	10 yr
≥50	3.4x	7.6x	57.7x	4	2	1	0	5	2	1	0
≥45	3.0x	6.4x	41.1x	5	2	1	0	6	3	2	1
≥40	2.7x	5.4x	28.9x	6	3	1	1	7	4	2	1
≥35	2.5x	4.5x	20.1x	8	4	2	1	9	5	3	1
≥30	2.2x	3.7x	13.8x	10	5	3	1	12	7	4	1
≥25	2.0x	3.1x	9.3x	13	8	5	2	15	9	6	2
≥20	1.7x	2.5x	6.2x	18	11	8	3	19	13	9	4
≥15	1.5x	2.0x	4.0x	24	18	13	7	26	20	15	9
≥10	1.3x	1.6x	2.6x	35	29	25	17	36	31	26	19
≥5	1.2x	1.3x	1.6x	52	50	47	40	51	48	46	42
≥0	1.0x	1.0x	1.0x	73	76	77	79	68	70	72	76
Median				5.4	4.8	4.3	3.7	5.1	4.8	4.3	3.7

firms generate real asset growth of 15% or higher in any given year; 18% sustain this level or more for three years, and only 13% can grow at this level or more for five years. One-in-eight firms doubles its size over any five-year horizon. Dare we say it again: Growth is difficult to sustain.

The probabilities shown in Exhibit 10.6 are based on firms that survive for the number of years indicated. Since most firms survive in some form (only about 1%–1.5% of firms go bankrupt each year), the probabilities are valid for all firms for which an analyst is making a forecast and for which there is an expectation of corporate survival.

The empirical evidence on growth is clear: Growth rates are noisy, quickly revert to the mean, and are, at best, weakly persistent.

FORECASTING GROWTH

Measuring a Firm's Sustainable Growth Rate

A firm's sustainable growth rate (SGR) is the maximum rate at which a company can grow organically with the cash it generates from operations.[8] This rate is typically equal to ROE or ROIC after required distributions to debt and equity capital providers (interest and dividend payments). In a dividend discount model (DDM), $SGR_{equity} = Plowback\ ratio \times ROE$ where the plowback or retention ratio is the amount of earnings retained to fund growth.[9] If 100% of earnings are retained, then growth equal to ROE can be funded internally. The payout ratio equals one minus the plowback ratio, or $(1 - g/ROE)$ in the case of the DDM. Because the HOLT model uses free cash flow to the firm (FCFF), we need a measure of sustainable growth for the enterprise.

A firm's maximum sustainable growth rate equals its NOPAT as a percentage of its opening invested capital ($NOPAT/IC_{BOY}$). FCFF is the cash available to distribute to equity and debt providers after growth has been funded.

---

[8]R. C. Higgins, "Sustainable Growth under Inflation," *Financial Management* 10 (1981): 36–40.
[9]Richard A. Brealey, Stewart C. Myers, and Alan J. Marcus, *Fundamentals of Corporate Finance*, 3rd edition, McGraw-Hill, 2000. See page 99 for a proof. We also showed this relationship to be true in Chapter 2.

Like the equity-based formula, the sustainable growth rate of the firm equals:

$$SGR_{firm} = Plowback\ ratio \times ROIC$$

In HOLT, enterprise plowback equals total gross cash flow less an asset replacement charge, which represents the amount of depreciating assets that must be replenished each year due to obsolescence. If we imagine a company with no dividend or debt payments, then plowback is simply gross cash flow less retirement (Plowback = $GCF - R$).

Because many firms pay dividends and borrow debt, the actual calculation of plowback is necessarily more complex:

Gross cash flow
 − Interest expense
 − Dividends
 − Rent expense
 − Retirement (maintenance capex)
 = Plowback

The first two items below gross cash flow are payments to capital providers. Capital providers are entitled to these disbursements before cash can be reinvested in the firm. Interest must be paid to debt providers. Dividend payments are to common, preferred, and minority shareholders. Rental expense is a contractual obligation for the use of leased assets used to generate operating profits. The total rental expense includes both a depreciation charge on the assets and a financing charge for the use of someone else's capital, like interest expense on debt. Consequently, the full rental expense must be deducted, not just the depreciation portion. As discussed previously, retirements are the estimated value of depreciating assets that must be replaced. A typical DCF model assumes that depreciation is a useful proxy of the asset replacement charge each period. HOLT does not make this assumption, but instead adds depreciation back to gross cash flow and imputes a retirement charge based on a firm's asset age and its historical growth rate.

EXHIBIT 10.7 Amazon's sustainable growth rate.

Amazon.com Inc	2009	2010	2011	2012	2013
Inflation Adjusted Gross Cash Flow	2,761	3,426	4,457	6,475	9,480
− Interest Expense	34	39	65	92	141
− Rental Expense	171	225	362	541	759
− Common & Preferred Dividends	0	0	0	0	0
+ Stock Option Expense not incl in R&D	159	201	265	399	531
Simple Plowback	2,715	3,363	4,295	6,241	9,111
− Retirements	581	879	1,152	1,461	1,900
Sustainable Cash Flow	2,133	2,484	3,143	4,780	7,211
BOY Inflation Adjusted Gross Inv.	8,404	10,577	14,524	19,903	28,475
Sustainable Real Growth Rate	**25.4**	**23.5**	**21.6**	**24.0**	**25.3**
Real Asset Growth Rate	43.1	31.6	32.2	44.4	40.9

Using the formula for SGR, Amazon's sustainable growth rate is shown in Exhibit 10.7.

Amazon's sustainable growth rate in 2013 was 25.3%, but it has been growing far faster than its sustainable rate. Is there a better way to estimate forward growth?

Why HOLT Uses a Normalized Growth Rate

HOLT research on growth shows that the sustainable growth rate is an excellent proxy for estimating a firm's likely growth rate in assets. It works remarkably well over time for mature, stable companies. However, for companies experiencing high growth or meaningful changes in capital structure, a modification is necessary to better predict their growth. For this reason, HOLT uses a normalized growth rate (NGR) to estimate a firm's asset growth. Here is the formula for NGR:

$$NGR = \frac{Plowback + \Delta \ Net \ Capital \ Events}{BOY \ Assets}$$

Capital Events include equity and debt issuances and repurchases. These amounts must be material (greater than 2.5% of gross investment) and occur with regularity. The "net" in net capital events (NCE) is capital inflow less capital outflow. The inclusion of a materiality requirement restricts the application of this portion of the SGR to less than 50% of firms in any given year, which are typically early life-cycle businesses (higher share issuance) and cash cows that frequently repurchase shares. Intuitively, firms that spend large amounts of discretionary cash on stock buybacks will have less to reinvest in growth opportunities. The normalized growth rate is an adaptive formulation that elegantly describes the growth of companies at all phases of the competitive life-cycle.[10]

Let's compute the normalized growth rate for Amazon (Exhibit 10.8).

In 2013, Amazon's normalized growth rate exceeded its SGR. This is an immediate flag that the firm is issuing equity or debt to fund expansion. The details of Exhibit 10.8 show that AMZN borrowed $1.9bn, $3bn, and $1bn in debt in 2013, 2012, and 2011. Funds from debt issuance exceeded share repurchases across all three years, pumping up the firm's ability to grow. To smooth distortions in growth, HOLT uses a three-year median NGR when forecasting.

EXHIBIT 10.8 The calculation of Amazon's normalized growth rate.

Amazon.Com Inc	2009	2010	2011	2012	2013
Sustainable Cash Flow	2,133	2,484	3,143	4,780	7,211
Conditional Net Capital Events					
Net Equity Issue (Repurchase)	0	0	(277)	(960)	0
Net Debt Increase (Buyback)	863	472	1,074	3,025	1,953
Change in Leased Assets	54	270	692	913	1,120
Acquisition Adj. for Goodwill	1,251	216	839	838	191
+ Net Capital Events	(334)	526	650	2,140	2,882
= Dynamic Cash Flow	1,800	3,010	3,793	6,920	10,092
BOY Inflation Adjusted Gross Inv.	8,404	10,577	14,524	19,903	28,475
Normalized Growth Rate	21.4	28.5	26.1	34.8	35.4
3-year median NGR	20.1	21.4	26.1	28.5	34.8
Normalized Real Growth Rate (BOY)	20.1	21.4	26.1	28.5	34.8

[10]For a brief, but more technical description of the normalized growth rate, see *HOLT Notes: The Normalized Growth Rate.*

Forecasting Growth: Near-Term and Long-Term Dynamics

Because earning excess profits over a long period of time is difficult, a carefully designed DCF model will forecast cash flows over a reasonable horizon and squeeze out excess profitability by the terminal period.[11] A similar principle can be applied to corporate growth. Our research suggests that most firms quickly revert toward 5% growth over any five-year horizon and toward 2.5% thereafter.

Let's consider Tesla, which has averaged annual growth of over 100% for the last five years, driven primarily by sales of electric automobiles. Elon Musk, the billionaire CEO and savvy entrepreneur thinks sales can sustain 50% annual growth for the next decade.[12] Let's assume an 8% sales growth thereafter for our terminal growth rate.

Assuming Musk is correct (a grand assumption), Tesla will become 8% of global auto industry sales in just 10 years. That would be a spectacular achievement if he can pull it off. But what does the more modest 8% compound growth rate mean over time? It's hard to decipher how this translates into economic reality when one uses a growing perpetuity equation at the end of a forecast. Even a 40-year forecast may not reveal the problem if pencil isn't put to paper. Let's apply some logic.

The global automobile industry had sales of more than $2 trillion in 2015. Tesla earned a fraction of this potential revenue, about 0.2% with sales of $4 billion. Assuming Tesla can sustain growth of 50% for the next decade, Tesla's sales will balloon to $233 billion and it would be the third largest automobile manufacturer in the world, only slightly behind global giants, Toyota and VW (we're assuming everyone else grows at 2%).

Given this spectacular growth, which is based on Musk's own projections, but restricted to a ten-year window, what does the much lower 8%

---

[11] This could require forecasts of well over 20 years for companies with extraordinary economic moats and competitive advantages. The inclusion of an adjustable profitability fade rate for valuing the terminal period means that the forecast only needs to be until the firm is ex-growth.

[12] Tesla Motors, Inc. Q4 2014 Earnings Call, February 11, 2015. See FactSet: callstreet Transcript, page 7. According to Michael J. Mauboussin, the conference call transcript actually says "30 percent" but if you work out Musk's math, the only way to get to a market capitalization basically "the same as Apple's is today" is to assume a 50 percent growth rate.

growth rate translate into over time? Assuming the rest of the auto industry continues to grow at 2% annually, in how many years will it take Tesla to become 33% of total auto sales?

We can solve the equation easily:

$$y = \frac{\overbrace{4.05(1 + 0.50)^{10}}^{\text{first 10 years}} \times \overbrace{(1 + 0.08)^{n}}^{\text{terminal growth}}}{2134 \times (1 + 0.02)^{n+10}} \quad \frac{Tesla}{Industry}$$

We will assume that Tesla isn't growing the overall market, only stealing market share from its competitors. We can solve for n after setting y to 0.33:

$$n = \frac{ln\left(0.33 \times \frac{2{,}134(1.02)^{10}}{4.05(1.50)^{10}}\right)}{ln\frac{1.08}{1.02}}$$

In just 23 years after its hyper-growth, Tesla would represent 33% of the entire global automobile manufacturing market! This is obviously absurd, and no rational analyst would intentionally forecast this outcome. Yet we have experienced similar egregious forecasts because the economic consequences of growth in a DCF model are often shrouded in the mathematics of compounding (Exhibit 10.9).

Ratcheting the sustainable growth rate down to 5% might seem like the solution. But even 5% is too high: In 45 years post hyper-growth, Tesla would represent 33% of global auto sales (or perhaps flying saucers by that date).

Instead, it makes sense to employ a sustainable growth rate that mirrors economic reality. In the United States, GDP averaged 3.2% growth net of inflation from 1950 until 2016.[13] HOLT's research shows that as companies mature, growth tends toward 2% to 3%, a level consistent with economic reality. Judging from real government bond yields in 2017 for developed economics, future growth might be more like 0% to 1%.

---

[13] Federal Reserve Bank of St. Louis, https://fred.stlouisfed.org/series/A191RL1A225NBEA.

EXHIBIT 10.9 **2015 automobile manufacturer sales as a percentage of total. 2025 assumes 2% annual sales growth versus 50% for Tesla. 2048 shows the effect of 8% compound annual growth for Tesla in the terminal period: Tesla has grown to become 33% of global auto manufacturer sales.**

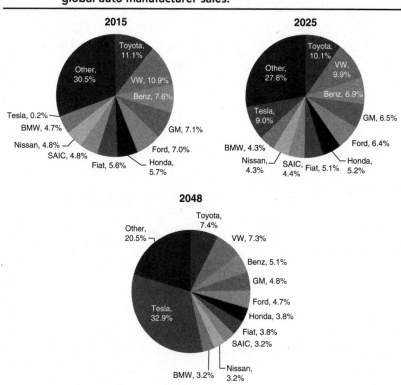

CONCLUSIONS

Forecasting growth is a serious challenge. Corporate capex patterns reveal idiosyncratic behavior. Economic cycles can result in a wait-and-see attitude as corporate executives look for signs of a cyclical upswing before committing capital reserves to fund projects. Even when times are good, growth can be outsized or miniscule.

Correctly anticipating a company's future growth can significantly enhance one's view of its intrinsic worth. As we saw in the chapter on competitive life-cycle dynamics, accurately gauging a growth stock's future pace of development is exceptionally hard. Investors tend to bid up growth stocks, anticipating that growth will be sustained for longer than actual outcomes tend to dictate. The worst thing you can do when forecasting growth is to extrapolate it. Growth stocks trade at large price multiples, but future share price performance is typically lackluster. Finding the next growth star probably involves more luck than skill. Our research on growth suggests caution: Like Spock, be logical—make a conservative growth forecast and consider the probability of it being attained.

11

EVALUATING MARKET EXPECTATIONS

"Stock prices are the clearest and most reliable signal of the market's expectations about a company's future performance."

—Alfred Rappaport and Michael J. Mauboussin, *Expectations Investing*

"It's a fun game. It never goes away."

—Bob Hendricks

KEY LEARNING POINTS

- The goal of value investors is to find stocks that can beat market expectations.
- Stocks with high expectations where profitability and growth are priced to increase dramatically tend to underperform.
- Stocks with low expectations where profitability is priced to crater tend to outperform, and might be good trades.

321

- Stocks that derive more than 40% of total value from expected growth opportunities are frequently lackluster investments.
- Before building a complex financial forecasting and valuation model for a company, try to back into its market-implied expectations. This is easy to do with HOLT Lens. The back-of-the-envelope pricing equations we derived in earlier chapters will prove useful.
- We provide tips on what to be aware of when considering HOLT's default valuations.

THE RELATIVE WEALTH CHART AS A DECISION AID FOR EFFICIENTLY ASSESSING STOCK OPPORTUNITIES

The rewards for anticipating the next Apple, Tesla, or Facebook will undoubtedly be large. Investors are motivated to find these winners, but how can they accomplish this aim? Is there a better way to find potential winners than by listening to the gossip about equity markets at the nearest watering hole or reading investment blogs?

To be effective, active investors cannot assess every available stock. They need to quickly and efficiently discard stocks with little chance of beating market expectations. They have to spot opportunities that others have missed.

Like grandmasters of chess, active investors benefit from "selective attention," skillfully tuning out unimportant details and focusing on what really matters. Experts use selective attention to rapidly evaluate options and make superior choices. Experts do not evaluate all possible options, just the better ones. Through practice, experts hone their decision-making skill. More thinking isn't better; better thinking is better.[1]

HOLT's Relative Wealth Chart gives portfolio managers a birds-eye view of the field. It provides high-level insight of what has happened (the company's historical track record of success), what is likely to happen (HOLT's default forecast, which is based on shared experiences of similar firms), and

[1] Bryant Matthews and David A. Holland, *Grandmasters: Lessons from Chess*, Credit Suisse HOLT, February 2017.

what others expect to happen (market-implied expectations indicated by HOLT's Green Dot).

We described the incredible loss of value experienced by U.S. department stores in 2016 in the Introduction to this book. The Relative Wealth Chart for legendary retailer Macy's is shown in Exhibit 11.1. Let's step through how it can help you assess our three key points: (1) how has the stock performed *historically*? (2) how is it priced to perform *prospectively*? and (3) how is it likely to perform *empirically*?

- Macy's has a history of successfully generating CFROI above its cost of capital, but assets have been shrinking. Over the past three years, CFROI has been fading, which has been matched by a sharp underperformance relative to the S&P 500.
- The default valuation indicates upside for the share price if Macy's can maintain its present CFROI and avoid further shrinkage. Unfortunately, HOLT's probabilistic forecast has no knowledge about the 800-pound gorilla called Amazon.
- The Green Dot indicates that CFROI will continue to fade sharply and real growth will remain negative. U.S. department stores are under tremendous pressure and must find new ways of creating sustainable competitive advantages.

The Green Dot allows you to read the opposing defense. How do other investors expect the future for a stock to unfold? If your competitors are reading the play wrong, you have an opportunity to score. As John Maynard Keynes observed, the heart of "successful investing is anticipating the anticipations of others."

DISTILLING EXPECTATIONS FROM A STOCK PRICE

Stock prices are a signal of expectations about a firm's prospects. The level of a stock's price tells us nothing about its investment merit or the expectations that are baked in. A $10 share price is a meaningless piece of information by itself. Each share of Apple currently trades at approximately $100

EXHIBIT 11.1   Macy's Relative Wealth Chart.

MACY'S INC

Sensitivity
Department Store
Market Cap: 7.058 B. USD

Price: 23.18 (Jun 28, 2017)
Warranted Price: 37.49 USD (62%)

CFROI & Asset Growth Inputs

	2012	2013	2014	2015	2016	t + 1	t + 10
Economic Return (CFROI %)	11.6	11.5	12.0	11.0	9.4	10.2	10.2
Real Asset Growth %	(6.4)	0.1	(5.7)	(7.9)	(9.8)	(0.0)	1.1
Discount Rate	5.84	4.91	4.78	4.98	4.93	5.65	

Warranted Valuation	Amount (MM)	Per Share
+PV Cash Flow Existing Assets	16,473	54.10
+NPV Cash Flow Future Investments	4,550	14.94
+Market Value Investments	0	0.00
Total Economic Value	21,023	69.0
−Market Value of Debt & Equivalents	9,607	31.55
−Market Value of Minority Interest	0	0.00
Warranted Equity Value	**11,416**	**37.5**
Shares Outstanding	305	upside 62%

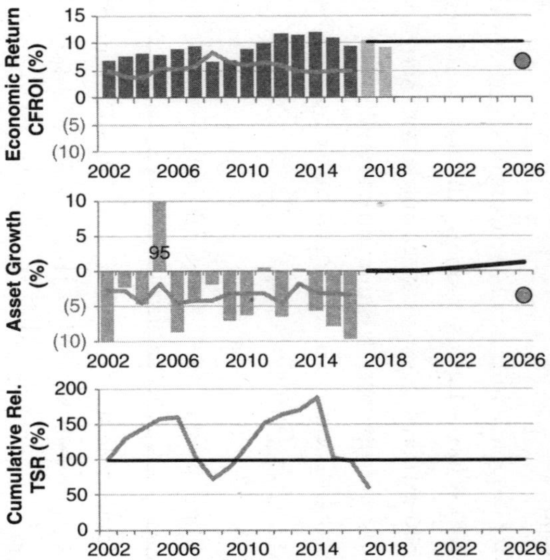

versus $200,000 for one class A share of Berkshire Hathaway. Which is the better investment?

A simple technique that offers a crude sense of a stock's relative value is to scale its price by book value or earnings. This results in a price-to-book (P/B) or price-to-earnings (P/E) multiple. Stocks with above-average multiples have above-average expectations, and vice versa. Stocks with the highest multiples have the highest expectations. Of course, we are assuming that the multiple is useful; for instance, earnings aren't negative. As we demonstrated in Chapter 2, even under the best conditions, a multiple is only a rough guide. Multiples should only be used as sanity checks, not as reliable valuation signals. For non-believers, Professors Lev and Gu provide plenty of evidence that the relevance of accounting figures has diminished.[2]

What expectations are we talking about? A P/E multiple does not provide any clarity into this question. Is there a better way to extract a stock's performance expectations from its price?

Let's re-examine the fundamental drivers of value creation expressed in the Gordon Growth Model, which we derived in Chapter 2:

$$P = \frac{D_1}{r_e - g} = B_0 \frac{(ROE_1 - g)}{r_e - g}$$

where D_1 = forward dividend, r_e = cost of equity, g = earnings growth, ROE_1 = forward return on equity, and B is book value. All drivers must be constant for the equation to hold.

This model suggests that the key drivers of equity value creation are a stock's return on equity and its earnings growth rate. Companies able to earn a return on equity above the cost of equity create economic value and should trade at higher multiples. There is strong empirical evidence that P/B is positively correlated to ROE.

We showed how to extend this model in the Introduction to valuing the firm, and introduced the fade rate as an adjustable value driver:

$$Enterprise\ Value = IC_0 \frac{(ROIC_1 - g + f)}{(r - g + f)}$$

---

[2] Baruch Lev, and Feng Gu, *The End of Accounting and the Path Forward for Investors and Managers*, John Wiley & Sons, 2016.

We term this equation the Fundamental Pricing Model.[3] We highly recommend that you memorize it. This equation offers superior insight into the drivers of value creation, and shrewd investors can put it to use to quickly gauge market expectations and test the sensitivity of firm value to changes in these value drivers.

A value driver's expected value can be backed out by setting it on the left-hand side and solving for it. For instance, the market-implied cost of capital r, which is equivalent to the expected return, can be derived given a mature firm's enterprise value-to-book ratio, profitability fade, long-term asset growth, and the forward return on invested capital $ROIC_1$:

$$Expected\ Return = \frac{IC_0}{EV}(ROIC_1 - g + f) + g - f$$

We could solve for each driver to judge market-implied expectations. For a mature firm with impressive profitability, it is highly informative to calculate the market-implied rate of fade and thus the company's market-implied competitive advantage period.[4] Understanding the level of operational performance required to justify today's price offers powerful insight into stock prices, and is an efficient method to analyze stocks. Investors can shift their focus from discussions of "what it's worth" to "what's priced in." When we look at equity prices this way, we can ask: "Can the stock beat market expectations?" Stocks from every phase of the life-cycle that have favorable odds of beating market expectations are sound fundamental investments.[5]

CAN IT BEAT THE FADE?

Anticipating whether a firm is likely to beat or miss expectations embedded in its price requires considerable skill. Bob Hendricks (the "H" in HOLT), a veritable wizard in the art of investing, ceaselessly drilled this point into

[3] This formula was developed by David Holland. A proof is available in Chapter 5 and fully derived in the report: "Don't Suffer from a Terminal Flaw, Add Fade to Your DCF" by David A. Holland and Bryant Matthews, Credit Suisse HOLT, June 2016.
[4] We showed that the expected competitive advantage period equals $1/f$, thus the market-implied rate of fade is the inverse of the market-implied competitive advantage period $MICAP$.
[5] Alfred Rappaport and Michael J. Mauboussin. *Expectations Investing: Reading Stock Prices for Better Returns*. Harvard Business School, 2001; Bartley J. Madden (1999), *CFROI Valuation: A Total System Approach to Valuing the Firm*, Butterworth–Heinemann.

HOLT employees and his clients every chance he could. He understood Keynes' insight.

As young acolytes at HOLT, we were required to analyze companies and present our views to peers. This setting could be simultaneously wonderful and terrifying. It mostly depended on whether you were on the giving or receiving end of the feedback.

Bob liked to say that HOLT employees needed to have "broad shoulders." You needed to be able to take criticism to grow. These were formative years during which we learned our craft from seasoned veterans. After carefully listening to a HOLT analyst expound on some company's fundamentals, Bob would laser in to the core of the investment thesis: "Okay, here's the big question," he'd drawl in his warm and encouraging way, and throw a zinger straight at you: "Can the stock beat the fade?"

This is a brilliant question. It cuts right to the heart of the matter. Even if a stock's intrinsic worth isn't that high, if other investors think its value is much lower, then companies that can beat those low expectations can turn out to be great investments. At HOLT, we heard the phrases "Can it beat the fade?" and "Fade happens!" thousands of times.

Whatever stock you are looking at adding to or removing from your portfolio, this is one of the most important questions you can ask. If the answer is "yes," even if the company seems about as exciting as mud, it's probably a good fundamental investment.

A great company is not always a great investment, and a bad company isn't always a bad investment. These points are as distinct as night and day, but too often confused by investors and linked as inseparable. Bob's focus on "Can it beat the fade?" slices through the confusion.[6]

How can we keep this idea of "beating the fade" front and center? That's what HOLT's Green Dot is for!

---

[6] We are of the view that it is best to invest in companies with proven records of excellent capital allocation decisions, especially if they can be bought at a reasonable price. These stocks tend to do well over the long term. Companies with records of poor operating returns that look cheap should be viewed as trades, and not as long-term holds. As Buffett said and we demonstrated in Chapter 8, "Turnarounds seldom turn."

EXHIBIT 11.2 **Amazon's Relative Wealth Chart as of April 30, 2014, indicates a prolonged period of value creation and growth. Shareholders have been handsomely rewarded.**

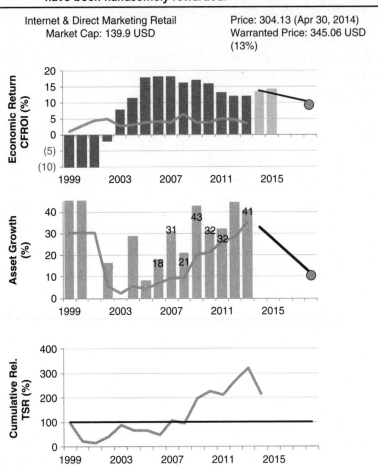

Internet & Direct Marketing Retail
Market Cap: 139.9 USD

Price: 304.13 (Apr 30, 2014)
Warranted Price: 345.06 USD
(13%)

THE GREEN DOT

HOLT's Green Dot is prominently visible on the Relative Wealth Chart (RWC). Exhibit 11.2 is the RWC for Amazon that we first encountered in Chapter 3 (Exhibit 3.32).

The top panel shows Amazon's historical track record of success as dark bars (CFROI). The first two light bars at the far right are forecast CFROI derived from consensus EPS estimates.[7] The Green Dot circle at the end is a "market-implied" CFROI, or the economic rate of return that is necessary by year five of the forecast to equate the present value of future cash flows to the firm's current price. Because this is the CFROI (at $t + 5$) that links together the future free cash flows to current price, it is "implied" by investors' expectations. We call it "market-implied CFROI" or the Green Dot. Remember, CFROI above 6% is generally indicative of a prosperous company. At a CFROI of 12% fading to 9%, Amazon is creating shareholder value.

What does Amazon's Green Dot tell us? We can see immediately that profitability is expected to decline over the next five years since the Green Dot is below the first forecast CFROI. We also see that the expected CFROI at $t + 5$ is below the level of profitability that Amazon has enjoyed over the past decade, suggesting a trough of sorts. The $t + 5$ CFROI is near 10% but not below 6%, which means that the firm is still expected to earn above-average profits. Some fade in profitability is being "priced in," but it is not extreme. Does this fade strike us as unrealistic? Will Amazon's profitability fall to a ten-year low?

Just by glancing at the Relative Wealth Chart, we have discovered three useful insights. First, the market is expecting profit erosion. This isn't unsettling since Amazon has been growing rapidly for an extended period (which isn't sustainable in the long term) and such high growth rates typically invite competition. (High profitability coupled with high growth is indicative of a nascent market; companies thirsty for profits will seek entry.) Second, Amazon is priced to remain profitable over the next five years, and is expected to enjoy more years of hearty growth. This also makes sense, as there is no obvious reason to anticipate that Amazon will be unprofitable or a cost of capital business in the next five years. Third, we have benchmarked Amazon's forecast CFROI against its historical track record. It's obvious that CFROI has been declining for the last ten years, so further decay appears reasonable. Amazon's growth more

---

[7]We also need the asset base in both years, which is grown out from LFY using HOLT's forecast normalized growth rate.

than offset the decline in profitability for the firm to continue growing economic profit.

In mere seconds, we have covered a lot of ground. Of course, the real work of deciding whether Amazon is a solid investment or not remains to be done, but as a start, we have gained some important insights quickly and efficiently. The Relative Wealth Chart is an exercise in selective attention. The Green Dot acts as a barometer, helping us to quickly gauge the expectations embedded in a stock's price. Stocks with high expectations should be avoided, and stocks with low expectations should be researched.

The Relative Wealth Chart is a remarkable picture that shows a firm's recent operational success, its likely near-term prospects, and its embedded *price expectations* all in one visual. It empowers an investor so that he or she can efficiently assess whether a stock's price expectations appear to be reasonable or excessive. Skilled users accomplish all of this in a blink. Is the Green Dot in line with the firm's history of CFROI? Is it unrealistically high or low? Is the firm's track record of operational success stable enough to develop a confident forecast, or is it volatile? What is driving the change in CFROI? Is the business model tuned to creating value or growing earnings at all cost? After becoming well-accustomed to the Relative Wealth Chart, and assuming some knowledge of the companies under analysis, the answers to these questions are intuited in a flash. The Relative Wealth Chart is a powerful tool in the hands of skilled users.

Until recently, the Relative Wealth Chart needed one more critical feature: It lacked the ability to benchmark a stock's expectations against the historical performance record of similar firms. This has been remedied and represents a major advancement. The benefit of seeing how firms with similar operating performance and growth subsequently performed is unparalleled. We can now understand the empirical likelihood of a firm achieving different scenarios. We can see its *probability of success.*

The adjusted Relative Wealth Chart looks like Exhibit 11.3.

For Amazon, there is a 51% probability that it will meet or exceed current price expectations. This probability is based on a sample of how

EXHIBIT 11.3 Factoring probability into Amazon's Relative Wealth Chart.

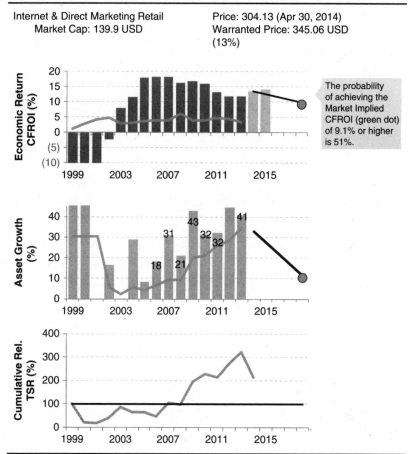

Internet & Direct Marketing Retail
Market Cap: 139.9 USD

Price: 304.13 (Apr 30, 2014)
Warranted Price: 345.06 USD
(13%)

The probability of achieving the Market Implied CFROI (green dot) of 9.1% or higher is 51%.

similar firms from history behaved over subsequent five-year periods. Similar firms had CFROI levels, growth rates, and operational stability like Amazon.

The 51% probability of earning a CFROI equal to or higher than 9% also reinforces the reasonableness of HOLT's default forecast, represented by the black line. In this example, HOLT's forecast CFROI mirrors what investors anticipate will happen with Amazon's profitability over the next five years. Investors expect an average outcome. Note that the probability model says nothing about how the firm will grow over the next five years. For now, it is a comment only about the probability of attaining forecast CFROI.

Most firms demonstrate mean-reverting CFROI. Investors expect the same from Amazon: While profitability is priced to decline only modestly, growth rates are assumed to have peaked. CFROI is expected to fall from 12% to 9%, which superficially (given a "blink") appears to be reasonable for a Star with a highly capable management team and a long track record of success.

How can investors act on this information? A shrewd portfolio manager, who anticipates Amazon can beat the fade and hold CFROI steady at 13% coupled with growth above 15%, will buy Amazon's stock, as more than 45% upside to fair value would be indicated. Her thesis that investors underappreciate Amazon's ability to maintain profits will likely be supported when Amazon reports stronger-than-expected earnings, and the stock price leaps. On the other hand, an investor who thinks CFROI will decline to 6% will sell or short the stock, believing that investors are overly optimistic about Amazon's future profits. In a flash, you have "anticipated what others are anticipating" about Amazon, and put this information to work.[8]

THINKING ABOUT EXPECTATIONS AT DIFFERENT LIFE-CYCLE STATES

"It is not just high CFROI that delivers great shareholder returns; it is all across the CFROI spectrum."

—Bob Hendricks

The HOLT framework is a wonderful tool for determining market expectations at any phase of the life-cycle. HOLT's default forecast and Green Dot estimates are particularly helpful for Stars, eCAPs, and Cash Cows. Each of these phases is expected to mean-revert, and most

---

[8] From the vantage of August 2017 before we go to press, Amazon has beaten the growth expectations of April 2014, and thus outperformed the market.

firms comply. In fact, about 70% of companies from each state fade toward the cost of capital over any five- to ten-year interval. eCAPs have unusual profit persistence, and HOLT recognizes this by flagging companies with stable profitability and extending the forecast horizon from five to ten years.

Early life-cycle firms and companies in a restructuring phase may require user intervention to better reflect their potential outcomes. For early life-cycle companies, possible outcomes may be wide-ranging and many will be priced to become Stars. HOLT's default expectation of mean-reversion may not be helpful for some of these firms. The Green Dot is only useful when its starting inputs are relevant. Tesla is an excellent case study.

In Exhibit 11.4, we re-created the default view of Tesla in HOLT Lens shortly after its IPO on June 30, 2010. Note that the HOLT forecast (the black line) assumes mean-reversion in CFROI (fading toward 6%) and growth (fading toward 2.5%). In contrast, the Green Dots for CFROI and Growth suggested that investors were expecting CFROI to climb from −30% to +25% and growth to follow suit. But, note critically, that these Green Dots are based on the starting estimates for CFROI and Growth in $t + 1$, which were both 0%. These starting values are almost certainly not what investors had in mind, given that growth in 2009 was 38% and growth in 2010 was expected to more than double. Can a more realistic view of the performance expectations that investors were embedding into the stock's price be determined?

A reasonable scenario is easily obtained by flexing forecast CFROI and growth. If we assume that Tesla focuses exclusively on its growth potential over the next five years, maximizing sales instead of profits, we can sensibly assume Tesla may become a cost-of-capital business over this interval. What growth rate is needed to equate the present value of forecast cash flows to the prevailing price of $23? Growth fading from 75% to 25% nicely fits the bill (Exhibit 11.5). This growth forecast reveals an aggressive firm and underscores investors' high expectations for success. It anticipates that Tesla's asset base will grow from $333 million to $2.4

EXHIBIT 11.4   Tesla's Relative Wealth Chart in HOLT Lens as of June 30, 2010.

TESLA INC

Sensitivity
Internet & Direct Marketing Retail
Market Cap: 2.219 USD

Price: 23.83 (Jun 30, 2010)
Warranted Price: 1.59 USD (~93%)

CFROI & Asset Growth Inputs

	2005	2006	2007	2008	2009	t + 1	t + 5
Economic Return (CFROI %)				0.0	(35.1)	(0.0)	6.1
Real Asset Growth %				0.0	38.4	(0.0)	1.8
Discount Rate				6.99	4.12	4.86	

Warranted Valuation	Amount (MM)	Per Share
Total Economic Value	245	2.6
–Market Value of Debt & Equivalents	97	1.04
–Market Value of Minority Interest	0	0.00
Warranted Equity Value	**148**	**1.59**
Shares Outstanding	93	downside −93%

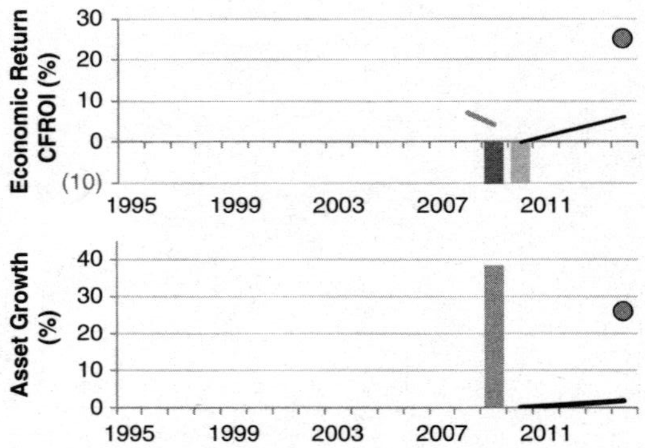

Economic Return CFROI (%) and Asset Growth (%) charts, 1995–2011.

EXHIBIT 11.5 Tesla's Relative Wealth Chart in HOLT Lens as of June 30, 2010, adjusted for CFROI fading to 6% from 0% and growth fading from 75% to 25%.

TESLA INC

Sensitivity
Restaurants
Market Cap: 2.219 USD

Price: 23.83 (Jun 30, 2010)
Warranted Price: 24.02 USD (0%)

CFROI & Asset Growth Inputs

	2005	2006	2007	2008	2009	t + 1	t + 5
Economic Return (CFROI %)				0.0	(35.1)	0.0	6.0
Real Asset Growth %				0.0	38.4	75.0	25.0
Discount Rate				6.99	4.12	4.86	

Warranted Valuation	Amount (MM)	Per Share
Total Economic Value	2,333	25.1
−Market Value of Debt & Equivalents	97	1.04
−Market Value of Minority Interest	0	0.00
Warranted Equity Value	**2,237**	**24.0**
Shares Outstanding	93	

upside
0%

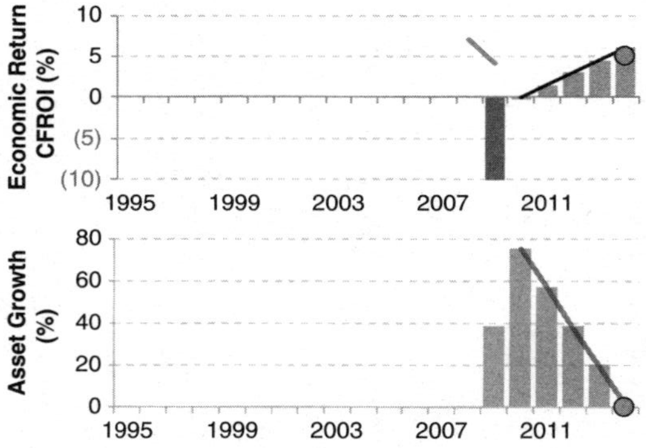

billion by 2015. This is probably a better reflection of what investors were expecting from Tesla. And yet, as aggressive as that sounds, Tesla bested these expectations and reached assets of nearly $9 billion by 2015. Investors who thought that Tesla could beat the fade and bought the stock were richly rewarded.

Clearly, the default HOLT forecast and Green Dots were not representative of Tesla's potential. Why is that? At the risk of being redundant, we want to stress that seven out of eight companies in the early life-cycle phase bypass stardom altogether. The odds of a firm succeeding like Tesla are small, and HOLT's default forecast assumes a prototypical outcome. Investors are encouraged to build their own scenarios, especially for early life-cycle firms and companies that can beat the fade.

Firms in a restructuring phase are also expected to mean-revert because HOLT treats these companies as going concerns. Under the going-concern principle, there is compelling economic rationale to assert that an unprofitable firm will eventually climb back to its cost of capital to remain competitive (and alive). In reality, many troubled firms fail to fully recover. HOLT research indicates that less than 10% of all firms in a restructuring phase successfully return to their cost of capital and sustain profitability at this level. Investors are similarly encouraged to develop scenarios for troubled firms, paying particular attention to the likelihood of full recovery or future profitability.

WHY THE GREEN DOT IS SO HELPFUL

Picking tomorrow's Apple today isn't the only path toward the coveted goal of shareholder gains. Whether a company is a growth star or an out-of-favor value veteran, a key to outperformance is detecting equities with unrealistic price expectations and using this information advantageously.

Exhibit 11.6 offers compelling evidence in support of this claim. We split stocks into five groups based on the CFROI *expected* five years from today that equates the present value of forecast future cash flows to

EXHIBIT 11.6 **Annualized excess shareholder return by CFROI relative achievement. Largest 1,000 stocks by market capitalization, U.S. equities. January 1976–March 2013.**

highest					
		−20%	−9%	−2%	2%	8%
		−17%	−7%	0%	4%	10%
		−14%	−6%	−0%	4%	11%
		−12%	−2%	1%	5%	12%
		−7%	0%	2%	6%	13%
		−−	−		+	++
lowest		lowest		*Relative Achievement*		highest

Expected CFROI (t + 5) is labeled along the vertical axis.

current price.[9] Expectation is ranked from high to low (top to bottom) along the vertical axis. Moving left to right, we separated stocks by their achieved CFROI less what was anticipated. The difference (achieved $CFROI_{t+5}$ − expected $CFROI_{t+5}$) represents relative achievement.

Exhibit 11.6 shows the annualized shareholder return to stocks based on whether they exceeded, met, or fell short of expectations. The center of the table represents the excess shareholder returns to stocks that perfectly met expectations. These shareholders netted zero excess gain. Many great companies fell into this middle bucket.

Companies that earned the lowest CFROI relative to expectations (negative relative achievement) are in the first column and show dismal stock performance. Companies that outpunched CFROI expectations are at the far right, which is where the juicy shareholder returns are located. The center column shows the average excess return to firms that met expectations.

If you focus on the center column only, notice that whether expectations were high or low, performance was hardly better than average for companies that met expectations. This is a key point: There is no excess reward to investors who buy stocks with high expectations of future performance when those stocks (subsequently) only meet expectations. This is

[9] We arrive at this market-implied CFROI by iterating until the resulting $t + 5$ CFROI is located that causes the present value of future cash flows to equal today's price. The $t + 5$ implied CFROI is used in combination with HOLT's forecast CFROI at $t + 1$. Linear fade is assumed between $t + 1$ and $t + 5$ and a 10% mean-reverting fade rate is used thereafter. When combined with a growth rate forecast, a stream of future cash flows can be determined which are then discounted to present.

one reason growth stocks often underperform. Growth stocks are priced with high expectations (high P/B multiples), but most growth companies are unable to exceed their price expectations.

Firms that beat expectations, especially when expectations are low, are the ones most handsomely rewarded. Keynes' quote captures this insight: "Successful investing is anticipating the anticipations of others." HOLT helps you quantify those expectations.

Gauging what investors *expect* to be delivered from what firms *actually* deliver is the essential task of the fundamental equity investor. Investors cannot hope to outperform over the long haul by gingerly selecting companies with high return on capital (quality) or naively picking value stocks in the hope of mean-reversion.

Look at the top two rows in the center. These are stocks that had high CFROI expectations. They delivered what was expected. Looking at the types of companies that make up this group over time shows that many of these stocks would be characterized as "high quality." And yet, even though they met demanding expectations of earning high economic returns, they yielded only benchmark gains. Quality stocks are excellent investments, especially when purchased at a fair price or on the cheap, but stocks that meet expectations do not generate excess gain.

Value stocks are located along the bottom row. Value stocks have low expectations of future performance (that is why their P/B multiples are below-average). Note that when value stocks beat expectations, they deliver superior shareholder performance.

Exhibit 11.6 shows the importance of understanding a stock's price expectations. Investors can win by picking stocks from any category (high expectations = growth, low expectations = value). The key is picking companies that can exceed expectations and "beat the fade."

HOLT Lens makes it easier to gauge expectations using the Relative Wealth Chart for individual company analysis. For bulk analysis, clients can use the Screening Tool. For instance, if we are interested in identifying stocks with high growth expectations, we can quickly and efficiently search for them. In Exhibit 11.7, we screened for firms with market capitalization

EXHIBIT 11.7 Screening for stocks with high growth expectations.

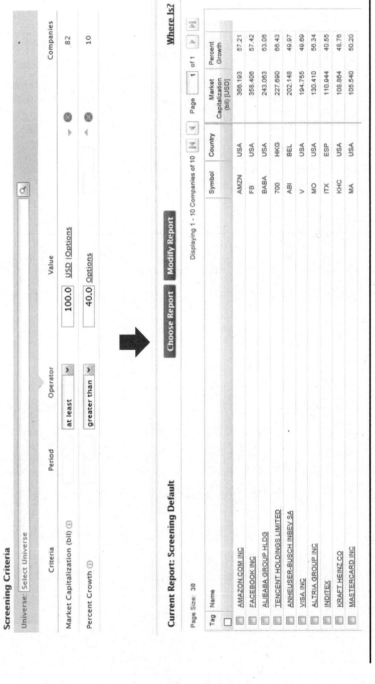

Screening Criteria

Universe: Select Universe

Criteria	Period	Operator	Value	Companies
Market Capitalization (bil) ⓘ		at least ▸	100.0 USD │Options	.82
Percent Growth ⓘ		greater than ▸	40.0 Options	10

Choose Report   Modify Report

Current Report: Screening Default   **Where Is?**

Page Size: 30   Displaying 1 - 10 Companies of 10 |◀ ◀   Page 1 of 1 ▲ ▶|

Tag	Name	Symbol	Country	Market Capitalization (bil) [USD]	Percent Growth
☐	AMAZON COM INC	AMZN	USA	366.193	57.21
☐	FACEBOOK INC	FB	USA	358.406	57.42
☐	ALIBABA GROUP HLDG	BABA	USA	243.063	63.06
☐	TENCENT HOLDINGS LIMITED	700	HKG	227.690	66.43
☐	ANHEUSER-BUSCH INBEV SA	ABI	BEL	202.148	49.97
☐	VISA INC	V	USA	194.765	49.69
☐	ALTRIA GROUP INC	MO	USA	130.410	56.34
☐	INDITEX	ITX	ESP	110.944	40.55
☐	KRAFT HEINZ CO	KHC	USA	108.864	48.76
☐	MASTERCARD INC	MA	USA	105.540	50.20

Source: Credit Suisse, HOLT Lens, April 2017.

EXHIBIT 11.8 Key phases of the competitive life-cycle.

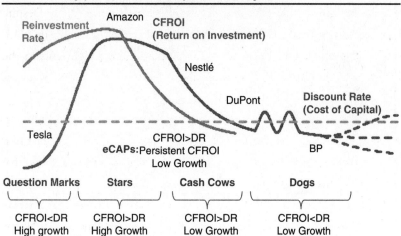

greater than $100bn and PVGO% above 40%. Ten firms passed muster. Are expectations too rich?

PICKING STOCKS ACROSS THE LIFE-CYCLE

Let's consider four stocks, one from each phase of the competitive life-cycle. How is the firm likely to profit and grow in future periods? What are the market's expectations regarding the company? What does HOLT predict will happen to future CFROI and growth over the next five years? Which scenario seems more likely: the market's or HOLT's?

Conveniently, HOLT Lens offers a probability assessment for both HOLT and market fair value scenarios. This fruitful exercise will underscore the power and strengths of the HOLT framework, but it will also expose areas where the default HOLT model may need to be fine-tuned in order to achieve a reasonable estimate of firm value. Exhibit 11.8 depicts the key phases, or states, of the competitive life-cycle.

Question Mark (Tesla)

Tesla is a fascinating example of a Question Mark.

With a market capitalization greater than $34 billion as of December 2016, sales growth has averaged over 100% a year since 2011. Despite this, Tesla has earned a CFROI above its cost of capital just once, in 2013. Reported profit is low, but expectations for profits are high, and so the firm trades at a HOLT P/B multiple above 5.0 (remember, the average is close to 1.5).

Tesla is no longer just a fledgling start-up. With more than $4 billion in revenue in 2015, it has demonstrated that it is a viable car manufacturer. Tesla is disrupting the status quo, but it earns only a sliver of the global auto sales. Tesla is a company with significant potential.

Exhibit 11.9 reveals Tesla's economic returns over time and its extraordinary growth. Shareholders have been vastly rewarded, and the stock has outperformed the S&P 500 by 531% over the most recent seven years. Market expectations remain high as indicated by the Green Dots on the Relative Wealth Chart at right, which show CFROI is expected to rise from 0% to above 10%, coupled with growth of 8.3% rising to 12.6%. Does HOLT's market scenario make sense? In contrast, HOLT is forecasting CFROI to rise from 0% to 2.5% over the next five years coupled with growth falling from 8% to 2.6%.

Tesla has been a winning investment for intrepid investors. Why is HOLT's forecast so dismal for a firm that has been beating expectations for several years?

The answer is rooted in HOLT's empirical research on corporate performance. The brutal reality is that few Question Marks ever become Stars. To remind you of the odds, only 1-in-8 Question Marks ever become a Star. 63% remain in place or transition to Dog, leaving only a handful that earns profits above the cost of capital. HOLT takes the outside view and forecasts Question Marks to become average. This is a winning proposition: 76% of Question Marks remain subpar performers.

When Question Marks win and become Stars, the payoff can be immense. HOLT's default forecast for Question Marks takes a dim view of their prospects based on overwhelming evidence. Investors

EXHIBIT 11.9 Tesla Flex Valuation and Relative Wealth Chart as of May 22, 2017.

TESLA INC

Sensitivity
Automobile Manufacturers
Market Cap: 50.14 USD

Price: 310.35 (May 22, 2017)
Warranted Price: 48.36 USD (−84%)

CFROI & Asset Growth Inputs

	2012	2013	2014	2015	2016	t + 1	t + 5
Economic Return (CFROI %)	(26.7)	1.7	(1.0)	(7.2)	(3.5)	(0.0)	2.5
Real Asset Growth %	34.8	102.9	114.3	40.9	147.9	8.3	2.6
Discount Rate	4.81	3.31	3.53	3.43	3.65	3.25	

Warranted Valuation	Amount (MM)	Per Share
+PV Cash Flow Existing Assets	22,874	141.58
+NPV Cash Flow Future Investments	3,574	22.12
+Market Value Investments	0	0.00
Total Economic Value	**26,448**	**163.70**
−Market Value of Debt & Equivalents	16,744	103.64
−Market Value of Minority Interest	1,890	11.70
Warranted Equity Value	**7,813**	**48.36**
Shares Outstanding	162	

downside
−84%

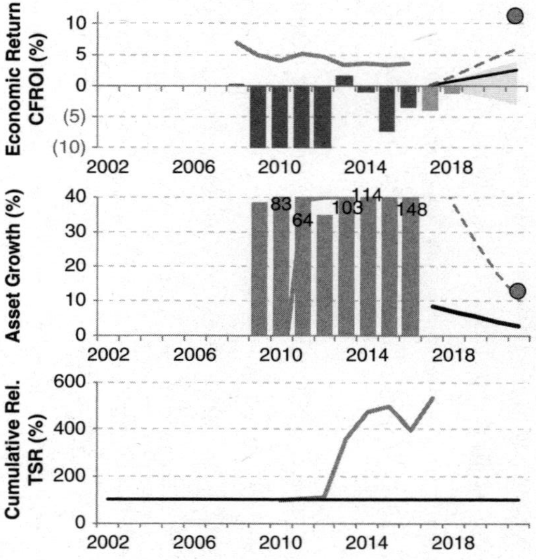

that see a Star in the making need to alter the HOLT default forecast to better assess the likely expectations embedded in the stock's price. A scenario that is probably closer to broad investor expectations has CFROI climbing from 0% to 6% over the next five years combined with growth falling from 50% to 10% (shown as dotted lines). The scenario results in a fair value warranted price. Elon Musk's bold prediction of 30% annual growth for the next decade results in 640% upside.

Question Marks Summary

HOLT's research indicates that Question Marks are likely to become average performers, not Stars. This is the default projection in CFROI and growth. Investors who are optimistic should override the CFROI and growth forecast. HOLT provides an empirical probability assessment in Flex Valuation of the user's CFROI forecast, which is a highly useful gauge for benchmarking and tapering undue optimism or pessimism.

Star (Amazon)

We've highlighted Amazon throughout the book as an extraordinary company with a strong commitment to shareholder value principles. It makes perfect sense to complete the circle and discuss this company's investment thesis, given its Star status.

Amazon's success has been otherworldly, driven in large part by its exceptional growth. CEO Jeff Bezos is not afraid to take calculated risks and has been successfully investing in R&D initiatives like Amazon Web Services (AWS) that are bearing much fruit. The decline in CFROI since 2010 has been more than offset by the firm's explosive growth, and economic profits have steadily increased.

HOLT loves Star companies. The default forecast does a remarkable job of anticipating the typical decline in CFROI and reinvestment from peak levels. For Amazon, HOLT's May 2017 default forecast predicts

CFROI will fall from 10.7% LFY to 8.5% over the next five years with growth declining from 34% to 9%. This is the trajectory of most firms, like Amazon, that have profitable CFROI well above the cost of capital coupled with attractive growth. Empirical evidence shows that most of these Stars are unable to sustain their high growth rates, and that over the next five years, revert toward 5% growth. HOLT kicks in a few extra basis points of growth for Amazon, given its slightly lower-than-average CFROI volatility and its exceptional size, which can work to stave off competition for a while longer (Exhibit 11.10).

The consensus CFROI and growth anticipated by investors are quite close to the default HOLT forecast. Market expectations have CFROI holding steady at 10% coupled with growth declining from 25% to 11%. This seemingly small difference in forecast profitability and growth versus the default HOLT estimate lifts the warranted price by 12% to a fair value price of $995 a share. Optimistically, if Amazon can sustain CFROI of 10% and maintain growth of 20%, +90% upside would be indicated. This might seem like a stretch, but Amazon has a solid history of beating the fade.

Star Summary

HOLT's base forecast of CFROI and reinvestment rate for Stars anticipates declining profitability and rapidly decaying growth rates. This default treatment is based on empirical evidence. The vast majority of Stars are unable to maintain both high CFROI and growth over any five-year horizon: More than 70% of Stars experience a decline in either CFROI or growth.

Given their profitability, Stars are often highly sensitive to growth rate adjustments. Even small increases in estimated growth can sometimes lead to meaningful improvement in intrinsic value. Growth stocks require careful deliberation about the level of profitability and growth that can be realistically sustained. Investors who are optimistic about a Star's ability to maintain or increase profitability or growth *must* alter the default forecast to capture these valuable benefits.

EXHIBIT 11.10 Amazon's Flex Valuation and Relative Wealth Chart as of May 30, 2017.

AMAZON.COM INC

Sensitivity

Internet & Direct Marketing Retail
Market Cap: 475.428 USD

Price: 994.62 (May 30, 2017)
Warranted Price: 870.58 USD (−12%)

CFROI & Asset Growth Inputs

	2012	2013	2014	2015	2016	t + 1	t + 5
Economic Return (CFROI %)	12.0	12.0	7.6	10.1	10.7	11.3	8.5
Real Asset Growth %	44.4	40.9	49.6	26.3	34.2	26.5	9.3
Discount Rate	4.61	3.47	3.60	2.90	2.73	1.94	

Warranted Valuation

	Amount (MM)	Per Share
+PV Cash Flow Existing Assets	132,459	277.11
+NPV Cash Flow Future Investments	312,880	654.56
+Market Value Investments	477	1.00
Total Economic Value	**445,816**	**932.7**
−Market Value of Debt & Equivalents	29,678	62.09
−Market Value of Minority Interest	0	0.00
Warranted Equity Value	**416,138**	**870.58**
Wind-down Value/Share		
Wind-down Ratio		
Shares Outstanding	478	

downside
−12%

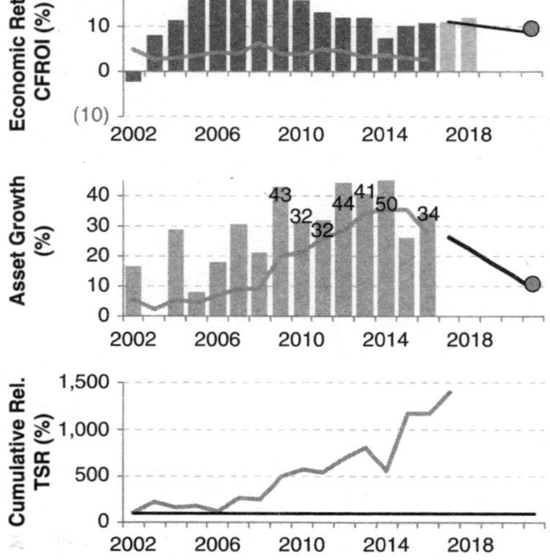

Economic Return CFROI (%)

Asset Growth (%)

Cumulative Rel. TSR (%)

eCAP (Nestlé)

It's not just the Swiss or Nespresso lovers like George Clooney that appreciate Nestlé. The firm has outperformed the MSCI Europe Index by 150% since 2002. Over the past 32 years, Nestlé has earned CFROI above 6%, never once faltering. Its profitability is enviable, with the firm ranking in the highest 10% of companies having durable profits. Nestlé has built a formidable moat to insulate profits with its numerous high-quality brands. The firm has ranked #1 in global food sales since 2014. Nestlé's motto, "Good Food, Good Life," offers lessons in simplicity, sincerity, and customer commitment. Nestlé is an admirable firm.

HOLT research on profit persistence flags companies like Nestlé because they exhibit unusually persistent profitability coupled with sustainable growth. This is a powerhouse combination that can lead to large shareholder gains over time for long-horizon investors. This is the type of company in which Warren Buffet likes to invest. Less than 5% of all publicly traded firms exhibit profit persistence like Nestlé, making this an elite investing category. HOLT calls these stocks "eCAPs" because they have empirically demonstrated that they possess competitive advantages. eCAP stands for "empirical Competitive Advantage Period." HOLT gives these firms a longer forecast horizon to acknowledge their greater profit persistence. Despite making up less than 5% of all traded companies, it should be noted that upwards of 40% to 50% of most size-weighted indices are comprised of eCAPs, which are concentrated amongst the largest firms.

The default HOLT forecast for Nestlé anticipates a minimal decline in CFROI over the next ten years from 14.8% to 14% (Exhibit 11.11). Growth is expected to be approximately 0%, or equal to the rate of inflation in nominal terms. This forecast leads to a warranted price of $66 compared to Nestlé's current stock price of $85, suggesting 22% downside.

Ongoing research at HOLT shows that superior firms like Nestlé tend to fade at close to 5% a year after the forecast horizon, not 10%. In this case, adjusting the fade rate from 10% to 5% ratchets up the warranted price

EXHIBIT 11.11 Nestlé's Flex Valuation and Relative Wealth Chart as of May 22, 2017.

NESTLÉ S.A.

Sensitivity

Packaged Foods and Meats
Market Cap: 263.089 USD

Price: 84.92 (May 22, 2017)
Warranted Price: 66.16 USD (−22%)

CFROI & Asset Growth Inputs

	2012	2013	2014	2015	2016	t + 1	t + 10
Economic Return (CFROI %)	14.0	16.0	13.9	16.0	14.1	14.8	14.0
Real Asset Growth %	4.9	(6.9)	6.9	(9.1)	10.5	(0.0)	1.0
Discount Rate	4.76	4.25	3.61	2.98	3.06	2.74	

Warranted Valuation	Amount (MM)	Per Share
+PV Cash Flow Existing Assets	153,044	49.40
+NPV Cash Flow Future Investments	75,898	24.50
+Market Value Investments	24,157	7.80
Total Economic Value	253,100	81.7
−Market Value of Debt & Equivalents	44,500	14.36
−Market Value of Minority Interest	3,623	1.17
Warranted Equity Value	204,977	66.2
Shares Outstanding	3,098	

downside
−22%

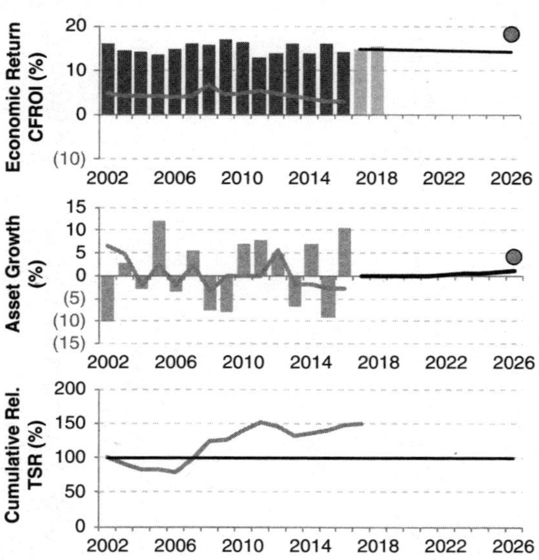

to $74, still 13% below current price. It is challenging to validate a fade rate below this level for any firm. As the story of Sears reveals, shocks and disruptions occur all the time and firms that fail to innovate and maintain peak efficiency will be quickly overtaken by competitors.

ecCAP Summary

eCAPs are Stars and Cash Cows that also exhibit durable profitability. These are enviable firms and can be excellent investments when purchased at a reasonable price.

The HOLT model works marvelously on eCAPs. eCAPs are awarded a 10-year forecast horizon, typically coupled with low growth and minimal fade in CFROI.

Investors should focus critically on the terminal fade rate. Will Nestlé suddenly become a riskier firm in year 11 of the forecast? The 10% fade rate implies a remaining CAP of just 10 years (CAP $= 1/f$). Investors examining firms like Nestlé or Kraft are wise to bear in mind the story of Sears or to recall Sara Lee's troubled years before altering the residual fade rate. Nonetheless, assessing the terminal fade rate is typically the chief consideration for eCAPs since growth is usually negligible. The fundamental pricing model can be used to assess the market-implied fade rate and CAP.[10]

Cash Cow (DuPont)

DuPont is a venerable Cash Cow. The firm flings off 60% of earnings each year and hands it back to shareholders as a dividend. It earns CFROI above its cost of capital. Although DuPont has struggled to grow, it has managed to keep pace with the S&P 500 since 2005. DuPont is nowhere near Star status and lacks the profit persistence and stability of eCAPs, but not by much. DuPont is an exciting investment idea precisely because it is possible for the firm to reinvigorate itself like Honeywell and generate large shareholder gains, or to stumble into oblivion.

---

[10]David A. Holland, "An Improved Method for Valuing Mature Companies and Estimating Terminal Value: Adding Fade to Your DCF Model," Credit Suisse Quant Conference, New York City, December 2016.

HOLT does an excellent job forecasting CFROI and growth rates for Cash Cows. Most Cash Cows tend to fluctuate around the long-term cost of capital of 6%, distribute dividends, and grow close to the rate of inflation. Cash Cow businesses need to dislodge entrenched bureaucratic tendencies, focus on increasing the efficiency of operations, motivate employees, and seek out innovations that can bring new life to the firm. This is a critical juncture.

DuPont earned a CFROI of 7.5% in 2016. HOLT anticipates a small decline in CFROI in 2017, fading back up to 7.8% by 2021. Growth is expected to remain at the level of inflation for the next five years. Beyond year 5 of the forecast, CFROI is expected to fade back toward 6%. The default HOLT forecast indicates 11% downside.

The big question for Cash Cows is: How much longer? For how many more years can the firm sustain above-average profits? This is easily tested in HOLT Lens using Flex Valuation (Exhibit 11.12). Interestingly, extending the forecast from 5 to 10 years leads to no improvement in valuation. It's hard to imagine that investors are anticipating growth above inflation for DuPont. More likely, investors are overly optimistic about the firm's penchant for profits. A 5% residual fade rate results in a fair value scenario, but this fade rate should be reserved for only the very best firms globally with exceptional records of profit stability.

Cash Cow Summary

The big question for Cash Cows is: How much longer can the firm earn excess returns? Flex Valuation in HOLT Lens provides immediate feedback on sensitivities that explore the terminal fade rate or increase or decreases in the cost of capital. Questions around capital structure changes can be directed to a HOLT Sector Specialist for bespoke and interactive simulations.

Dog (BP)

A dog may be a man's best friend, but Dog stocks are usually not much of a pal.

EXHIBIT 11.12 DuPont's Flex Valuation and Relative Wealth Chart as of May 22, 2017.

DUPONT

Sensitivity

Diversified Chemicals
Market Cap: 67.046 USD

Price: 77.34 (May 22, 2017)
Warranted Price: 68.46 USD (−11%)

CFROI & Asset Growth Inputs

	2012	2013	2014	2015	2016	t + 1	t + 5
Economic Return (CFROI %)	9.0	8.4	7.9	8.2	7.5	7.1	7.8
Real Asset Growth %	(0.6)	2.3	(0.3)	(19.4)	0.5	(0.0)	0.0
Discount Rate	5.34	4.40	4.08	3.65	3.30	2.91	

Warranted Valuation	Amount (MM)	Per Share
+PV Cash Flow Existing Assets	63,863	73.67
+NPV Cash Flow Future Investments	20,766	23.95
+Market Value Investments	650	0.75
Total Economic Value	85,280	98.4
−Market Value of Debt & Equivalents	25,104	28.96
−Market Value of Minority Interest	825	0.95
Warranted Equity Value	**59,350**	**68.5**
Shares Outstanding	867	

downside −11%

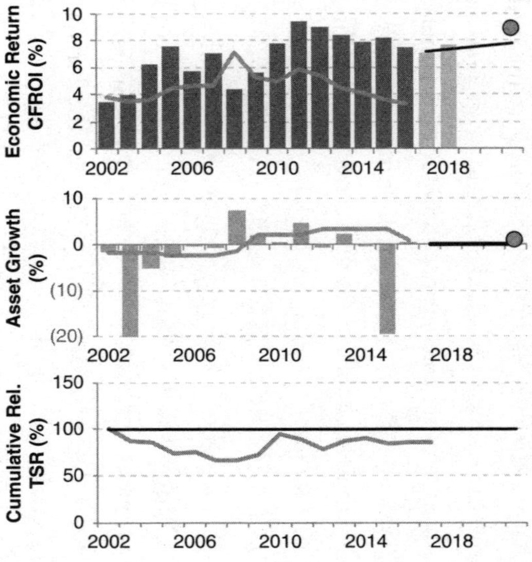

Economic Return CFROI (%)

Asset Growth (%)

Cumulative Rel. TSR (%)

Companies in the Dog category have experienced a material decline in CFROI, which is below the cost of capital. Many firms in this position attempt to grow their way out of trouble. This is a losing prospect. Instead, Dogs need to shed unprofitable businesses and revitalize their operations.

Empirical evidence suggests that about 30% of Dogs recover back to the cost of capital. However, only about 5% of Dogs maintain improvements. The rest slip backwards into oblivion, merge, or eventually de-list from their exchange.

Many Dogs are cyclical firms that have fallen on hard times. BP is a good example, up to a point. Oil prices are far below record highs, and BP is smarting. However, the firm is also a laggard compared to peers in terms of operational effectiveness. Of late, BPs R&D efforts have not been as rewarding as peers.

HOLT's default forecast for Dogs is that CFROI will revert back toward the cost of capital. This is a reasonable assumption if the firm continues to be priced as a going concern. For BP, HOLT forecasts CFROI to climb from 0% to 3.5% over the next five years combined with 0% real growth (Exhibit 11.13). This forecast is close to market expectations, which anticipates that CFROI will climb back to 2%. The significant valuation swing from +25% to 0% based on a one percentage point decline in CFROI from 3% to 2% highlights the onerous debt burden of the firm and its effect on small changes in profitability.

Dog Summary

If a firm is expected to survive, it makes sense that CFROI will climb back toward the cost of capital when it is far below it. HOLT anticipates mean-reversion in profitability for Dogs. At times, the HOLT forecast for Dogs is too generous. Dogs can get stuck in the mud for long stretches of time, and there is never any guarantee that they will re-emerge as a profitable firm. Most Dogs fail to fully fix their businesses.

A concern for investors in Dogs is whether or not HOLT's replacement charge is appropriate. HOLT imputes a retirement charge based on the firm's historical growth rate. The very low growth rate of most of these

EXHIBIT 11.13 BP's Flex Valuation and Relative Wealth Chart as of May 22, 2017.

BP PLC

Sensitivity
Integrated Oil & Gas
Market Cap: 121.62 USD

Price: 6.18 (May 22, 2017)
Warranted Price: 7.71 USD (25%)

CFROI & Asset Growth Inputs

	2012	2013	2014	2015	2016	t + 1	t + 5
Economic Return (CFROI %)	4.0	5.1	3.3	0.1	(0.7)	0.5	3.4
Real Asset Growth %	1.7	11.1	1.7	(2.2)	(7.4)	(0.0)	0.2
Discount Rate	5.98	5.42	5.26	5.15	5.41	4.85	

Warranted Valuation	Amount (MM)	Per Share
+PV Cash Flow Existing Assets	275,949	14.02
+NPV Cash Flow Future Investments	(4,780)	(0.24)
+Market Value Investments	26,180	1.33
Total Economic Value	297,350	15.1
−Market Value of Debt & Equivalents	143,291	7.28
−Market Value of Minority Interest	2,420	0.12
Warranted Equity Value	151,639	7.7
Shares Outstanding	19,676	upside 25%

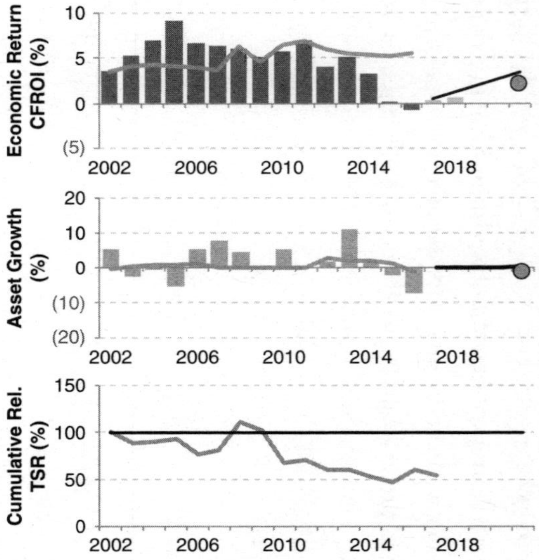

Economic Return CFROI (%)

Asset Growth (%)

Cumulative Rel. TSR (%)

firms ensures the maximum retirement amount is being charged against the firm's typically meager cash flows, often resulting in a negative net cash receipt. This is probably a reasonable expectation, but investors will want to dig into this area when necessary, particularly for asset-intensive companies with long-lived projects and low corporate growth.

FINAL REMARKS

We should never forget market prices are transient. What is expensive today can be cheap tomorrow and vice-versa. McDonald's is a great example. In January 2003 the stock was trading at a HOLT P/B ratio of 1.0. Investors had priced the stock to earn only its cost of capital into the hereafter. We've recreated the pricing dynamics as exhibited in HOLT in Exhibit 11.14.

The hashed bars in the top panel show McDonald's subsequent CFROI performance. The Green Dot shows low market expectations. McDonald's trounced investors' expectations and the share price rocketed upwards.

How does McDonald's look today? Investors are excited about CEO Steve Easterbrook's renewed focus on operational excellence and his expansive vision that includes bringing back fresh (unfrozen) hamburger. The stock is priced for CFROI to climb from historically high levels up to 14% coupled with continued real growth of 2.5%. In contrast to 2003, MCD is now trading at a HOLT P/B multiple of 3.6.

HOLT shows that about 25% of historical observations like McDonald's met or exceeded the high expectations embedded in MCD's stock price. This can be determined by noting that the CFROI Green Dot is near the upper boundary of the blue triangle (Exhibit 11.15). The triangle represents the upper and lower 25th percentile of CFROI outcomes for firms with the same starting profitability and growth as McDonald's. These very high expectations warrant caution. More often than not, stocks with high expectations fail to meet or exceed what's priced in, and the stock price suffers as a result.

The McDonald's examples capture Bob Hendricks assertion: "It is not just high CFROI that delivers great shareholder returns; great investments

EXHIBIT 11.14 McDonald's Flex Valuation and Relative Wealth Chart as of January 31, 2003.

MCDONALD'S CORP

Sensitivity
Restaurants
Market Cap: 18.075 USD

Price: 14.24 (Jan 31, 2003)
Warranted Price: 20.52 USD (44%)

CFROI & Asset Growth Inputs

	1997	1998	1999	2000	2001	t + 1	t + 5
Economic Return (CFROI %)	8.7	8.8	9.1	8.9	8.1	7.5	7.7
Real Asset Growth %	5.8	6.4	2.0	2.8	3.5	3.6	2.6
Discount Rate	4.39	3.36	2.05	3.21	3.63	5.62	

Warranted Valuation

	Amount (MM)	Per Share
+PV Cash Flow Existing Assets	38,627	30.43
+NPV Cash Flow Future Investments	3,209	2.53
+Market Value Investments	990	0.78
Total Economic Value	42,826	33.7
−Market Value of Debt & Equivalents	16,776	13.22
−Market Value of Minority Interest	0	0.00
Warranted Equity Value	26,050	20.5
Shares Outstanding	1,269	

upside
44%

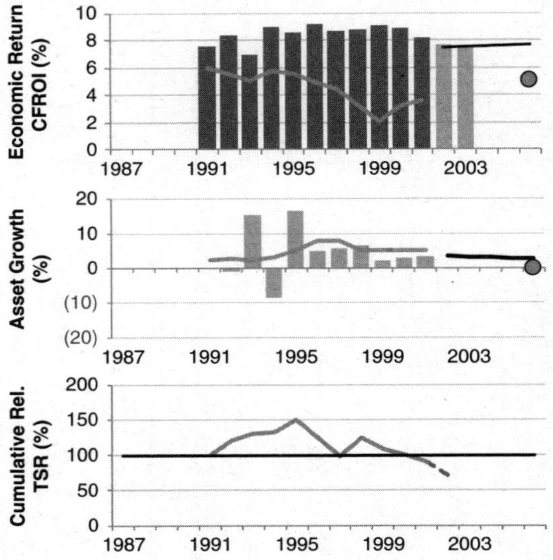

EXHIBIT 11.15 McDonald's Flex Valuation and Relative Wealth Chart as of May 22, 2017.

MCDONALD'S CORP

Sensitivity
Restaurants
Market Cap: 120.473 USD

Price: 147.82 (May 22, 2017)
Warranted Price: 108.36 USD (–27%)

CFROI & Asset Growth Inputs

	2012	2013	2014	2015	2016	t + 1	t + 5
Economic Return (CFROI %)	11.0	10.8	10.4	9.8	11.3	11.2	10.9
Real Asset Growth %	3.9	3.8	(2.1)	1.3	(12.3)	2.4	2.4
Discount Rate	5.23	4.39	4.44	4.35	4.00	3.66	

Warranted Valuation

Warranted Valuation	Amount (MM)	Per Share
+PV Cash Flow Existing Assets	92,605	113.63
+NPV Cash Flow Future Investments	38,475	47.21
+Market Value Investments	726	0.89
Total Economic Value	131,805	161.72
–Market Value of Debt & Equivalents	43,491	53.36
–Market Value of Minority Interest	0	0.00
Warranted Equity Value	**88,315**	**108.36**
Wind-down Value/Share		
Wind-down Ratio		
Shares Outstanding	815	

downside
–27%

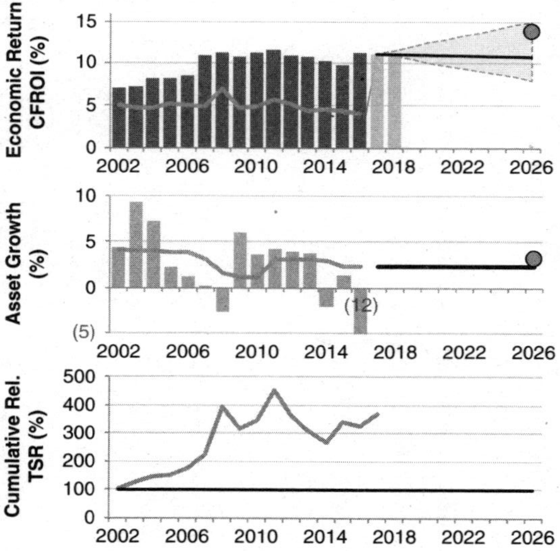

355

are found across the CFROI spectrum." In a recent interview, Hendricks stressed to both authors his fundamental belief that "there is no single magic pattern [for winning at investing]. There are multiple patterns for the multiple business models out there. Part of the challenge of investing is framing." Bob spent time considering and looking for changes in a company's operating drivers. If a new CEO was hired, he would ask if the CEO was an asset turns or margin guy. If the company had poor turns and the CEO had a track record of focusing on turns, then Bob would get excited, particularly if the Green Dot was low. Once you connect with the Relative Wealth Chart and its relationship to value drivers, as Bob pointed out, "the examples jump off the page. It's a fun game, it never goes away."

CHAPTER APPENDIX: GAUGING EXPECTATIONS USING PVGO

The present value of growth opportunities (PVGO) is the percentage of total value expected to be earned from future investments. Exhibit 11.16 shows that a firm can be deconstructed into two components: an existing business that is maintained into perpetuity and all new projects. The profitability of the existing business is expected to fade. These components can be valued separately, which creates an exciting opportunity to assess the value of different profit streams. Imagine, for instance, that Starbuck's expands into gourmet burgers. We would be wise to value its existing coffee franchise separately from its burger business.

HOLT's measure of PVGO is determined by first estimating a valuation for the core business that assumes continual replenishment of assets necessary to operate, zero growth, and reversion to the mean for profitability. This estimate is conservative, suggesting average performance for the existing business over time. We subtract this value (the present value of the existing business) from the firm's market value to arrive at an estimate of the value investors are anticipating from future growth opportunities.

EXHIBIT 11.16 PVGO = Market Enterprise Value less the present value of the existing business (wind-down + replacement value).

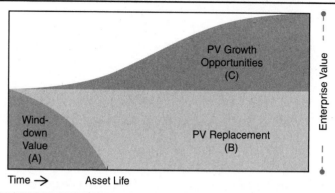

HOLT's measure of PVGO is reliable, and investors are smart to take notice. Here's why. Because of a growth stock's potential for outsized shareholder gains, the allure of growth is often irresistible, and many investors overpay for these stocks. HOLT research shows that there is a well-heeled limit to what investors should typically pay for growth: Stocks with more than 40% of total value attributable to growth (PVGO) should be avoided.

Instead of chasing sexy growth stories, investors benefit from a dispassionate approach that evaluates a firm's growth expectations and exposes this to the cleansing light of historical benchmarks. What emerges from the empirical evidence is compelling: Betting on growth can be costly. Investors should remember that growth is elusive and stocks with high growth expectations often fail to deliver. Eliminating stocks with PVGO greater than 40% of total value might save you from losses.

12

CLOSING THOUGHTS

We opened by recalling the words of Albert Einstein: "Everything should be as simple as it can be but not simpler." We will summarize some of the lessons from this book we would like to leave you.

Don't forget the golden rule of corporate finance.

A vital responsibility for corporate executives and their boards is capital allocation. Managers who focus relentlessly on building and maintaining a sustainable competitive advantage are more likely to allocate capital successfully into positive NPV strategies and maximize the firm's value (Exhibit 12.1). Decision analysis can help objectify the process. Corporate executives must go beyond earnings and manipulating earnings for the benefit of the media and their bonuses. Managers must focus on joining strategy and valuation at the hip, and invest in positive NPV strategies.[1] Corporate boards would be wise to remunerate executives on economic value creation, not earnings. Investors will excitedly queue to fund companies that allocate capital effectively.

---

[1] Michael Mauboussin likes to remind his audience that strategy and valuation are not two separate tasks but rather, they should be joined at the hip. We agree wholeheartedly.

EXHIBIT 12.1 We believe that the purpose of a firm is to build and maintain a sustainable competitive advantage. These are the elements that will help it succeed.

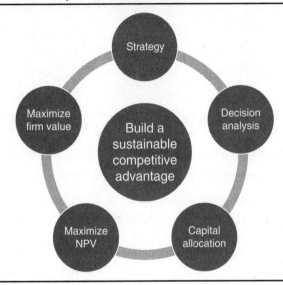

Choose financial performance metrics that best reflect a firm's economics.

A firm's economics should guide the selection of its financial performance metrics and the adjustments necessary to calculate those metrics. ROE is poor measure of a firm's profitability since it focuses only on equity investors and not the quality of the firm's operations. Earnings can be gamed by accounting shenanigans and are also dependent on a firm's leverage. In short, earnings and ROE are not to be trusted. ROIC is a better measure of profitability but liable to accounting distortions. Although it takes more effort to calculate CFROI, it is a comprehensive measure of a company's profitability. Because CFROI reverses accounting distortions and adjusts for inflation, it is comparable across borders and industries, and over time. This is highly advantageous to corporate and fund managers when assessing profitability and the plausibility of forecast profitability. What's the upside? A better measure of profitability results in improved capital allocation decisions and fundamental valuation. Keep metrics as simple as possible, but not simpler.

Shareholders' equity is not free.

The biggest issue with an income statement is that it contains no charge for shareholders' equity, implying that equity is free. Economic profit corrects for this oversight by subtracting a capital charge from the after-tax operating profit. The capital charge is an opportunity cost on the funding provided by all capital providers. We prefer the economic profit approach when discussing valuations since the present value of future economic profits equals the total NPV of all present and future investments. We showed the connection between IRR and CFROI, and project NPV and HOLT EP. These relationships connect project economics to corporate valuation. For companies with long-lived assets, it is advantageous to use inflation-adjusted gross investment instead of net assets (invested capital) in the assessment of economic profit. Significant intangible expenses such as R&D should be capitalized and placed on the balance sheet. Again, keep it as simple as possible, but not simpler. You must go beyond earnings and never forget that earnings have an opportunity cost.

Fade happens.

We provide empirical evidence throughout the book that fade happens. Asset growth fades quickly, so beware of extrapolating high growth in forecasts. Profitability is stickier but it does fade, and its fade dynamics differ by industry. Although fade happens, it is rarely an explicit driver in a DCF model. We introduced our Fundamental Pricing Model and showed how fade can be added as a value driver to perform back-of-the-envelope valuations of mature firms, or used to estimate the terminal value in a DCF valuation. The sensitivity of a firm's valuation to changes in its competitive advantage period can be assessed. An improved understanding of fade results in more accurate fundamental valuations and better insights into the probability of forecasts being realized. We remain active on this research front.

Market-implied expectations provide free and valuable information.

It is highly beneficial to reverse engineer a valuation into determining a stock's market-implied expectations. This provides a betting line and free information into how the market is pricing the company's future. HOLT Lens makes this quick and easy, and allows you to assess the combination of CFROI and asset growth implied by a share price. We recommend that you take two perspectives:

- Assume the market is correct and analyze what the expectations mean for a company and its industry. How plausible are they and what is the market signaling?
- Assume the market can be inefficient and identify how a company might outperform or underperform the market's expectations. How plausible are your reasons, and what's the probability of your forecast profitability?

For high-quality companies with exceptional returns on capital, don't forget the neglected value driver: the rate at which profitability fades to the cost of capital. We showed that the inverse of fade equals the competitive advantage period, and that changes in CAP can have a dramatic impact on valuation.

Although we prefer companies with proven records of effective capital allocation and value creation, they tend to be priced at a premium. The basic objective of a value investor is to "buy low and sell high." Improved forecasting and an understanding of market-implied expectations can help fundamental investors improve their odds of outperformance. Don't waste time if you can buy a high-quality stock at an attractive price. Our studies indicate that companies with poor profitability tend to remain stuck in the mud. When investing in low-quality stocks, remember Buffett's warning that "turnarounds seldom turn" and don't fall in love with the stock.

Lastly, please remember that a valuation is an opinion at a given point in time. As information changes, so could your forecast and valuation.

INDEX